Successful
Baccalaureate
Social Work
Programs

Successful
Baccalaureate
Social Work
Programs

A GUIDE FOR CURRENT AND FUTURE LEADERS

EDITED BY
**Susan Mapp and
Needha Boutté-Queen**

P R E S S

Alexandria, Virginia

ISBNs: 978-0-87293-217-3 (paperback); 978-0-87293-218-0 (eBook)

Printed in the United States of America.

CSWE Press
333 John Carlyle Street, Suite 400
Alexandria, VA 22314
www.cswe.org

First Printing, September 2023

Cover and text design by Kathleen Dyson

Contents

Section One
Program Director Responsibilities

CHAPTER 1

Being a BSW Program Director

Susan C. Mapp

Baccalaureate-level social work is a growing field: The number of students increased 7.5% from 2010 to 2020. The number of accredited baccalaureate social work (BSW) programs continues to grow as well, having increased 16.6% in the same period (Council on Social Work Education [CSWE], 2021). To meet accreditation standards, each of these programs must have a designated program director. This is a complex position with numerous and varied responsibilities, especially if the individual is also chair of the department (see sample job description in the appendix). Those in this role must not only ensure that the program is meeting accreditation standards but also grapple with issues common to undergraduate students, including academic concerns (e.g., fulfilling general education requirements) as well as social and emotional concerns (e.g., traditional-aged students dealing with identity issues and nontraditional students navigating barriers in their return to school).

Given their role of overseeing social work educational programs, BSW program directors have issues in common with their MSW program director colleagues. However, their work with undergraduate students and its above-noted challenges mean that their responsibilities also can be more akin to those of department chairs, even when they do not have the title. The occupation of this liminal space means that they overlap with both of these groups but are not fully in one or the other. Despite these challenges, resources for these professionals have been few and far between, a situation not unique to social work. This lack of scholarship on program administration has also been noted in the nursing literature (e.g., Delgado

& Mitchell, 2016), where the skills needed for leadership—"budget, politics, policies, accreditation requirements, leadership and management"—do not align with "the disciplinary and scholarly knowledge" taught in doctoral programs (Berman, 2015, p. 298).

In 2017, the last year for which the Council on Social Work Education (CSWE) reported faculty statistics, a third of social work faculty were at or near retirement age (55 or older) (CSWE, 2018). Therefore, it is essential that the profession support its current and future leaders. This challenge is clearly addressed by CSWE in its current strategic plan, in which Goal 3 states, "Develop future leaders and administrators for social work education" (CSWE, 2019).

It is the intent of this book to provide information to aid in the myriad tasks common to BSW program directors, aimed at both current program directors and those who aspire to leadership (or find themselves in leadership roles regardless of aspirations). To do so, it is helpful to describe the development of undergraduate social work education in the United States and the power dynamics that led to the development of the Association of Baccalaureate Social Work Program Directors (BPD). Following that is an overview of the little existing literature related to BSW program directors that exists, and then an overview of the book's structure.

History of BSW Education

Formal social work education is generally recognized to have begun in 1898, with the summer training class organized by the New York Charity Organization Society at Columbia University; this short course evolved into full-scale degree programs (Austin, 1997). These new degrees were primarily at the master's level because it was believed that many of those who were interested in enrolling would have already obtained an undergraduate liberal arts degree—most of them women (Austin, 1997). Although the first association for schools of social work—the American Association of Schools of Social Work (AASSW)—initially included undergraduate programs, this quickly changed. After Dr. Abraham Flexner infamously declared in 1915 that social work was not a profession, it was generally accepted that social work would be better recognized as such if it concentrated on graduate education (Stuart et al., 1993).

Early social work education also had a private-public split. Private universities were concentrating on preparing graduates for practice in nongovernmental organizations through master's-level education. In contrast, public organizations, which needed workers as a result of the development of governmental programs such as formal child welfare offices or programs created through the New Deal, did not see a master's degree as the level of education required for such positions (Stuart et al., 1993). Therefore, public universities focused on developing undergraduate programs to train these workers, many in rural areas (Austin, 1997; Watkins & Holmes, 2008). The schools with undergraduate social work programs then developed the National Association of Schools of Social Administration (NASSA), which accredited undergraduate social work programs (Stuart et al., 1993).

When looking at social work leaders in this era, few were to be found, even though the Great Depression was a time of great need in the country, and social workers were providing many of the services. This was likely due to the preponderance of women in the profession and the prejudice against seeing women as leaders (Atwater, 1950, as cited in Sullivan, 2016). However, leadership as an area of focus for academic study grew in the 1950s (Sullivan, 2016).

In 1952, NASSA and AASSW merged into the organization we have today, the Council on Social Work Education. However, the focus on graduate education remained because only those programs that defined undergraduate education as "preprofessional" were admitted (Stuart et al., 1993). This may be because of the heavy imbalance in the number of programs at the beginning—59 graduate programs as compared with only 19 undergraduate programs (Kendell, as cited in Watkins & Holmes, 2008). Additionally, CSWE did not permit undergraduate programs to be accredited, in part as a result of the lingering influence of Flexner and social work was striving to be recognized as a "profession," an impact that was even greater because social work was female dominated (Austin, 1997).

However, the growth of social service programs in the 1960s again raised the need for more trained social workers, much as it had in the 1930s. The 1962 Social Security Amendments required trained individuals to work in areas such as foster care and public assistance, and the demand was estimated to exceed the numbers that graduate programs could produce (Stuart et al., 1993). The 1965 report by the Department of Health, Education, and Welfare—*Closing the Gap in Social Work Manpower*—called for a continuum of social work education from paraprofessional to baccalaureate to masters (with federal funding) and explicitly recommended professional recognition of social work education at the baccalaureate level. This coincided with the work that CSWE was doing, starting in 1960, to explore the expansion of its work to include undergraduate education (Stuart et al., 1993).

In 1967, Congress appropriated $5 million for social work education to be evenly divided between the undergraduate and graduate levels. This was followed by additional funding through the National Institute of Mental Health to train social workers to work in the area of mental health (Stuart et al., 1993). This funding led to an expansion of programs and requests to CSWE for help in developing those programs. A series of standards developed throughout the 1960s culminated in a system to formally approve baccalaureate programs in 1970 and ultimately led to an accreditation process in 1974. This was almost concurrent with the 1969 decision by the National Association of Social Workers (NASW) to "recognize the BSW as the first level of professional practice" (Stuart et al., 1993, p. 7).

The Association of Baccalaureate Social Work Program Directors

Concerns about the lack of involvement of undergraduate faculty in developing the CSWE accreditation standards and how they would be implemented helped lead to the development of a group focused on these issues. Additionally, graduate faculty had formed their own interest group—the Conference of Deans—and NASW was similarly seen as unwelcoming (Stuart et al., 1993). Therefore, the existing Southern Association of Baccalaureate Social Workers provided leadership for the Undergraduate Program Director's Constituency Group of CSWE to develop a national organization focused on undergraduate social work education. This group quickly became a strong advocate for undergraduate education. Even during its formative period, the steering committee not only developed the structure for the new organization but was also active in advocating for continuation of the federal funding provided in the 1960s and for inclusion in NASW and CSWE (Stuart et al., 1993). The Association of Baccalaureate Social Work Program Directors (BPD) was officially formed in March 1975, held its first conference in 1983, and was formally incorporated in 1988 (Stuart et al., 1993).

EPAS Program Director Requirements

As noted, accreditation standards from CSWE require that every BSW program have an identified program director. The 2022 Educational Policy and Administration Standards (EPAS) requires the following in Accreditation Standard 4.3, "Administrative and Governance Structure" (CSWE, 2022):

> 4.3.4.(a) The program has a program director who administers all program options. The program director has a full-time appointment

to social work, with a primary assignment to the program they administer. Institutions with accredited baccalaureate and master's social work programs have a separate director appointed for each program.

B4.3.4(c) The baccalaureate program director has sufficient assigned time for administrative oversight of the social work program, inclusive of all program options. It is customary for the program director to have, at minimum, 25% assigned time to administer the social work program.

The requirements had not changed a great deal when reviewing the available accreditation standards from the last 40 years until the 2022 revision. In the 1984 accreditation standards, in addition to a full-time appointment to the program, BSW program directors were required to have *either* a bachelor's or a master's degree in social work (MSW). If they did not have an MSW, then a doctoral degree in social work was required (CSWE, 1984). The requirement for release time of 25% was added in the 1994 standards, together with the description of leadership ability; "leadership ability" had already existed in the 1984 standards for MSW program directors (CSWE, 1984, 1994). It was not until the 2015 EPAS that the requirement to have an MSW was added, rather than the option of a BSW with a doctoral degree in social work if the master's was in another field (CSWE, 2015).

The 2022 standards, however, removed the preference for a doctoral degree for the BSW program director. More controversial was the removal of the requirement of a minimum 25% release time. The Commission on Higher Education Accreditation (CHEA) had stated that accreditation standards cannot be prescriptive in such matters, so they had been removed for both BSW and MSW program directors. However, when the draft was released, the outcry among program directors was immediate, as they feared that their institutions would remove this amount of release time if it were not required. The final 2022 standards reflect a nonprescriptive balance that refers to a "customary" release time for carrying out duties associated with administering a program. From there, the program is required to address the director's overall workload, specify the amount of assigned time to carry out administrative functions at their institution, and discuss how this amount is derived, as well as the sufficiency of the release time noted (CSWE, 2022). Each program tells its own story.

Thus, the current list of requirements is not extensive. The program director must have earned an MSW and have a full-time appointment to the program, sufficient release time, and "leadership ability." There are no requirements for being tenured or even tenure-track, which can make it difficult for the program director to advocate for their program given their relative vulnerability. "Leadership ability" is a vague concept and can be difficult to determine. Thus, it is important to discuss the difference between leadership and management and explore the existing literature on BSW program director leadership.

Leading the BSW Program

As noted above, in 1994, accreditation standards began requiring that the BSW program director demonstrate "leadership ability" (CSWE, 1994). Program directors are responsible for both the management and leadership of their programs, and it is important to understand the difference between the two. Leadership "is about influencing, developing, coaching, guiding, mentoring or supervising people" (Allen, 2018, para. 10). The difference can be thought of as, "The manager's job is to plan, organize, and coordinate. The leader's job is to inspire and motivate" (Hardesty, 2011, para. 2). Management involves completing tasks such as handling budgets, monitoring workloads, overseeing promotion and tenure processes, and running effective meetings. Leadership helps the unit move forward and involves duties such as recruiting and retaining effective faculty, handling conflict productively, managing change, and supporting the professional development of faculty and staff (Rodriguez et al., 2016). In essence, tasks are managed, and people are led (Allen, 2018). The concept of leadership and what it entails are further explored in Chapter 2.

People can be good at leadership and bad at management or vice versa, but the effective program director needs to be proficient at both. Management can be disparaged at times in contrast to its flashier cousin, leadership, but completing tasks effectively and efficiently is also essential to a well-functioning department. In addition, part of the work of the program director is making sure that people are led well so that they can successfully complete tasks. Clearly, both are needed.

In 1995, Macy, Flax, Sommer, and Swaine published a book on being a BSW program director (Macy et al., 1995) with chapters on academic and student affairs, accreditation, fiscal and physical resources, faculty and staff resources, and program governance, all essential subjects for the program director. A second edition was published in 2000 by Macy, Turner, and Wilson (Macy et al., 2000). However, because of marked changes in both social work education and higher education in general, this classic is now outdated in many respects, as discussed next.

The authors identify academic affairs as the "heart of the academic enterprise" (Macy et al., 2000, p. 8) and explain that the program director is responsible for completing administrative tasks related to all curricular activities as well as providing leadership for them. This responsibility includes not only supporting and ensuring the development and delivery of an effective curriculum, but also supporting faculty research and faculty and staff development. Macy et al. note that there was often a tension between university scholarship expectations and the type of scholarship "appropriate to professional disciplines" (p. 31). However, since that time, accreditation standards have moved academic requirements from prescribing what courses are taught to a competency-based model. Additionally, in response to the fiscal crunch discussed later, more social work departments, particularly at Research 1 (R1) institutions, have been increasing faculty expectations to obtain federal grants in order to secure the overhead dollars that come with them (Lightfoot, 2019).

When looking at student affairs, one must consider areas such as recruitment, retention, advising, and gatekeeping—all of which are covered in EPAS under Accreditation Standard 4.1, "Student Development— Admissions; Advisement, Retention, and Termination; and Student Participation." How students are recruited to any program has changed greatly since 2000 and now includes methods such as social media advertising and geocaching, as well as traditional means such as college fairs and in-person visits. Because of their status as professional programs that educate students to serve vulnerable and oppressed populations, all social work programs are required to detail their admission standards as part of the accreditation process and to explain how admission decisions are made.

In addition, programs must explain how decisions to terminate students from the program are made, which can occur because of both academic and professional performance concerns (Standard 4.1, CSWE, 2022). These processes, commonly known as gatekeeping, can be fraught with difficult issues and were the focus of an almost-500-page book edited by Gibbs and Blakely (2000). However, given the book's age and the changing legal and social landscapes, much of the information from Gibbs and Blakely is also outdated. For example, many schools have had to evolve their professional performance expectations to include such things as social media expectations. However, attempts to terminate students from the program for performance concerns can face impediments. With the increasing competitiveness of higher education and decreasing funding, institutions are often eager to hold on to their students and their tuition dollars and may balk at the social work program dismissing one, even for flagrant violations of professional conduct. Thus, program directors may have to navigate tensions between the Code of Ethics and pressure from the administration.

As noted, financial resources have become increasingly scarce in higher education, even before the impact of the COVID-19 pandemic. In the 2022 EPAS, Section 4.4, on Resources, requires the following:

> Adequate resources are fundamental to creating, maintaining, and improving an educational environment that supports the development of culturally competent social workers. Social work programs have the necessary resources to carry out the program's mission and to support learning and professionalization of students and program improvement. (CSWE, 2022, p. 34)

EPAS requires fiscal (a sufficient budget), informational (adequate library resources and technology), physical (office and classroom space), human (faculty and support staff), and sufficient resources to increase accessibility and equity for students. Macy et al.'s (2000) most recent book was written before the devastation to higher education budgets. As of 2019, state funding of higher education had decreased 9% since the 2008 Great Recession and 18% since the 2001 tech bust (Whitford, 2020). Between 2008 and 2018, almost all states ($n = 41$) reduced the amount they spend per student by an average of 13%. However, in six states (Alabama, Arizona, Louisiana, Mississippi, Oklahoma, and Pennsylvania), it was more than 30% lower (Mitchell et al., 2019). It is important to emphasize that these numbers were calculated before the financial devastation caused by the COVID-19 pandemic. All of these cuts have resulted in reduced numbers of full-time faculty and reduced academic and student support offerings.

Within the chapter in Macy et al. (2000) on faculty and staff resources is a discussion of various topics, including both management and leadership responsibilities. These include recruitment of personnel and assignment and oversight of appropriate duties, as well as handling personnel conflicts, mentoring, and supporting development—which includes assisting with developing a scholarly agenda as appropriate. As noted, this last piece has been growing at many institutions, and the pressure to produce scholarship in "top" journals and obtain government grants can conflict with the desire for quality teaching and student mentoring that bring many faculty members to baccalaureate teaching.

The last area, program governance, can be a tricky line to walk, especially for a program director who is not the head of a department, such as being combined with other majors that are not accredited professional programs. Program directors may need to make decisions regarding risk management, dealing with grievances (from faculty, staff, or students), and oversee internal committees such as curriculum committees. In these cases, program directors have responsibilities but little power to make the decisions they believe are needed. This can be exacerbated in cases where policies or actions are needed for accreditation.

Research on Baccalaureate Program Directors

The job of program director comes with a great deal of responsibility, but as noted, there is little in the scholarly literature regarding this position. Cassie et al. (2006) discussed the leadership duties of the BSW program director and noted a wide range of skills needed for the role. Similar to what Macy et al. (2000) discussed, Cassie et al. (2006) stated that these leaders operate in an environment of shared governance where they serve as middle managers, both representing their faculty and implementing the requirements of administration. They are charged with leading their faculty, which requires skills in conflict management, motivation, and communication. They oversee recruitment and retention of students as well as monitoring the curriculum and learning outcomes (Cassie et al., 2006). The skills needed to be a successful social work program director include managing the curriculum, making decisions, time management (including work-life balance), and maintaining positive working relationships, which includes managing conflict, communication with outside groups, and managing change (Cassie et al., 2007; Mapp & Boutté-Queen, 2021b).

The only recent research relating to the role of the BSW program director was conducted by the editors of this book (Mapp & Boutté-Queen, 2021a; 2021b). We held two focus groups of current BSW program directors to explore preparation for the role, its stressors and joys, and areas in which they would like training. Results showed that the vast majority had no training before becoming program directors, and their training needs included information on leadership and management, gatekeeping, and accreditation-related issues (Mapp & Boutté-Queen, 2021a).

These focus group results were used to develop a national survey of BSW program directors, which found that two-thirds were untenured at the time they assumed the position, and while most respondents indicated being in a BSW-only program, only 38% reported being chair of the department. Respondents stated this lack of formal authority created issues when the program director was responsible for making sure that accreditation standards were met but had no power to make any needed changes (Mapp & Boutté-Queen, 2021b).

When asked about stressors of the position, accreditation was the most common, followed by stressors created by lack of time, which qualitative comments indicated resulted from balancing numerous tasks and competing priorities. This is despite the fact that almost 30% reported working between 50 and 54 hours a week and that 25% worked even more than that—up to 80 hours a week. It is unclear why prior EPAS standards required only a 25% release for BSW programs, but a 50% release for MSW programs, given that undergraduate program directors were struggling to complete all their required responsibilities. Although the requirement for these releases was removed in the 2022 EPAS, this disparity of "customary" release time was retained. Despite this workload, 80% reported being satisfied or very satisfied with their jobs, most commonly because of their work with students.

A lack of training was common, with only 12% of these program directors reporting having received any training prior to assuming the role, and when they did, it was usually about accreditation and only rarely on other issues such as faculty development, faculty evaluation, or maintaining a positive work climate. A little more than half reported receiving training once they started the job, again most commonly on accreditation, and they indicated a need and desire for more information (Mapp & Boutté-Queen, 2021b).

Training for Program Directors
To help meet this need for training, CSWE offers the Program Director Academy, a leadership certificate program offered every two years to a selected cohort of new program directors, defined as those who have been in their position for 3 years or less. In addition, CSWE financially supports individuals to attend summer leadership trainings through either the Harvard Institutes for Higher Education or the Higher Education Resource Services (HERS) Institute: Higher Education Leadership Development Program. BPD has offered a preconference workshop for new program directors each year, and the editors have twice offered a session for experienced program directors at the conference. In 2010, BPD selected five early career faculty as "Emerging Leaders" to be involved

with the Social Work Congress that year; this cohort then held a series of roundtables with other early career faculty around developing new leaders (Bryan et al., 2020).

However, as indicated by research, these trainings do not fully meet the need, in part because they are primarily aimed at new program directors and because of the cost associated with them. The Program Director Academy has a fee of $1,200, in addition to travel costs, and attending the Harvard or HERS summer leadership institutes is approximately $10,000, of which CSWE covers half. The preconference trainings at BPD incur an additional fee to the membership and conference fees, as well as travel costs. Some institutions are able to support these costs, but others are not, leading to a disparity in access to education and knowledge. Thus, there remains a gap in access to updated, relevant knowledge, which is likely to have been enlarged as a result of COVID-19's effects on faculty retirements, other losses, and reduced fiscal resources at universities.

The Contributions of This Text

This book was developed to meet the need for more information voiced by program directors, both in the survey and beyond. Chapters were conceptualized based on the feedback, and knowledgeable program directors and faculty were recruited to write them. The book is organized in sections about the managerial and leadership duties of program directors, programmatic issues, and topics relating to faculty and students.

EPAS requires a program director to have "leadership ability," so it is helpful to first think about one's own leadership style. To this end, Chapter 2 discusses leadership in social work, along with several different leadership models that fit well with social work to help program directors think about what their own model is. This is followed by Chapter 3, on accreditation—the program director task identified as the most stressful. In this chapter, the roles of the Commission on Educational Policy and CSWE's accrediting body are explored in relation to developing the EPAS. The various types of feedback avenues and processes are discussed, together with initial benchmarking processes, reaffirmation, and changes over time, especially those occurring because of COVID-19.

However, using data effectively should not be limited to accreditation requirements, and thus Chapter 4 helps program directors think about how else they can use data to support their programs. In these days of ever-tightening budgets, program directors need to think about their financial reality in the face of EPAS and other institutional realities. Thus,

Chapter 5, on developing and administering budgets in line with accreditation standards, comes next.

Section 2 looks at topics related to the program. Chapter 6 looks specifically at creating a new BSW program. As indicated by CSWE statistics, the number of BSW programs continues to grow to help meet the need for more social workers, and this chapter is written to assist those who are contemplating such a venture or have already begun it. Many programs are expanding their online offerings, so Chapter 7 explores online education in BSW programs. It can be difficult to conceptualize how to manage an effective program and complete gatekeeping responsibilities if students are not on campus, and this chapter explores those tensions.

It should not be assumed that directing will be the same for all BSW programs, as there are important variations, especially related to the size of the program. Large programs will have more faculty and students to accomplish goals but may be less flexible and unable to provide personalized experiences for students. Conversely, smaller programs can be more flexible and able to build more individualized experiences but may be limited in what they are able to take on because of their smaller numbers. Therefore, Chapters 8 and 9 explore the unique characteristics of each and share tips for success.

An issue that cuts across standards for students and faculty is ensuring an equitable and inclusive environment for all. This essential responsibility needs to start with the program director engaging in individual introspection and then developing a scaffolded approach across the program, including the physical environment, staff, advisors, faculty, departmental policies and programming, and the curriculum. For inclusion to thrive, all faculty must model cultural consciousness across macro and mezzo systems to help students develop their individual cultural consciousness and cultural humility. This requires all members of the department to engage in introspection and trainings that focus on building cultural consciousness, and Chapter 10 details important steps in how to accomplish this.

EPAS does not dictate how education is delivered, and new technology is opening up possibilities undreamed of at the time Macy et al. (1995; 2000) wrote their books. In the survey by Mapp and Boutté-Queen (2021b), the areas in which program directors indicated the strongest desire for information were technology and remote education. Technology has opened new doors to how students can be educated and programs can be administered; however, because of the rapid evolution of these tools, faculty may find it difficult to keep up. In the 2017 Annual Survey, 60% of full-time faculty were 45 years of age or older; thus, they are not "digital natives" (CSWE, 2018). Therefore, Chapter 11 explores purposes of technology and current tools to accomplish these purposes.

Section 3 looks at issues related to the faculty. Standard 4.2 requires each program to have qualified faculty; thus, recruiting and retaining such persons is essential to the success of any program, which is explored in the four chapters in this section. The first one (Chapter 12) discusses methods for how to recruit faculty who are well suited to the particular program and presents important legal considerations. Once faculty are brought on board, the program director is then often the one charged with helping fulfill Standard 4.2, demonstrating that faculty are provided with "opportunities, resources, and support for professional growth and innovation." Program directors can support their faculty members through effective supervision and faculty development, which includes giving them useful evaluations to help guide them—explored in Chapter 13. However, it should not be assumed that all faculty are tenure-track or even full-time, as more programs are using adjunct and contingent faculty to help teach their courses. Because of their status, adjunct faculty are often left out of faculty development and conversations, but it is essential that they are supported if they are to be quality instructors, and Chapter 14 explores this.

Interpersonal difficulties can require a huge amount of time from program directors, and thus thinking proactively about how to handle them is important. Standard 4.2 states that faculty should "model the behavior and values" of the profession. Therefore, the last chapter in this section, Chapter 15, discusses how to build and maintain a collegial department.

Section 4 relates to student issues. With the expanding number of BSW programs comes increased competition for students, which is critical to the survival of any program, especially because the number of graduates is not increasing at the same rate as the number of programs (CSWE, 2021). Chapter 16 therefore discusses methods to successfully recruit and retain students, whether they are coming from off campus or are already on campus.

However, not every student who seeks to be a social worker is well suited for the profession—thus the need for gatekeeping, as explored in Chapter 17. Standard 4.1 requires that programs identify their criteria and processes for admission to, and termination from, the program. Although social work ethics require us to support a broad variety of students in successfully completing their degree, these ethics also require us to prioritize the needs of clients who may be harmed if those unable to appropriately fulfill their duties are graduated and thus certified as ready for practice.

However, it is essential to follow the law while gatekeeping, and Chapter 18 provides guidance on these issues. Program directors must stay aware of the rapidly changing landscape concerning students and their rights. An important part of this is the legal landscape that helps to set guidelines for programs to achieve Standard 2.0, on Anti-racism, Diversity, Equity, and Inclusion (ADEI) in both explicit and implicit curricula. For example, the evolving interpretation of the Americans With Disabilities Act means that mental health issues are now included, giving these issues appropriate parity with physical health issues. Program directors thus may be responsible for determining what is and is not a reasonable accommodation for field practice. Federal and state law protects students by guaranteeing them equal protection and rights to due process, and program directors must be aware of important legal protections afforded to students on campus from admission to program completion, and every step in between.

All of the chapters integrate pieces to help readers think more deeply about the subject matter, such as reflection questions, case studies, and practice tips. They all also provide additional readings to locate more information on the topic. It is hoped that this handbook will help program directors gain access to important information to help them in the oversight of their programs. BSW education is an essential piece of the social work education continuum, and it must be done well.

References

Allen, T. (2018, October 9). What is the difference between management and leadership? *Forbes.* https://www.forbes.com/sites/terinaallen/2018/10/09/what-is-the-difference-between-management-and-leadership/#4a4a172674d6

Austin, D. M. (1997). The institutional development of social work education. *Journal of Social Work Education, 33*(3), 599–612. https://doi.org/10.1080/10437797.1997.10778897

Berman, A. (2015). Academic leadership development: A case study. *Journal of Professional Nursing, 31*(4), 298–304. https://doi.org/10.1016/j.profnurs.2015.02.006

Bryan, V., Krase, K. S., McLaughlin, A., & Meyer-Adams, N. (2020). BPD emerging leaders 2010–2016: Identifying and responding to the need for new academic leadership. *Journal of Social Work Education, 56*(2), 286-300. https://doi.org/10.1080/10437797.2019.1656576

Cassie, K. M., Sowers, K. M., & Rowe, W. (2006). Leadership in baccalaureate social work education: Preparing for the role of academic chair. *Journal of Baccalaureate Social Work, 11*(1), 1–20.

Cassie, K. M., Sowers, K. M., & Rowe, W. (2007). Ready, willing, and able: An assessment of academic leadership preparation and interest. *Journal of Baccalaureate Social Work, 13*(1), 115–127.

Council on Social Work Education. (1984). *Handbook of accreditation standards and policies.* Author.

Council on Social Work Education. (1994). *Handbook of accreditation standards and policies.* Author.

Council on Social Work Education. (2015). *Educational and policy accreditation standards.* https://www.cswe.org/getattachment/Accreditation/Accreditation-Process/2015-EPAS/2015EPAS_Web_FINAL.pdf.aspx

Council on Social Work Education. (2018). *2017 statistics on social work education in the United States.* https://www.cswe.org/Research-Statistics/Research-Briefs-and-Publications

Council on Social Work Education. (2019). *2020 strategic plan.* https://www.cswe.org/About-CSWE/2020-Strategic-Plan

Council on Social Work Education. (2021). *2020 statistics on social work education in the United States.* https://www.cswe.org/getattachment/Research-Statistics/Annual-Program-Study/2020-Annual-Statistics-On-Social-Work-Education-in-the-United-States.pdf.aspx

Council on Social Work Education. (2022). *Educational and policy accreditation standards.* https://www.cswe.org/accreditation/info/2022-epas/

Delgado, C., & Mitchell, M. M. (2016). A survey of current valued academic leadership qualities in nursing. *Nursing Education Perspectives, 37*(1), 10–15. http://doi.org/10.5480/14-1496

Gibbs, P., & Blakely, E. H. (2000). *Gatekeeping in the BSW program.* Columbia University Press.

Hardesty, C. (2011, March 25). What is the difference between management and leadership? *Wall Street Journal.* https://guides.wsj.com/management/developing-a-leadership-style/what-is-the-difference-between-management-and-leadership/

Lightfoot, E. (2019, October). *How neoliberalism in higher education is changing the landscape of PhD programs.* Paper presented at the 65th Annual Program Meeting of the Council on Social Work Education, Denver, CO.

Macy, H., Flax, N., Sommer, V., & Swaine, R. (1995). *An ecological perspective: Directing the baccalaureate social work program.* Association of Baccalaureate Social Work Program Directors.

Macy, H. J., Turner, R., & Wilson, S. (2000). *Directing the baccalaureate social work education program* (2nd ed.). Eddie Bowers Publishing.

Mapp, S. C., & Boutté-Queen, N. (2021a). The role of the baccalaureate social work program director: A qualitative understanding. *Journal of Social Work Education, 57*(1), 127–137. https://doi.org/10.1080/10437797.2019.1661922

Mapp, S., & Boutté-Queen, N. (2021b). The role of the US baccalaureate social work program director: A national survey. *Social Work Education: The International Journal, 40*(7), 843-860. https://doi.org/10.1080/02615479.2020.1729720

Mitchell, M., Leachman, M., & Saenz, M. (2019). State higher education funding cuts have pushed costs to students, worsened inequality. *Center on Budget and Policy Priorities.* https://www.cbpp.org/research/state-budget-and-tax/state-higher-education-funding-cuts-have-pushed-costs-to-students

Rodriguez, T. E., Zhang, M. B., Tucker-Lively, F. L., Ditmyer, M. M., Back Brallier, L. G., Karl Haden, N., & Valachovic, R. W. (2016). Profile of department chairs in U.S. and Canadian dental schools: Demographics, requirements for success, and professional development needs. *Journal of Dental Education, 80*(3), 365–373.

Stuart, P. H., Leighninger, L., & Donahue, J. N. (1993). *Reviewing our past: A history of the Association of Baccalaureate Social Work Program Directors.* https://www.cswe.org/getattachment/About-CSWE/CSWE-A-Brief-History/References/History-(2).pdf

Sullivan, W. P. (2016). Leadership in social work: Where are we? *Journal of Social Work Education, 52*(S1), S51–S61. https://doi-org/10.1080/10437797.2016.1174644

Watkins, J. M., & Holmes, J. (2008). Educating for social work. In K. M. Sowers and C. N. Dulmus (Eds.), *The comprehensive handbook of social work and social welfare* (pp. 25–36). Wiley. https://doi.org/10.1002/9780470373705.chsw001006

Whitford, E. (2020). Public higher ed funding still has not recovered from 2008 recession. *Inside Higher Ed.* https://www.insidehighered.com/news/2020/05/05/public-higher-education-worse-spot-ever-heading-recession

CHAPTER 2

Finding Your Leadership Approach

Susan C. Mapp

The 2022 Educational and Policy Accreditation Standards (EPAS), established through the Council on Social Work Education (CSWE), set forth a requirement for "leadership ability" in its directors—both program and field. For the program director, EPAS states that this person must have the "ability to provide leadership through teaching, scholarship, curriculum development, administrative experience, and/or other academic and professional activities in social work" (CSWE, 2022b, p. 31).

Kwame Christian of the American Negotiation Institute noted that once we achieve a certain level in our professional career, competence is typically assumed, but what makes a leader stand out is the "ability to interact with others, especially under pressure" (Christian, 2020, p. 134). As noted in Chapter 1, CSWE sees part of its role as helping to develop these leaders, as exemplified in its 2020 strategic plan, in which one of the strategies to achieve Goal 3—support the career development of students, faculty members, and administrators—is to "develop future leaders and administrators for social work education" (CSWE, 2020, Goal 3c).

By necessity, much of this leadership learning and training often comes after one has earned a social work degree. Although aspects may be integrated into a BSW or MSW program, there is a paucity of MSW programs focusing on leadership, though the number is growing. The number of MSW programs offering concentrations in management or administration has grown slightly, to 50 of 349 programs that offer a concentration and another nine that offer a certificate as of May 2022 (a total of 17%), from the 11% noted by Peters (2018) as of 2015 (CSWE, 2022a).

Like other forms of social work practice, leadership works best when the individual is clear about their theoretical approach. There is no dearth of models, which is important to note; too often, people do not see themselves as leaders because they do not fit the charismatic, extroverted leader model, sometimes referred to as the "Great Man" model, when in fact other forms of leadership are equally successful. In addition, some may believe that leadership is an innate quality when in fact leadership is a skill that can be developed, like any other. Pittman (2020, p. 128) noted, "Leadership is not just a position, but a grounded set of behaviors," while others have noted that leadership does not even require the position but can be exhibited by people at any level of the organizational hierarchy (Wergin & Leslie, 2006).

> **REFLECTION QUESTIONS:**
>
> Think about leaders you admire/have admired as effective.
>
> - How do/did they accomplish their work?
> - What traits did they exemplify, and how did they interact with others, both peers and subordinates?

Because a full review of leadership approaches and their evolution is beyond the scope of this chapter, this chapter focuses on a few models that fit well with social work values and ethics: strengths-based leadership (two variations), servant leadership, and the social change model. Readers are encouraged to think about what fits well with their style. Program directors can think about which suits them or, like clinicians, be familiar with several models that can be used in different situations. In all instances, it is essential that program directors use an approach that suits their personal style; to do otherwise would result in being inauthentic and thus would fail. Before moving into the specifics of these approaches, it is important to first ground the discussion in why leadership development is important, together with a discussion of what research has found to be general traits associated with good leaders.

Why Is Leadership Development Important?

Leadership development can have numerous positive impacts across all system levels of the program. At the individual level, through the requisite ongoing self-assessment and self-improvement, McCauley et al. (2010) note that this reflection can improve the ability to lead oneself through "self-awareness, the ability to manage conflicting demands, the ability to learn, and leadership values" (p. 14). Self-awareness requires us to think deeply about our areas of strengths and therefore the areas where we are not as strong as well.

Leaders naturally have conflicting demands, as any program director knows; they may feel caught between the demands of administration, students, and faculty, and must be able to balance these in an ethical manner. They may feel caught between the demands of the job and the needs of their personal life—a tension that has always existed but has been exacerbated by the impacts of the COVID-19 pandemic with nontenured faculty and those from marginalized populations, such as women, people of color, and members of the LGBTQ+ population, being disproportionately affected (Kotini-Shah et al., 2022; Tugend, 2020). Thus, the need for self-awareness and the importance of good leadership has only grown.

Looking at the mezzo level, McCauley et al. (2010) discussed the impact of leadership development on the ability to lead others through the improved "ability to build and maintain relationships (particularly with people who are different from oneself), the ability to build effective work groups (including the ability to bridge differences), communication skills, and the ability to develop others" (p. 16). Because leadership is inherently an interactive activity, McCauley et al. (2010) stated that the foundation of the ability to have effective relationships is "the capacity to respect people from varying backgrounds and to understand and value the diverse perspectives that they bring" (p. 16).

Similarly, program directors need to have people, whether faculty, staff, or students, maintain effective relationships with one another, as reflected in the ability to build effective work groups. Communication skills encompass not just the ability to tell others what we are thinking (expressive), but also the ability to truly hear and understand others' thoughts (receptive). Here, the skills of reflection and paraphrasing learned in social work education can help to ensure that one is listening to understand and not listening to respond. And program directors must be able to help others develop their own abilities to achieve these things.

Last, at the macro level, leadership development can positively affect programs and organizations through "management skills, the ability to think and act strategically, the ability to think creatively, and the ability to initiate and implement change" (McCauley et al., 2010, p. 17). Management skills, as discussed in Chapter 1, reflect the ability to accomplish the work of the organization. This day-to-day work needs to be balanced with the long-term direction of the organization, and thus BSW program directors must also be able to think strategically to determine the shared vision of the future and then ensure that the work is aligned with that path. Because higher education as a whole, as well as the context of social work, is rapidly evolving, the ability to think creatively is essential, which McCauley et al. (2010) defined as "seeing new possibilities, finding connections among disparate ideas, and reframing the way one thinks about an issue" (p. 17). An effective leader must then be able to put these creative possibilities into action, and thus the last ability is to initiate and implement change.

Although the business world is awash in scholarship on leadership and how to be an effective leader, there has been little scholarship on leadership in social work education, though there is some for social work in general. Multiple authors have noted that many business leadership models are not a good fit for social work because of not only to the different missions but also the value fit (e.g., Peters, 2018; Sullivan, 2016). As noted by Peters (2018), these traditional models are based on a more militaristic model with strict hierarchies and assume competitions with a winner and loser, in contrast to social work, which tends to have a strong emotional aspect in its organizations and consideration of multiple system levels.

Even a century ago, Mary Parker Follett, a pioneer management theorist and social worker, noted that organizations thrive through power-sharing and focusing on "power with," not "power over" ("Mary Parker Follett," 2020). Rank and Hutchison (2000), in their survey of social work leaders, found that respondents perceived five things that made social work leadership different from that in other professions: adherence to the Code of Ethics, a systems view, participatory leadership style, altruism, and concern about the public image of the profession (p. 493).

Sullivan (2016) further examined how human service organizations can differ from for-profit businesses, and much of what he wrote can be applied to universities as well. He cited Hasenfeld in noting differing factors, such as the use of professional staff, the focus on relationships between staff and clients, "the moral nature of the work," as well as the institutional setting (p. S54). With universities relying on faculty with advanced degrees, typically doctorates, to serve students—often conducting this work through the strong relationships they develop with students, especially at the baccalaureate level—the parallels are clear.

Sullivan (2016) continued on to note the need for agencies to be responsive to a diversity of stakeholders, who often hold different views about the role of the agency, and that these views can also change across time, with positive views often waxing and waning with the economy, again much like universities. He added, "Although these dilemmas have always confounded human service organizations, today, agencies deal with an increasingly diverse clientele with complex problems and needs and operate in the face of growing, and at times, unrealistic expectations," a sentiment with which many academics likely agree (Sullivan, 2016, p. S54).

Culture and Leadership

Effective leadership styles vary by cultural norms in areas such as power distance (whether subordinates are able to contradict superiors), collectivism (whether the group or the individual is more valued), the acceptability of assertiveness, perceived locus of control (whether people believe they have control over things that happen), and whether performance or care for others is rewarded (Northouse, 2019). Effective program directors must be able to align their own style with the style of those they aim to lead.

Who is able to rise to a formal leadership position is still heavily concentrated among those from historically privileged groups. In looking at the reasons for this as it relates to gender, Simon and Hoyt (2019) discussed the "leadership labyrinth," which can be extrapolated for other historically marginalized groups. They examined three central areas affecting who is able to navigate to the center of the labyrinth and achieve a leadership position: human capital, gender differences, and prejudice.

Human capital encapsulates the ability to access the opportunities necessary to be able to rise in leadership, the effect of a lack of access to which has been termed the "leaky pipeline," where those on a leadership path are unable to stay on it. These opportunities include education, work experience, and development opportunities, and can be limited by things like work-home conflict, where caregiving roles affect the ability to put in the time for the extra work often seen as necessary to be a "successful leader." These individuals may also not even be offered these opportunities due to an implicit belief that they would not be successful in them.

Assumptions about gender differences, which can be expanded to cultural differences, first center on style and effectiveness. Although a traditionally "male" leadership style is seen as more favorable in the workplace, women who adopt such a style are rated negatively by male peers and subordinates. Women have been found to lead in a more participatory style, though not a more interpersonally oriented style (Simon & Hoyt, 2019). Second, tied to their gender role, women are often seen as less committed or motivated, though research has not borne this out. Lloyd-Jones extrapolates from this to note that women of color often say that they are not seen as "legitimate" leaders (2016).

Third, the willingness to be a self-promoter affects the ability to move into leadership positions. Men have been found to be more comfortable self-promoting, identifying with and using power, and identifying themselves as a leader as opposed to a facilitator, the facilitator role being one with which women tend to identify themselves (Simon & Hoyt, 2019). Last in this category is the willingness and ability to negotiate. Not only have women been found to be less willing to negotiate, but the framework within which these negotiations occur is typically unstructured and ambiguous, which acts to the detriment of women and other disempowered groups (Simon & Hoyt, 2019).

The last barrier concept relates to prejudice, looking first at the impact of stereotypes of traditional cultural roles of who is a leader and what is needed to be a leader. First, looking specifically at women, this relates to the concept that their role is the family caretaker rather than a business leader, and that skills that are stereotyped as feminine, such as caring and empathy, are not seen as translating into effective leadership. These biases are often implicit, and people do not realize they are acting on them. Second, biased perceptions and evaluations relate to the previously discussed concept that although "masculine" traits are seen as favorable, women who adopt them are rated harshly, as was seen in Hillary Clinton's 2016 presidential run (Simon & Hoyt, 2019).

Third is whether and how the person chooses to react to these prejudices, which is often affected by how many stereotypes they face. The last concept examines the impacts of the intersection of identities, noting that Black women often face different barriers in the workplace than their peers from other races (Simon & Hoyt, 2019). Lloyd-Jones (2016) also noted that women of color may encounter a "chilly climate" in which they may be relegated to tracks that focus on their identity, such as teaching about race, mentoring students of color, or service on diversity committees, rather than opportunities that lead to higher prestige.

REFLECTION QUESTIONS:

- How do your identities help or hinder you in the leadership process?
- What culture exists to support or subvert your leadership—both at the program level and the institutional level?

All leaders must be able to critically reflect on their own positionality through the intersection of their identities and how it affects their leadership. As noted by Santamaría et al. (2016), leaders must ask themselves questions such as: How do these elements create barriers or facilitators to recognize other points of view and perspectives? What blind spots exist because of them? What privilege has been created that can be leveraged to advocate for others?

Higher educational institutions were established by and for those traditionally in power—wealthy White men. As other groups have slowly been allowed in, systems have not necessarily evolved to include them, but rather have worked to adapt them to existing systems. As social work educators and leaders, it is part of our ethical mandate to work to create more socially just systems, including within our own institutions and programs. Resources have been distributed inequitably, both between and within institutions, with female-dominated disciplines like social work often being allocated fewer tangible resources as well as intangible resources such as attention and prestige (Kezar & Posselt, 2020). With the continual reduction of financial resources from federal and state governments to higher education, the financial burden has shifted to institutions and thus often to students. Departments that are unable to demonstrate financial viability are being closed, primarily in the humanities, but in other areas as well, including social work.

Pushing back against a neoliberal focus driven by finances are calls for focusing on social justice and equity-mindedness. *Equity-mindedness*, as described by the Center for Urban Education at the University of Southern California, "refers to the perspective or mode of thinking exhibited by practitioners who call attention to patterns of inequity in student outcomes" (USC Center for Urban Education, n.d., para. 1). These leaders turn a critical eye both to themselves and to their institutions with an awareness of how the systems in which they were educated were developed and the impact they have as a result. They are "evidence-based; race conscious; institutionally focused; systemically aware; and equity advancing" (USC Center for Urban Education, Figure 1).

These individuals have learned to slow down the decision-making process to engage in reflexive practices to ensure that they are not replicating previous practices that perpetuate inequality. As BSW program directors, there are places where we hold power and places where we lack power. Through our social work education, we learned to recognize interlocking systems of power and how intersecting identities can create or block access to them. Undergraduate education is often seen as "lesser" than graduate education, and those who teach it are stigmatized, much as how social workers are stigmatized for their association with the disempowered and disenfranchised in our society. As stated, we are also often lower on the ladder of privilege due to the profession being female dominated. This is essential to recognize because "socially just leadership means being aware of the way that power shapes administrative structures and culture," and leaders must have a sense of their own role and positionality within it (Kezar & Posselt, 2020, p. 12).

> **REFLECTION QUESTIONS:**
> - How can we operate with students at the center of what we do?
> - How do our systems create barriers or springboards for different types of students?

Social work program directors must also challenge unjust systems on their campus for employees. Although most institutions have a faculty governance body to speak for the rights of faculty, staff all too often lack a similar voice and power. Many promotion and tenure systems favor traditional modes and methods of scholarship over those seen as more feminist, such as qualitative research or community projects. Many institutions now push grants as a mechanism to recover some of the traditional funding streams that have been lost over recent decades (Lightfoot, 2019). However, grantors, especially those of major grants from the federal government with a high indirect rate, often privilege certain areas and types of research to the exclusion of those that would question the very systems on which they are built. Therefore, as anti-racist and anti-oppressive social work leaders, we must continually use a reflexive approach to ourselves, our leadership style, and the systems within which we operate.

Leadership Traits in Higher Education

A number of studies have been conducted to determine what makes an effective leader in higher education. When looking at common traits of "Great Colleges to Work For," leaders are credible and capable, communication is transparent and interactive, there is a focus on achieving goals through collaboration and contribution (putting people in the right positions to maximize their contributions), and respect is demonstrated through fairness and acknowledgment (Ruben et al., 2017, p. 72). Integrating findings across studies, the common traits of higher education leaders are listed next (Bernotavicz et al., 2013; Bliss et al., 2014; Holosko, 2009; Lamb & Clutton, 2014; Peters, 2018; Pittman, 2020; Sullivan, 2016; Vito, 2015; 2020):

- acceptance of individuals and a welcoming of their perspectives
- adaptive
- authentic
- collaboration
- communication
- focus on the mission
- inspiring and empowering others to act to achieve a shared vision
- integrity
- modeling values
- positivity
- problem solving
- teamwork
- transparent
- trust

In one of the only studies to include social work faculty, Rank and Hutchison (2000) surveyed social work deans and heads of National Association of Social Workers (NASW) chapters regarding perceptions of leadership. They found five common elements: proaction (defined as acting in anticipation of future problems), values and ethics, empowerment, vision, and communication (p. 492). These leadership traits align well with the five exemplary leadership practices identified by Kouzes and Posner (2016): Model the Way, Inspire a Shared Vision, Challenge the Process, Enable Others to Act, and Encourage the Heart.

Model the Way means that leaders act in ways that exemplify shared values, and *Inspire a Shared Vision* has leaders enlisting others in working to achieve an exciting future. Leaders who *Challenge the Process* seek opportunities to innovate, often looking outside of their organization for inspiration, and take risks and experiment to achieve small wins and constantly move the organization forward. When leaders *Enable Others to Act*, they empower all to do their best work through developing collaborative relations built on trust. Lastly, leaders *Encourage the Heart* when they recognize and demonstrate appreciation for the work that individuals do and create community through a celebration of values and victories (Kouzes & Posner, 2016).

These practices are assessed through their Leadership Practices Inventory (see https://www.leadershipchallenge.com), an instrument that can be completed through a self-assessment and/or through a 360 process. The internal reliability of the subscales that measure the five practices is consistently strong, with Cronbach's alpha generally ranging between 0.8 and 0.9; test-retest reliability has also been strong. Female respondents and respondents of color tend to score significantly higher on these practices than men or White individuals, respectively (Posner, n.d.).

Leadership Models

But the question is then how to demonstrate these traits and values in our work as program directors. Much like social work clinical practice, there is no one right way, but the approach will vary based on the clinician and the client system. Also similarly, the approach must align well with the leader, or it will be inauthentic and thus ineffective. As noted, many social work leaders receive little formal education about leadership development, which includes learning about different leadership models. Determining one's "leadership philosophy" is the first step in Ruben et al.'s (2017) model of effective leadership development. This includes determining one's:

- Vision of leadership: the leader you aspire to be;

- Leadership identity: how you would like to be viewed by colleagues;

- Leadership brand: what you would like to be uniquely known for; and

- Leadership legacy: the lasting contribution you want to make (p. 170).

Determining the model of leadership with which one most closely identifies is an important part of clarifying this philosophy, and thus the following models are discussed: Strengths-based leadership (both for leading oneself and leading others), servant leadership, and the social change model. As noted, these are by no means the only approaches, and readers are referred to the suggested readings at the end of the chapter for more resources.

Strengths-Based Leadership

Although strengths-based leadership has been critiqued for being more of a pop culture phenomenon than an academically based theory (Dugan, 2017), it is widely used, and by its very name, it is clearly aligned with social work principles. *Strengths-based leadership* is a term that has been used in a variety of contexts: focusing on the strengths of the leader or the leader focusing on the strengths of those on their team, or both. Systems are set up to focus on what is wrong—we take points off a paper for errors; we write up employees for their mistakes—but strengths-based leadership requires that we focus on what is *right* and what people are naturally good at. The idea is that if we focus on that, both people and outcomes will thrive. The model is still grounded in the concept that leadership is learned, but that this learning should be focused on areas of innate strength (Dugan, 2017). Although the social work literature has not looked at using this approach, a meta-analysis of studies assessing the implementation of this approach in businesses found improvements across all domains examined: reduced turnover and safety incidents and increased profit, sales, and engagement of both employees and customers (Asplund et al., 2016).

Those encouraging the leader to focus on their own strengths note that people are more engaged in their work and thus more productive when the leader is operating based on their strengths. In addition, when leaders are aware of their own strengths, they are able to more thoughtfully assemble a team that complements, not duplicates, these areas, meaning that everyone will be more successful (Rath & Conchie, 2008). Focusing on the strengths of the team and enabling people to work on the things they are passionate about and good at will lead to outcomes that are good for everyone.

One of the leaders in this area has been Dr. Donald Clifton, who developed the StrengthsFinder assessment (now called CliftonStrengths). This tool, based in positive psychology, encourages people to focus on what they are naturally good at. Its premise is that people often do not recognize these abilities as strengths because they come so naturally to them, but if they do, and coordinate their work based on their strengths, they will be more successful. Teams are also encouraged to use this tool to work together more effectively.

The assessment consists of 177 semantic differential phrases, and the test taker chooses the ones that are more like them. Based on that information, an individual's top five strengths are identified out of 34 possibilities. Although there is an upgrade report ranking all 34, it goes against the ethos of the assessment to discover what you are *not* good at. Test-retest validity for the scale over 6 months is 0.70, and Cronbach's alpha for each theme ranges from 0.52 to 0.79. Its validity also appears to be strong, including construct, congruent, and discriminant validity (Asplund et al., 2014). Although it is not free, it is low cost ($20 as of this writing), and there are packages for universities that want to use it across the institution.

The 34 themes are organized into four broader categories, or domains, as they term them: Executing, Influencing, Relationship-Building, and

Strategic Thinking (Rath & Conchie, 2008). Those strong in *Executing* excel in accomplishing tasks and seeing projects completed. Within the domain, a person might have the strength *Deliberative*, in which they think deeply and contemplate the anticipated obstacles before making decisions, while a person with *Focus* follows through with commitments, including making any adjustments needed to accomplish the goal (Rath & Conchie, 2008). People whose strengths are in the domain of *Influencing* help spread ideas. Someone with *WOO* (Winning Others Over) loves to meet new people and develop a positive relationship; strangers are just friends they haven't yet met. A person with the strength of *Command* excels at being a leader; they are good at being in charge and bringing along others with them (Rath & Conchie, 2008).

The *Relationship-Building* domain focuses on those skilled at bringing a team together in order to make the most of these strengths. For example, someone with the strength of *Developer* is able to spot the potential in a person and provide them with opportunities to develop that potential. Those with *Individualization* are interested in learning the unique qualities of each person and then building on those strengths in a way that maximizes them (Rath & Conchie, 2008). People strong in the *Strategic Thinking* domain "absorb and analyze information that informs better decisions" (Gallup, 2020a, para. 3); they use this information to help their team think about what *could* be. In this domain, those with *Ideation* as a strength are fascinated by ideas and seek connections between them, and those with *Futuristic* are excited by the potential that the future can hold (Rath & Conchie, 2008).

As an example to give readers an idea of how these come together, I discuss my top five strengths below:

> My top five strengths are *Analytical, Learner, Input, Maximizer,* and *Relator.* The first three of these fall into the *Strategic* domain; *Maximizer* is in *Influencing* and *Relator* is in *Relationship-Building.*

> My focus on research as my focus in social work is no surprise once you know I am strong in *Analytical*—which focuses on identifying reasons and causes through understanding patterns and connections. *Learner* is common to academics because people in this domain have a "great desire to learn and want to continuously improve. The process of learning, rather than the outcome, excites them" (Rath & Conchie, 2008, p. 199). This complements my theme of *Input*: "People strong in the Input theme have a craving to know more. Often they like to collect and archive all kinds of information" (Rath & Conchie, 2008,

p. 191). This explains why I was the only college student I knew who bought a filing cabinet to save articles I had read and papers of which I was particularly proud (some of which I still have).

Relators love deep connections with people and draw enjoyment and strength from meaningful; genuine relationships; they enjoy working with those they know well. My co-editor of this book has been my friend and colleague since the last century (we've lost count of the exact number of years). My *Maximizer* strength means I am looking for strengths in order to take work from good enough to great. The description of *Maximizer* is one of my favorites: "Excellence, not average, is your measure. Taking something from below average to slightly above average takes a great deal of effort and in your opinion is not very rewarding. Transforming something strong into something superb takes just as much effort but is much more thrilling" (Gallup, 2020b, para. 1). Helping students achieve more than they thought they were capable of is one of my great pleasures. One of my students once wrote on an evaluation, "Dr. Mapp sets the bar high, but because she believed in me that I could achieve it, I believed in myself."

Strengths-Based Leadership for Others

When social workers think about being strengths-based, they are more likely to think about focusing on the strengths of others rather than their own. Although Rath and Conchie's model focuses more on the leader than on those they supervise, it can be adapted for this purpose. When leaders know and use the strengths of those around them, work assignments can be better aligned. This is outlined in the ABCD model of strengths-based leadership (Walter, 2013):

A—Align, don't fix: Employees should be able to volunteer for projects that interest them, rather than be assigned to ones for which they may have no interest or natural talent.

B—Build diverse teams: Research has found that teams produce better outcomes when they are composed of diverse people. This includes not only diverse strengths but also age, sex, gender, race, ethnicity, background, perspectives, and so forth.

C—Create a culture of transparency: For you to truly learn about your faculty, and thus their strengths and passions, they must be able to trust you.

D—Don't manage, empower: Let your faculty solve problems that arise, rather than stepping in and doing it for them. The diverse teams and their different viewpoints will naturally lead to a conflict of opinions, but as long as the conflict remains healthy, it is more productive to let them work it out themselves—both for the quality of the outcome and the development of your team.

The ABCD model transitions to other models of strengths-based leadership, in which focusing on your own strengths is not the primary method. In other models, rather than naming specific categories of strengths, strengths-based leadership is about identifying strengths in those you supervise and building on them. Much as when social workers use a strengths approach with clients, the focus is not on what is going wrong, but on what strengths the person has, because it is also based in positive psychology. It is centered in the belief that every person has potential and that capacity building is both a process and a goal. Much like entropy in systems theory, the concept here is that change is inevitable, but that positive change occurs through authentic relationships that value differences that come together in an inclusive process (Hammond, 2010).

Here the core values are identified as empowerment, empathy, self-reflection, cultural humility, and a genuine mutual respect (Byczkowski & Scott, 2020). It centers the concept of curiosity—learning from others to help move them and the organization forward. This can encompass learning from them about their strengths and what they believe is going well and exploring what needs to be changed in processes. When something is not going well, rather than assigning responsibility and blame, or telling the person how to do it correctly, this approach emphasizes learning from them about how they see the situation and how their personal strengths and values are at play within it. Thus, collaboration is key (Byczkowski & Scott, 2020).

> **PRACTICE TIP:** When you need to have a meeting with someone (faculty, staff, or student) about something that is not going well, start by asking them about their perception of the situation and their understanding of the task. Once there is a shared understanding of the task, you can work together to identify strengths for its accomplishment.

Empowerment can be both structural and psychological. Psychological empowerment encompasses four domains: competence, impact, meaning, and self-determination. *Competence* means that people feel confident in their skills to do their jobs, and *impact* assesses whether employees believe they have influence over what occurs in their workplace. *Meaning,* as it relates to psychological empowerment, is whether they believe that their work is "meaningful;" that is, that it helps them to achieve the type of world in which they would like to live. *Self-determination* in this context means that employees believe they have autonomy in determining how to accomplish their jobs (Byczkowski & Scott, 2020).

The four dimensions of structural empowerment are information, opportunity, resources, and support. *Information* relates to knowledge of the current state of the organization, including the fit of their unit in the overall structure, as well as the goals and values of administration. *Opportunity,* as it relates to structural empowerment, assesses whether the employee is provided with challenging work and the opportunity to learn skills and take on new roles. To assess *resources*, it is necessary to determine whether employees are given what they need to do their jobs, whether that be time or resources (including human resources), as well as have input on decisions related to obtaining these. *Support* means that people receive the support they need to obtain the resources discussed previously, but also strengths-based feedback that is specific and regular enough to be useful (Byczkowski & Scott, 2020).

This approach does not mean that people are only ever told positive things, but leaders need to work to ensure that these aspects of empowerment are met in order to set the employee up for success. Then if something does appear offtrack, rather than scolding the employee or telling them what they did wrong, a strengths-based leader approaches the conversation with "compassionate curiosity," to learn about the situation from their point of view (Christian, 2020). Readers are referred to Christian (2020) for a full discussion of this cognitive-behavioral therapy-based framework and its three steps: acknowledge emotions, get curious with compassion, and joint problem-solving.

Christian (2020) noted that we tend to avoid difficult conversations because of fear and anxiety, and thus we must start with our own internal psychology to ensure that we are centered for the discussion. Only once that occurs can we engage and connect with the other person. He discussed the importance of active listening to ensure that the other person feels truly heard, remembering that we are there to learn about their perspective, not to defend our own perspective or ourselves. This does not mean that our perspective is unimportant, but if the goal is to solve the problem, we need to do it together. Christian discussed the necessity of addressing issues while they are small, because the longer an issue is unaddressed, the longer we are implicitly saying that the other person's behavior is acceptable. You can also watch his Ted Talk at https://www.ted.com/talks/kwame_christian_finding_confidence_in_conflict.

> **PRACTICE TIP:** Before important conversations, be sure to take some time to center yourself and identify your true concern or goal. Are you simply reacting to things not being done as you would do them, or is there an important outcome that will not be achieved?

Servant Leadership

Although the concepts that form the basis of servant leadership go back millennia, it was Robert Greenleaf who developed the term "servant leadership" in a 1970 essay to explain the idea of a leader for whom the focus is not power or money, but rather the development of others (Northouse, 2019; Tarallo, 2018). In 1977, Greenleaf published a book in which he expanded these ideas—*Servant Leadership*. Servant leadership falls into the realm of transformational leadership theories. Leaders with a transformational style focus not just on the outcome but also on the process of developing their "followers" as well as the broader community (Dugan, 2017, p. 189).

There is a lack of agreement in the literature on servant leadership about its exact characteristics, but common ones include "authenticity, humility, integrity, listening, compassion, accountability, courage and altruism" (Northouse, 2019, p. 231). A servant leader focuses primarily on the growth and well-being of people and the communities to which they belong through a focus on emotional needs, empowerment, and being an ethical model to others. While traditional leadership generally involves the accumulation and exercise of power by the one at the "top of the pyramid," servant leadership is different. The servant leader shares power, puts the needs of others first, and helps people develop and perform as highly as possible (Greenleaf Center, 2018). This then helps the organization reach its potential. Rather than working as managers who ensure the timely and accurate completion of assigned tasks, servant leaders seek to "develop and align an employee's sense of purpose with the company mission" (Tarallo, 2018, para. 6). Servant leaders are drawn to leadership by a deeply held motivation to serve others that permeates all aspects of their life (Dugan, 2017).

It has been stated that servant leadership is an effective model to reengage employees as people return to a more "normal" workplace as COVID-19 restrictions are relaxed (Connor, 2022), but this can be true for any workplace where normalcy and trust have been disrupted. The central tenets of listening and empathy to truly understand people's experiences can be used to create a path for healing within the organization when combined with putting other people's needs first and fostering growth and development (Connor, 2022).

To actualize servant leadership, the thoughts and opinions of faculty, staff, and students should be continuously sought, starting from the first day of orientation, to let them know that their input is truly desired. Servant leaders maintain their focus on "talent development" throughout an employee's tenure; in fact, some say that if a leader is not spending 25% of their time developing future leaders, then they are not truly a leader (Tarallo, 2018). The servant leader operates from the perspective that they have a moral obligation to help others develop to their fullest potential (Dugan, 2017). Similar to the strengths-based model, the servant leader approach focuses on the strengths of those the leader supervises and tries to align tasks with these areas. These leaders will also work to give away power whenever possible to empower others (Tarallo, 2018).

> **REFLECTION QUESTIONS:**
>
> - What ongoing processes do you have in place to solicit feedback from all program members (faculty, staff, students, and community stakeholders)?
> - What mechanisms exist for supportive leadership development for all?

Servant leaders also recognize the importance of asking good questions and listening deeply to the answers, similar to the "compassionate curiosity" previously discussed (Christian, 2020). This is true for both questions asked by the leader, as well as those asked of them (Tarallo, 2018). Use of "powerful questions" is also an important way to accomplish this. The concept of powerful questions comes out of the World Café model and focuses on developing and asking open-ended questions that truly evoke deep thinking (Vogt et al., 2003). The intent of powerful questions is to help the person being questioned to move closer to their goals, and thus the questions are intended to "lead to discovery, insight, and commitment to action" (Kee et al., 2010, p. 63). Powerful questions presume positive intent on the part of the questioner and focus on the past only for how it can inform the present and the future, rather than forcing the person to justify previous actions (Kee et al., 2010).

Vogt et al. (2003) noted that U.S. culture focuses on the importance of having the right answer, rather than posing the right question, and that we are thus drawn to quick fixes and either/or thinking. However, posing the right question at the start of a discussion can lead us to deeper thinking, provoking insight and innovation that can truly propel our institutions forward. It calls us to question our assumptions and think about what is *not* being discussed. According to Vogt et al. (2003, p. 4), a powerful question has the following characteristics:

- generates curiosity in the listener
- stimulates reflective conversation
- is thought-provoking
- surfaces underlying assumptions
- invites creativity and new possibilities
- generates energy and forward movement
- channels attention and focuses inquiry
- stays with participants
- touches a deep meaning
- evokes more questions

A list of powerful questions can be found in Vogt et al. (2003), but readers should not limit themselves to those. For example, the League of Women Voters offers a set of powerful questions developed by Diversity Dimensions Consulting (2018), such as:

- "What does success look like?"
- "What resonates for you?"
- "What are you holding on to?"
- "Who are you becoming?"

PRACTICE TIP: You can preidentify powerful questions before a meeting to guide the conversation, but don't limit yourself to them. Be guided by responses.

However, like all theories, servant leadership has its weaknesses. As a developmental model, it takes time to see results, and it is time-consuming for the leader. "Followers" must also desire this approach for it to be effective, otherwise it can be seen as micromanagement or overly personal (Northouse,

2019). It has also been critiqued in a feminist analysis by Eicher-Catt (2005), who noted the difficulties in juxtaposing a traditionally masculine concept—leadership—with a traditionally feminine one—servant—as one often comes at the expense of the other. She also noted that simply because a company espouses a servant leadership ethos does not mean that it actualizes it in terms of who is placed in positions of power. Although the tenets of empathy, deep listening, and caring for the whole person align well with culturally feminine characteristics, this does not mean women are actually placed in positions of power. As of 2022, in the executive leadership stratum of one of the more famous companies to adopt it, Southwest Airlines (2022), there are no visible people of color and the proportion of women remains low, at only 25%.

Social Change Model

Like servant leadership, the social change model is a transformational leadership theory, originally developed as a conceptual model for students to learn about and develop leadership skills (Dugan, 2017; Komives et al., 2009). It has expanded to professionals, and its tenets are a good fit with social work values because of its focus on positive social change through relationships, which align with the social work values of the *importance of human relationships* and *social justice*. It is focused on two goals—self-knowledge and leadership competence—and has six basic assumptions on which it is structured (Komives et al., 2009, p. 50):

- The purpose of leadership is to create positive social change.
- Leadership is a collaborative process.
- Leadership can be undertaken by any person, and it does not rely on a formal position.
- Leadership is inclusive and accessible to all.
- Leadership should be based on values.
- Service is an excellent method to develop leadership skills.

Thus, the social change model focuses not just on the outcomes but on how they are achieved. This model seeks to be expansive and inclusive regarding who can be involved in change efforts and how goals are achieved. It is dynamic, in that it is meant to be adapted depending on the context and those applying it (Dugan, 2017).

The seven basic values for the social change model are grouped into what Komives et al. (2009) referred to as "interacting clusters or dimensions"

(p. xiii), but social workers will recognize them as system levels. Each of these values has associated "Knowing, Being and Doing," in the terms of Komives et al. (2009), but social work educators likely recognize them as knowledge, values, and skills. The societal or community dimension has one value: *citizenship*. In this model, *citizenship* refers to responsible connections to one's community (or society) and working for positive social change within it. This requires a knowledge of how systems operate and advocacy skills, for example (Dugan, 2017; Komives et al., 2009).

The next level, *group*, includes the values of common purpose, collaboration, and controversy with civility. *Common purpose* is the concept that all members of the group are working toward a shared vision, thus creating trust among group members. Among the things necessary to achieve this are an understanding of how to develop a functioning group and the skills to do so (Dugan, 2017; Komives et al., 2009). *Collaboration* then uses this trust and shared vision to build on relationships among group members, focusing particularly on their strengths and diversity, to bring multiple perspectives to every effort. Group members need to "engage across difference and share authority, responsibility, and accountability for its success" (p. 54). This will clearly require effective active listening and a commitment to equitable and inclusive environments (Dugan, 2017; Komives et al., 2009). Working across differences means that as a result, there will be different perspectives of what is occurring and how to proceed. This leads to the last value in this category, *controversy with civility*, which requires open discussion of these different perspectives to develop effective solutions. Managing this kind of discussion requires mediation skills and empathy (Dugan, 2017; Komives et al., 2009).

The last level, *individual*, includes the values of consciousness of self, congruence, and commitment. *Consciousness of self* is the self-knowledge referred to in the goals of this model. Leaders must be aware of their own knowledge, values, and skills, including their attitudes and emotions as well as the impact of their own social position (Dugan, 2017; Komives et al., 2009). Ongoing reflexive practice and mindfulness facilitate the insight required for leaders to be effective. *Congruence* is that the leader's actions are in line with what they know about themselves through the consciousness of self, thus reflecting the honesty and integrity discussed earlier in this chapter as an important piece of effective leadership. The last value, *commitment*, signals that the goal of this model, positive social change, "requires an intrinsic passion, energy, and purposeful investment toward action" (Komives et al., 2009, p. 54). The leader must truly believe that their efforts can make a change and be able to adapt to barriers that are encountered (Dugan, 2017; Komives et al., 2009).

Research on the social change model is most commonly conducted with the Socially Responsible Leadership Scale, which has demonstrated strong reliability and validity. This research has demonstrated that the knowledge, values, and skills that undergird the model's key concepts are learnable, as longitudinal gains have been documented (as discussed in Dugan, 2017). It is available online and currently priced at $8.

Putting It Into Action

As a program director, once you have determined your preferred leadership theoretical framework, or perhaps an intentional combination of multiple models, you then need to determine how to put it into action. Like social work practice, work as leaders is a continuous process of growth and improvement (or should be!). Just as faculty members are required to assess students' achievement of the social work competencies and then use the results to continually improve programs, the same should be true of leadership. How do we continually assess the impact and outcomes of our work, determine what we should keep doing, and identify what needs to change? This requires a level of reflexivity, self-awareness, and openness to feedback and growth. We will never have all the answers, but every step forward brings us closer to them, to the benefit of our programs and those within them.

Ruben et al. (2017) laid out their model for becoming a better leader, much like the continuous improvement processes of assessment, as an ongoing loop of gathering information, intentional action and assessment, and then applying that knowledge. To facilitate reflection on application of one's leadership model and philosophy, they offered the following questions:

1. What was I trying to accomplish?

2. What understandings—theories or concepts—guided my actions?

3. How effective was I at translating my understanding into practice?

4. Was the outcome what I expected or hoped for? If not, why not?

5. What options should I have considered?

6. What refinements should I consider for the future in my understanding and my actions? (p. 176)

I would also append the following to question 4—if yes, why? It is as important to understand why things went as we hoped as to understand why they did not. Thus, in question 6, "What should I keep doing?" can be added. Through honestly answering these six questions, we can gain insight into what is helping us achieve our leadership goals and what we need to adjust. We should also seek feedback from others on their perceptions. We can then apply that knowledge to our future actions and assess the outcomes. Through engagement in this ongoing loop, we continue to improve as leaders.

Conclusion

Like clinical work, leadership works best when we are thoughtful about our approach and understand why we believe a certain approach is most effective, assess the research supporting that belief, and align our work mindfully with it. By considering the models presented here, or others (there are many others), social work leaders regardless of their formal position can work to ensure that their work is aligned with social work values and aims to accomplish the goals of the program for the good of all stakeholders.

Suggested Readings

Christian, K. (2020). *Finding confidence in conflict: How to negotiate anything and live your best life*. American Negotiation Institute.

Diversity Dimensions Consulting. (2018). *Powerful questions*. https://www.lwv.org/sites/default/files/2018-07/Powerful%20Questions.LWV%20DEI%20Training%20Resource.pdf

Dugan, J. P. (2017). *Leadership theory: Cultivating critical perspectives*. John Wiley & Sons.

Northouse, P. G. (2022). *Leadership: Theory and practice* (9th ed). Sage.

Ruben, B. D., De Lisi, R, & Gigliotti, R. A. (2021). *A guide for leaders in higher education: Concepts, competencies, and tools* (2nd ed.). Stylus Publishing.

Vogt, E. E., Brown, J., & Isaacs, D. (2003). *The art of powerful questions: Catalyzing insight, innovation, and action*. Whole Systems Associates. https://umanitoba.ca/admin/human_resources/change/media/the-art-of-powerful-questions.pdf

Temple University online strength-based leadership certificate: https://noncredit.temple.edu/public/category/courseCategoryCertificateProfile.do?method=load&certificateId=34037371

References

Asplund, J., Agrawal, S., Hodges, T., Harter, J., & Lopez, S. J. (2014). The Clifton StrengthsFinder 2.0 technical report: Development and validation. *Gallup*. https://www.gallup.com/services/176321/clifton-strengthsfinder-technical-report-development-validation.aspx

Asplund, J., Harter, J. K., Agrawal, S., & Plowman, S. K. (2016). The relationship between strengths-based employee development and organizational outcomes: 2015 strengths meta-analysis. *Gallup*. https://www.gallup.com/cliftonstrengths/en/269615/strengths-meta-analysis-2015.aspx

Bernotavicz, F., McDaniel, N. C., Brittain, C., & Dickinson, N. S. (2013). Leadership in a changing environment: A leadership model for child welfare. *Administration in Social Work, 37*(4), 401–417. https://doi.org/10.1080/03643107.2012.724362

Bliss, D. L., Pecukonis, E., & Snyder-Vogel, M. (2014). Principled leadership development model for aspiring social work managers and administrators: Development and application. *Human Service Organizations: Management, Leadership & Governance, 38*(1), 5–15. https://doi.org/10.1080/03643107.2013.853008

Byczkowski, N., & Scott, C. (2020). *Strengths-based leadership: An overview* [Workshop]. Temple University Strength-Based Leadership Program.

Christian, K. (2020). *Finding confidence in conflict: How to negotiate anything and live your best life.* American Negotiation Institute.

Connor, C. (2022, April). Using servant leadership to motivate post-pandemic, disengaged employees. *The ACAD Leader.* https://acad.org/resource/using-servant-leadership-to-motivate-post-pandemic-disengaged-employees/

Council on Social Work Education. (2020). *2020 strategic plan.* https://www.cswe.org/About-CSWE/2020-Strategic-Plan

Council on Social Work Education. (2022a). *Directory.* https://www.cswe.org/accreditation/directory

Council on Social Work Education. (2022b). *Educational and policy accreditation standards.* https://www.cswe.org/accreditation/info/2022-epas/

Diversity Dimensions Consulting. (2018). *Powerful questions.* https://www.lwv.org/sites/default/files/2018-07/Powerful%20Questions.LWV%20DEI%20Training%20Resource.pdf

Dugan, J. P. (2017). *Leadership theory: Cultivating critical perspectives.* John Wiley & Sons.

Eicher-Catt, D. (2005). The myth of servant-leadership: A feminist perspective. *Woman and Language, 28*(1), 17–25.

Gallup. (2020a). *An introduction to the strategic thinking domain themes.* https://www.gallup.com/cliftonstrengths/en/252080/strategic-thinking-domain.aspx

Gallup. (2020b). *What is the definition of maximizer?* https://www.gallup.com/cliftonstrengths/en/252299/maximizer-theme.aspx

Greenleaf, R. (1977). *Servant leadership.* Paulist Press.

Greenleaf Center. (2018). *What is servant leadership?* https://www.greenleaf.org/what-is-servant-leadership

Hammond, W. (2010). Principles of strength-based practice. *Resiliency Initiatives.* https://greaterfallsconnections.org/wp-content/uploads/2014/07/Principles-of-Strength-2.pdf

Holosko, M. (2009). Social work leadership: Identifying core attributes. *Journal of Human Behavior in the Social Environment, 19*(4), 448–459. https://doi.org/10.1080/10911350902872395

Kee, K., Anderson, K., Dearing, V., Harris, E., & Shuster, F. (2010). *Results coaching: The new essential for school leaders.* Corwin.

Kezar, A., & Posselt, J. (2020). Introduction. In A. Kezar, & J. Posselt (Eds.), *Higher education administration for social justice and equity: Critical perspectives for leadership* (pp. 1–18). Routledge.

Komives, S. R., Wagner, W., & Associates. (2009). *Leadership for a better world: Understanding the social change model of leadership development.* Jossey-Bass.

Kotini-Shah, P., Man, B., Pobee, R., Hirshfield, L. E., Risman, B. J., Buhimschi, I. A., & Weinreich, H. M. (2022). Work–life balance and productivity among academic faculty during the COVID-19 pandemic: A latent class analysis. *Journal of Women's Health, 31*(3), 321–330. http://doi.org/10.1089/jwh.2021.0277

Kouzes, J. M., & Posner, B. Z. (2016). *Learning leadership: The five fundamentals of becoming an exemplary leader.* Wiley.

Lamb, B., & Clutton, N. (2014). Leadership development for interprofessional teams to drive improvement and patient safety. In D. Forman, M. Jones, & J. Thistlethwaite (Eds.), *Leadership development for interprofessional education and collaborative practice* (pp. 47–68). Palgrave Macmillan. https://doi.org/10.1057/9781137363022_4

Lightfoot, E. (2019, October). *How neoliberalism in higher education is changing the landscape of PhD programs.* Paper presented at the 65th Annual Program Meeting of the Council on Social Work Education, Denver, CO.

Lloyd-Jones, B. (2016). Women of color and applied critical leadership: Individual, professional, and institutional strategies for advancement. In L. J. Santamaría & A. P. Santamaría (Eds.), *Culturally responsive leadership in higher education* (pp. 61–75). Routledge.

McCauley, C. D., Van Velsor, E., & Ruderman, M. N. (2010). Introduction: Our view of leadership development. In E. Van Velsor, C. D. McCauley, & M. N. Ruderman (Eds.), *The center for creative leadership handbook of leadership development* (pp. 1–26). Jossey-Bass.

Mary Parker Follett. (2020, November 13). In *Wikipedia.* https://en.wikipedia.org/w/index.php?title=Mary_Parker_Follett&oldid=988432814

Northouse, P. G. (2019). *Leadership: Theory and practice* (8th ed). Sage.

Peters, S. C. (2018). Defining social work leadership: A theoretical and conceptual review and analysis. *Journal of Social Work Practice, 32*(1), 31–44. https://doi.org/10.1080/02650533.2017.1300877

Pittman, A. (2020). Leadership rebooted: Cultivating trust with the brain in mind. *Human Service Organizations: Management, Leadership & Governance, 44*(2), 127–143. https://doi.org/10.1080/23303131.2019.1696910

Posner, B. Z. (n.d.). *Bringing the rigor of research to the art of leadership: Evidence behind the five practices of exemplary leadership and the LPI®: Leadership Practices Inventory®.* Wiley. https://www.leadershipchallenge.com/LeadershipChallenge/media/SiteFiles/research/TLC-Research-to-the-Art-of-Leadership.pdf

Rank, M. G., & Hutchison, W. S. (2000). An analysis of leadership within the social work profession. *Journal of Social Work Education, 36*(3), 487–502. https://doi.org/10.1080/10437797.2000.10779024

Rath, T., & Conchie, B. (2008). *Strength-based leadership: Great leaders, teams, and why people follow.* Gallup Press.

Ruben, B. D., De Lisi, R., & Gigliotti, R. A. (2017). *A guide for leaders in higher education: Core concepts, competencies, and tools.* Stylus Publishing.

Santamaría, L. J., Jeffries, J., & Santamaría, A. P. (2016). Unpacking institutional culture to diversify the leadership pipeline. In L. J. Santamaría & A. P. Santamaría (Eds.), *Culturally responsive leadership in higher education* (pp. 17–30). Routledge.

Simon, S., & Hoyt, C. L. (2019). Gender and leadership. In P. G. Northouse (Ed.), *Leadership: Theory and practice* (8th ed., pp. 403–431). Sage.

Southwest Airlines. (2022). *Executives.* Retrieved May 7, 2022 from https://www.swamedia.com/executives

Sullivan, W. P. (2016). Leadership in social work: Where are we? *Journal of Social Work Education, 52*(S1), S51–S61. https://doi.org/10.1080/10437797.2016.1174644

Tarallo, M. (2018, May 17). *The art of servant leadership.* Society for Human Resource Management. https://www.shrm.org/resourcesandtools/hr-topics/organizational-and-employee-development/pages/the-art-of-servant-leadership.aspx

Tugend, A. (2020). "On the verge of burnout": Covid-19's impact on faculty well-being and career plans. *The Chronicle of Higher Education.* https://connect.chronicle.com /rs/931-EKA-218/images/Covid%26FacultyCareerPaths_Fidelity_ResearchBrief_v3%20 %281%29.pdf

USC Center for Urban Education. (n.d.). *Equity mindedness.* https://cue.usc.edu/about /equity/equity-mindedness/

Vito, R. (2015). Leadership support of supervision in social work practice: Challenges and enablers to achieving success. *Canadian Social Work Review, 32*(1–2), 151–165. https://doi.org/10.7202/1034148ar

Vito, R. (2020). How do social work leaders understand and ideally practice leadership? A synthesis of core leadership practices. *Journal of Social Work Practice, 34*(3), 263–279. https://doi.org/10.1080/02650533.2019.1665002

Vogt, E. E., Brown, J., & Isaacs, D. (2003). *The art of powerful questions: Catalyzing insight, innovation, and action.* Whole Systems Associates. https://umanitoba.ca/admin/human _resources/change/media/the-art-of-powerful-questions.pdf

Walter, E. (2013, August 27). Four essentials of strength-based leadership. *Forbes.* https://www .forbes.com/sites/ekaterinawalter/2013/08/27/four-essentials-of-strength-based-leadership /#68b7667464c9

Wergin, J. F., & Leslie, D. W. (2006). *Leadership in place: How academic professionals can find their leadership voice.* Jossey-Bass.

CHAPTER 3

Accreditation and Reaffirmation

Tips to Help Navigate the Process

Needha Boutté-Queen
Stacey Borasky

Without a doubt, securing initial accreditation or reaffirmation is one of the most important tasks for social work program directors, with accreditation-related activities among the top stressors for undergraduate program directors (Mapp & Boutté-Queen, 2020). We wholeheartedly believe that attaining accreditation or reaffirmation, despite being viewed as a stressful undertaking, is inherently doable, provided that processes and timelines are followed as noted by your institution and the Council on Social Work Education (CSWE).

However, this chapter is not intended to be a step-by-step guide for how to achieve the accreditation or reaffirmation goal. Rather, it provides a higher education accreditation overview, along with insight, resources, and tips that can be used by new and seasoned program directors across all program levels, specifically those at the baccalaureate level of social work education. For a more detailed guide, readers are referred to the resources available on the CSWE website and encouraged to engage the assistance of the *accreditation specialists*, CSWE staff specially trained to support programs through the accreditation and reaffirmation processes.

Over time, we have learned that knowing and understanding the policies, procedures, and entities associated with accreditation benefited our collective ability to participate in both social work and institutional accreditation processes. Therefore, to help program directors better understand where social work education policies, standards, and processes fall in the overall scheme of accreditation, the chapter begins with a discussion of the current higher education accreditation structure in the United States. From there, this chapter moves to a brief discussion of CSWE's governance structure, including an overview of the commissions and councils that contribute to the policies, standards, and curriculum associated with social work education under the CSWE umbrella.

We then move to a discussion on the do's and don'ts associated with the initial accreditation and reaffirmation processes. Finally, the chapter ends with an overview of some of the changes that have occurred with social work education accreditation processes and procedures over time. Included throughout are practice tips based on our experience with successful program development and renewal. The suggested readings are intended to benefit all program directors as they undertake these crucial processes.

Higher Education Accreditation in the United States

Accreditation of degree programs at the undergraduate and graduate levels provides the public with an assurance of quality. Accrediting bodies for each degree are composed of peers who write accreditation standards, develop policies and procedures for program review, and make decisions regarding a program's compliance with the accreditation standards. The Commission on Higher Education Accreditation (CHEA), a body that recognizes accreditors of both institutions and programs, explains why accreditation is important:

- Students who want federal (and sometimes state) grants and loans need to attend a college, university, or program that is accredited.

- Employers ask if a college, university, or program is accredited before deciding to provide tuition assistance to current employees, evaluating the credentials of new employees, or making a charitable contribution.

- The federal government requires that a college, university, or program be accredited in order to be eligible for federal grants and loans or other federal funds.

- State governments require that a college, university, or program be accredited when they make state funds available to students or institutions and when they allow students to sit for state licensure examinations in some professional fields (CHEA, n.d.a, para. 3–7).

According to the Federal Code of Regulations (Education, 34 C. F. R. §602 (2021)), the United States Department of Education (DOE) also recognizes programmatic and regional accreditors with its own set of standards for recognition. The reference to regional accreditors may be new to some program directors, as many are quite familiar with their institution's accrediting commission, but most are probably not familiar with the names or requirements of the others. There are six accreditation regions in the United States, and seven commissions oversee institutional accreditation activities (CHEA, n.d.b). The institutional accrediting commissions in the United States are:

- Northwest Commission on Colleges and Universities
- Higher Learning Commission
- Accrediting Commission for Community and Junior Colleges, Western Association for Schools and Colleges
- Southern Association of Colleges and Schools Commission on Colleges
- Middle States Commission on Higher Education
- New England Commission on Higher Education
- WASC Senior College and University Commission

Though CHEA standards provide the template for regional accrediting bodies, each commission has its own process and set of standards to which institutions must respond in order to receive or maintain accreditation.

PRACTICE TIP: Look for commonalities and differences in the accreditation standards used by one other accrediting body compared with those used by your institution. From there, look at how programmatic accreditation feeds into both sets of standards.

As noted above, the DOE recognizes program and regional body accreditation, but it does not operate in an accreditation vacuum. The National Advisory Committee on Institutional Quality and Integrity (NACIQI) makes recommendations and provides information about accreditation processes, institutional eligibility, and other accreditation-related issues directly to the DOE (NACIQI, n.d.). Federal aid to students and many federal grant opportunities require universities to be recognized by accreditors with

NACIQI recognition. For this reason, all regional accreditors seek NACIQI recognition, as do many programmatic accreditors.

CSWE's Board of Accreditation (BOA), as the Accrediting Body, is recognized by the CHEA as the sole accrediting body for social work education in the United States. The BOA must be reviewed periodically by CHEA to ensure that it continues to meet those standards in order to maintain its recognition. Although recognition by NACIQI is possible for the BOA, it is not required, given that social work programs are housed in colleges and universities that are regionally accredited, which makes social work programs eligible for federal funding opportunities.

Although this entire discussion may sound overwhelming or present like a multifaceted, complex bureaucratic process, it is really very simple: Your program sits in a college or university that has its own institutional accreditation. When you engage in reaffirmation of your program's accreditation, your efforts help your institution meet its accreditation expectations as well. In some instances, because of the rigor associated with social work program accreditation, institutions may mirror processes used by social work programs during the self-study writing process or engage social work faculty in the institutional reaffirmation efforts.

For example, when each of our universities was last reviewed by its regional accreditor, the social work program's assessment plan and use of data for programmatic change served as a model for how other university programs and majors could structure their continuous improvement processes. Further, the social work programs' examples were used in both authors' 5-year interim reports, required by the regional accreditor to demonstrate continued adherence to the standards between reviews. In addition, social work program directors and faculty may be tapped to assist with regional accreditation because of familiarity with accreditation at the programmatic level and experience in systematic review and improvement.

REFLECTION QUESTIONS:

- What is your institution's regional accrediting body?
- When was the last time your institution's accreditation was reaffirmed?
- Beyond supplying data, how were you involved with your institution's reaffirmation?

- What knowledge and skills do you have that would contribute to your institution's reaffirmation efforts?
- What steps can you take now to get involved in your institution's next report or reaffirmation processes?

CSWE and Accreditation

From the larger framework of higher education accreditation, we now move into the specifics of CSWE's role in the social work education accreditation process. The introductory chapter of this text introduced the reader to CSWE's history, including program affirmation. As noted there, initially, only master's programs in the United States and Canada were accredited by CSWE, largely because it was commonly thought that formal professional practice education for social workers existed only at the master's level (CSWE, n.d.a). As time passed, accreditation of programs in Canada became the responsibility of what is now known as the Canadian Association for Social Work Education, leaving CSWE to focus solely on programs in the United States, which include, starting in 1974, those at the undergraduate level (CSWE, n.d.b.). Likewise, as program growth continued and leaders at that time began to formally address concerns, various programs, initiatives, task forces, and councils emerged and the CSWE governance structure evolved (CSWE, n.d.b).

Governance

Starting from a simple organization, CSWE is now a formal and complex organization that consists of multiple departments, as well as volunteer-based commissions and councils. For those interested in learning more about each, a visit to the CSWE website is highly recommended. There, readers not only have direct access to information about the history, but they will also find detailed information about the governance structure, membership benefits and membership programs, accreditation and reaffirmation, and opportunities to serve in various capacities.

Although CSWE has a highly knowledgeable, skilled, and diverse paid staff, its governance structure consists of a volunteer body divided into a Board of Directors and commissions and councils composed largely of social work educators. These volunteers develop and implement policy and help guide and focus the work critical to quality social work education in the United States, Guam, Puerto Rico, and the U.S. Virgin Islands. Understanding the roles and responsibilities of each is helpful to those who are not familiar with how social work education and the accreditation and reaffirmation processes work and how they are influenced by internal and external variables.

Critical to this governance structure is the requirement that, excluding private members, volunteers must be CSWE members to serve on the Board of Directors, commissions, and councils. While Board members are elected by the membership, every year an email call for applications is distributed as an opportunity to indicate one's interest in serving on councils and commissions, and when the call closes, applications are reviewed (CSWE, n.d.c). From the pool of qualified applicants, the chair of the CSWE Board of Directors appoints members to each of the commissions and councils, and those members serve for 3-year periods, which may be renewed for a subsequent term (CSWE, n.d.c). Currently, there are six commissions that contain 11 councils, with commission chairs serving as ex officio, nonvoting members on the Board of Directors. The six commissions are:

1. Board of Accreditation (BOA) (also known as the "accrediting body")

2. Commission for Diversity and Social and Economic Justice

3. Commission on Educational Policy (COEP)

4. Commission on Global Social Work Education

5. Commission on Membership and Professional Development

6. Commission on Research

Most relevant to the topic of this chapter are the BOA and the COEP, and thus we explain their structure and purpose. For detailed information on the remaining commissions, readers are encouraged to visit the CSWE website.

Commission on Educational Policy

Consisting of 16 members and a chair, the Commission on Educational Policy (COEP) creates the educational policies noted in the accreditation process. According to CSWE (n.d.d), included in the seven tasks assigned to this commission are "establish priorities for action in the area of educational policy and planning" (para. 5) and "prepare a statement of social work curriculum policy to encourage excellence in educational programs and to be used by the Board of Accreditation in formulating and revising accreditation standards" (para. 3).

The COEP identifies future issues that will likely face social work education and practice. This work is done through a variety of methods, but typically includes surveys of CSWE members, literature reviews on practice trends and issues that affect practice, consultation with the National Association of Social Workers and other practice-focused organizations, as well as employment projections and other data from the Bureau of Labor Statistics. For example, in the Educational Policy and Accreditation Standards (EPAS, 2015, p. 7), the COEP added "environmental justice" to Competency 3: Advance Human Rights and Social, Economic, and Environmental Justice (CSWE, 2015). This addition resulted from COEP's research, identifying such issues as the impact of climate change and toxic waste on vulnerable communities as critical issues for social workers to address in practice.

The two councils under the COEP are the Council on Field Education and the Council on Practice Methods and Specializations. These councils may be viewed as those that most directly influence the field- and practice-related policies as they carry out their stated functions and through their service as advisors to COEP on matters related to those two areas. For example, according to CSWE (n.d.e), the Council on Field Education, which has six specific functions, is the council that most directly engages various field education stakeholders in order to "advance the role of field education as the signature pedagogy in social work education" (para. 1). Further, CSWE (n.d.f) indicates that, through the processes associated with its three functions, the Council on Practice Methods and Specializations "identifies and responds to issues relevant to the preparation of students in the context of current and emerging social work practice" (para. 1).

Board of Accreditation (CSWE Accrediting Body)

Because of its direct connection with accreditation and reaffirmation, the Board of Accreditation (BOA) is the most familiar commission to social work program directors and faculty. Despite being familiar with CSWE as the overarching organization and with the BOA itself, many program directors do not know that the BOA is the only body recognized by the CHEA to accredit undergraduate- and master's-level social work programs in the United States. As noted previously, CSWE does not accredit programs; the BOA does. Thus, although the BOA is a commission that currently consists of 28 commissioners, a chair, and a co-chair, its relationship to CSWE is different from that of other commissions, and this is a CHEA requirement. Three additional, noteworthy pieces about the BOA (or CSWE Accrediting

Body) are that it is the only commission with a full staff and operating budget; that programs, not institutions, are accredited; and that, as the landscape of education and program offerings change, we expect that BOA's role in the accreditation process will change as well. This kind of landscape shift occurred several years ago, when the resurrection of clinical or "practice" doctoral social work programs (DSWs) became more common and resulted in a push for accreditation of these programs. The pilot accreditation process for these degrees began in fall 2021 (CSWE, n.d.g).

> **PRACTICE TIP:** Remember, because there are differences between program levels and because the BOA is not recognized to accredit schools of social work or whole institutions, BOA accreditation occurs at the program level only.

We have found that understanding the relationships between the COEP and BOA and between BOA and CHEA can save program directors time and frustration when learning what is required during the candidacy, initial accreditation, and reaffirmation processes. CHEA recognition requires BOA to undergo a self-study and review the process periodically. Just as CSWE-accredited programs must meet and respond to certain standards, so must the BOA respond to CHEA. In fact, it is the review, response, and feedback process that sometimes leads to changes in what BOA requires or requests of programs to get accredited.

For example, as this chapter was being written, there was discussion about the draft of the 2022 EPAS. Although many program directors, faculty, field staff, and other stakeholders were against some of the proposed changes, such as the elimination of required release time and faculty-student ratios, the BOA was in fact responding to feedback from CHEA indicating that some standards may have been too prescriptive in nature. Ultimately, the issues were resolved, and changes are reflected in the 2022 EPAS. The point here is that not sufficiently acknowledging, or failing to address, CHEA feedback can lead to the loss of CHEA recognition and the ability to accredit programs, and damage the reputation of CSWE and the BOA.

In addition to having to undergo a re-recognition process and abide by the standards under which it is recognized, the BOA must carry out several functions related to accreditation and reaffirmation. These are clearly noted in Memorandum of Agreement Between the Council on Social Work Education Board of Directors and Accrediting Body (CSWE, 2022a, para. A 1-5):

1. The AB has sole authority to define the scope of accreditation evaluation and services for social work programs.

2. The AB has complete autonomy in making the determination if a program is or is not in compliance with the accreditation standards.

3. AB has sole authority to execute periodic reviews, revisions, and publication of accreditation standards, policies, and procedures including timeline for reviews, execution of review and revision processes, final approval of standards, accreditation policies, procedures, and publication of finalized accreditation materials and decisions.

4. The petitions, reports, and correspondence related to the AB recognition shall be made available to the CSWE President and CEO and the CSWE Board of Directors, provided that the AB is not obligated to provide confidential or program-specific information contained in such materials and that such access does not compromise the autonomy of the accrediting body.

5. The development of new Educational Policy and Accreditation Standards (EPAS) is a collaborative effort between the AB and the CSWE Commission on Educational Policy (COEP). A joint writing committee comprised of AB and COEP members draft an integrated set of competencies and educational policies to inform the accreditation standards.

    The CSWE Board of Directors approves the educational policies and competencies to support continuity between the AB and CSWE vision for social work education.

At the time of this writing, the BOA, or AB, has begun the process of piloting accreditation of social work practice doctoral programs. Before requesting to take on additional accreditation responsibilities, the BOA must demonstrate that it has the capacity and ability to do so success-fully. Thus, the pilot process with two programs must be completed and reviewed by CHEA before CHEA can approve the BOA for granting accreditation at the doctoral level (CSWE, n.d.h).

The BOA does not develop the standards under which programs are accredited or reaffirmed in isolation; those result from a process that involves a joint committee. Although the standards are formed by the BOA, the basis for the accreditation standards is the statement on curriculum policy developed every 7 years by COEP (refer to the COEP discussion above).

Because COEP's work involves ascertaining how the practice landscape of social work needs to change, the educational policy (the "EP" in EPAS) statements are critical to forming accreditation standards for the programs that prepare the next generation of social work practitioners.

To ensure clear and accurate interpretation of the curriculum policy statement as it informs accreditation standards development, representatives from the BOA and COEP, together with Department of Social Work Accreditation staff members and a representative from the Research Committee (the joint committee), review each standard as it responds to the written policy statement. This requires considerable effort and many hours of discussion, review, and revision, and the work does not stop there. The process of arriving at a final Education Policy and Accreditation Standards document also involves getting input from other members of the BOA, COEP, CSWE membership, and other social work education stakeholders as drafts are disseminated and feedback is considered for incorporation (CSWE, 2022b). In fact, this is a multistep process that occurs with the goal of excellence in social work education in each step and every discussion.

PRACTICE TIPS:

- During each EPAS development cycle, attend as many feedback sessions as possible. The discussion will contribute to your understanding of the document, which will improve your ability to write your self-study to accurately address it.

- Be certain to give your own feedback on the drafts. As noted, the document is shaped by us, not an unknown "them."

As new program directors, we knew little about CSWE's governance and all that went into developing the standards under which our respective programs were accredited or reaffirmed. It was only through ongoing involvement with CSWE, as volunteers and (for one) as an employee, in the accreditation and reaffirmation processes, and study of what is presented here, that we came to better understand and appreciate the work of our colleagues charged with setting the quality standards we now know as the EPAS. We cannot stress enough that this section has provided only a glimpse into the governance structure of CSWE and how that structure contributes to social work education and accreditation. Included are what we consider to be the most important aspects of each commission as it contributes either directly or indirectly to social work education accreditation and reaffirmation, but there is so much more to know.

PRACTICE TIP: Maintain CSWE membership and volunteer to serve in CSWE governance. Getting to know more about the organization and those in other programs will be benefit you in your own process.

Undertaking the Initial Accreditation Process: History and Lessons Learned

A brief search on the keywords *social work education, accreditation,* and *reaffirmation* yields hundreds of matches that reflect decades-long study and input on these overarching topics. Examples of these matches can be grouped under these headings: accreditation decisions (Mabrey, 1998), advanced standing (Bremner & Zastrow, 2008), assessment (Buchan et al., 2004; Drisko, 2014; Horner & Borrero, 1981; Krase et al., 2021; Rahill et al., 2016; Sellers & Neff, 2019), autonomy (Koerin et al., 2001; Wayne & Hull, 1992), change (Lewis, 1981; Vernon et al., 2009), competencies (Holden et al., 2017; Voss et al., 2017), critique/reinventing (Drolen, 1999; Friedman, 2009; Robbins, 2014; Stoesz & Karger, 2009; Thyer, 2009; Watkins, 2009; Wolk & Wertheimer, 1999); curriculum (Cheung et al., 2019; Holosko et al., 2010; Lewis, 1981; van Wormer & Snyder, 2007), distance education (Vernon et al., 2009; Wilson, 1999), education policy (Jeffery, 2007), field education (Bogo, 2015; Bogo & Sewell, 2019; Dwyer & Urbanowski, 1981; Harris et al., 2016), performance/outcomes (Holden et al., 2002), and location as it relates to any number of topics, as well as geographic locations such as Australia (Pawar & Thomas, 2017), Cuba (Dubus & Greene, 2015), and the United Arab Emirates (Veeran, 2013).

These writings and many others offer colleagues a sound basis to learn about historic and current frameworks and understand each of these topics as they relate to accreditation, provide research findings, suggest new insights and opportunities, and even offer critiques abut accreditation processes. Yet, although accreditation-related topics have been addressed in the literature many times over the years and offer sound suggestions for change or further review, program directors can still benefit from more practical "life lessons" to support their accreditation efforts. These include the do's and don'ts: practical steps to avoid pitfalls and to help you develop and submit to the BOA a high-quality benchmark or self-study document for review. Building upon what we have offered in this chapter thus far, we now address those things from candidacy, where benchmark documents are developed and submitted to the BOA, through reaffirmation, where programs prepare self-study documents for review.

Candidacy

Before a program director submits any documents to CSWE, their broader institution should explore in depth what is required to start a new social work program. As explained in more depth in Chapter 8, launching a new program is a multistep, multilayered process. The BOA views the candidacy process as not only providing oversight as the program develops, but also as an opportunity to ensure new programs address resources, processes, and procedures that lead to equity, viability, and program sustainability. A program director would likely be the first program hire (even if they are not new to the institution) and would work closely with the university administration to seek regional accreditation approval (if required) to start a new program prior to seeking candidacy with CSWE; this approval is a requirement of CSWE as part of the Candidacy Eligibility Application.

Each regional accreditor has its own requirements for notifications of substantive changes at a university, including adding new programs. The importance of having a team to support this process cannot be overstated. Institutions typically have at least one person tasked with overseeing university compliance with accreditation standards—the designated Accreditation Liaison Officer. As a program director, you would partner with this person to complete the necessary components of a substantive change proposal, if required. Once the proposal is submitted, the regional accreditor may require a site visit, depending upon each accreditor's rules and the substance of the change requested. Once regional accreditation approval is in place to launch the program, it is time to begin the candidacy process with CSWE.

The BOA uses a 3-year benchmark process, beginning with determining eligibility to host a program at the college or university. Then a series of benchmark document submissions ensues, along with visits by a commissioner to the campus (or virtually) over 3 years, culminating in a final review for initial accreditation. The benchmark process divides the accreditation standards into two developmental reviews and one final review for compliance with all accreditation standards. The BOA determined that some standards require compliance from the beginning, such as having in place a mission and goals, admissions policies and procedures, and directors of programs and field education. These enable students to be admitted to the program during the first year or the precandidacy phase.

Other standards, such as curriculum mapping and syllabi, field education, and assessment, are considered "draft" standards. The commissioners provide feedback to the program about the draft standards, so that when the program is expected to be compliant (in Year 2), programs have guidance to assist in responding to those standards. This process continues into the second year. In the final year, Benchmark III or Initial Accreditation, the program is expected to demonstrate compliance with all standards.

The CSWE Accreditation Department team, especially the program's accreditation specialist, is of great assistance with the process. Although they cannot deem a program compliant with any standard, they can provide the program director with support through training and ongoing consultation throughout the process.

PRACTICE TIPS:

- Attend all offered trainings and workshops from CSWE, and network with others who have started a program. Never be afraid to contact your accreditation specialist, whose job is to help support you.

- Remember, though the BOA is looking for programs to address minimum compliance, the stronger the document(s) submitted, the better structured the educational experience for students, faculty, and other stakeholders will be. Thus, always strive for the best the program can offer.

Curriculum and Competencies: Foundation for the Social Work Program

All social work curricula are based upon the competencies for practice, as outlined in the EPAS and written by the COEP. The competencies reflect the knowledge, values, skills, and cognitive and affective processes social workers need to effectively practice with individuals, families, groups, organizations, and communities. Faculty design courses so that the requisite material is included to develop competence and the assignments provide formative and summative methods of evaluating student progress. Therefore, the curriculum is the core of a social work program.

PRACTICE TIP: Curriculum development and review are not just for new programs. Existing programs should also review their curricula on an ongoing basis to ensure continued relevance of their program context, including a review of assessment outcomes.

In our experience, there are multiple ways to tackle the task of developing and revising curricula. Best practice is to begin with the competencies. Each competency description in the EPAS provides details about what type of content is necessary to build competence in students. The knowledge, values, skills, and cognitive and affective processes are within the competency description; the program has a clear guide for what should be taught. The program director and faculty members have the power to design courses and scaffold them as they see fit. It is important to understand various theoretical perspectives and models for curriculum development, so that you can choose what works best for your program's context and mission. In the next paragraph, we offer some relevant theories and an example of using theory to explain the rationale for curriculum design.

It is crucial to familiarize yourself with educational theories for curriculum development, such as andragogy (theory of adult learning), the constructivist perspective, Bloom's Taxonomy, backwards design, concept mapping, and horizontal and vertical integration, to name a few. Theories help the program leaders and faculty explain to the BOA the rationale for the curriculum design, and the program director's knowledge of theories is critical to telling the story of the program's approach to teaching their students.

For example, the following is a competency description and behaviors taken from the 2022 EPAS.

Competency 2: Advance Human Rights and Social, Racial, Economic, and Environmental Justice

Social workers understand that every person regardless of position in society has fundamental human rights. Social workers are knowledgeable about the global intersecting and ongoing injustices throughout history that result in oppression and racism, including social work's role and response. Social workers critically evaluate the distribution of power and privilege in society in order to promote social, racial, economic, and environmental justice by reducing inequities and ensuring dignity and respect for all. Social workers advocate for and engage in strategies to eliminate oppressive structural barriers to ensure that social resources, rights, and responsibilities are distributed equitably and that civil, political, economic, social, and cultural human rights are protected.

Social workers:

- advocate for human rights at the individual, family, group, organizational, and community system levels; and

- engage in practices that advance human rights to promote social, racial, economic, and environmental justice.

The description above lays out for faculty the content (knowledge, values, skills, and cognitive and affective processes) and the behaviors that will enable them to demonstrate the competency in practice. The content should be included in some parts of the curriculum, such as "global intersecting and ongoing injustices throughout history that result in oppression and discrimination" (knowledge) or "evaluate the distribution of power and privilege in society in order to promote social, racial, economic, and environmental justice" (skill).

Let's use Bloom's Taxonomy to imagine where this competency might be taught and how it would result in assignments, readings, and activities, based upon the order in which the courses are taken. The Vanderbilt University Center for Teaching (n.d.) created an updated graphic for Bloom's Taxonomy (Figure 3.1).

FIGURE 3.1

Bloom's Taxonomy

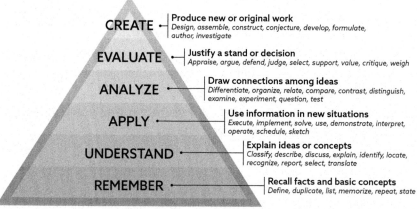

Vanderbilt University Center for Teaching

One might imagine that an introductory course in social work or in diversity, equity, and inclusion might focus on building knowledge and understanding of historical oppression and discrimination. In Bloom's Taxonomy, this type of knowledge lays the foundation for the ability to analyze how those historical practices led to the distribution of power and privilege today. That skill might be taught in a policy analysis course or an advanced course in social justice, or might be integrated into various practice classes.

Where that information is offered in a program's curriculum and where students learn skills is up to the faculty of the program. Therefore, there are no prescriptive courses or structure for the curriculum; there is the expectation that this competency and all competencies are woven into many courses, with some educational theoretical underpinning for how, when, and where this competency is taught and evaluated. Not only is this important information for a program director to have, but it is also critically important that all faculty understand the placement and reasoning to ensure a single voice to any commissioner, site visitor, or other program stakeholder. Engaging faculty throughout curriculum design discussions and benchmark document review will help reduce errors in writing as well as ensure the clarity of the program's narrative.

PRACTICE TIPS:

- Start with the competency.
- Ensure that the program is engaged and that faculty are clear on relevant theories that support the curriculum.
- Engage in faculty review of each piece of the self-study. This helps to ensure accuracy and identify writing challenges or issues that may impede the clarity of your program's narrative.
- Consider getting involved as a site visitor so that you can learn more about what the BOA is looking for.

Reaffirmation

Although it may sound like a cliché, the process of reaffirmation begins immediately following the last decision, whether that be initial accreditation or reaffirmation. This means that good recordkeeping is key, especially as it pertains to assessment and making changes as a result of assessment review. It is also helpful to shift the program to the most current EPAS as soon as is feasible. This will give you time to discover pieces that are not being adequately addressed or need to be refined long before you submit the self-study to the BOA.

Think of accreditation as continuous quality improvement. It is not meant to be something we think about only every 8 years; it is truly a process for examining the program in every aspect, across all standards and substandards in the EPAS. If you see accreditation this way, you will learn to build annual processes that make writing a reaffirmation self-study much easier. Some steps toward this end include annual assessment and analysis of competency data, documenting programmatic changes based on data, and evaluation of the program's efforts to continually provide a learning environment that is inclusive and a place for students and faculty to thrive.

Self-Study Preparation

Although CSWE provides a reaffirmation timeline (which is very helpful in tracking due dates for reaffirmation applications, fees, site visit forms, etc.), it is also important to create your own checklist and due dates for internal processes. Work backward from the date that your first document or fee is due to CSWE, using the timeline associated with the BOA meeting attached to your reaffirmation. Determine what your internal teams need in order for you to submit that first document (reaffirmation eligibility application and fees). This may involve working with several offices at the university, including the president's office, as the president must certify that the program is seeking reaffirmation and is eligible to do so.

Follow this with an internal timeline for completing the self-study document and assign tasks to faculty as needed, including reviewing sections of the self-study; reviewing assessment data and subsequent decisions made since your last review; and evaluating your program's efforts at creating a safe, supportive, inclusive, and anti-racist learning environment as required by the 2022 EPAS. Consider multiple methods of doing that evaluation, including surveys, focus groups, regular meetings with student leaders, and the like. For each standard in the self-study, list the key personnel in the program or university who will assist you in responding to the standard. For example, your program's field director is a key person to respond to the field education standards and make the connections between classroom and field or practicum. In summary, make a plan well ahead of—at least 3 years—your program's review for reaffirmation.

PRACTICE TIPS:

- Attend a reaffirmation workshop and be sure that all those who will assist with the process either attend or review the materials presented by the CSWE staff. This will help ensure that everyone is familiar with the most current standards.

- Schedule a session with your accreditation specialist to answer any questions you have if the standards or expectations have changed since your last review.

Writing for Accreditation

We believe that writing a self-study, whether for initial candidacy, accreditation, or reaffirmation, involves skills that many of us have not used for a while, because a self-study document is not a typical research article or book chapter. This kind of process is more like a "call and response," where the EPAS document is the "call" and the program's benchmark, or self-study document, is the "response." In fact, while the EPAS provides the format via the call, program directors need to remember that there may be many pieces addressed in a single standard, and not responding clearly to each may mean that the response is then identified as a concern or the standard not being in compliance.

Something being marked as a concern or not in compliance is not necessarily the end of a program's chances for candidacy, accreditation, or reaffirmation. It is, however, an experience that provokes anxiety that might have been avoided if the response was clearly linked to each part of the call. All too often, programs provide steps in the process (procedures), but not the criteria or the policy of the action. Examples of where multiple requirements or criteria, policies, and procedures are required are areas that address the generalist practice curriculum, field education, and assessment.

PRACTICE TIP: As you write, be sure you are responding to each part of the standard. Where there is an and, respond to everything that is requested. Likewise, where asked for criteria, policies, and procedures, be sure to clearly discuss each.

Writing the Reaffirmation Self-Study

Your self-study is a narrative. Tell the story of your program. Where have you been? What are your strengths and concerns? What changes have you made? Where are you going? This narrative is similar to a grant proposal in terms of how it is structured and what you are expected to cover. If you have ever applied for a grant as a practitioner or a researcher, you know that grants have specific areas to which you must respond. In the practice tips in the "Candidacy" section, we mentioned the importance of responding to each part of the standard. That is obviously the same guidance for reaffirmation. So, while the self-study is a narrative—your program's story—it is also meant to help the BOA determine your compliance with the standard.

For you to tell your program's story accurately, note in your reaffirmation document what happened between the benchmark and self-study periods. Once your program's initial accreditation or reaffirmation has been obtained, begin keeping a record of what changes occurred from term to term or year to year, and why. This may include information from faculty meeting minutes, curriculum or assessment committee records, and your program's assessment outcomes over time. A record of this nature is especially helpful when documenting changes that occur as a result of assessment findings.

Avoid the temptation to include things that, while interesting and perhaps proud accomplishments, are not necessary to demonstrate compliance. Remember that while your institution may have multiple initiatives that affect your students and faculty, the BOA is most interested in what *your program* is doing; this is a programmatic self-study, not an institutional self-study. The BOA wants to see how the program ensures compliance with the accreditation standards.

Give yourself time to draft each standard thoroughly and then time for a final review before submission. Rushing to write a self-study in a semester might not allow you the opportunity to respond as clearly and accurately as needed for the BOA to determine program compliance upon first read. In fact, beginning a working draft of the self-study document years out may be useful for reducing some of the last-minute pressures associated with the reaffirmation process. Keeping this document in a shared folder is also a good idea so that others may contribute as they have time, and the document will be easy to locate should program leadership change.

PRACTICE TIP: At the *very* latest, begin your writing at least 3 years before your submission deadline because editing is easier than writing entire sections.

In some areas, the standards ask for evidence, and site visitors may also request the same. With that in mind, be sure that you have supporting documentation or evidence of claims made and that this information is the same no matter where the program directs the reader. For example, if you are discussing admission criteria, policies, and procedures, make sure that the student handbooks, catalog, and other materials where such policies are contained are all up to date and accurate. If you are citing assessment data, make sure these data are accurate both online and in the documents you provide. It is easy to miss things if you do not regularly update them yourself as the program director but instead rely on other offices to do so.

> **PRACTICE TIP:** When making changes in various documents (e.g., self-study, student handbook, field manual, online assessment records), be sure to change the information in each location before moving to another task.

Although there are different approaches to writing the self-study, you should most definitely have faculty involved in self-study development, by writing specific sections and/or reviewing drafts. One school of thought is that "one person–one voice" is the best approach, with the program director writing the entire document but having faculty provide input and reviews. Others believe that it is better to divide the writing among a team of faculty, so that each person can concentrate on their area of expertise or the area over which they have authority or oversight. Who writes the document may end up being simply a function of the size of the program and availability of others to assist. At the end of the day, the program director is responsible for ensuring that the program remains compliant with the accreditation standards and for submitting a high-quality self-study on behalf of the program. However, this does not mean that the actual writing is a single-person task.

> **PRACTICE TIP:** Avoid writing the self-study by yourself. Not only is this an unnecessary exercise in inducing stress, but writing alone also does not allow program faculty to take ownership of the reaffirmation process.

According to a recent CSWE Department of Social Work Accreditation (DOSWA) presentation (CSWE DOSWA, 2021), among the standards cited most frequently by the BOA for site visitors to explore are faculty-to-student ratio, curriculum matrices, assigned time for the field director, assigned time for the program director, field education, diversity in the implicit curriculum, and assessment. Common threads running through the reason for citations are the lack of specificity or the lack of clarity.

The site visitor will always ask about mission and goals, diversity, and assessment, even if the letter of instruction does not ask specific questions about those areas. Given that many programs experience challenges in responding to these standards adequately, consult your accreditation specialist for guidance and consider bringing in a consultant (if your budget allows) to read your drafts and offer feedback, editing, to meet with administrators, and so forth, as you deem necessary. Although CSWE does not endorse consultants or recommend specific individuals to serve in that capacity, your social work education colleagues will likely know of experienced individuals who may be available. Before engaging with a consultant, the program should a) identify consultants who have experience with EPAS and knowledge of the timelines and processes, and b) review both the pros and cons of doing so. Some of the pros and cons are presented in Table 3.1.

TABLE 3.1

The Pros and Cons of Hiring a Consultant

Pros of Using a Consultant	Cons of Using a Consultant
A consultant can provide a second set of eyes to review documents.	The consultant's reader bias might lead to recommendations that go beyond the "minimal compliance" expectation of the BOA.
Consultants have experience with the process.	The expense might be cost-prohibitive.
Consultants understand the expectations of the BOA.	A consultant cannot ensure compliance; only the BOA can make that determination.
A consultant could advocate for the program with administration to help maintain compliance with standards.	Consultants without administrative experience in higher education might not be as valuable to the program.
Consultants from similar types of institutions bring expertise and understand the strengths and challenges.	Response times might hinder the program's ability to move forward as originally planned.

The need for consultants differs based on various factors, from the institution's complexity to the program options offered to students. Because institutions and programs are different, accreditation activities and internal timelines will vary. Table 3.2 provides a brief look at factors affecting the reaffirmation processes as well as how a consultant may be of value to a program director.

TABLE 3.2
Factors Affecting the Process

Factor Affecting Reaffirmation Process	Implications to the Timeline	Consultant Services
Program context	The type of institution and the position of the program within the university (separate department, school, college, etc.) can simplify or complicate the timeline.	A consultant could help identify all of the people at the administrative level who must be involved and in what ways they should be involved. Your job would be to help create a realistic timeline, roles, and responsibilities.
Institutional supports	Some institutions offer support with assessment of student outcomes, reviews and edits of documents, project management for large changes, or accreditation offices. These supports could affect the internal timeline.	A consultant might know what supports are available and the specific ways in which they can help (e.g., institutional research may assist with the assessment standards in EPAS); thus, new directors could benefit from a consultant in this area.
Change processes	Each institution has an infrastructure and processes for implementing changes in academic programs; the numbers of departments and people involved, the types of changes made to respond to EPAS, the time frames under which committees operate, etc., all affect the timeline.	A consultant who comes with reaffirmation experience at different institutions could help the program director create a timeline so that all who need to be included or give approvals would be involved prior to the document submission to CSWE.

(continued)

Table 3.2 (cont.)

Technology	Use of technologies can simplify some processes (e.g., data collection and analyses, field education, and curriculum mapping) and affect the timeline. However, using fewer technologies than needed might lengthen the timeline internally.	Program directors could explore with a consultant and university leadership technologies for data collection and analyses, online tools, and other means of supporting the program's ability to respond efficiently and effectively to each standard.
Faculty workload	Time to focus on the self-study process differs by institution. If possible, it is preferable to spread the workload among a team, which would release faculty from teaching or other responsibilities so they could assist with the reaffirmation process.	A consultant could assist with assembling a team of people to work with various pieces of the self-study; a consultant could then recommend the best use of the faculty and director's time.

PRACTICE TIP: When possible, leave sufficient time for faculty review and feedback or have a colleague outside of your program review the self-study for clarity and consistency before submission.

Writing the Benchmark Documents for Candidacy

The primary difference between writing a reaffirmation self-study and the candidacy benchmark documents is simply the time frame when the documents are submitted, based on the process. Writing for candidacy mirrors writing the reaffirmation self-study; you must address each standard and each piece of the standard as required. The same call-and-response format applies. Again, because the process of candidacy is developmental, the BOA does not expect full compliance with every standard until the program is in Year 3, the initial accreditation submission of a full self-study. At this point, the documents are exactly the same as those submitted for reaffirmation: the self-study, the syllabi, and all other supporting documentation.

PRACTICE TIPS:

- You don't have to be perfect, but be planful. Remember, the BOA only requires that programs demonstrate minimal compliance to standards and that programs are timely with document submission. Too often, program directors place unnecessary stress on themselves and others by writing too much. Add to this unforeseen delays that may prevent opportunities for program or external review prior to submission. Combined, these things often negatively affect the quality of the program's story and lead to BOA citations or questions.

- Don't make promises you can't keep, and don't say things that don't exist just to impress commissioners.

- Because field education is the signature pedagogy of social work education, it is important to consider it at all stages of program development and reaffirmation. With that in mind, never, ever forget field education, even during initial program development stages.

Field Education: The Signature Pedagogy

Field education is a crucial part of the candidacy and reaffirmation processes. A mistake that program faculty and administrators sometimes make is to consider field education as separate from the curriculum, rather than as the culminating experience of the curriculum. Further, because field education has its own director or coordinator, as required by the EPAS, programs sometimes operate as though the two sides of the curriculum are independent of each other in both curriculum and operations. This is a mistake we encourage you to avoid.

Field education is considered the "signature pedagogy" of social work education, and program faculty and administrators should therefore envision the field experiences of students and practice settings as they design curriculum, assignments, assessments, and so forth. Keep in mind that each course and its content affect the preparation of students for practice. In the same vein, without the ability to integrate what they learn in class into the practicum setting with actual clients, students are operating in a vacuum, relying solely on the field instructor.

Best practice is a full and clear integration of content from courses in assignments connected to the field placement and/or seminar courses attached to the field placement. Programs should require students to reflect on what they have learned and how that learning prepared them for practice. Therefore, we strongly encourage program faculty and administrators to include field education staff and field instructors in curriculum development and review, along with review of data from all assessments across the curriculum. The better the team is integrated with faculty, the more integrated the curriculum will be. Given that such integration must be articulated in the self-study (Accreditation Standard 3.3: Field Education in 2022 EPAS [CSWE, 2022]), program directors should be purposeful in their approach to the signature pedagogy and its design within the curriculum.

Changes Over Time

One thing we have learned over the last 25 years is that, even with accreditation and reaffirmation, change is certain. When we first embarked upon our journeys, we wrote as though each word was forever, until the next reaffirmation. So, we wrote with the kind of certainty that allowed us to rest and take a deep breath at the end of a job well done. What we did not fully grasp is that there are many variables that influence BOA's ability to accredit programs, educational policy, accreditation standards, and programmatic outcomes.

For example, as the BOA learns about changes to CHEA's requirements for accrediting bodies, it must adapt to maintain its status. This may or may not coincide with a program's reaffirmation timing and may require changes in what a program does. One example of this is the requirement that the program's current assessment outcomes data be posted on the program's website so that stakeholders and the public at large can always see it and make informed determinations about a program's effectiveness.

Another change is the use of multiple measures that do not include the students' self-assessment of content mastery. At one time, a program could simply submit field instructors' evaluations and student self-evaluations as evidence of compliance if benchmarks were clearly set and a description of how the data were derived accompanied the submission. Although this was simple and clean in terms of data collection, it was later determined that student self-evaluation data were inadmissible when determining benchmark attainment. This was because the students were still in learner mode, not yet graduated professionals, and therefore they could not determine mastery. Although student self-assessment can be an important learning tool for them, it is considered "indirect assessment" and thus inadequate for accreditation purposes.

Submission Process

Some changes have absolutely nothing to do with CHEA but are more practical in nature. Earlier candidacy, accreditation, and reaffirmation processes involved mailing multiple volumes of printed self-studies to the CSWE offices, site visitors, and commissioners for review. Not only was this process costly for programs (paper, toner, and postage), but it also created storage challenges for each person involved, whose office shelves were often lined with program documents that would rarely serve a purpose beyond the decision-making process. Thankfully, the documentation can now be submitted via email. Once it is received, a cloud-based program is used for dissemination to commissioners and site visitors, who can then print the documents if they wish or simply conduct the reading review on their computers.

Increased Use of Technology

Another practical change is the increased use of technology over time, which has led to having information at one's fingertips. For example, changes to the CSWE website include the addition of PowerPoint slides, which provide information previously only available through phone calls, emails, or conference attendance. In addition, this mode of communication enhances the ability of the DOSWA to communicate one message succinctly. Visitors to the site will see messages related to the accreditation process, student assessment, COVID-19, and even those standards, excluding assessment, that received the highest number of citations presented at CSWE's most recent Annual Program Meeting. Assessment, as anyone writing a self-study can understand, stands alone.

Benchmarks Decreased

One of the changes embraced by those seeking program accreditation was the reduction in time and benchmarks it took to reach the goal. The candidacy process for accreditation evolved over the years. At one point, it took 4 years to achieve full accreditation through a process of benchmark submissions and reviews of the program. Now, benchmarks are collapsed, and the entire process can be accomplished in 3 years, saving time, energy, and money for all involved.

EPAS Handbook and Glossary Added

To provide clarity and allow for a single point of reference, a handbook and glossary were developed and are available to all via the CSWE website.

From a commissioner's perspective, these documents were welcomed resources. They removed the potential for confusion—that is, for a program director to understand a term one way, the BOA representative to understand it another, and the accreditation specialist to be caught in the middle. Such confusion might have been detrimental to the program's accreditation process.

COVID-19

Over the years, the initial accreditation and reaffirmation processes had remained relatively stable in terms of types of program and field requirements, modalities of site visitor and commissioner visits, and so on, with the exception of one notable change: the expansion of the initial accreditation term from 4 to 8 years. However, the arrival of COVID-19 during the spring of 2020, with risks of infection, the absence of vaccinations, and uncertainties around transmission methods, led to near-immediate responses from CSWE and other accrediting bodies to ensure the health, safety, and well-being of students, faculty, staff, and all stakeholders.

Among the changes to social work education because of COVID-19 were the ability of programs to switch to online instruction, a reduction in the number of required field hours students had to complete, and the ability of students to complete required field hours through online assignments. For some program and field directors, the latter two presented challenges, given that many believed that one had to have a minimum of 400 hours to fully demonstrate mastery of practice behaviors and competencies, and others believed that traditional field placements occurred only in particular physical settings. However, for still others, it was an opportunity to reinforce the belief that field education is an integral part of the program, the outcomes of which are not limited to face-to-face interactions. Thus, those programmatic shifts from traditional face-to-face programs to online learning would also include opportunities for online field education. More than 2 years later, many program directors and faculty are looking back at how far they have come since March 2020, with both exhaustion and pride.

The same can be said for the BOA, which, because of COVID-19's presence, shifted to online meetings, where program accreditation and reaffirmation decisions were made. Further, to help ensure the safety and well-being of commissioners, site visitors, and program constituents, face-to-face visits to programs shifted to online formats using whatever platform the program made available. Although initially intended to be short term, both of these changes have influenced how the BOA inter-acts today. The number of face-to-face visits to programs has decreased permanently, as has the number of in-person meetings required for the conducting of BOA business. These actions also led to cost savings for programs and the BOA.

Conclusion

This chapter has taken readers on a journey through the overall accredita-tion structure in higher education in the United States, offered a glimpse into the governance structure of CSWE and how the BOA and COEP contribute to social work education, and discussed the initial do's and don'ts of the candidacy and reaffirmation processes. Finally, we noted some of the changes that have occurred over time, showing that accredita-tion and reaffirmation are neither monolithic nor static in nature. Several variables must come together to ensure accreditation oversight with integ-rity and transparency, and these variables may result from or contribute to changes eventually experienced at the programmatic level. It is our hope that this chapter provides program directors and those wanting to become program directors with a framework from which to build their accredita-tion and reaffirmation knowledge.

Suggested Readings

Commission on Higher Education Accreditation. (n.d.). *About accreditation.* www.chea.org /about-accreditation

Council on Social Work Education. (2022). *2022 Educational policy and accreditation standards.* https://cswe.org/Accreditation/Information/2022-EPAS

Council on Social Work Education. (2021). *About CSWE accreditation.* https://www.cswe.org /Accreditation

Mapp, S., & Boutté-Queen, N. (2020). The role of the US baccalaureate social work program director: A national survey. *Social Work Education: The International Journal, 40*(7), 843–860. doi.10.1080/02615479.2020.1729720

References

Bogo, M. (2015). Field education for clinical social work practice: Best practices and contemporary challenges. *Clinical Social Work Journal, 43*, 317–324. http://doi.org /10.1007/S10615-015-0526-5

Bogo, M., & Sewell, K. M. (2019). Introduction to the special issue on field education of students. *Clinical Social Work Journal, 47*(1), 1–4. http://doi.org/10.1007 /s10615-018-0696-z

Bremner, J., & Zastrow, C. (2008). Advanced standing revisited: Current status, structure, and issues. *Journal of Teaching in Social Work, 29*(1/2), 101–116. http://doi. org/10.1080/08841230802179068

Buchan, V., Rodenhiser, R., Hull, G., Smith, M., Rogers, J., Pike, C., & Ray, J. (2004). *Journal of Social Work Education, 40*(2), 239–253. http://doi.org/10.1080/10437797

Cheung, M., Zhou, S., Narendorf, S. C., & Mauldin, R. L. (2019). Curriculum mapping in a social work program with the 2015 Educational Policy and Accreditation Standards. *Journal of Social Work Education, 55*(1), 23–33. http://doi.org/10.1080/10437797.2018.1508392

Commission on Higher Education Accreditation. (n.d.a). *About accreditation.* www.chea.org/about-accreditation

Commission on Higher Education Accreditation. (n.d.b). *Regional accrediting organizations.* https://www.chea.org/regional-accrediting-organizations-accreditor-type

Council on Social Work Education. (2015). *2015 educational policy and accreditation standards.* https://www.cswe.org/Accreditation/Standards-and-Policies/2015-EPAS

Council on Social Work Education. (2022a). *Commission on Accreditation.* https://www.cswe.org/About-CSWE/Governance/Commissions-and-Councils/Commission-on-Accreditation

Council on Social Work Education. (2022b). *2022 Educational Policy and Accreditation Standards.* https://cswe.org/Accreditation/Information/2022-EPAS

Council on Social Work Education. (n.d.a). *The road to 1952: AASSW and NASSA.* https://cswe.org/About-CSWE/CSWE-A-Brief-History/The-Road-to-1952

Council on Social Work Education. (n.d.b). *Concerns of the profession.* https://cswe.org/About-CSWE/CSWE-A-Brief-History/The-Concerns-of-the-Profession

Council on Social Work Education. (n.d.c). *Governance.* https://cswe.org/About-CSWE/Governance

Council on Social Work Education. (n.d.d). *Commission on educational policy.* https://cswe.org/About-CSWE/Governance/Commissions-and-Councils/Commission-on-Educational-Policy.aspxhttps://cswe.org/About-CSWE/Governance/Commissions-and-Councils/Commission-on-Accreditation.aspx

Council on Social Work Education. (n.d.e). *Council on field education.* https://cswe.org/About-CSWE/Governance/Commissions-and-Councils/Council-on-Field-Education.aspx

Council on Social Work Education. (n.d.f). *Council on practice methods and specializations.* https://cswe.org/About-CSWE/Governance/Commissions-and-Councils/Council-on-Practice-Methods-and-Specializations.aspx

Council on Social Work Education. (n.d.g). *Professional practice doctoral program accreditation.* https://cswe.org/Accreditation/Information/Profession-Practice-Doctoral-Program-Accreditation

Council on Social Work Education. (n.d.h). *Commission on accreditation.* https://cswe.org/About-CSWE/Governance/Commissions-and-Councils/Commission-on-Accreditation.aspx

Council on Social Work Education Department of Social Work Accreditation (CSWE DOSWA). (2021). *Frequently-cited standards.* https://www.cswe.org/getmedia/21f83609-fcdc-410f-9f57-dc26642d0322/Frequently-Cited-Standards-FINAL.pdf

Drisko, J. (2014). Competencies and their assessment. *Journal of Social Work Education, 50*(3), 414–426. http://doi.org/10.1080/10437797.2014.917927

Drolen, C. S. (1999). Do accreditation requirements deter curriculum innovation? Yes! *Journal of Social Work Education, 35*(2), 183–186. http://doi.org/10.1080/10437797.1999.10778958

Dubus, N., & Greene, R. (2015). Can the Council on Social Work Education Educational Policy and Accreditation Standards be exported to Cuba? *Journal of Human Behavior in the Social Environment, 25*(1), 67–76. http://doi.org/10.1080/10911359.2014.953432

Dwyer, M., & Urbanowski, M. (1981). Field practice criteria: A valuable teaching/learning tool in undergraduate social work education. *Journal of Education for Social Work, 17*(1), 5–11. http://doi.org/10.1080/00220612.1981.10778523

Education, 34 C. F. R. § 602 (2021).

Friedman, R. A. (2009). "Reinventing social work accreditation": Write on! *Research on Social Work Practice, 19*(1), 124–126. http://doi.org/10.1177/1049731508318555

Harris, H., Yancey, G., & Myers, D. (2016). Social work field education in and with congregations and religiously-affiliated organizations in a Christian context. *Religions, 7*(5), 52–66. http://doi.org/10.3390/rel7050052

Holden, G., Barker, K., Kuppens, S., & Rosenberg, G. (2017). Self-efficacy regarding social work competencies. *Research on Social Work Practice, 27*(5), 594–606. http://doi.org/10.1177/1049731515586466

Holden, G., Meenaghan, T., Anastas, J., & Metrey, G. (2002). Outcomes of social work education: The case for social work self-efficacy. *Journal of Social Work Education, 38*(1), 115–133. http://doi.org/1.1080/10437797.2002.10779086

Holosko, M., Skinner, J., MacCaughelty, C., & Stahl, K. M. (2010). Building the implicit BSW curriculum at a large southern state university. *Journal of Social Work Education, 46*(3), 411–423. http://doi.org/10.5175/JSWE.2010.200900068

Horner, W., & Borrero, M. (1981). A planning matrix for Standard 1234A. *Journal of Education for Social Work, 17*(1), 36–43. http://doi.org/10.1080/00220612.1981.10778527

Jeffery, D. (2007). Managing race in social work education policy. *Journal of Education Policy, 22*(4). 429–454. http://doi.org/10.1080/02680930701390578

Koerin, B., Reeves, J., & Sheridan, M. (2001). BSW autonomy issues in combined BSW/MSW programs. *Journal of Social Work Education, 37*(2), 309–313. http://doi.org/10.1080.10437797.2001.10779056

Krase, K., DeLong Hamilton, T., Harris-Jackson, T., Gerritsen-Mckane, R., Christenson, B., Sullivan, D. J., Danhoff, K., & Freedman, D. (2021). Exploring correlates of implicit curriculum for accreditation outcome evaluation: Results of student evaluations. *Social Work Education.* Advance online publication. http://doi.org/10.1080/02615479.2021.1925241

Lewis, H. (1981). Are the traditional curriculum areas relevant? *Journal of Education for Social Work 17*(1), 73–80. http://doi.org/10.1080/00220612.1981.10778532

Mabrey, T. (1998). Accreditation decisions in social work education: Looking for patterns, 1985–92. *Social Work Education, 34*(1), 21–30. http://doi.org/10.1080/10437797

Mapp, S., & Boutté-Queen, N. (2020). The role of the US baccalaureate social work program director: A national survey. *Social Work Education: The International Journal, 40*(7), 843–860. http://doi.org/10.1080/02615479.2020.1729720

National Advisory Committee on Institutional Quality and Integrity. (n.d.). *Welcome.* https://sites.ed.gov/naciqi/

Pawar, M., & Thomas, M. (2017). Social work education in Australia and the USA: Comparative perspectives and contemporary issues. *Social Work Education, 36*(6), 648–661. http://doi.org/10.1080/02615479.2017.1335699

Rahill, G. J., Joshi, M., Lucio, R., Bristol, B., Dionne, A., & Hamilton, A. (2016). Assessing the development of cultural proficiency among upper-level social work students. *Social Work Education, 52*(2), 198–213. http://doi.org/10.1080/10437797.2016.1152134

Robbins, S. (2014). From the editor—accreditation, competency-based education, and EPAS revisions. *Journal of Social Work Education, 50*(4), 581–586. http://doi.org/10.1080/10437797.2014.947893

Sellers, W., & Neff, D. (2019). Assessment processes in social work education: A review of current methods. *Journal of Teaching in Social Work, 39*(3), 212–225. http://doi.org/10.1080/08841233.2019.1610544

Stoesz, D., & Karger, H. J. (2009). Reinventing social work accreditation. *Research on Social Work Practice, 19*(1), 104–111. http://doi.org/10.1177/1049731507313976

Thyer, B. A. (2009). The CSWE and social work accreditation: Not guilty on all charges. *Research on Social Work Practice, 19*(1), 127–130. http://doi.org/10.1177/1049731508318632

Vanderbilt University Center for Teaching. (n.d.). *Bloom's Taxonomy.* https://cft.vanderbilt.edu/guides-sub-pages/blooms-taxonomy/

Veeran, V. (2013). Reframing the discourse on social work in the Arab world: Considerations for the accreditation of social work in the UAE. *Social Work Education, 32*(8), 1075–1088. http://doi.org/10.1080/02615479.2012.730512

Vernon, R., Pittman-Munke, P., Vakalahi, H., Adkins, L. F., & Pierce, D. (2009). Distance education programs in social work: Current and emerging trends. *Journal of Social Work Education, 45*(2), 263–278. http://doi.org/10.5175/JSWE.2009200700081

Voss, R. W., Bolton, D. L., Dente, C. L., Ingersoll, T. S., Bartholomew, J., & Rolly, H. F. (2017). A qualitative study of an international social work course in German, using the EPAS core competencies and behaviors as the coding scheme. *International Social Work, 60*(4), 990–1000. http://doi.org/10.1177/0020872815594864

Watkins, J. M. (2009). Response to Stoesz and Karger's article, "Reinventing social work accreditation." *Research on Social Work Practice. 19*(1), 112–113. http://doi.org/10.1177/1049731508317255

Wayne, J. H., & Hull, G. H. (1992). Autonomy and visibility in undergraduate social work education. *Journal of Social Work Education, 28*(3), 312–321. http://doi.org/10.1080/10437797.1992.10778784

Wilson, S. (1999). Distance education and accreditation. *Journal of Social Work Education, 35*(3), 326–330. http://doi.org/10.1080/10437797.1999.10778971

Wolk, J. L., & Wertheimer, M. R. (1999). Generalist practice vs. case management: An accreditation contradiction. *Journal of Social Work Education, 35*(1), 101–114. http://doi.org/10.1080/10437797.1999.10778950

van Wormer, K., & Snyder, C. (2007). Infusing contact on oppression into the social work curriculum. *Journal of Human Behavior in the Social Environment, 16*(4), 19–35. http://doi.org/10.1300/10911350802081568

CHAPTER 4

Using Data Effectively

Assessing Beyond Assessment

James W. Drisko

Ruiz-Primo (2020, p. 1) stated that "assessment comes from the Latin word *assidere*, meaning 'to sit beside.'" But she added that in most U.S. educational institutions, assessment rarely feels like companionable support—more likely it takes the form of "high-pressure tests that play an outsize role" (p. 1) for learners and faculty, potentially with significant consequences. For social work BSW programs and their directors, assessment is also a demanding, high-pressure process that supports or challenges overall educational effectiveness and program quality (Stage & Manning, 2003). The stakes are high for directors, faculty, placement agencies, alumni, students, and institutions. Yet there are many potential benefits as well.

Banta and Palomba (2015) stated that assessment is the systematic collection, review, and use of data about educational programs to improve student learning and development. Social work education views educational assessment somewhat more broadly as improving student learning and guiding program improvement, yet also supporting accountability and informing the public (Council on Social Work Education [CSWE], 2022). Assessment is a professional obligation, a way to learn what we, as program directors and educators, do well and what we need to strengthen. It is a key part of *all* quality social work services, allowing formative evaluation of needs, processes, and summative evaluation of outcomes. Assessment keeps us honest and grounded in real evidence. As a component of accreditation, assessment requires careful thinking, development of a multiyear plan, and ongoing care in its implementation. Yet the same assessments, and some modest alterations to accreditation requirements, can also guide other aspects of program review and development. The very process of assessment can help guide and enhance internal program quality.

Assessment and Reaccreditation

Summative competency assessment was first incorporated into the Educational Policy and Assessment Standards (EPAS) developed by CSWE (2008). The purpose of the emphasis on assessment was to more fully and explicitly document that students actually learned from social work education programs. That is, greater accountability was sought to show accreditors, students and their families, the public, and future employers that program graduates were truly professionally capable. This contrasted with the emphasis on detailing the planned course of study and syllabi that had oriented prior accreditation standards. Evidence was sought to assess the yield of an educational experience. It is worth noting that assessments or user evaluations are also required by most state-level licensing standards. *Showing* that we learn from paid educational and training programs has become part of professional culture.

Under 2008 EPAS, each social work program had to first define its own mission and goals, which are both linked through a logic model to each social work competency and practice behavior. A logic model is a planned description of the chain of factors that generate effects. In this case, the logic model details how the social work program, through specified components and processes, helps learners develop the required social work competencies. Under 2015 EPAS (CSWE, 2015) and continued in 2022 EPAS (CSWE, 2022), CSWE required that the logic model be presented in narrative as well as graphic format (the competency assessment matrix).

Programs must set their own benchmark standards that define adequate levels of summative endpoint performance. Benchmarks are usually set as a total percentage of all the students, in a given cohort or year, who meet the standard for each competency assessment measure. For example, 92% of the graduating cohort were assessed as competent for ethics Competency 1; the benchmark was set at 85% by the program. Thus, this program met its benchmark standard. Benchmarks can be set at any percentage: Obviously, the higher the standard is, the better a program will appear to the public, potential students, and the profession.

In addition to the explicit student-focused curriculum, program leaders were further required under 2008 EPAS to undertake general assessments of their programs' internal organization, practices and processes, diversity, and structures—called the *implicit* curriculum. "The implicit curriculum consists of the student learning experience and the program context or environment" (CSWE, 2022, p. 24). It is composed of all the elements of the learning environment that are not specifically parts of the student curriculum per se. These elements include admissions, policies, administrative structures, participation in program governance, and human, social, and racial diversity. Because these implicit curriculum elements set the tone of the overall learning environment, they are assessed to show how they support educational excellence and social work purposes and values. 2022 EPAS further strengthens requirements to examine how equity and diversity are addressed by programs.

2008 EPAS was criticized for requiring too much detail, with each competency further operationalized into component "practice behaviors" that each needed to be measured. Yet assessment formally documented the proportion of students in a program that met established program outcome benchmarks. Students and applicants could easily learn how effective each program was in delivering its intended quality social work education. Internally, learning from both what was done well and what needed improvement allowed competency data to guide future program renewal, revisions, and additions. The process also showed faculty and students that social work evaluation processes and procedures applied to our own programs as well as to the progress of clients and communities. It reinforced the concept that assessment and evaluation are key parts of all social work practices.

2015 EPAS and 2022 EPAS

2015 EPAS continued the focus on summative assessment of competence in several areas, but sought to reduce the overall number of assessments to be completed. 2022 EPAS continues and extends this practice. Under 2022 EPAS Standard 5.0.1(a), a systematic plan for assessment is required. Two different measures are currently required for each of the social work competencies. One assessment measure must be based on real or "simulated" social work practice in field education. The other can be based on academic or classroom activities known as "indirect assessments," which support or guide practice (Drisko, 2015). Such indirect assessment does not directly examine actual practice. Pairing both types of assessment was designed to provide a more robust measure of competence in action.

Under 2022 EPAS, Form AS 5.0.1(a) (available from CSWE) is used to detail how assessment is undertaken. Each instrument used must be described, along with the assessment process: When and by whom the process is undertaken must be stated clearly. Next, target levels of expected student achievement for each assessment instrument, and how they are calculated, along with copies of these instruments, must be included in the self-study. Further, all assessments must be completed by program-designated personnel, including field staff. They may not be completed by students or by persons who are not part of the social work program. All nine social work competencies and any additional program-developed competencies must be assessed.

Another 2015 EPAS policy change continued in 2022 EPAS required that these competencies each be assessed in terms of four "dimensions": knowledge, values, skills, and cognitive and affective processes. The goal was to assess "holistic competence"—actual practice capability integrating these four dimensions—rather than to break the competencies down into separate, siloed components (Bogo et al., 2014). In recent accreditation practice, CSWE requires that at least two dimensions of each competency be measured, but not all four dimensions (CSWE, 2019, slide 13). For Competencies 6 through 9, while each point to five levels of practice (individuals, families, groups, organizations, and communities), assessment does not need to include all five levels (CSWE, 2019, slide 15).

Under 2022 EPAS, programs must also have a method for analyzing their collected assessment data. This begins with completing Form AS 5.0.1(b) for the most recent year assessed by Form 5.0.1(a), described above. This process details the calculations made for the nine competencies (and any program-added competencies). How all calculations are made for each competency is described, including naming all of the instruments used. Next, the outcomes are compared with the program's benchmark levels of student achievement. Outcomes for both the program as a whole (in aggregate) and for each program option are to be specified.

2022 EPAS Standard 5.0.1(c) describes the process to formally review the assessment plan and collected data. Although not required, describing who does this review, how frequently the review occurs, and with what focus is useful to state. Most often, programs have a committee charged with this ongoing review process. The purpose of this review is to describe any needed changes to the explicit curriculum based on the latest assessment data—which will change annually. Specific changes made to the curriculum based on the collected data are detailed across all program options.

2022 EPAS 5.0.1(d) requires that each program post both its assessment plan and a summary of assessment outcomes on its web page using Form

AS 5.0.1(d). This form differs for BSW and MSW programs. These must be updated online at least every 2 years. The self-study must include the hyperlink or URL on the program's web page where the assessment plan and outcome data are located. These online postings must address both the program as a whole and any differences across different program options.

To this point, 2022 EPAS refines the model used in 2015 EPAS. 2022 EPAS Standard 5.0.2(a) is a new requirement under 2022 EPAS and addresses anti-racism, diversity, equity, and inclusion (ADEI) efforts. Under Standard 2.0, programs must engage in specific and continuous efforts related to ADEI. Assessment Standard 5.0.2(a)(a) requires that programs identify at least one effort related to the implicit curriculum and develop an assessment plan for these efforts, including identification of which stakeholders are involved in the ADEI work and its assessment. As required for the explicit curriculum assessment, the program must explain its data collection procedures and provide copies of all assessment instruments used for the ADEI effort(s) across all program options.

Standard 5.0.2(b) requires description of the process used to review the ADEI efforts and to detail changes made based on this assessment. (This process parallels that required under Standard 5.0.1(a) for the explicit curriculum.) ADEI outcomes for the most recent year must be presented, along with a description of the process used to review both the ADEI *assessment plan*, 5.0.2(b)(b), and the *process* used to formally review the outcome data, 5.0.2(b)(c). Again, who does this review, how often, and with what focus should be stated clearly. Changes made to ADEI efforts based on these data are detailed under Standard 5.0.2(b)(d) and must address all program options, as stated in 5.0.2(b)(e).

2022 EPAS newly obligates assessment of overall program outcomes. Standard 5.0.3 requires monitoring of graduation rates *and* at least one other outcome (i.e., employment rates, higher education acceptance rates, and time to program completion). Annual collection periods for these data are determined by the program. Obviously, graduation rates may be easier to determine for each class yearly, while employment rate data may take a longer time period. Overall assessment is documented using Form AS 5.0.3 (available from CSWE). The outcomes monitored are identified in 5.0.3(b). Benchmarks for overall graduation rates are set, along with benchmarks for the other program-identified outcome(s), in 5.0.3(c).

A rationale for how the benchmark is set is provided in Standard 5.0.3(d), and how graduation rates and program-identified outcomes are calculated from the available data is provided in 5.0.3(e). Next, graduation rates and program-identified outcomes must be provided along with supporting data according to 5.0.3(f). These data must be presented in aggregate for the program as a whole, as well as separately for each program option, according to 5.0.3(g). Finally, the program explains how these data are used for continuous program improvement of overall graduation rates and for the program-identified outcomes, per 5.0.3(h), stating by whom, how frequently, and for what purpose.

Although the assessment standards have different foci, what is asked of programs is mostly similar or parallel across the three major assessment standards. Assessment— 2015 EPAS Standard 4—remains the most-cited concern in reaffirmation reviews by CSWE. It is a time-consuming process that requires care, but can also build program cohesion, develop skills, and support high-quality education.

CSWE Assessment Support

In online documents and examples, as well as in many types of training opportunities, CSWE provides guidance for creating the required summative assessment plan. As noted in Chapter 3, starting the accreditation self-study years before materials are due is the key to success. Working closely with the program's CSWE accreditation specialist will help the program director obtain support and answers to specific questions. (Contact CSWE to learn which accreditation specialist is assigned to your program if this is not already known.)

Many new assessment-related forms are available online. Reviewing, updating, and clarifying the program's mission and goals begin the process and point to key educational targets. Courses and assessment measures are then updated to clearly link to the program's own mission and goals, as well as to map out the competencies and dimensions the program seeks to highlight. The rationale for each assessment measure should be clearly stated to all faculty and students, and must also be stated in the accreditation narrative. Benchmarks are set, assessment matrices are developed for the program competencies, and measures are detailed. Full copies of all measures must be included in the self-study documents. Grading rubrics should be reviewed and updated to show how assessment measures will be operationalized, aggregated, and summarized. Examples of such materials are available on the CSWE accreditation web pages. CSWE (2020b) also offers a very detailed online template for Volume 1 of a self-study under 2015 EPAS that clarifies what is expected for each accreditation standard. Updated examples for 2022 EPAS will be available as it is implemented.

Formative and Summative Assessments

Assessments are often described as either *summative*—done at the conclusion of an intervention to measure its final overall effectiveness—or as *formative*—done before or during an intervention to identify baseline knowledge and skills. Formative assessments measure an intervention's impact at different points in time during its delivery and the process of the intervention's impact (Dolin et al., 2018). Some argue that the current educational literature highly values formative assessments but denigrates summative evaluation. Yet Man Sze Lau (2016) pointed out that both forms of assessment are inherently connected and work best when combined. The two types of assessment have different purposes.

Summative Assessments

CSWE's accreditation process centers on an overall summative assessment of student competence. Such assessments do document overall student performance in the cohort or cohorts studied. Programs could identify an individual student's progress on meeting the competencies, but this is rarely done—and may be a loss to the programs and their students. (Should we not seek to graduate only students who are each fully competent in all the require areas?) Aggregated across an entire class cohort of students, assessment results are then compared with the program's established competency benchmarks. This allows determination of meeting, exceeding, or not reaching the program's own benchmark standards. Completed at the end of a term or year, or at the end of the program, such assessments provide summative measures of educational effectiveness.

Summative assessments help identify strengths, deficits, and areas where attention is needed in educational programs. As CSWE obligates, such summative outcome data must be combined with identifying and planning to revise and renew areas of the program that did not meet benchmarks (for the explicit curriculum) or program expectations (for the implicit curriculum). Thus, good assessment data shape program review and improvement. However, assessment data alone do not necessarily point to ways to make improvements. Faculty must review and understand any summative deficits found and identify ways to improve program delivery to ameliorate these deficits. Summative data may, or may not, clearly point to ways to improve prior practices. Creativity and consultation are indicated where the needed changes are not conspicuous or where potential methods to address them differ. Leaders of very small programs may find it useful to involve outside consultants in the assessment development and in using assessment data to guide program renewal.

Summative Assessment Measures

There are several standardized tests of professional learning, though CSWE does not specifically endorse any of them (CSWE, 2019, slide 14). However, CSWE does not prohibit their use, so long as the measure clearly addresses a *specifically designated competency* and its dimensions as defined by the relevant EPAS. A rationale for using such tests, or specific items on a test, for competency assessment is also required in the program narrative. Standardized tests appear to emphasize academic learning (knowledge and skills) and do not often directly assess actual, real-world practice performance (Drisko, 2014). This may mean that they can only be used for indirect or academic assessment, but not for actual practice assessment for accreditation purposes.

In some parts of the United States, program directors may find that such standardized tests profile their students in ways that allow comparison and contrast with results from students pursuing other majors or in other programs. This may be particularly useful in areas such as writing proficiency and critical thinking, which are key dimensions of undergraduate learning. Program-generated assessment measures should be clearly focused on important areas of learning and practice. Such measures may be developed with multiple dimensions and draw upon real-world practice activities (Drisko, 2014, 2015).

Most programs use existing assessment measures for accreditation reviews. Real practice can be assessed using field placement evaluations with carefully targeted questions. Many programs use recordings of practice in supervision and field advisement, which typically link to real practice. Transcriptions, videos, and process recordings of practice may also draw on real practice (Fitch et al., 2008). Practice requires that learners create and test out hypotheses about client system needs. Skills in how practice is done, and the knowledge and values that inform learner choices, are on display explicitly or implicitly. Sometimes knowledge, values, and skills are apparent only through omission. Cognitive and affective processes may be assessed using self-reflective write-ups, conversations, or formal exams. Here, assessment or evaluation items must be focused on specific competencies. What we use to assess the program as a whole for accreditation is based on summarizing the results across each student. The same assessment information is used by instructors and faculty to guide each student's learning. Program assessment draws on the everyday assessments by field instructors and faculty; the same data do double duty.

Portfolios

A portfolio is a compendium of a student's work in a specific area (Alvarez & Moxley, 2004; Schatz, 2004). Portfolios are often used as final capstone projects, which may address several competencies (Fitch et al., 2008). The portfolio is also a lasting archive of accomplishments that can be available throughout the student's time in a program and afterward. Portfolios help to clarify how learning and sophistication develop through comparison with earlier and later materials. Portfolios may be used as summative assessments for accreditation purposes so long as they focus on a specific competency or multiple specified competencies (Carten & Finch, 2010; Drisko, 2015). A narrative rationale for the use of a portfolio is also required by CSWE, along with rubrics to show how the portfolio is evaluated to document competency compared with benchmark standards. Many students find that creating a portfolio increases their motivation to learn (Carten & Finch, 2010).

Several software products can be used to create digital portfolios, such as FlipGrid (Microsoft, 2020) and BookCreator (Tools for Schools, 2019). Both are free to use, though BookCreator requires a fee for more than 40 books. Both online and paper portfolios also raise the issue of student privacy. If portfolios are exhibited or are available online, students must choose to give their voluntary consent. Such consent is not required for in-classroom use, though consent should be sought if the content of the portfolio includes sensitive material that may be shared with the class. Portfolios provide a valuable learning resource and may be a useful basis for summative competency assessment (Fitch et al., 2008).

Structured Examinations of Simulated Practice

Regehr et al. (2007, p. 327) sought to "build a better mousetrap" to improve competency assessment in field instruction. One development was the objective, structured, clinical examination (OSCE; Bogo et al., 2011). Although the exam is labeled "clinical," its purpose is to assess closely simulated practice. It may be adapted to assess other forms of practice. The first part of the OSCE is a 15-minute interaction between a student and a trained actor meant to provide a consistent scenario across students.

Great care must be taken to ensure adequate detail and ambiguity are included in the scenario and case materials. Solid and consistent acting is also required, building on a script that includes all the specific elements to be assessed. The OSCE is structured such that a specific scenario and format serve as a consistent exposure to practice for students. Performance is rated on a rubric that scales the results and provides feedback to the student. To ensure objectivity, the rating is done by an independent rater, not the field instructor or an involved faculty member. Results may be used as a summative measure of competence, demonstrating closely simulated practice on dimensions of knowledge, values, skills, and cognitive and affective processes. Complex chains of behavior are assessed, including critical thinking and the integration of values and ethics into practice. Both the client actor(s) and the rater give feedback directly to the student.

The second part of the OSCE asks the student to respond in writing to structured questions that require reflection (cognitive and affective processes), as well as to integrate knowledge in specific practice topics (Bogo et al., 2011). Issues of diversity, ethics, social justice, and more may be specifically targeted—and used for CSWE accreditation assessment. A fact sheet for field instructors detailing the OSCE process is online (University of Toronto, n.d.). Bogo et al. (2014) describe many uses of the OSCE in *Using Simulation in Assessment and Teaching: OSCE Adapted for Social Work.*

Research Proposals and Policy Analyses: Actual Practice in an Assignment

For research and for policy practice, creating a research proposal or completing a policy analysis *is* a form of real practice. Ideally, students select their own topics (demonstrating applicable knowledge, values, skills, and cognitive processes) and then demonstrate competence by preparing a research proposal or a policy analysis. Such assignments are widely used because of their proximity to practice, and templates for what should be addressed are readily available. The components of such assignments may also address other EPAS competencies (e.g., ethics, diversity, and social justice). With some forethought, a single assessment tool may measure several different summative competencies as well as their different dimensions (knowledge, values, skills, and cognitive and affective ability).

Summative assessment tools may be linked to program or institutional needs beyond CSWE accreditation. By engaging other stakeholders in assessment, the social work program's community connections can be expanded. Student and alumni input to the program can also be enhanced, showing the program's energy and encouraging enthusiasm from the groups who generate future applicants. Implicit curriculum and ADEI assessment may serve as a means for improving community awareness of the program or one of its projects. Explicit curriculum measures of actual world practice may be used over time to support community changes.

Summative assessment is the focus of accreditation standards, and it is a terrific tool to document overall student learning. To complement summative evaluation, formative or in-progress assessments are also useful.

Formative Assessment Measures

In contrast to the summative, final-outcome assessment approach used by CSWE for accreditation, formative measures help guide and focus in-progress education (Schneller & Brocato, 2011). Formative assessment measures often begin with baseline assessments, which simply document the knowledge, values, skills, and other attributes of learners before an intervention is begun, such as at the start of a social work program (Kealey, 2010). This provides a basis to demonstrate that future learning is due to the program's impact and that it adds value to the student's education. A baseline is the starting point for before-and-after comparisons of each learner's progress. In the aggregate, such baseline assessments easily profile an entire cohort.

Oddly, few programs and few professional accreditation models begin with a baseline assessment. This undermines a stronger before-and-after comparison model, which could show the program's impact on learners. It also misses an opportunity for the faculty to learn about strengths and limitations of each student's initial learning styles and methods. A baseline assessment could help guide remedial efforts for students to support their learning and to aid their retention and progress within the program. Outside of social work education, there are arguments for giving students' credit or its equivalent for their demonstrated areas of competence while redirecting education to those areas in which the students have more to learn and master. This would both reduce costs and better individualize education. Such a process must begin with a baseline assessment.

Assessing the Implicit Curriculum

CSWE requires that at least one aspect of the implicit curriculum be assessed along with the explicit curriculum. Under 2022 EPAS, explicit examination of ADEI efforts is newly mandated in the implicit curriculum assessment Standard 5.0.2(a). The implicit curriculum refers to all aspects of the educational program that are not contained in the explicit curriculum. Areas of the implicit curriculum include, but are not limited to, diversity, student development, faculty, administrative and governance structure, and resources. For example, a program might review the impact of its policies and procedures for terminating students or the assets and limitations of its guiding faculty code or similar governance documents. Assessment requires gathering data on the implicit curriculum to "continuously inform and promote change in the ... implicit curriculum" (CSWE, 2020a, p. 9). These data are used to guide program renewal, change, and innovation under 2015 EPAS.

2022 EPAS, as noted above, requires specific attention to ADEI in practice for assessment of the implicit curriculum. The program must have a systematic plan to assess ADEI efforts within the program's implicit curriculum under Standard 5.0.2(a). Programs may, of course, do additional assessment of the implicit curriculum for their own needs and internal interests. Although 2015 EPAS allowed wide-ranging targets and methods for implementing assessment of the implicit curriculum, 2022 EPAS focuses specifically on assessing ADEI efforts as part of the implicit curriculum (as detailed above.)

For programs using 2015 EPAS, the online CSWE *Self-study, Volume 1, Optional Template* (CSWE, 2020b) outlines an approach to assessing the implicit curriculum. Specifically, it calls for the program to describe the areas of the implicit curriculum addressed, the methods of this assessment used, the specific stakeholders who are the sample for the assessment, the specific procedures that shaped the assessment, and the tools or instrument used in the assessment. The outline also requires a narrative or table explaining the findings in detail and a plan for making specific changes (immediately or in the future). The outline follows a typical needs assessment or research proposal format, augmented with detailed findings from the assessment and a plan for using the data to guide program change and renewal. (This model is applied to the ADEI assessment under 2022 EPAS with a different, required focus.)

Formative Assessment and the Implicit Curriculum

At the program level, aspects of the implicit curriculum can be assessed through surveys, focus groups, and community discussions. Both quantitative and qualitative models are appropriate (Schneller & Brocato, 2011). Formative ideas relating to how a given concern is understood, and how it might be better addressed, are sought from various groups. These approaches allow stakeholders to voice their concerns and to appreciate strengths publicly.

Surveys provide privacy for critical statements and public discussions do not, but they allow for more direct and interactive conversation about issues of interest. Directors should ensure that the focus of a survey or discussion is clear, with boundaries and expectations formally established. Electronic recordings are useful for keeping and summarizing results. Using more than one recorder is likely to improve the details of results. Future summative assessment plans may also be shaped via formative community input. In this way, the EPAS-required assessment of the implicit curriculum can be viewed as a form of formative assessment—one that guides future efforts.

Formative Assessment and Student Learning

Turning from the implicit curriculum back to the explicit curriculum, 2015 EPAS added "cognitive and affective processes" to the long-standing trio of knowledge, values, and skills as educational outcomes. This phrase refers to metacognitive processes that shape both learning and professional practice. Cheetham and Chivers (2005) found that empathy, resilience, self-confidence, communication, and listening skills all influence learning and service delivery in addition to knowledge, values, and skills. They also found that reflection was a "super meta-competency" (p. 112).

Reflection is the ability to identify and think about one's inner thoughts and feelings, the work environment and its goals, and the needs of clients or constituents. In the list of professional metacompetencies, social workers might also include reflexivity, the ability to analyze power dynamics, assumptions, and presumptions in a situation (Drisko, 2015). Several studies by Holden and colleagues (2002) also demonstrate that learner self-efficacy—that is, one's belief about one's personal capabilities to organize and execute the courses of action required to produce given attainments—enhances educational progress. Similarly, Schneller and Brocato (2011) found that the use of portfolios increased both student motivation and overall learning. Formative assessment may improve student learning outcomes.

Suto (2012) reviewed several methods to explore rater cognition, or why they gave the responses they gave. The purpose of the research was to assess raters' rationales and reasons for a given response. Two methods were proposed that help learners identify and reflect on their cognitive and affective process. One is called "thinking aloud," in which the learner is simply asked to explain their thinking and feelings. The method is based upon teams of learners, but faculty can set up student-run thinking-aloud assignments. Suto stated that thinking aloud "yielded important insights into the competencies needed for scoring expertise, as well as the sequences of mental activity that scoring typically involves" (p. 21).

The thinking-aloud technique may be used far beyond assessment of how raters give ratings. It could be used to reflect on diversity in the program and institution, or on student group processes, or ways to more fully involve community members in program planning. Social workers may note that traditional process recording involves a similar reflective process while also requiring the learner to document client statements. Using multiple columns to record statements, thinking, and alterative interventions documents the learner's cognitive and affective processes in detail. Such steps can be extremely useful for supervision and in field seminars.

Suto (2012) described another method called "simulated reflection," in which learners explain to an instructor or a peer why they did what they did in practice. Like thinking aloud, simulated reflection asks the learner to look back at past actions and identify the rationale for their actions and reflect on their own cognitive and affective processes. Here too, elements of the traditional process recording are used to promote self-reflection and to develop confidence in one's professional actions. Of course, it is possible for the learner to highlight positive actions and omit questionable actions. All three methods—thinking aloud, simulated reflection, and the process recording—are time-intensive undertakings for students and for faculty raters. Yet they offer depth and detail that are not obtained in summative outcome assessments. Such information can be used to improve student learning outcomes and build confidence and self-efficacy.

Students may also be asked to identify and rate their own learning styles and investment. Many models exist to help students better understand and articulate *how* they learn. Models typically distinguish intellectual, active, affective, and intuitive dimensions—though many other styles may also be listed. In my teaching, students find it very useful and easy to reflect on their learning styles. For example, an intellectual learner may want to read an article on depression before meeting a depressed client, while a student with an active learning style may find it more useful to meet the client and then read the article.

In my experience, most students identify two stronger (of these four) learning styles. The student and I would then agree that one task of their learning will be to keep an eye on the two weaker styles and to find ways to use them. Often the strong learning styles can be used to complement the weaker ones. The student becomes a more able learner who can better help others. Several students have stated that the exercise has helped them orient their field instructors and faculty. Self-ratings are often valuable forms of formative assessment.

Most programs require students to complete a learning plan, which may include a written self-assessment. Such assessments document the student's concerns and can be structured to include attention to learning strengths and challenges. Formative assessments using the student's own self-evaluation can be very useful in developing reflective abilities. Coupled with direct instructor assessment, self-assessments help to focus the student on learning and point out that there are many ways of knowing and many different starting points among students. In addition to explicit course content, instructors might focus on building self-efficacy, confidence, and ability. Combining student self-assessment with formal instructor observations can make difficult-to-understand concerns clear. Here a professional skill (e.g., writing or critical thinking) may be assessed to guide and promote learning but with no linked summative assessment.

Conclusion

Both formative and summative assessments are useful tools in social work education. Formative assessments can help us better understand how students learn and which materials and learning opportunities promote the most progress, as well as document the processes of education. Formative assessments help guide program renewal and change. Summative assessments document final learning and competency. They help students, educators, potential employers, and the public know the expectations for program graduates—and that these have generally been well met. Summative assessments are required currently for social work program accreditation because they document what students have gained from a program. 2022 EPAS adds overall assessment of graduation rates along with a focused assessment of ADEI efforts in the implicit curriculum.

Assessment is best as an ongoing process. It is best done on a routine basis. It is not wise to wait for reaccreditation to push attention to assessments of the social work competencies. Accreditation in social work is structured to draw on assessment results as data to guide program renewal and improvement. There is little reason for programs not to continue such assessments between accreditation cycles.

Assessments of both the explicit curriculum and the implicit curriculum are now required by CSWE. Assessments of the explicit curriculum are very detailed by CSWE and summative in nature, although assessments of the implicit curriculum are meant to be structured but may address a wide range of issues and stakeholders. Useful guidance is available from online resources or from CSWE accreditation specialists.

By demonstrating the merits of assessment to the program, we, as program directors and educators, also show our students the professional benefits and importance of assessment. We demonstrate how assessment may be used to support individuals and to evaluate programs. Many different approaches to assessment are available for higher education assessment. Assessments do take thoughtful formulation to create and some ongoing effort to complete. Yet they are key parts of social work practice at all levels of scale.

Suggested Readings

Banta, T., & Palomba, C. (2015). *Assessment essentials: Planning, implementing, and improving assessment in higher education* (2nd ed.). Jossey-Bass.

Council on Social Work Education. (2022). *2022 educational policy and assessment standards.* https://www.cswe.org/accreditation/policies-process/2022epas/

Drisko, J. (2014). Competencies and their assessment. *Journal of Social Work Education, 54*(3), 1–14.

Drisko, J. (2015). Holistic competence and its assessment. *Smith College Studies in Social Work, 85*(2), 110–127.

Kealey, E. (2010). Assessment and evaluation in social work education: Formative and summative approaches. *Journal of Teaching in Social Work, 30*(1), 64–74.

References

Alvarez, A., & Moxley, D. (2004). The student portfolio in social work education. *Journal of Teaching in Social Work, 24*(1/2), 87–103.

Banta, T., & Palomba, C. (2015). *Assessment essentials: Planning, implementing, and improving assessment in higher education* (2nd ed.). Jossey-Bass.

Bogo, M., Rawlings, M., Katz, E., & Logie, C. (2014). *Using simulation in assessment and teaching: OSCE adapted for social work.* CSWE Press.

Bogo, M., Regehr, C., Logie, C., Katz, E., Mylopoulos, M., & Regehr, G. (2011). Adapting objective structured clinical examinations to assess social work students' performance and reflections. *Journal of Social Work Education, 47*(1), 5–18.

Carten, A., & Finch, J. (2010). An empirically based field-education model: Preparing students for culturally competent practice with new immigrants. *Journal of Public Child Welfare, 4*(3), 365–385.

Cheetham, G., & Chivers, G. (2005). *Professions, competence and informal learning.* Edward Elgar Publishing.

Council on Social Work Education. (2008). *Educational policy and assessment standards.* Author.

Council on Social Work Education. (2015). *Educational policy and assessment standards.* Author.

Council on Social Work Education. (2019). *Assessment of student learning outcomes.* https://www.cswe.org/CSWE/media/AccreditationPDFs/(Public)-4-0-Assessment-Session-APM-2019.pdf

Council on Social Work Education. (2020a). *EPAS 2015 interpretative guide.* https://www.cswe.org/CSWE/media/AccreditationPDFs/2015-EPAS-Interpretation-Guide-v-11-05-20.pdf

Council on Social Work Education. (2020b). *Self-study, volume 1, optional template.* https://www.cswe.org/CSWE/media/AccreditationPDFs/Self-Study,-Volume-1,-Optional-Template-2-27-20.docx

Council on Social Work Education. (2022). *2022 educational policy and assessment standards.* https://www.cswe.org/getmedia/8d7dade5-2683-4940-9587-5675f6ef5426/2022-EPAS.pdf

Dolin, J., Black, P., Harlen, W., & Tiberghien, A. (2018). Exploring relations between formative and summative assessment. In J. Dolin & R. Evans (Eds.), *Transforming Assessment* (pp. 53–80). Springer.

Drisko, J. (2014). Competencies and their assessment. *Journal of Social Work Education, 54*(3), 1–14.

Drisko, J. (2015). Holistic competence and its assessment. *Smith College Studies in Social Work, 85*(2), 110–127.

Fitch, D., Peet, M., Reed, B., & Tolman, R. (2008). The use of ePortfolios in evaluating the curriculum and student learning. *Journal of Social Work Education, 44*(3), 37–54.

Holden, G., Meenaghan, T., Anastas, J., & Metrey, G. (2002). Outcomes of social work education. *Journal of Social Work Education, 38*(1), 115–133.

Kealey, E. (2010). Assessment and evaluation in social work education: Formative and summative approaches. *Journal of Teaching in Social Work, 30*(1), 64–74.

Man Sze Lau, A. (2016). Formative good, summative bad? A review of the dichotomy in assessment literature. *Journal of Further and Higher Education, 40*(4), 509–525.

Microsoft Corporation. (2020). FlipGrid. https://info.flipgrid.com/

Regehr, G., Bogo, M., Regehr, C., & Power, R. (2007). Can we build a better mousetrap? Improving measures of social work practice performance in the field. *Journal of Social Work Education, 43*(2), 327–343.

Ruiz-Primo, M. A. (2020). *Beyond tests and quizzes: Getting creative with assessment during Covid-19.* Stanford University Graduate School of Education. https://ed.stanford.edu/news/beyond-tests-and-quizzes-getting-creative-assessment

Schatz, M. (2004). Using portfolios: integrating learning and promoting for social work students. *Advances in Social Work, 5*(1), 105–123.

Schneller, D., & Brocato, J. (2011). Facilitating student learning, the assessment of learning, and curricular improvement through a graduate social work integrative seminar. *Journal of Teaching in Social Work, 31*(2), 178–194.

Stage, F., & Manning, K. (2003). *Research in the college context: Approaches and methods.* Brunner-Routledge.

Suto, I. (2012). A critical review of some qualitative research methods used to explore rater cognition. *Educational Measurement: Issues and Practice, 31*(3), 21–30.

Tools for Schools. (2019). BookCreator. (software). https://bookcreator.com/

University of Toronto. (n.d.). *OSCE adapted for social work: Fact sheet.* https://socialwork.utoronto.ca/wp-content/uploads/2015/09/OSCE-Fact-sheet-for-Field-Instructors.pdf

CHAPTER 5

Budgeting

It's Not Just Numbers

Carolyn J. Tice

This chapter is designed to assist both newly appointed and experienced social work program directors regarding budget development and monitoring. In this context, a "director" is the administrator responsible for a social work program. A prevailing theme throughout the chapter is that directors must remain diligent and flexible when considering and describing their programs' funding sources and allocations. Smart budget management offers opportunities for directors to bring their programs' goals to the attention of not only upper administrators but also a wide constituency of stakeholders within and outside of their institutions. As stated in the Educational Policy and Accreditation Standards (EPAS) of the Council on Social Work Education (CSWE, 2022), it is crucial that directors demonstrate how budget allocations "achieve its mission and continuously improve the program" (Accreditation Standard 4.4.1).

It is not uncommon for program directors and faculty to have limited training or experience in finance (Lees et al., 2019). However, the task of budgeting for a social work program requires financial literacy that emphasizes knowledge, skills, behaviors, attitudes, and available resources to make wise choices (Birkenmaier et al., 2013). Informed financial choices promote programmatic fiscal security and the ability to engage in meaningful exchange even with budget constraints.

For social work program directors, program budgeting is relevant to social and economic justice. Within the program, budget management should promote fair and open distribution of resources to faculty and staff toward the achievement of the program mission while constantly improving the program's curricula and field education. Directors must also ensure financial accountability to the university community and adherence to accreditation standards for both social work and regional accreditors.

This chapter offers content and exercises to support directors' transparent and active participation in budget and management processes. A 5-point process is introduced: (1) exploring the mission statement, goals, and objectives; (2) understanding the budget structure; (3) soliciting direction and input; (4) budget advocacy; and (5) assessment and evaluation. This process is designed to establish an ongoing system of accountability that supports inclusion, goal planning, and observable and measurable program evaluation.

Exploring the Mission Statement, Goals, and Objectives

A social work program's *mission statement* provides a point of reference for all planning and budgeting activities. It communicates the overall purpose and goals of the program and distinguishes the program from other academic departments within the university. Indeed, a clear, concise mission statement provides the basis for establishing program goals and objectives and allocating resources. (CSWE, 2022, Educational Policy 1.0).

In a broad way, the mission statement reflects the beliefs and values of the social work profession (CSWE, 2022, Educational Policy 1.0). The program's mission statement should complement the mission of the university, college or school, and department. This is typically accomplished through defining the program's learning opportunities and unique educational features, such as a rural or urban focus, that distinguish the program from others. Equally as important, the mission statement informs students of the learning expectations related to social work purpose and values (CSWE, 2022, Accreditation Standard 1.0).

Used as a guiding principle, the mission statement can generate attention, support, and understanding from those outside the university who are important to the program's success. These could include agency personnel, social workers, government officials, community members, donors, and clients. By sharing why the program matters, the mission statement provides a direction or pathway for subsequent assessment and evaluation. To help ensure that a mission statement is relevant, programs might consider the needs that the program addresses and specific learning opportunities associated with the program, such as a focus on child welfare, gerontology, or substance misuse (University of Connecticut, 2016).

When creating or revising a mission statement, be sure to do the following:

- Solicit formal (through meetings and retreats) and informal (during conversations and discussions) input from faculty, staff, students, and alumni. Consensus on the mission is critical to program success.

- Survey the program's key community constituents to find out what they think would define the program's purpose in the context of social work practice and policy.

- Keep it short. Because the program's mission needs a clear focus, the mission statement should be only a few sentences. In fact, some programs use elements of their mission statement as a slogan, such as *Community Organization Fosters Change* or *Inclusion Means Action*.

- Make it individualized. A program faculty and administration may think that their particular program's mission is unique, but given the many other social work programs across the nation, that is not always the case. Take time and use input from others to describe the key features of your program (Ford, 2018).

The mission statement provides insight into the program's aspirations and sense of direction on social work education. To measure achievement in relation to the mission statement, a program needs articulated *goals*. Goals provide motivation, a clear focus, and clarity of importance (Corporate Finance Institute, 2020). By setting goals, the program has measurable and observable targets to achieve and, if achieved, results that will demonstrate success.

A SMART—specific, measurable, achievable, realistic, and timely—framework is used to help guide goal setting:

Specific: Well defined, clear, and unambiguous. A specific goal should answer questions like these: What needs to be accomplished? Who is responsible for it? What steps are needed to achieve it?

Measurable: Specific criteria that measure progress toward the accomplishment of the goal. Quantifying program goals makes it that much easier to monitor progress and know when desired outcomes are achieved.

Achievable: Realistically attainable. Is the goal, as outlined for the program, reasonable? Is it something that the program could realistically accomplish? Consider any conditions or limitations that might impede attainment.

Realistic: Within reach and relevant to the program's mission. Consider why the goal is important to the program and the university as a whole.

Timely: With a clearly defined timeline that informs program faculty and staff when a goal has been reached and indicates why the achievement was made (Corporate Financial Institute, 2020). Keep in mind that SMART goal statements should be informed by and consistent with the program's mission statement. Goals should be fully integrated with one another, because changes in one goal could have implications for others.

> **REFLECTION QUESTION:**
>
> Design a professional objective for yourself using the SMART goal format. What aspect of the format was most helpful to you, and why?

The steps needed to reach a goal are *objectives*. An objective represents a defined action or an incremental step taken to achieve a stated program goal. Thus, objectives are approaches or methods to reach goal attainment. Objectives are specific actions that occur in the context of a designated time frame. Ideally, objectives help faculty, staff, and students to maintain and celebrate the incremental achievement of goals related to a mission statement.

Although the common perception is that they are the same, a goal and an objective are distinctly different. A goal represents an aim or a desired outcome for the program. An objective is a step to achieve the goal. The major differences between goals and objectives are:

- Goals are broad statements of values and beliefs, which are achieved through continuous actions taken in a particular direction.

- A goal represents a primary outcome, whereas an objective is a stepping stone for achieving the goal.

- Goals are based on ideas, whereas objectives are fact based.

- Objectives should be attained in a given period or time frame.

- Goals are difficult to measure; objectives are designed to be measurable and observable.

- Goals are abstract; objectives are concrete.

- Goals require general actions to be attained. Objective attainment needs specific actions (Krysik & Finn, 2018).

An effective objective for a social work program might be to have faculty complete course rubrics associated with CSWE's nine competencies at the end of each semester. The goal is to achieve program accreditation. Said another way, accreditation supports academic standards for excellence in keeping with social work's purpose of promoting human and community well-being (CSWE, 2022). Consider the ways in which the achievement of objectives can be announced and celebrated and why this might be significant to goal attainment.

REFLECTION QUESTIONS:

- List the publications, websites, and other locations where the program's mission statement, goals, and objectives are provided or posted. Identify an additional way to increase their visibility as a way to educate others about your program.

- Identify the parties responsible for designing the program's mission statement, goals, and objectives. Determine where and how stakeholders, including students and alumni, are involved in the formation and adoption of the program's mission statement, goals, and objectives. List two ways the program can solicit more input on the mission statement from a wider range of people, including community members.

- Review the mission statements of at least three other social work programs. Describe what you perceive to be the strengths of the statements and how you would improve the statements. Consider how these statements reflect the 2022 EPAS.

Understanding the Budget Structure

A budget represents an outline of the costs associated with achieving the mission, goals, and objectives of a social work program. The resources allocated to the budget indicate the university's commitment to the program and its mission. Consequently, the annual program budget is more than a financial plan; it is the university's resource endorsement of the program. In the case of state-funded universities, the funding decisions are made by the state legislature, usually in May or June of each year. Unlike state-funded universities, private institutions receive no state appropriations, and annual budgeting is more driven by revenue from tuition and fees along with endowments, if any.

In many ways, the budget lays a foundation for planning, administering, and evaluating the program. The director must be familiar with the intricacies of the budget and have the ability to manage the program's financial affairs. For example, the links among enrollment figures, faculty recruitment and development, scholarship or research funding, and service are both complex and critical to effective budgeting. Certainly, this may be the case for program directors who are in colocated or multidisciplinary departments. In this situation, program directors may advocate, negotiate, and collaborate with other directors for resources.

Becoming familiar with basic budgetary elements, including relevant terminology, is essential to understanding the sources of funds that support a program. Although budget models in higher education vary greatly, a program director needs to understand some common models, such as responsibility center management (RCM) and centralized budgeting, and how their features are associated with funding and contribute to the budget structure.

The incremental budget model is often used in universities. In this model, the year-to-year budget is generally based on the previous year's budget. Usually, only small increases or decreases occur in the budget from one year to the next. These changes are primarily based on whether university revenues increased or decreased during the academic year.

In RCM, individual programs or departments are responsible for generating their own revenue, such as by increasing student enrollment, introducing a new program feature, or increasing external funding (Lees et al., 2019). The role of the university's central administration is minimized in the RCM model because programs and departments are primarily in control of both generating and spending funds and management.

In contrast to RCM, centralized budgeting requires substantial involvement and control of funding by the institution's senior administration. Indeed, all funding allocations and decisions related to budget management are made by the institution's administration (Kosten, 2016). Shortcomings of this model include little input from the social work program members in terms of priorities relevant to practice and policy. However, it is commonplace for universities to combine aspects of centralized budgeting with decentralized budgeting (Lees et al., 2019). Such a budgeting combination allows program directors to participate more actively in the budget-making process. Whatever budget model is used at a university, budgets usually comprise two broad components:

The personnel budget is composed of the salaries and fringe benefits of all tenured and tenure-track full-time faculty, instructors, adjunct instructors, and staff. It is critical that the university have recurring funding for tenured faculty, because they are appointed without term. Tenure-track faculty should also be supported by recurring funds, given that the university and program's goal is for tenure to be achieved. The funding commitment for adjunct instructors may vary depending on teaching needs and enrollment. Salaried staff may be permanent or temporary—the funding commitment depends on the hiring process. Benefits available to faculty and staff are defined and applied by the university. Often, the costs of benefits are covered centrally with no direct cost to the program.

The operating budget is used to pay for expenditures like office supplies, travel, mailings, equipment, guest speakers, and furniture. Item lines tend to vary depending on what is needed and the availability of funds. Unlike a personnel budget, an operating budget allows the program director some discretionary spending.

The basic budget structure—including where the program director has control over spending—highlights the need for the program director to understand that effective administration means that the budget is a tool rather than a document. Budget review should be done with an understanding of EPAS to ensure that the budget is aligned to help achieve the standards. By using a working budget, the director will become better at ensuring that funds are available to achieve the program's mission, goals, and objectives. This is important when the university's fiscal situation is sound and even more so when financial cutbacks occur.

REFLECTION QUESTIONS:

- Identify your institution's budget model. How familiar are you with the model? Identify the institution's personnel responsible for budget development and their roles in the process.

- Identify the role of shared governance (the interface of faculty working with university administrators) in the budget's formation and resource distribution. Determine if and how the university's budget is shared with the campus community.

- If possible, review your program's personnel budget or that of the university. What do the salary allocations tell you about your faculty now, and what can you forecast for future resource needs? For example, are there faculty members who are moving toward tenure or retirement? What effect will faculty changes have on your program's budget?

- During the COVID-19 pandemic, virtual teaching dominated universities across the nation. How do you think this teaching format affected operating budgets? What impact would furloughs have on the personnel budget?

- Consider your need to recruit a new tenure-track faculty member. How would the recruitment and hiring process affect your personnel and operating budgets?

- How does your budget align with your program's mission, goals, and objectives? You should consider not only the amount of total funds, but also how those funds are allocated. Do you have sufficient faculty to maintain reasonable course sizes? Do you have funds to support a vibrant implicit curriculum?

Soliciting Direction and Input

An important aspect of addressing budget issues is the relationship and trust between the program director and the upper-level administrators who authorize resource allocation and approve budgets. In some social work programs, the director solicits direction and input from one or all administrators, including the provost, chief financial officer, and/or dean or chair. The program's administrative assistant is likely to be involved in the communication process as well.

If the program director of a multidisciplinary department or a shared undergraduate-graduate program does not have direct control, then shared governance becomes critical. Shared governance of the budget and resources creates opportunities. Specifically, it should enrich communication patterns, improve understanding of resource distribution, help forecast future resource needs, and contribute to the overall success of the program and university. Other possible opportunities or benefits include the following:

- **Support for participation in external conferences and meetings.** Resource requests and allocations could enable attendance at events like the annual CSWE and Association of Baccalaureate Social Work Program Directors (BPD) conferences. Conference settings facilitate interaction with colleagues from across the country and provide an opportunity for attendees to gain a wide range of perspectives and ideas on the educational and scholarly initiatives at other institutions, as well as accreditation tips.

- **Regular administrative meetings.** When sponsored by the dean or provost, such meetings provide the time for discussions on matters of mutual interest, like accreditation. Regular meetings provide a time for sharing thoughts on operational issues, policies, practices, accountability, and faculty recruitment and promotion.

- **Dean, provost, or chair meetings.** Regular, formal meetings should be held, at least annually, between senior administrators and program chairs where progress and barriers toward achieving goals are reviewed. Ideally, the provost or dean will also offer an annual orientation for the new chairs (Lees & Malik, 2020).

Universities usually have a faculty senate or an equivalent and may also have a standing faculty committee that contributes to institutional planning and budgeting. In a faculty senate, a faculty representative from each program serves on the senate to both share and gather information pertinent to their program. In some institutional settings, budget-related issues, like faculty and staff benefits or student services, are on the meeting agenda. An open discussion of such topics is both informative and supportive of a more transparent university community.

Where present, a university's standing committee on budget and planning is usually composed of appointed members across all faculty ranks. The provost and vice president for finance and/or the chief financial officer often present key financial matters such as student enrollment figures, faculty raises or furloughs, and grant funding. Through shared governance, this committee may have the authority to request certain detailed information and pose questions on funding streams and subsequent allocations. Meetings may be recorded and distributed to members.

Material and information gathered from such meetings and any other relevant gatherings with university administrators and faculty should be shared with program faculty at regularly scheduled meetings. All faculty meetings should be recorded and distributed to faculty members, with a copy to appropriate senior administrators. Included in the information should be updates on budget issues; this is especially critical when the budget has a surplus or deficit. In this way, faculty will be kept informed of the budget's status, and their input will be solicited and considered valuable.

Whatever meeting the director is attending or soliciting information from, some prevailing lines of questioning include the following (adapted from Lees et al., 2019):

- What are the factors—internal and external to the university—that influence the program's budget?

- What are institutional budget priorities, and how do they match with the program's budget?

- What must the program pay for from its operating budget?

- What program costs can be shared with the university or another program or department?

- Who is responsible for explaining the university's budget reporting system to a newly appointed director?

- How is the operating budget provided—in a lump sum or by categories?

- What happens if there is a budget surplus or deficit?

- Is there a carryover policy when excess program funds are available?

- How much flexibility in the personnel and operating budget does the director have in relation to vacant staff and faculty positions?

What becomes obvious when soliciting direction and input on the program budget is the need to know the internal rules and norms. Relevant questions might be: What is the chain of command in the budget-making process? How much flexibility does the director have in implementing the budget? And, to whom does one go with questions about incidental or daily budget matters? Request and read documents such as the university's faculty handbook and/or university policies on regulations and procedures, along with the student guides, many of which outline budget-related program goals and community efforts. Further, much can be learned by reviewing websites, minutes from faculty senate meetings and budget hearings, and senior administration announcements. Particularly critical points should be shared with the program's faculty and staff.

When communicating with senior administrators like the dean or provost, the program director should forecast the program's needs for office supplies, equipment (e.g., computers, laptops, and printers), and organizational memberships, both personal and programmatic. If the time for reaccreditation is approaching, the director should plan ahead—at least a few years—by requesting additional funding before the anticipated self-study and site visitations are scheduled. Also, the costs related to student field trips, guest speakers, conferences, and field education programs should be considered.

Documentation of the budget procedures and processes is essential to the follow-up of significant issues and talking points. To structure communication and support documentation, meeting agendas should be constructed and distributed before the meetings start, and the meeting minutes distributed afterward. The formality of both the agenda and the written or recorded minutes might vary according to the meeting content; a more informal meeting could be documented through a follow-up email listing topics discussed, decisions reached, action steps required, and so forth. Whatever the format, documentation serves as a history of what was discussed and/or decided during a meeting. Such documentation may be distributed to meeting attendees and nonattendees as appropriate.

REFLECTION QUESTIONS:

- Identify the administrator(s) at your university who authorize resource allocation and approve your program's annual budget. How often do you meet with these individuals, and do the number and content of meetings meet your program needs? Please consider what you would change about both the meeting schedule and content.

- In what ways does the program keep senior administrators informed of budget issues related to the EPAS?

- The faculty senate (or similar body) usually represents a key feature of the university's governance. What committees could you or faculty members serve on to enhance your program's representation in governance while gaining insight into budget-related decision making?

- Identify the primary methods or strategies you use to keep faculty and staff informed and involved in the program's budget. How do you address program deficits and surpluses?

- Does your university carry over budget funds from one year to the next? Describe how your university's carryover policy is particularly important to you as program director. Specifically, consider how you might use additional funds in either your personnel or your operating lines. How would such funds add to the achievement of program goals and objectives?

- A decrease in student enrollment as a result of the COVID-19 pandemic or other situations out of your control is likely to affect your program's personnel and operating budgets. What strategies can be used to guide the program through challenging budget times? For example, funding allocations could be reduced with minimal impact to your program operation and educational goals.

Budget Advocacy

One essential role of the program director is to champion the social work program whenever possible. This means that *budget advocacy* is an ongoing process to help ensure that adequate funds are available to support and enhance the program's mission, goals, and objectives in a comprehensive manner.

Based on professional experiences, budget advocacy tends to be most effective when combined with at least three key features. The first feature is a budget analysis which enables the program director and relevant staff to secure all budget information so that they can understand the details of the personnel and operating budgets. With this information, the program director should be in the position to explain the budget implications in a clear and concise way to various audiences, including faculty, staff, and students. Budget information can be regularly included at program meetings so that faculty and staff can ask questions, provide ideas, and remain informed of the budget's status.

At social work faculty meetings, budget advocacy strategies may emerge when a particular need or idea is introduced. For example, faculty members might describe a community-based project that corresponds with the program's mission, goals, and objectives, but will need funding to "buy out" some faculty time or support student involvement. It will be up to the program director, with support from faculty and staff, to move the request forward to find funding within the existing budget or to advocate for additional funds from senior administrators. In either case, this advocacy strategy follows a bottom-up process of recognizing a need or an opportunity and moving the funding request up the university's organizational structure.

A second broad budget advocacy strategy involves collaborations with other academic and/or service programs within the institution. This advocacy strategy requires an interdisciplinary need or project where the expansion or redirection of funds supports more than one academic unit. An example might be a local community conference sponsored by the social work, psychology, and sociology programs, where students would present on social justice initiatives based on their volunteer experiences or agency placements. Although food, advertisement, and rental costs would be minimal, one program would not support the event alone.

In a collaborative event such as this, the director of one of the programs would initiate contact with the other directors to advocate for a cost-sharing agreement while petitioning the dean for additional funding should it be needed. Through consultation and flexible negotiations and with student and faculty input, an interdisciplinary effort can take shape and gain support. In this situation, funds from a program's operating budget could be used to support the collaborative effort. Simultaneously, additional funds could be requested from the senior administration. Thus, interdisciplinary budget advocacy expands the possible funding base when projects and initiatives support mission statements, goals, and objectives across multiple programs.

Finally, budget advocacy strategies can be created and implemented by groups affiliated with the program. For instance, if an advisory board suggested a project—for example, a luncheon to honor students or a scholarship fundraiser—that board might request program funds, along with their private contributions, to launch the event. The director would identify funds in the operating budget or the donor account in the development or scholarship office, but it may be that board members would request a meeting with a senior administrator to pitch their idea and gain a funding commitment. The commonalities that budget advocacy strategies share involve leveraging assets, building on relationships, and connecting requests to the program mission, goals, and objectives.

In the three budget advocacy approaches described, a prevailing theme is the need to analyze the budget and processes before advocating for a desired goal. From this analysis, an argument based on the evidence for additional funding can be used to advance goals and help to ensure program accreditation. Thus, budget facts and figures become evidence in the advocacy effort to show the gap between available funds and what is needed to ensure goal attainment (Ubogu, 2003). As illustrated by the three examples here, evidence-based budget advocacy helps to accomplish the following (adapted from Ubogu, 2003):

- Empower faculty, staff, students, alumni, and community members to participate in the program budget through their aspirations and goal setting.

- Facilitate informed debate about budget allocations and redistribution.

- Consider possible policy and procedure changes to the budget process.

- Support interdisciplinary collaboration.

- Enhance shared governance up, down, and across the university's organizational structure.

- Promote more transparent, participatory, and accountable budgetary processes.

- Enhance the creditability and success of advocacy budget strategies.

REFLECTION QUESTIONS:

- Identify three times when you have advocated for your program. For each, describe why you advocated, when you advocated, how you advocated, and to whom you advocated. For each example, what advocacy strategies proved successful, and why? What are the takeaway points learned from your experiences?

- Identify at least three types of requests for which faculty might advocate that would likely result in budget increases or decreases. What tops the list, and why?

- Discuss with your program faculty the programs, projects, or services at your university with which your program could collaborate. How would the program advocate for additional funding, if necessary, for each?

- Describe at least three ways in which shared governance could intersect and enhance budget advocacy.

Assessment and Evaluation

Budget evaluation is the final stage of the budget cycle; assessment indicates to what extent allocated resources have been used appropriately and effectively to meet the program's mission, goals, and objectives. The director should ensure that assessment and evaluation processes and findings are used to inform and improve the mission, goals, and objectives of the program. Consequently, budget *assessment* and *evaluation* provide important information for future program planning.

As the program director executes the budget throughout the academic year, the data from the budget tell the story of how funds are being spent, which then shows how program needs are being met. Assessment and evaluation occur when the initial budget figures in the personnel and operational lines are compared with expenditures and reflect what funds are likely to be left at the end of the academic year.

Tracking program spending should be done monthly to monitor when, how, and why funds are allocated. This usually involves a budget spreadsheet, software, and perhaps an online application. In this way, financial surprises are kept to a minimum. As a result of this process, the director, often in conjunction with an administrative assistant, is kept informed if expenditures are over, under, or remain on budget during each month and throughout the year (Caldwell, 2020).

It is expected that in some months, program expenses will exceed allocations. This may occur at the start of the academic year with the purchase of office supplies. Ideally, the director will reduce spending later in the academic year to cover the previous costs or anticipated expenses. With careful tracking of the budget, the director will stay informed of budget expenditures and be able to take action and engage in advocacy when necessary to help ensure that funds are not depleted before the next funding cycle begins.

In some universities, the chair, dean, or chief financial officer meets with the social work program director and the administrative assistant regularly. During these meetings, the budget is reviewed in great detail and projections are made regarding future outlays. Factors influencing the budget are discussed, including the fiscal status of the university. Such meetings are not only helpful in understanding how campuswide finances work, but they also give the program director an opportunity to advocate for the program.

Faculty and staff need to be kept informed of what the budget assessment and evaluation reveal. The chair should provide a budget update at least quarterly based on the data collected. Budget information should also be shared with senior administrators so that there is a clear understanding of the factors influencing the budget figures in light of the program's mission, goals, and objectives. Such updates lay the foundation for possible future funding for the program.

> **REFLECTION QUESTIONS:**
> - If available to you, take time to review your university's budget. What costs and allocations come as a surprise to you, and why?
> - Determine whether your program has surplus or deficit spending. What are the ramifications? How will the university's policy on carryover affect your program during the next fiscal year?
> - Determine whether it is possible at your university to move funds among budget categories. Consider whether this would be beneficial, and how.
> - Describe the ramifications, both programmatic and institutional, of your program ending the academic year with a deficit.

Conclusion

For social work program directors, the budget is part of everyday interactions. With a broad dual focus, the director is ever mindful of monitoring the costs associated with operating the program. Essential to this focus are the program's mission, goals, and objectives. As described throughout this chapter, program directors need a general understanding of budgeting to administer their program effectively and efficiently in the complex university setting. Ideally, the introduction of basic budget concepts, terms, and processes will help directors in their program's budget development while enhancing their ability to advocate for funding support within and outside of their university.

Suggested Readings

Buller, J. L. (2015). *The essential academic dean or provost: A comprehensive desk reference.* Wiley.

Heinzman, L. N., Kay, L. A., Rhodes, S. J., & Lees, N. D. (2018). Marketing strategies to engage current students, alumni, and donors. *The Department Chair, 29*(2),11–13. https://doi.org/10.1002/dch.30218

Lees, N. D. (2016). Planning department staffing to meet academic needs. *Academic Leader, 32*(8), 5–6.

Rhodes, S. J., Heinzman, L. N., & Lees, N. D. (2018). Maximizing the benefits of an external advisory council. *The Department Chair, 28*(4), 14–16. https://doi.org/10.1002 /dch.30189

References

Birkenmaier, J., Sherraden, M., & Curley, J. (Eds.). (2013). *Financial capability and asset development: Research, education, policy, and practice.* Oxford University Press.

Caldwell, M. (2020). How to evaluate your budget. *The Balance.* https://www.thebalance .com/how-to-evaluate-your-budget-2385694

Corporate Financial Institute. (2020). *What is a SMART goal?* https://corporatefinanceinstitute .com/resources/knowledge/other/smart-goal/

Council on Social Work Education. (2022). *Educational policy and accreditation standards.* https://www.cswe.org/accreditation/standards/2022-epas/

Ford, M. (2018). Do's and don'ts: Mission and vision statements. *Business Administration Information.* https://www.businessadministrationinformation.com/general-business /how-to-write-clear-mission-and-vision-statements

Kosten, L. A. (2016). Outcomes-based funding and responsibility center management combining the best of state and institutional budget models to achieve shared goals. *Lumina Foundation.* https://www.luminafoundation.org/files/resources/obf-and -responsibility-center-management-full.pdf

Krysik, J. L., & Finn, J. (2018). *Research for effective social work practice* (4th ed.). Routledge.

Lees, N., Malik, D. J., & Williams, J. R. (2019). *Budgeting basics for new academic chairpersons.* Keynote presented at 36th Academic Chairpersons Conference, Houston, TX. https://newprairiepress.org/accp/2019/keynote/1/

Lees, N. D., & Malik, D. J. (2020). Effective communication, part 2: Improving chair-dean communication. *The Department Chair, 31*(1), 10–12. https://doi.org/10.1002/dch.30329

Ubogu, F. N. (2003). Competing for a slice of the budget cake: An academic library perspective. *African Journal of Library, Archives and Information Science, 13*(2), 175–186. https://www.ajol.info/index.php/ajlais/article/view/26138

University of Connecticut. (2016). *How to write a program mission statement.* https://assessment .uconn.edu/wp-content/uploads/sites/1804/2016/06/HowToWriteMission.pdf

Section Two

Program Topics

CHAPTER 6

Starting a BSW Program

Jo Daugherty Bailey

Starting a baccalaureate social work (BSW) program is an entrepreneurial enterprise. It entails envisioning a purpose, consulting with administrators, meeting with various stakeholder groups, collecting and analyzing data, developing detailed plans for program structure and curriculum, creating and managing a budget, and more. It is not an easy process; it takes years and requires countless hours of attention and labor to build. And, it is simultaneously a creative and exhilarating venture. The development of a BSW program is an opportunity to collaborate with colleagues to craft a program that addresses the social service needs of the community and offers students a path toward realizing their professional goals and dreams. Knowing that the design and implementation of the program will affect many clients and communities is a humbling reminder of the seriousness of the endeavor.

To develop a viable program, a multistage process that allows for deliberation and thought is required (see Figure 6.1). To develop a proposal for the institutional, regulatory, and accrediting bodies, it is necessary to begin with forming a rationale for and a conceptualization of the program. This rationale demonstrates the need for the program and clarifies the availability of resources. Elements of conceptualization include developing the program's purpose: What skills, what students, and what gaps in the area's educational offering will the program address? Once these are identified, you are set to build out the curriculum, policies, and structures that will sustain the program.

FIGURE 6.1

Steps to Proposal

Determining Need

Before you commit to the idea of developing a BSW program, you must first ask whether it is necessary and prudent to do so. This might seem like an odd start to a chapter dedicated to describing how to develop a program, but given the stakes (i.e., costs to students and the university should your efforts fail), these are critical questions to consider thoroughly and objectively. As of this writing, there are 541 BSW programs accredited by the Council on Social Work Education (CSWE, 2022a). Although most programs are successful, some are not; 46 BSW programs have closed in this century (CSWE, 2021b). And although some of these were in small, private colleges where the entire school closed, not all were. To explore the need for a program, one factor to consider is the initiating event that prompted the possibility of creating a program: Did the request emanate from college or university leaders, from students, or from the community? The reasons for this request as provided by the initiator will prove worthwhile when preparing the justification for the program.

It is essential to undergo due diligence to assess the level of student interest, community support, and, most especially, university investment. To explore program viability, areas of inquiry include current and potential students' level of interest in the degree, whether other colleges and universities in the area have BSW programs, and, if so, whether those programs produce a sufficient number of graduates for the community's needs. That is, will a new program fulfill an unmet need for students and the community? Following this, the major issue is whether or not the university has, and is willing to devote, sufficient resources for the program's development and sustenance. To answer these questions, you must gather data.

Feasibility Study

The initial exploration begins with a feasibility study, which is a comprehensive evaluation of the need (and demand) for and cost of operating the program (see Box 6.1). The information collected for the feasibility study will then allow the university to determine the overall value of the program. Program need is based upon two major constituencies: the labor market and potential students. (The following assumes that the data collection and analyses are performed by university personnel, although there are private firms that offer this service for a fee.)

Market Considerations

For a BSW program, the labor market includes agencies and organizations that employ baccalaureate-level social workers. Nationally, these tend to include for-profit, nonprofit, and governmental agencies in the following sectors: individual and family services, human resources, residential facilities, and medical facilities (Salsberg et al., 2017). You can find information on the state of employment for social workers in a number of reports (see Box 6.1). It will also be necessary to assess local employers' need for your graduates (this gets a little trickier if your institution has a large regional or national draw of students). In whatever way the university's community is defined, potential employers in the community should be queried about their interest in your graduates (and students).

The key questions pertain to whether the queried organization employs baccalaureate-level social workers, if they predict a need for them in the future, and how large the need is (i.e., an estimate of how many graduates they might employ in a given time frame). This information can be collected via interviews, surveys, or focus groups. Other potential sources are reports and papers produced or commissioned by national, state, or local agencies that identify present and future service gaps. Such reports may be population based (e.g., services for older adults) or service based (e.g., housing) and can provide a more focused picture of the local service landscape.

BOX 6.1

Resources for Feasibility Study	Source (see references for details)
Knocking at the College Door: Projections of U. S. High School Graduates	Western Interstate Commission for Higher Education (2020)
Occupational Outlook Handbook, Social Workers	Bureau of Labor Statistics (2021)
Results of the Nationwide Survey of 2017 Social Work Graduates	Salsberg et al. (2018)
Profile of the Social Work Workforce	Salsberg et al. (2017)
The Social Work Profession: Findings From Three Years of Surveys of New Social Workers	Fitzhugh Mullan Institute for Health Workforce Equity (2020)
From Social Work Education to Social Work Practice	Salsberg et al. (2019)
Resource Guide: Feasibility Studies	Tennessee Higher Education Commission (2017)
4 Critical Steps to Optimize Degree Program Portfolios	Hanover Research (2020)
Student Interest Assessment Handbook	Hanover Research (2014)

Assessing whether the program will attract an adequate number of students to sustain itself is another key element of the feasibility study. The most natural population to query is students, particularly students currently majoring in related fields like psychology and sociology, at the home institution. Students who have not yet declared a major are also a potential source to evaluate the degree of student interest. Additional student populations that may be helpful to include are those from local high schools and community colleges as well as current staff in social service agencies who desire a bachelor's degree. The answers that students and potential students give will indicate their level of interest in the prospective major at your institution, whether they are interested in full- or part-time study, and what their career aspirations may be.

Other potential sources for determining student demand are faculty and staff in related programs (e.g., social and behavioral sciences) and school counselors at the local high schools and community colleges. Finally, a description of the projected student pipeline from high schools and community colleges, often available through the state-level Department of Education, is a way to ground your predictions. For example, data on the number of students who will be graduating from your state's high schools over the next 5 to 10 years will provide you with reliable evidence of the potential student pool for the program (see Box 6.1).

Although the aforementioned sources may indicate student demand and interest, you will also need to ascertain if the educational market is already saturated or nearly saturated. For this, search for social work programs in colleges and universities in your state or region by reviewing the directory of accredited BSW programs on the CSWE website. Once you have a list of undergraduate programs in your designated area, you can research the number of students in their programs and the trends in enrollment over time, through their respective offices of institutional research and the National Center for Education Statistics Integrated Postsecondary Education Data System. Increases in enrollment may indicate high demand in the region, while decreases in enrollment, especially if the decrease is occurring in several programs in the region, could point to market saturation.

Resource Considerations

If the data indicate a probable need for the program, the next phase of the feasibility study is to appraise the resource and budgetary needs associated with starting and maintaining the program. Among the needs to be identified are those around library resources, technology, classrooms, offices, and marketing. Library needs pertain to the databases, books, and journals currently available in the system. The school's librarian can run a report and help to assess the sufficiency of the current collection and what purchases may be required.

Technology, classroom, and office needs will vary upon program aims and size. Programs that anticipate the use of technology in the classroom (e.g., digital learning tools) or online course offerings will have greater technology needs. The number of classrooms needed will depend on program size and scheduling. To estimate program size, refer to the data gathered on student interest, projections of high school and community college graduates over time, and trends in nearby institutions' enrollments. To forecast scheduling, the number of projected part- and full-time students and the delivery method (i.e., on campus, online, hybrid) are correlated with the plan of study (i.e., the order of courses students take). This information will help you determine the number of classes to be offered in a classroom each semester and thus the number of classrooms required.

The amount of office space needed is related to the estimate of the program's size, that is, the projected number of students. The program's size will indicate the number of staff and faculty necessary to run the program. Finally, there are the costs associated with the accreditation process (a minimum of $30,000 at this time) (CSWE, 2022c), which include an application fee, costs associated with the site visit, and the annual program fees, which depend on the size of the prior year's graduating class. Fees associated with reaffirmation must also be included in planning, both short and long term.

The largest budgetary costs are those associated with staffing. Calculating these costs has been simplified to some extent by the requirements set by CSWE (see CSWE, 2022b). These requirements do change with each new version of the Educational Policy and Accreditation Standards (EPAS); what is presented here is based on the 2022 EPAS (CSWE, 2022a). At the time of this writing, BSW programs are required to have at least a program director and a field director, each with primary assignment (51% or more) to the program. CSWE requires that each of these positions have sufficient time designated for administrative duties. Under the previous EPAS, the minimum administrative time was required to be 25% for each of these directors, but the requirement has been removed from the 2022 EPAS and is now referred to as a "customary" amount of administrative time. From personal experience, 25% assigned time is challenging for a small, two-person program because of the host of administrative activities necessary to create a successful and supportive program for students, and of course the load grows heavier as the number of students in the program increases.

According to CSWE (2022b), the majority of full-time faculty members must have an MSW from an accredited program, and those who teach practice courses must have 2 years of post-MSW practice experience, in accordance with Accreditation Standard 4.2. Although CSWE does not specify a minimum number of faculty (beyond having the program and field directors), the program must demonstrate it has a sufficient workforce to carry out its mission and goals. The 2022 EPAS requires a faculty-to-student ratio of 1:25 for BSW programs; if unmet, the program must provide evidence of effectiveness. CSWE also does not specify how many staff members are required, but rather indicates that the program must demonstrate adequate staff support. The costs of faculty and staff are unique to each university, and human resource personnel can help determine these costs. The actual number needed will also depend on the projected size of the program: As the number of students increases, the number of staff and faculty necessary to run the program and teach classes may also increase.

It may be tempting to estimate the faculty and staff needs at the lowest level possible to appear economically attractive to university reviewers. This is inadvisable because of the enormous amount of work involved in managing a social work program. Among the list of activities required by CSWE, and which are essential for the program's success, are the following:

- administering the admissions and field placement processes;
- ensuring student support through advising;
- facilitating student engagement;
- coordinating recruitment activities;
- conducting ongoing program assessment;
- handling student issues;
- responding to student questions and concerns;
- developing and maintaining agency and community relationships;
- managing and revising curriculum; and
- overseeing the budget.

And, to do these well, staff and faculty must have sufficient time beyond their other university duties allocated for these activities. At the very least, it is prudent to employ at least one full-time staff member and to advocate for reassigned time for the directors to support these vital administrative functions.

Justification

Once feasibility is established, the program's leadership will have an understanding of the need the program will fulfill and be able to argue the rationale for it. Components of the program's justification include the students it will serve, how the community will benefit, and the program's connection to the university's mission. From the feasibility study, the program will have information about both its potential competition and the students it will serve. This information will serve as a guide to creating the mission and goals for the program. In addition, the reason given by the initiator of the request for a program merits exploration, if not already addressed in the feasibility study. For example, if a leader from a local graduate-only school of social work originated the conversations for a potential program in your university, it would be beneficial to obtain a letter of support from them to include in your submissions to the university and accreditors.

A first step in determining the program's unique contribution, which essentially will serve as a component of the justification to seek approval, is to develop a market comparison of other programs in the region. This comparison will include developing profiles of the competitor programs and their institutions' missions, goals, cost, and student demographics. (This information is readily available via the websites of the universities and programs you are looking at, as well as the National Center for Education Statistics Integrated Postsecondary Education Data System.) You should develop a document with the descriptions of the programs and their institutions, as this information will be required in the approval process. Your program leaders can then compare their university's mission and student population with these other programs and their institutions to illustrate potential gaps your program will fill.

The program leaders' ability to demonstrate that the program will meet some unaddressed need strengthens the argument for approval. To identify these needs, local agencies, community leaders, and news organizations may have information regarding service gaps or pressing social problems. For example, reports of racialized police violence indicate an urgent need for justice system reform, and a BSW program dedicated to social justice can articulate its ability to prepare students to contribute to reform efforts. Additionally, other programs may be too far away to serve the local community, or the proposed program may aim to serve a different population of students than other schools in the region do. On this latter point, the ability and commitment to serve a diverse student body and historically underserved students are not only core to social work values; they also bolster the case for a program's approval. While serving these students is a valuable goal, the program must intentionally establish practices, policies, and curriculum that truly support and promote the strengths of underserved populations and students of color (see Box 6.2 for suggestions).

BOX 6.2

Inclusive Practice Considerations

The creation of a system and culture of inclusivity—one that is anti-racist, anti-ableist, nonclassist, pro-Indigenous, pro-LGBTQIA+, and supportive of first-generation students—can be institutionalized when incorporated into program conceptualization. Ideas for this include the following:

- mechanisms to solicit input from a variety of voices
- recruitment of diverse students, staff, faculty, field instructors, and committee and board members
- application and enrollment support services
- academic and study support services
- availability of supportive advising and mentoring of students
- courses focusing on diverse populations
- class material from diverse authorities
- universal design in teaching, learning, and services
- opportunities for gathering, collaboration, and celebration
- staff and faculty development opportunities
- ongoing inclusive-practices training of staff and faculty

Adapted from U.S. Department of Education (2016) and Burgstahler (2021).

From here, the program faculty and administrators develop the mission and goals. Although BSW programs are generalist by design and share educational standards as determined by CSWE, they still must be able to establish their particular niche (i.e., why is another program necessary?). A program's mission illustrates its reason for being and articulates its purpose, distinguishing it from other programs ("Mission, Vision, and Values," 2019). The mission statement serves as a guidepost for the program upon which future decisions and actions will be grounded. A good mission statement is clear and succinct; the management literature is rife with cautions against nebulous, wordy, and overreaching mission statements. From the mission, the program's goals are developed, and these will then direct the program's activities and curriculum, which effectuate the EPAS. Information from the feasibility study and the justification will form the basis for the proposals to be submitted to approving entities (see Figure 6.1).

Program Proposal Process

Before pursuing CSWE accreditation, the program must have received approval from the university and, in many cases, from the university's regional accreditor and the state's higher education coordinating or governing board. Although most states require new program approval for public institutions, requirements vary by state and according to the type of institution—public or private (Venters, 2021). The proposal process may be unique for each of the particular entities, but there are some common elements among them (see Figure 6.2). First, each will have its own form and format, which typically are available on its website. Your institution's accreditation liaison officer is likely able to point you to this information and tell you whose approval is needed and in what order. Generally, the information needed for the approval phase will include the results from the feasibility study and the justification elements (as described previously).

In addition to these results, proposals will include descriptions of faculty (e.g., degrees, experience, and expertise), course plans and syllabi, an outline of the admission criteria and process, and an assessment plan. Some institutions may also require external evaluation or letters of support from community partners. Once approval is gained from the institution (including its governing board), the proposal is submitted, along with signatures from academic leadership, to the state's coordinating or governing board of higher education (if required) and to the university's regional accreditor. Upon approval from these entities, which may take a year or more, the program can seek CSWE accreditation.

FIGURE 6.2
Proposal Elements

Accreditation Process

Arguably, the most rigorous approval process step is the professional accreditation process for social work programs. Fortunately, CSWE provides extensive guidance and support for programs applying for candidacy and full accreditation. This support is in the form of the accreditation handbook (available on the CSWE website; see CSWE 2022a), forms (also on the website; see CSWE 2022c), the assignment of an accreditation specialist, and trainings and workshops on the accreditation process. The process toward accreditation is itself supportive and consists of a series of incremental stages (see Figure 6.3), which will aid the program in building the elements of a program over the course of approximately 3 years. The following information is found in the EPAS Handbook (CSWE, 2022c), with the exception of insertions of my personal thoughts. The sections of the handbook are referenced, as applicable.

Precandidacy

The program submits the Application and Letter of Institutional Intent. These are rather straightforward documents that indicate the prior levels of approval, the identification of the program director, and the administration's support for the program. Upon approval, CSWE assigns an accreditation specialist and the program submits the draft of the Benchmark I document and the review brief form (CSWE 2022c). (See Box 6.3 for tips on writing the Benchmark document). The accreditation specialist reviews the documentation and provides feedback regarding any additional information or clarification needed.

After approval by the specialist, a site visit is held by a commissioner. During the visit, the commissioner, who is a trained volunteer social work educator, interviews program personnel, university leadership, and students (and potentially other groups; you will be told in advance who they need to meet) (3.3.8). The commissioner will hold an exit meeting with program and university leadership that highlights their initial impressions (3.3.8). During this exit meeting, the commissioner will indicate if there are any areas of concern or noncompliance. Having this information in advance of the commissioner's report, the program can then begin to work to address the issues in order to offer a timely response to CSWE.

BOX 6.3

Writing the Benchmark Document

- The Benchmark Review Brief serves as an outline and a check for the Benchmark document. The brief lists each of the Accreditation Standards and the corresponding compliance statements.

- CSWE provides a template that programs can use to draft and write the Benchmark document (CSWE, 2021a). Standards that begin with the letter *B* apply to BSW programs. Standards that begin with the letter *M* apply to MSW programs and can be removed for BSW programs.

- It is helpful to review and utilize these documents as a guide while preparing program curriculum and elements prior to preparing the Benchmark itself. This work will help with ensuring complete and thorough documentation of the program's attainment of all the standards.

After the visit, the commissioner submits a report noting any areas of concern or noncompliance to be addressed (3.3.9), to which the program must prepare a response to the agency (3.3.10). For areas of noncompliance, the response must demonstrate how it has been addressed. For areas of concern, the response may correct the area or provide explanation and an argument for the area of concern. The commissioner may also include in their report additional notes on the program. These are provided to support the program and address issues that, while not meeting the bar of "concern" or "noncompliance," the program should also consider and address in their response (see Box 6.4 for suggestions on preparing the response).

Commissioners on CSWE's accrediting body consider not only the Benchmark document and the commissioner's report, but also the program's response in its decision on the program's status. It is therefore important to demonstrate how all of the standards are being met by the program. All of the documentation is provided to the commission members, who then vote on the program's status for candidacy, which may be granted, deferred until the next meeting (in pursuit of additional information), or denied (3.3.11).

BOX 6.4

Writing the Response

The commissioner's report is written in the Review Brief document. The report will identify concern, compliance, or noncompliance for each standard. The commissioner's report will include notes that fully describe what they see as a problem and will offer guidance on how to address the issue.

For each problematic area (concern or noncompliance), copy and paste into a document the standard and the commissioner's notes on it. Then, below each, write the heading "Response." Fully explain and describe how the issue has been (or will be) fixed. Be specific and offer a thorough enough explanation to demonstrate how the solution meets the standard.

Candidacy

When notified of candidacy status, the program has 1 year to prepare and submit the Benchmark II document. Another visit is scheduled approximately a year after the first visit. Once again, the commissioner visits the various constituencies and writes a report regarding areas of noncompliance or concern (3.4.5). The program responds to any remarks (3.4.7); see the recommendations described in Box 6.4. Once again, the accrediting body considers all of the information from the commissioner and program and votes on whether the program may continue in candidacy, defers a decision until the next meeting (in pursuit of clarifying information), or removes the program from candidacy (3.4.8).

Initial Accreditation

The final phase of the process involves submitting Benchmark III and a final site visit, again approximately one year after Benchmark II and the second visit. The commissioner meets with constituencies and provides a report regarding areas of noncompliance or concern (4.5.1). The program once again responds to the report (4.5.2). In the following Board of Accreditation (BOA) meeting, one of six different decisions may be issued: (1) grant initial accreditation for 8 years, (2) grant initial accreditation with a requirement of reporting from the program to be reviewed by the program's accreditation specialist, (3) grant initial accreditation with a requirement of reporting from the program to be reviewed by the BOA, (4) defer a decision until additional information can be provided by the program for the next BOA meeting, (5) order another year of candidacy, or (6) or deny accreditation. It bears repeating that the accreditation process is a supportive one. CSWE is invested in helping programs develop over time in such a way that they will achieve full accreditation. To wit, in a review of the past 5 five years of accreditation decisions, not one program was denied accreditation. The commissioner and the accrediting body members are clear in their feedback regarding precisely how the program needs to be updated to address any concerns. At any point in the process, when a program director is unsure about how to incorporate the feedback, they are able to meet with their accreditation specialist to problem-solve.

FIGURE 6.3

The Accreditation Process

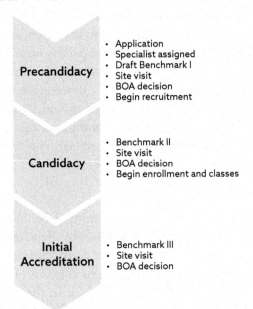

Precandidacy
- Application
- Specialist assigned
- Draft Benchmark I
- Site visit
- BOA decision
- Begin recruitment

Candidacy
- Benchmark II
- Site visit
- BOA decision
- Begin enrollment and classes

Initial Accreditation
- Benchmark III
- Site visit
- BOA decision

Planning and Implementation

Curriculum

Although the information and support for the accreditation process provided by CSWE is comprehensive, the elements of curricular planning are complex and merit additional consideration. The broad pieces of curricular planning are the required general education coursework, prerequisites, and program courses. The state and institution set the minimum number of credit hours for a bachelor's degree, typically 120 hours (American Council on Education, 2019). Institutions determine the required general education content for all undergraduates, which can range between one-quarter and one-half of undergraduate degree hours (Bowen, 2004). One way to conceptualize the degree requirements is to work backward, starting with the EPAS competencies, as these form the basis for the student learning outcomes.

First, the program faculty and administrators determine the connections of the program's mission and goals to these competencies, identifying where the program goals map onto the competencies. From here, courses are created, with the goal of each of the competencies having representation in the curriculum. This does not mean that each competency must have its own course, but rather that the content exists within one or more courses (the program and field directors must also be able to demonstrate that all competencies are met in the field component). Then, the program faculty and administrators can devise the plan of study outlining the course sequencing, that is, the order in which students may take the courses. Here, the program faculty and administrators should be thinking through how the social work curriculum builds knowledge and skills over time.

When developing the draft of social work courses, the program faculty and administrators should consider the knowledge or skills the student must already have when entering into each course. In developing the course-sequencing outline, the program faculty and administrators must determine which courses will serve as pre- or corequisite courses. Some courses are foundational, introducing the students to the basics of the social work knowledge base (e.g., the profession's history and values). They may also draw from the general education curriculum to determine if a particular course may serve as a foundation for one or more social work courses.

For example, a social work course in policy may require the student to have knowledge of the legislative process, which may be found in government courses in the general education curriculum. Or, before a course in which students will be required to craft a research proposal or conduct a research project, it may be useful for them to have taken a course in research methods or statistics from the general education curriculum. It is possible that courses outside the general education curriculum may also serve as prerequisites. It is necessary to think through whether or not co- and prerequisites are absolutely necessary, as the greater the number of these, the less flexibility there will be for students, which can affect retention and completion rates (Mertes & Jankoviak, 2016).

Policy

Another substantial project involves the development of admissions and other program policies and processes. Admissions policies include acceptance criteria (e.g., completion of general education coursework, if necessary; prerequisite completion, if applicable; and/or minimum grade point average [GPA]), application requirements (i.e., the elements required of the applicant), and types of acceptance (e.g., full, conditional, and denied). An admissions process must be devised, outlining how the admissions process will work: when applications will be accepted, who will review them, and the timeline and method for communicating an applicant's status (see Chapter 17 for further information on gatekeeping).

The program must also establish policies for field education for both agencies and students. One of the obligations for field agencies is that the agency provide appropriate experiences for the student and properly supervise students in accordance with CSWE requirements. The program should have an application available for students to enter a field placement, and there should be some sort of matching process (perhaps asking students about their interests). The program faculty and administrators would need to develop policies regarding professional and academic expectations for field placements.

Finally, the program must establish policies and processes for the students to remain in the program, including both academic and professional performance expectations. Academic expectations pertain to minimum grades in coursework, minimum GPA requirements, and following the plan of study to remain in the program and graduate. Professional performance expectations relate to minimal behavioral standards, which may be adherence to the university's code of conduct as well as the social work professional Code of Ethics (NASW, 2021). It is extremely important to explain to students these expectations in detail and the consequences for the specific types of violations. It is advisable to have university guidance and approval for the expectations, consequences, and processes; when a serious infraction occurs, it behooves the program to have systems in place that have the full support of the administration.

Operations

Beyond attending to curriculum and policy, the program faculty and administrators must establish mechanisms to recruit and support students, given that attaining initial accreditation is contingent upon the program having matriculated at least one cohort of students. Recruitment activities and communication in the precandidacy and candidacy stages are crucial for developing student interest. Chapter 16 discusses recruitment in general, and it is definitely trickier to do during this phase of a program. During this early period, some potential students will be understandably reluctant to enter a program that is not yet fully accredited. Be ready to explain the accreditation process, even if briefly, during your recruitment activities. A key component of this explanation is that candidacy is a phase of accreditation.

Because enrolling students is required for accreditation, the program must engage in intensive recruiting efforts during precandidacy and early candidacy. Holding recruitment events, working with university advisors to gain assistance in spreading the word about the program, sending email blasts to students, disseminating flyers on campus, creating web pages about the program, opening social media accounts, presenting in classrooms, getting a profile in the university's media forms, and holding meet and greets are all ways to generate student interest. Outside of the university, distributing materials to or meeting with advisors, faculty, and chairs in community colleges and high schools can inform the potential student population in the area. Some of these schools may allow you to present to their students. If your budget permits, you can advertise in newspapers, radio, websites, social media, or television. Messaging for recruitment could include the value of a social work degree, highlights of program strengths, and program timelines for application and enrollment. On a final note, recruiting may begin in precandidacy, but in order to graduate from an accredited program, students cannot start in the program before the academic year in which candidacy is granted (CSWE, 2022c, 1.1.4).

It is wise, especially for any external communications, to work with the university's communication office to ensure compliance with the institution's rules and proper institutional branding. Additionally, seeking the consultation of the university's marketing experts can be fruitful in developing a comprehensive, effective marketing campaign. Recruiting for the program does not happen for just a few years; rather, it takes an ongoing commitment to education and reeducation of the university and larger community about the program.

Once in the program, students will need support systems to help them through enrollment, academic demands, personal issues, and field placement. These supports should be identified and in place before student enrollment, and descriptions of these systems should be included in the benchmark documents. An essential support for students is advisement on course enrollment to make sure that the student follows the plan of study appropriately. In some universities, this advising may be done by program staff or faculty or by college- or university-level advisors.

To ensure inclusivity, consider the types of supports that strengthen persistence rates for first-generation students and students of color, such as mentorship, tutoring, and other practices recommended by the U.S. Department of Education (2016). For other issues, such as handling the demands of the material, balancing other obligations, and experiencing personal and family crises, faculty and staff are often the first point of contact for students. Although some of these issues may be handled by program personnel (e.g., discussing social work content and ethics), in other cases, such as mental health concerns or writing needs, a referral to an institutional support (e.g., counseling or tutoring services) may be more appropriate.

It is therefore important that the program has an ongoing way to inform all students about the institutional supports available to them. Some students may not seek support, which is common for first-generation students and students of color (U.S. Department of Education, 2016), so offering at least an annual advisement meeting with a faculty member is one way to both circumvent potential student problems and provide students with mentorship and support their development as social workers.

Additional critical support is provided by field faculty and field instructors who meet with students regularly as a function of their roles. This is one reason that developing a clear field manual and a guide for field instructors is so critical. To the extent that everyone knows what is expected of them, what the requirements and rules are, what to do when they are having issues, and whom to consult with when concerns arise, the program is able to prevent or readily handle serious disruption in a field placement.

Program personnel must also develop solid relationships with the community and demonstrate this in benchmark documents and during site visits. Importantly, program faculty and administrators must demonstrate that the program has a sufficient pool of agencies able to serve as field placement sites for undergraduate students. Field agencies not only must ensure that students will have opportunities to meet the competencies and be assigned appropriate tasks and duties to build their professional skills, but also must commit staff to offer ongoing, frequent, and culturally competent supervision to the student. The field instructor needs to have an understanding of their role and the time to properly train students for their tasks within the agency and to support students' learning. Holding an orientation for field instructors before they begin in this role will provide quality assurance as well as an opportunity to build collaborative relationships with instructors and their agencies. These associations are important not only to ensure placements for students, but also to demonstrate to CSWE the program's connections within the community.

To enhance these community connections, the program faculty and administrators may want to develop an advisory board or committee to bring in leaders from agencies and the larger community. Building a board or committee takes consideration: Think carefully through its purpose, which will help guide its composition and activities. Write out the board's or committee's charge, that is, its mission and terms of service (e.g., length of appointment, expectations of members), in advance. Some programs have field committees that bring in representatives from all of their placement agencies; some may have committees to determine the relevance of a program's curriculum (i.e., whether or not they are preparing students well for the type of work they will be doing); and some may have advisory boards to help in large initiatives like fundraising. Regardless of its particular purpose, each will aid the program personnel in understanding the community and communicating the program's interest in the community, and as such, it is vital to ensure diverse representation on boards and committees.

Conclusion

As presented in this chapter, the process of creating and starting a BSW program is tiered in its approach. The work needed at the front end (i.e., the feasibility study) is crucial in order to prepare subsequent proposals, which in turn assist in building the benchmark documents required for accreditation. At every step in this process, you will need a broad array of input, guidance, resources, and support from the university community. These supports will undergird the program and help secure the program's success. Hopefully, you will also be able to build a network beyond the university, where you can seek opinions, advice, and support.

When I went through the process of starting a program, I was astounded by the amount of helpful information and support that I received from colleagues at other universities. At the end of the day, we are all social work educators, with all that the term implies. And while I used the term *competitor* earlier, in no way did I get the sense (and still do not) from peers that we are competitive with one another. As long as your market area is not saturated, you can carve out your niche and develop a program in a way that fulfills the needs of your students, university, and community.

Suggested Readings

Dee, J. R., & Heineman, W. A. (2016). Understanding the organizational context of academic program development. *New Directions for Institutional Research, 2015*(168), 9–35. https://doi.org/10.1002/ir.20158

Ginsberg, L. H. (2008). *Management and leadership in social work practice and education*. Council on Social Work Education.

Hanover Research. (2019). *The case for data-driven program development*. https://www.hanoverresearch.com/reports-and-briefs/case-for-data-driven-program-development/

References

American Council on Education. (2019). *U.S. higher education: A brief guide*. https://www.acenet.edu/Documents/brief-guide-to-US-higher-ed.pdf

Bowen, S. H. (2004). Reality check: What's in a name? The persistence of "General Education." *Peer Review, 7*(1). https://www.aacu.org/publications-research/periodicals/reality-check-whats-name-persistence-general-education

Bureau of Labor Statistics, U.S. Department of Labor. (2021). *Occupational outlook handbook, social workers*. https://www.bls.gov/ooh/community-and-social-service/social-workers.htm

Burgstahler, S. (2021). *A framework for inclusive practices in higher education*. DO-IT University of Washington. https://www.washington.edu/doit/framework-inclusive-practices-higher-education

Council on Social Work Education. (2021a). *Accreditation process*. https://www.cswe.org/Accreditation/Accreditation-Process

Council on Social Work Education. (2021b). *Formerly accredited or approved baccalaureate social work programs*. https://www.cswe.org/Accreditation/Directory-of-Accredited-Programs/Formerly-Accredited-or-Approved-BSW-Program

Council on Social Work Education. (2022a). *2022 Educational policy and accreditation standards (EPAS) for baccalaureate and master's social work programs*. https://www.cswe.org/accreditation/standards/2022-epas/

Council on Social Work Education. (2022b). *About CSWE accreditation*. https://www.cswe.org/Accreditation.aspx

Council on Social Work Education (2022c). *Accreditation process*. https://www.cswe.org/accreditation/accreditation-process/

Fitzhugh Mullan Institute for Health Workforce Equity. (2020). *The social work profession: Findings from three years of surveys of new social workers*. https://www.cswe.org/getattachment/a75b244d-5831-4d51-b59c-1e51de32b93e/SW-Workforce-Book-2020.pdf?lang=en-US

Hanover Research. (2014). *Student interest assessment handbook*. https://www.minnstate.edu/system/asa/academicaffairs/programs/docs/program-planning/Student-Interest-Assessment-MnSCU.pdf

Hanover Research. (2020). *4 critical steps to optimize degree program portfolios*. https://www.hanoverresearch.com/reports-and-briefs/four-critical-steps-to-optimize-programs-in-an-era-of-uncertainty/

Mertes, S. J., & Jankoviak, M. W. (2016). Creating a college-wide retention program: A mixed methods approach. *Community College Enterprise, 22*(1), 9–27.

Mission, vision, and values. (2019). In *Encyclopedia of Management* (8th ed., vol. 2, pp. 742–746). Gale.

National Association of Social Workers. (2021). Code of ethics of the National Association of Social Workers. https://www.socialworkers.org/About/Ethics/Code-of-Ethics/Code-of-Ethics-English

Salsberg, E., Quigley, L., Acquaviva, K., Wyche, K., & Sliwa, S. (2018). *Results of the nationwide survey of 2017 social work graduates*. https://cswe.org/Centers-Initiatives/Initiatives/National-Workforce-Initiative/Survey-of-2017-SW-Grads-Report-FINAL.aspx

Salsberg, E., Quigley, L., Mehfoud, N., Acquaviva, K. D., Wyche, K., & Sliwa, S. (2017). *Profile of the social work workforce.* https://hsrc.himmelfarb.gwu.edu/sphhs_policy _workforce_facpubs/16/

Salsberg, E., Quigley, L., Richwine, C., Sliwa, S. Acquaviva, K., & Wyche, K. (2019). *From social work education to social work practice.* https://www.cswe.org/CSWE/media /Workforce-Study/2018-Social-Work-Workforce-Report-Final.pdf

Tennessee Higher Education Commission. (2017). *Resource guide: Feasibility studies.* https://www.tn.gov/content/dam/tn/thec/bureau/aa/academic-programs/program-approv /aca-pol/THEC_Resource_Guide_Feasibility_Studies_July_2017.pdf

U.S. Department of Education. (2016). *Advancing diversity and inclusion in higher education.*

Venters, M. (2021). State-level program approval and review. *State Higher Education Executive Officers Association (SHEEO).* https://sheeo.org/wp-ontent/uploads/2021/09 /SHEEO_ProgApp.pdf

Western Interstate Commission for Higher Education. (2020). *Knocking at the college door: Projections of U. S. high school graduates.* https://knocking.wiche.edu/

CHAPTER 7

Launching and Coordinating Online Undergraduate Social Work Programs

Jennifer R. Jewell
Kathleen Arban
Heather Diehl

As the demographics of college students have shifted, so too has the delivery of education. Even before the COVID-19 pandemic forced much of higher education online, many postsecondary students were engaged in online education. During the 2019–2020 academic year, 31% of undergraduate students (6.8 million) took at least one online course, and 19% of undergraduate students (4.2 million) were enrolled in fully online programs, which means that 50% of all students were engaged in some level of online learning (U.S. Department of Education, National Center for Education Statistics, 2020). Although that year did include the early months of the pandemic in the United States, universities were instructed not to count courses that were moved online because of the pandemic.

Social work education has also embraced online education as an effective course delivery option. Most social work programs offer students the option of completing at least some of the program online (56.1% of baccalaureate programs; 66.2% of master's programs; Council on Social Work Education [CSWE], 2021). Although not as common at the BSW level as at the MSW level, 6.5% of undergraduate and 28.9% of MSW social work programs offered an entirely online option in 2020 (CSWE, 2021). This data point is similar to the national data; 37% of graduate students are enrolled exclusively in online programs, and undergraduate students are enrolled at a rate of 19% (U.S. Department of Education, National Center for Education Statistics, 2020).

Given the limited number of online baccalaureate programs, decreases in some BSW enrollments, and the changing demographics of students, some program faculty and administrators may be thinking strategically about starting an online undergraduate social work program or option. For example, Walden University and Maryville University have an entirely online BSW program, and Simmons University and the University of Louisville offer hybrid social work programs (both in-person and online options). However, launching and coordinating an entirely online BSW program or a hybrid program presents multiple unique factors, such as responding to student need, allocating resources, providing faculty training and support, and meeting accreditation standards. This chapter will explore these factors within the context of the opportunities and potential challenges of providing undergraduate education in a completely online format.

Distance education is an umbrella term that describes education when the instructor is not in person (e.g., online, satellite or wireless communication, or audio- and videoconferencing), which can be either synchronous or asynchronous (National Center for Education Statistics, n.d.). Online education is a type of distance education that "uses the internet as a delivery modality to offer thoughtfully designed, quality, student-focused learning experiences, built on proven best practices that create effective interactions between learners, peers, instructors, and content" (Mathes, 2020, para. 5). Although many programs use some aspects of technology to enhance and reinforce learning and some programs offer portions of the course online in a blended or hybrid format, this chapter will focus on the implementation and coordination of undergraduate social work programs that are offered completely online.

Online Education

No longer viewed as a passing fad, online education has grown exponentially over the last few decades (U.S. Department of Education, 2018). Moreover, after being forced to move teaching and learning online to maintain education during the COVID-19 pandemic, a growing number of institutions plan to continue distance education, which will expand the number (Lederman, 2021). The research comparing traditional in-person and online learning varies depending on the subject area and the courses offered, the characteristics of the students, and the instruction being offered, which makes a case for either one or both being more or equally effective, depending on the variables examined (Bates, 2021). Some studies suggest that online education is less effective (Alpert et al., 2016; Xu & Jaggars, 2014), but other studies show no significant differences between online and in-person learning or, in some cases, improved outcomes in short- and long-term student performance in online versus in-person learning (Faulconer et al., 2018; Paul & Jefferson, 2019). In a meta-analysis funded by the U.S. Department of Education, online learning was shown to be as effective as face-to-face instruction (Means et al., 2013), and Fischer et al. (2021) found that when students took online courses required for their major at a large public California university ($N = 10,572$), they were more likely to graduate within 4 years, and their time to degree was slightly accelerated. Afrouz and Crisp (2021) conducted a scoping review of the social work literature to synthesize research on online social work education, which revealed no differences in grades and academic performance.

Within social work education, online programs at both the under-graduate and graduate levels are growing (CSWE, 2021). Although social work education was later than other professional disciplines to adopt technology, over the last decade the field of social work has embraced the use of technology in both education and practice, as evidenced by the accreditation of online social work programs by CSWE and the adoption of *Standards for Technology in Social Work Practice* by several social work professional organizations (National Association of Social Workers [NASW], 2017).

This transition was important because the demographics of college students have been shifting; the number of traditionally aged students (18–22 years old) is shrinking because of the declining birth rate. The rate of decline is expected to be more than 15% after 2025 (Barshay, 2018). Nontraditional adult learners, defined as those 25 and over, have long been a neglected student population, yet many universities and colleges have started to actively recruit them. Given the necessity for institutions of higher education to recruit and retain more nontraditional students, social work is positioned well to serve this population, as the profession has attracted many adult learners (CSWE, 2021), who tend to respond favorably to competence-based education (Chen, 2017).

Expanding social work education online offers many benefits for social work students, particularly nontraditional students, as it is more flexible, which allows for the balance of education with other responsibilities, such as work and family (Ilgaz & Gulbahar, 2017; Tzavara & Wilczek, 2019). Online education is also more accessible, as anyone with a reliable internet connection can take courses, which has increased access to individuals living in more remote areas.

As noted, while only 6.5% of undergraduate social work programs were offered entirely online in 2020, 28.9% of MSW programs offered their entire degree online (CSWE, 2021). According to the *Directory of Accredited Programs* on the CSWE website (https://www.cswe.org/accreditation/directory/?) in late fall 2022, of 536 accredited undergraduate programs, 89 are online (17%), and of the 312 accredited MSW programs, 156 (50%) offer an online program option. Although there is a discrepancy between the numbers reported in that directory and *2020 Annual Survey* (CSWE, 2021), the number of online MSW program options is far outpacing the number of online BSW programs, which may be explained by the added considerations for starting online BSW programs, such as addressing general education requirements. Yet, online BSW programs extend social work education beyond brick-and-mortar buildings to reach students where they are, helping to ensure accessibility for more students.

Launching an Online Program

The Salisbury University School of Social Work (SU SSW), with which the authors were or are associated, has a long commitment to providing social work education in multiple modalities to ensure access to student populations. All three authors have served at various levels of administration at SU SSW, including the Director of the School of Social Work, MSW Program Chair, and Site Coordinator. SU SSW first ventured into distance education in the form of satellite programs in 2006. In 2014, SU SSW partnered with the University of Maryland Global Campus (UMGC), a sister institution in the University System of Maryland, to provide social work education to military-connected students in Europe under a U.S. Department of Defense contract, thus launching an online undergraduate and graduate social work option. A regional online MSW option in the United States was launched shortly after the SU-UMGC partnership, and SU SSW most recently launched a regional BSW online program option in fall 2022. Given the varied experiences of launching multiple online programs, this chapter integrates both research and practice experience into the development of online program options in general.

Institutional Support and Program Buy-In

Extending to online has allowed higher education institutions to expand the target market to mitigate declining enrollments while creating additional revenue streams. Yet, although launching online options can be beneficial for colleges and universities, an investment of time and resources must be established to help with a successful launch. Institutional support is imperative for launching a new program option, and that support must encompass technological infrastructure, a technology plan, and incentives for faculty (Pedro & Kumar, 2020; Phipps & Merisotis, 2000). In their review of 13 online education quality frameworks, Pedro and Kumar (2020) contend that "the transition to online education necessitates changes within institutions and the provision of various types of support for stakeholders (e.g., faculty, students) and processes (e.g., course development) to ensure its success" (p. 50). Program directors should use a quality assurance framework from the beginning to furnish a blueprint for development. The Online Learning Consortium (2022) embraced the "Five Pillars of Quality Online Education": learning effectiveness, faculty satisfaction, student satisfaction, access, and scale.

Programs interested in launching an online BSW option must complete some market research and create a feasible program proposal (see Chapter 6 for information on starting a BSW program). Program directors need to secure the support of university administrators to ensure adequate resources are allocated to assist with a successful launch, such as a dedicated instructional designer to help with course conversions. Given the cost of employing additional technology specialists for online courses, program directors will need to secure the ongoing institutional commitment to invest in this type of instructional support. They will also need to collaborate with a technology team to develop an online course quality assurance plan, such as the use of Quality Matters (2022), that sets universal course design and online course delivery standards.

> **PRACTICE TIP:** Advocate with your institution to hire an instructional designer to provide individualized support to social work faculty, including devising standardized course templates so faculty can focus on course content.

Not only can the shift to online delivery present a steep learning curve for some instructors (Dawson & Fenster, 2015), but skepticism also persists about the effectiveness of online education to achieve student learning outcomes (Jaschik & Lederman, 2019). This skepticism, particularly for practice-oriented competencies, exists within social work education (Levin et al., 2018). Some faculty, particularly those who have not taught online, perceive online social work education as less effective (Levin et al., 2018). Other studies indicate that faculty regard teaching online as more challenging compared with in-person classes (Leary et al., 2020; Rhode et al., 2017; Seaman, 2009). Whether online education is considered less effective or more work for instructors, these perceptions can hinder acceptance of online education.

Even with the best plan and an established infrastructure, digital divides exist for students, including the availability of broadband infrastructure, affordability of internet access at home, and the accessibility of adequate devices to complete schoolwork. Internet speed varies according to region and availability, which can affect a student's ability to participate in live class sessions, complete exams, and watch videos and prerecorded lectures. Students use a range of devices to access course materials, ranging from cell phones to PCs, which affects object image clarity and thus the students' ability to use certain applications, and some platforms malfunction.

Although access to technology and the internet has increased significantly in the United States (Pew Research Center, 2021), limited data capacity, broken hardware, and subpar connectivity present challenges for college students that can affect their academic performance (Gonzales et al., 2018). About 9% of college students do not have access to a laptop to use for schoolwork (Galanek et al., 2018). These challenges create equity issues for some students. Means and Neisler (2020) found that although only 8% of students in their study experienced serious hardware or software issues, rates were higher among Black (15%) and Latino (10%) students than White students (6%). These rates were also higher among students with households earning under $50,000 (11%) than households earning more than $100,000 (4%).

Given the necessity of adequate technology when engaging in higher education, particularly online education, some postsecondary institutions, such as Wake Forest University, the University of Michigan, and Indiana State University, now provide laptops or other technology for students to keep or borrow during their time as students. Some programs provide laptops to all students, and other programs require that students must meet some criteria, such as being eligible for a Pell Grant, to access a laptop or other equipment. Although these examples demonstrate wide institutional support for technology accessibility, program directors can advocate for similar provisions for online students if the programs do not already exist at their institutions.

Another significant factor is the availability of online general education courses and/or the support from the liberal arts programs to develop online courses if they do not exist. Depending on the level of institutional support, upper administration can help to persuade other units to move some courses online, such as prerequisites for the program. While lack of availability does not have to hinder the development of an online BSW option, it does change the nature of the program, which will be addressed later in this chapter.

Faculty Readiness

Successfully transitioning to online instruction is "not a simple matter of transferring face-to-face approaches" (Bower, 2011, p. 79). Rather, faculty need a skill set that combines up-to-date technology and pedagogy (Mayer & Sekayi, 2018). Identifying the needs of faculty (both full- and part-time) will help to ensure that the professional development and mentoring opportunities match the gaps in knowledge and skills for online education. Although faculty buy-in is crucial, program directors can also incentivize faculty development.

Faculty readiness to teach online should explore skills and knowledge in course design, course communication, time management, and technical competence, such as navigating the learning management system (LMS), creating and editing videos, and using online collaborative tools (Los et al., 2021; Martin et al., 2019). Investing in faculty training will contribute to the retention of students, because faculty members will learn to create effective assessment procedures, enhance faculty engagement in online courses, and utilize online tools to increase social interactions in class (Seery et al., 2021).

Inadequate technological preparedness has been shown to be a barrier to the acceptance of online education (Wingo et al., 2017). Developing both comfort with technology and enhanced technical competencies, including knowledge on how to use various systems and the ability to troubleshoot difficulties, enhances favorable views of online education and student outcomes (Levin et al., 2018; Wingo et al., 2017). Moreover, faculty can utilize technology that is not available in traditional face-to-face settings to promote collaboration and build community online. As research demonstrates, "activities in live classrooms do not always translate into online environments" (Washburn & Zhou, 2018, p. 1). Thus, in making the transition to an online modality, instructors will need to rethink their goals and adopt effective pedagogical practices, not only new teaching strategies and new technologies but also new views of teaching and learning (Feist, 2003). Program directors can assist faculty in exploring these aspects of online teaching preparedness by providing professional development opportunities.

> **PRACTICE TIP:** Have faculty (both full- and part-time) complete a training for readiness for online teaching that explores technology, pedagogy, communication, and organizational skills, along with attitudes related to online teaching.

Los et al. (2021) offered the Online and Blended Teaching Readiness Assessment (OBTRA) as a tool to assess faculty readiness and inform professional development opportunities. Faculty professional development can take a variety of forms, including books, workshops, peer collaboration and mentorship, seminars, and certification programs. Program directors can be instrumental in creating these opportunities and encouraging participation. Whatever the form, professional development should include contingent faculty as well as full-time faculty, be flexible in nature, and provide support and community to instructors, which can diminish feelings of isolation sometimes experienced with teaching online (Pedro & Kumar, 2020).

At SU, with the support of an instructional designer, the SSW developed a Certificate of Online Learning and Teaching, which provided "technology skills for instructors, online pedagogy, building community and instructor presence, and Quality Matters" (SU, 2022). Although contingent faculty initially received a small stipend and supplemental materials for completing the training, the training later became a required component of the contract. This course was later modified and adopted by the university at large.

The Online Learning Consortium and other higher education institutions, such as the University of the District of Columbia and Columbia University, offer comparable certificate programs (Alston et al., 2017; Creswell Báez et al., 2019). Responding to feedback from contingent faculty on a survey similar to the OBTRA, SU SSW developed a series of trainings designed to better prepare instructors for the transition to online course delivery, particularly in the wake of the COVID-19 global pandemic. Given the political and social landscape, the workshops incorporated a trauma-informed lens with a focus on student engagement, instructor presence, equity and inclusion, and student well-being. At the university level, instructional design and delivery staff members may be available to provide workshops on a variety of topics ranging from instructional software to Quality Matters.

> **PRACTICE TIP:** Include both full-time faculty and contingent faculty members in professional development opportunities. Consider offering the trainings in the evening or on weekends to accommodate the schedules of contingent faculty members.

Knowles (2007) analyzed interviews with 30 educators and administrators who developed online programs in Canada. He grouped obstacles to the development of programs into the following categories of challenges: professional, pedagogical, faculty, and administrative (p. 17). Within the area of faculty engagement, Knowles identified "the need for faculty dialogue on a number of levels that include philosophical dialogue, pedagogical dialogue, and dialogue and input into program planning and policies" (p. 27).

Dawson and Fenster (2015) applied principles from Knowles's (2007) research in creating faculty support for the change to online instruction. One strategy they employed was the creation of a technology committee that served as the mechanism by which faculty members were involved in the process of planning and implementation. Through ongoing dialogue, the process was "owned by the faculty as a whole" (Dawson & Fenster, 2015, p. 370). For faculty, course design can feel like the most daunting component of creating an online program option. Faculty may be more receptive to moving courses online if they are provided some choice regarding teaching strategies (i.e., asynchronous online, synchronous online). In some cases, the program director may explore course downloads or stipends for faculty who take on the lion's share of course conversions (Dumont et al., 2021).

> **PRACTICE TIP:** Encourage faculty to participate in interest-based task groups to facilitate collaborative action in revising the curriculum, thus spreading the work among faculty members.

Program directors should attempt to create an "environment that not only fosters faculty development and knowledge and skills related to online teaching, but also recognizes and rewards faculty engagement in such learning as needed" (Pedro & Kumar, 2020, p. 60). The conversion of courses to online should be acknowledged in the tenure and promotion process as part of the scholarship of teaching (Pedro & Kumar, 2020).

Although many full-time faculty are aware of professional development workshops and trainings within their institutions, contingent faculty may not be aware of these opportunities or believe that they have the time to commit. Because most contingent faculty teach only one or two courses a year, teaching is not their primary focus. To encourage contingent faculty to broaden their skill set, provide multiple options to engage in the training, such as synchronous and asynchronous. Incentives can also be offered, such as continuing education units, and free books and materials.

> **PRACTICE TIP:** Include participation in an orientation course in contingent faculty contracts. Within the orientation, provide an overview of the resources available to instructors to support them in their role.

Peer mentoring is another way for instructors to build skills and confidence as they transition from the physical to the virtual classroom. Within SU SSW, contingent faculty are also invited to a monthly meeting that serves as a time for training and support as faculty troubleshoot issues experienced in the class and training. Sharing a common discipline permits instructors to exchange not only technical expertise but also technology grounded in the curriculum. On occasion, an instructional designer attends to introduce new instructional software or demonstrate a feature in the LMS. Topics have included how to promote student engagement in both synchronous and asynchronous courses, tools to further teacher presence, and how to provide useful feedback.

The use of assistant instructors or technicians can benefit instructors and students in a variety of ways, including effective learning as well as faculty and student satisfaction (Armstrong et al., 2021). Within synchronous sessions, assistants can admit students from the waiting room, facilitate breakout group discussions, monitor the chat, and assess student participation (Armstrong et al., 2021; Center for Teaching and Learning, n.d.; Venable, 2012). Assistant instructors can also be instrumental in building a sense of community among students, grading, corresponding with students, responding to student questions and concerns, sharing materials with the class, conducting review sessions, summarizing themes from discussion posts, creating rubrics, and hosting virtual office hours (Center for Teaching & Learning, n.d.; Herrman & Waterhouse, 2010; Talbot et al., 2015; Venable, 2012). The use of assistant instructors permits the instructor to focus on the class content and provides the necessary support to students (Armstrong et al., 2021).

Policy Development

Several researchers argue that it is essential for institutions to develop policies related to privacy, confidentiality, and field participation that are specific to online instruction (Phipps & Merisotis, 2000; Reamer, 2013). When considering the development of an online program option, program leaders should consider the following when formulating policy: audience (transfer students, traditional students pursuing a premajor, or nontraditional students), catchment (will the program be regional or national in scope?), advisement, existing technology, and infrastructure to support faculty and students.

When developing an online undergraduate program, first a few policies must be developed to determine who is eligible for the program. Some universities and colleges, such as Walden University and Touro University Worldwide, have the infrastructure to offer all general education courses online, and thus, undergraduate students can start pursuing an online BSW degree during their first year. For institutions that do not offer general education courses online, students interested in pursuing an undergraduate BSW will have to complete their general education courses at another institution and then transfer into the online program. For example, to pursue the BASW online degree option at Millersville University, students must complete their associate's degree or have completed at least 60 previous college credits before applying to the program. These factors determine who can access the program and when.

Program directors should also consider the catchment area for the program, which involves determining the preferred geographic scope of the program and ensuring that the institution of higher education is approved to operate in a state. As outlined in Part H: Program Integrity of the Higher Education Opportunity Act (2008), postsecondary educational programs must be registered and approved to operate within a state (Fountain, 2021). The National Council for State Authorization Reciprocity Agreements (NC-SARA; https://nc-sara.org) was established in 2013 to ensure comparable standards for distance education programs and assist with implementation of reciprocity agreements across states. Program directors should check the NC-SARA directory for their institution, and if their school is not a member, discuss with administration about becoming a member if the institution meets the eligibility criteria.

Once you have established that reciprocity exists for a program to operate in another state, you can decide on the geographical scope of the program. Some undergraduate online social work programs are offered nationally, such as those at Western Kentucky University and the University of Kentucky. Other institutions intentionally restrict where the online program option is offered. Salisbury University's BASW online option is available only in Maryland and nine surrounding states, and Missouri State University's BSW online option is available in Missouri and three surrounding states. Programs may restrict access for a number of reasons, such as to hamper rapid growth, the ability to adequately support field placements, and/or the desire to create a regional reputation.

Technology is an area in which policies and practices need to be crafted to anticipate potential oversights. Some may be familiar with the concept of "Zoombombing," when unwanted participants gain access and disrupt synchronous course sessions or workshops. The development and implementation of a carefully crafted technology plan can mitigate these anomalies. Online programs should have a technology plan that includes "learning management systems, library systems, mobile technologies . . . hardware (computers, telecommunications and ancillary equipment) and networks, both internal and external," all of which have costs in terms of resources, time, and money (Sankey et al., 2014, p.19). The plan should clearly delineate program policies in relation to access, support, and maintenance of technology.

Research has demonstrated that technical support for both students and faculty to successfully navigate and interface with various systems is vital to the development of a quality online program (Pedro & Kumar, 2020; Sankey et al., 2014). Of course, instructors are not expected to become experts in instructional design or technology; when institutions provide training and technical support, faculty will feel more confident about teaching online. This support should also be responsive to evolving student and faculty needs (Pedro & Kumar, 2020).

The nature of internet communication creates additional challenges in maintaining student privacy and confidentiality (Reamer, 2013). Because the content in social work courses can prompt student self-disclosure, an "unscrupulous or insensitive classmate might choose to print out a confidential message and share it with a third party" (Reamer, 2013, p. 379). Reamer (2013) contended that in addition to meeting the benchmark of developing a technology plan that incorporates security measures (Phipps & Merisotis, 2000), instructors should broaden discussions of expectations related to student behavior and confidentiality to include respecting classmates' privacy in online communication. The SU SSW developed the Social Media and Digital Technology Policy (in the student handbook) to set professional behavior in the use of social media and other technologies (Salisbury University, n.d.). This policy incorporates guidance from the NASW Code of Ethics (NASW, 2021), the Standards for Technology in Social Work Practice (NASW, 2017), and CSWE (2022) EPAS competencies.

Student Recruitment

Online students tend to have different characteristics from students who are seeking a brick-and-mortar experience (as discussed earlier), and given this reality, recruitment strategies used for on-campus students can be largely ineffective for engaging online students. Thus, marketing and recruitment strategies for online students must be distinctive and targeted, taking into consideration the unique background characteristics and academic needs of this population. Given the differences in these two student populations, many online program options are complementary and not in competition with existing on-campus programs (Ortagus & Tanner, 2019).

Program directors should assess whether sufficient infrastructure exists to support recruitment and marketing efforts. In schools where few online programs exist, social work program directors may consider outsourcing these efforts, but this will come with a cost, given that many of these companies require a high percentage of the tuition charged for a number of years. When not using a third party, program directors, working with other university personnel, should construct a profile of prospective online students, using a data-informed picture of who enrolls in similar programs at peer institutions.

After a student profile is constructed, a recruitment and communication plan with concrete goals with specific strategies and practices to recruit exclusively online students is paramount to the growth and sustainability of online program options. When location is no longer a determining factor in selection, program faculty and administrators have to identify what makes their program different from other online BSW programs. This messaging should highlight what is unique when compared with other competitors, such as delivering high-quality education, providing personalized interaction, or being attached to a reputable institution. Leveraging the institutional brand, particularly for highly regarded schools, can be an advantage, as these institutions usually have a distinctive brand and name recognition, which often connotes legitimacy (Ortagus & Tanner, 2019).

> **PRACTICE TIP:** Send a handwritten note or make a personal call to each student once they are admitted to the program. Small touches go a long way.

Personalizing student interaction during the recruitment process is a strategy that demonstrates the program may be more inclusive and accessible than prospective students might have thought (Ortagus & Tanner, 2019). SU SSW holds virtual information sessions hosted by the program chairs and other full-time faculty. Full-time faculty leading the sessions demonstrate the importance the program places in the recruitment process. Salisbury University has also engaged social work student workers and graduate assistants to make telephone calls to prospective students. These high-touch, low-cost efforts can influence a student's decision in this competitive market.

Field Education

The effective management of field instruction is another consideration in the development of an online program. Securing field placements in other locations can be challenging given the limited knowledge of the area, and agencies often prefer to work with local institutions with whom they are familiar. This requires field personnel to develop relationships in new areas that may require a significant amount of cold-calling. Given the time needed to find new placements year after year based on the new cohort of students, program directors should advocate for the hire of a field coordinator dedicated to cultivating online field placements.

Other suggestions for securing new placements include optimizing relationships gained through field director consortiums to locate viable placement options, geo-mapping regions where students reside, and collaborating with other social work programs in the region (Sankar, 2012). Many programs put the onus on students to identify agencies and contact people in their area where they may want to complete an internship, given that many know their own community better than university personnel.

Nontraditional students may also be able to utilize their existing networks and employment to secure work-based field opportunities (which have been expanded in 2022 EPAS; see CSWE, 2022). Once potential agencies are identified, programs need an established process to vet agencies to ensure quality control. To maintain quality control throughout the placement, programs can offer field seminar instructor training and conduct virtual visits with the student and field instructor to ensure compliance with CSWE standards and adherence to school policies (Sankar, 2012).

Alternatively, some programs have developed simulations to replicate client interactions as a way for field students to enhance skills and for field instructors to assess a student's skills prior to placement in the field. Virtual field experiences, which include synchronous and asynchronous learning activities, simulated client interaction, training in evidence-based interventions, and faculty and peer feedback, can be an effective way to impart essential practice behaviors (Phillips et al., 2018). In response to COVID-19, the University of Toronto expanded the use of simulation-based learning, affording students the opportunity to engage, assess, and intervene with "clients in the current context of the COVID-19 pandemic and the global movement for anti-racism" (Kourgiantakis & Lee, 2020, p. 763).

Similarly, Griffith University created an online course—the "COVID-19 Alternative Placement Course"—for students who were unable to remain in their placements. "The COVID-19 pandemic has created new social work research agendas concerning how to effectively promote learning in online field placements, the evaluation of alternative field placements and their impact on student efficacy and competence and future viability" (Fronek et al., 2021, p. 11). While the COVID-19 pandemic created many challenges for higher education, it also opened up opportunities for learning, including the development of more virtual field placements and the increased use of telehealth.

Student Retention Efforts

Retention rates among students taking online courses tend to be lower compared with those of students enrolled in face-to-face or blended courses. James et al. (2016) reported that retention rates at 4-year institutions for fully online students were 60–65% compared with 75–80% retention rates for students enrolled in face-to-face or blended courses. Many factors can affect retention rates, and as such, program directors should proactively implement and advocate for strategies to combat attrition. Seery et al. (2021) identified several types of retention strategies through a systematic review of the literature: course development strategies, social engagement strategies, comprehensive student integration, student success support strategies, faculty involvement strategies, and emotional engagement strategies.

Online students tend to be more diverse than their on-campus counterparts: The online population contains more older students, students from a lower socioeconomic status, students with disabilities, and first-generation college students (Ilgaz & Gulbahar, 2017; Moore et al., 2015). In recognizing the increased diversity of online students, student retention efforts must address the unique needs of these students, both inside and outside the classroom. While individual attributes, such as time and effort invested and perceived utility of learning, contribute to student persistence, programs can have more influence over the program factors that contribute to student retention (McGee et al., 2017; Yang et al., 2017).

Creating a Sense of Community

Creating a welcoming space and building opportunities for students to feel connected and supported are essential to student success and student retention. Within the virtual classroom, faculty presence in courses helps to enhance the perception of community and connectedness and decrease feelings of isolation, increase student retention, and increase student satisfaction and learning outcomes (Sheingold et al., 2013). Program directors can help to create a sense of community among social work students outside of the virtual classroom in small and significant ways, such as advocating for the provision of student IDs that directly connect the student to the institution or offering virtual orientations and clubs, where students can connect to one another.

Social work students in the online program option at Salisbury advocated for IDs, stressing that they did not have access to student discounts without a school ID, something that administrators had not considered. Given that SU SSW provides social work education to a diverse student population located across the United States and Europe, program administrators for both the BASW and MSW programs have been intentional in providing opportunities for students to connect through biannual virtual town halls and workshops. In addition, a few student organizations (i.e., Social Workers for Racial Justice and Asian Student Social Workers) have migrated online to recruit more diverse participation. Creating intentional ways to build a sense of community among students outside the classroom helps to address feelings of isolation, thus assisting with retention (Skelcher et al., 2020; Yang et al., 2017).

Whether orientation is completed on campus or online, holding an in-depth orientation prepares online students for the start of their academic career at the institution. Some argue that in-person orientation, even for online students, will lead to better academic success, because the students can practice the technology with support (Safford & Stinton, 2016). Yet, given that many students enroll in an online program because of the flexibility, attendance at an in-person orientation may not be feasible. While attending in-person orientation can assist in generating a sense of community (Lieberman, 2017), virtual, synchronous orientations can incorporate activities to encourage students to make connections among themselves.

PRACTICE TIP: Recognizing that one purpose of orientation is the development of a sense of community, build in small group exercises or encourage the students to use the chat feature to get to know one another during the virtual orientation.

Given the barriers to attending an in-person orientation, some programs have migrated orientation to the virtual world for all students. MacDonald Kuhn and Wyskocil Garcia (2020) discussed the use of an online orientation consisting of podcasts or videos on information, such as the nature of online courses, navigating the LMS, logging in to courses, and how to access help depending on the nature of the problem. Participation in online orientation has been shown to increase utilization of student support services and campus resources and to increase retention rates (Jones, 2013; Rose, 2018; Stoebe, 2020). Abdous (2019) found that an online orientation boosted students' academic self-efficacy, particularly students' self-confidence in using the LMS online tools and interacting with other students and instructors.

PRACTICE TIP: Be sure to integrate authentic learning activities within the online orientation that mimic course activities, allowing students to practice before starting on graded assignments.

The SU SSW students attend a synchronous, virtual orientation, during which program directors highlight key policies, important dates, and upcoming student activities. A keynote speaker helps to set the tone of the academic year, and the students engage in small group discussions on transitioning into school. Students can engage with one another across the different modalities (e.g., residential, satellite, and online options), which is a purposeful initial step in building connections.

SU SSW students are also required to complete an asynchronous component to orientation prior to the synchronous portion, which takes students on a virtual tour of the university. The asynchronous orientation ends with a short quiz that is submitted to the program director. Examples of modules are:

- welcome videos from academic leadership

- program overview

- faculty introduction videos

- social work ethics

- professionalism

- SSW online student support

- student connections, which includes student clubs and organizations, social media, and professional networking

- stress management and self-care

- university support services, including the Disability Resource Center and the Counseling Center

- advising

Online Academic Advising

Academic advising is a way advisors can connect with and support students on their academic journey. Academic advisors help students navigate the university, provide information on programs and resources, communicate policies and procedures, and help students problem-solve (Smith & Allen, 2014). Although this describes the purpose of academic advising, whether face-to-face or online, there are other factors to consider when connecting with advisees online. Phone and video advising are commonly used for distance advisors, with emails as a follow-up that include links to resources or that summarize the meeting.

Creating a culture where students feel comfortable with advising services can be supported by implementing policies and practices, such as requiring advising meetings prior to registration; using easy tools, such as Calendly, to schedule appointments; and ensuring that advising services are conveniently timed to accommodate the schedules of online students, including evening hours (MacDonald Kuhn & Wyskocil Garcia, 2020).

> **PRACTICE TIP:** Organize advisees by program option, which allows advisors to develop a greater depth of knowledge of effective ways to advise the specific student population.

SU SSW has academic advisors trained to work with online students and who are available to meet with students in the evenings and weekends. All students are enrolled in an "Advising Hub," an online course in the LMS where online students can connect with one another and quickly access needed resources and information. Online advisors also hold a live, virtual town hall with all advisees the week before the fall semester to build community among the online students and answer any questions that arise after completing the online orientation. To keep the lines of communication open, advisors also send out monthly communications to advisees to check in, as well as to inform students about upcoming dates and events. Columbia College, in Missouri, uses an appreciative advising model, in which the online student and advisor cocreate a student development plan built on the student's strengths and meet regularly to foster the relationship. This model proved to be helpful for online students on academic probation (Miller et al., 2019).

> **PRACTICE TIP:** Prioritize video advising over phone advising, as it can cut down on other distractions and allows the advisor to read the student's facial expressions. Another advantage is that the advisor can share their screen if necessary.

Student Support Services

Accessing support resources for students who attend a brick-and-mortar institution can be as easy as consulting a campus map to locate the tutoring center, writing center, or counseling center and walking across the quad for an appointment. For online students, accessing these resources can be a challenge or, in some cases, impossible if the supports do not exist virtually or outside of traditional business hours. With the increase in online program options and with prompting by regional accrediting bodies, such as the Southern Association of Colleges and Schools Commission on Colleges (2020), universities are recognizing that equitable access to basic student support services is a key component to student persistence and student success in higher education. Student support services can be a much-needed source of support while pursuing education, especially for nontraditional students, who often must balance multiple responsibilities.

At some institutions with a history of providing education to off-campus students, adequate student supports for online students may exist; in others, program administrators may need to advocate for adequate online student supports. Beginning in 2021, Salisbury University offered all students TimelyCare, a downloadable app that offers 24/7 on-demand mental health support in addition to scheduled appointments with a counselor and on-demand or live educational sessions to improve mental health. Although the provision of this service was prompted by the limited number of counselors available to see students face-to-face, this new service expands services to all students, including those in the online social work program. Prior to this, the onus was on the social work program to help an off-campus student find and access counseling services, and the university would pay the provider directly. Although the university was responsive in providing support services when needed, these programs were not initially set up with the launch of the online option. As program directors are considering new online program options, they should work with colleagues in student affairs to ensure adequate and equitable access to student services from the onset of the online program.

Library and Research Services

Information literacy is essential to student success, and working with a librarian has been shown to increase student retention, contributing to academic success (Catalano & Phillips, 2016; Murray, 2014). Librarians are tasked with finding and creating materials that students find supportive, useful, and relevant to their assignments. When students cannot locate or access the materials they need, they can become discouraged. Recognizing the growth of distance education programs, including online options, the American Library Association (ALA) established the Standards for Distance Learning Library Services in 2008 and revised them 8 years later (ALA, 2016). When planning the launch of online program options, program faculty and administrators can work with colleagues in the library to ensure that the library is equipped with the resources to support online programs, such as a sufficient number of online teaching librarians and adequate online databases and ebooks.

Salisbury University promotes library access to online students in several ways. The library's *Online Library Resources* website is easy to navigate, and the SU Librarian of External Resources provides asynchronous and synchronous library instruction via Zoom to teach students how to find, use, and evaluate resources. Students can also borrow books and have them shipped directly to their homes. SU SSW has a dedicated library liaison who has created *The Social Work Guide*—a web page for hybrid and online social work students with library instruction sessions and a live chat feature for students to easily access all of the library services (https://libraryguides.salisbury.edu/sowk). Faculty can incorporate graded, interactive discussion boards into their classes with the library liaison as a guest speaker or have the library liaison be a regular part of the course, bringing the library liaison directly to the students. To accommodate the schedules of students, the social work library liaison offers one-on-one virtual appointments with students in the evenings and on weekends.

Conclusion

Although online education has become an established modality in higher education, undergraduate programs have not shifted to online at the same pace as graduate programs. Yet, with faculty growing more confident with the use of technology (Bajaj et al., 2021) and some skepticism about online education waning (Jaschik & Lederman, 2019), some schools of social work may be considering the addition of an online option. This chapter has explored the development of an online undergraduate program option, which starts with securing the buy-in and support of both social work faculty and the institution as a whole. Although online programs can generate revenue, the institution will need to invest resources to help the program launch successfully. This support may be somewhat easier to secure because most institutions have had to adapt in some way to provide education and student supports online during the COVID-19 pandemic. Launching online undergraduate social work programs allows social work educators to bring social work education to a more diverse student population that has had limited access to higher education, which aligns with our Code of Ethics (NASW, 2021).

Suggested Readings

Bates, A. W. (2019). *Teaching in a digital age* (2nd ed.). Tony Bates Associates. Free digital download at https://pressbooks.bccampus.ca/teachinginadigitalagev2/

Jaschik, S., & Lederman, D. (Eds.). 2019 survey of faculty attitudes on technology: A study by Inside Higher Ed and GALLUP. *Inside Higher Ed.* https://www.insidehighered.com /system/files/media/IHE_2019_Faculty_Tech_Survey_20191030.pdf

Salisbury University. (2022). *Certificate for online learning and teaching—social work.* https://succeed.salisbury.edu/browse/chhs/socialwork/courses/sw-colt

Seery, K., Barreda, A. A., & Hein, S. G. (2021). Retention strategies for online students: A systematic literature review. *Journal of Global Education and Research, 5*(1), 72–54. https://www.doi.org/10.5038/2577-509X.5.1.1105

References

Abdous, M. (2019). Well begun is half done: Using online orientation to foster online students' academic self-efficacy. *Online Learning Journal, 23*(3), 161–187. https://doi.org /10.24059/olj.v23i3.1437

Afrouz, R., & Crisp, B. R. (2021). Online education in social work, effectiveness, benefits, and challenges: A scoping review. *Australian Social Work, 74*(1), 55-67. https://doi.org /10.1080/0312407X.2020.1808030

Alpert, W., Couch, K., & Harmon, O. (2016). A randomized assessment of online learning. *American Economic Review, 106*(5), 378–382. https://doi.org/10.1257/aer.p20161057

Alston, S. T., Moore, C. S., & Thomas, M. (2017). Strategies for enhancing online teaching in social work education. *Journal of Human Behavior in the Social Environment, 27*(5), 412–423. https://doi.org/10.1080/10911359.2017.1311817

American Library Association. (2016). *Standards for distance learning library services.* https://www.ala.org/acrl/standards/guidelinesdistancelearning

Armstrong, S., Lupinski, K., Burcin, M., Kato, K., & Kaufman, M. (2021). Evaluation of a teaching assistant program in online education. *Journal of Educational Research and Practice, 11*, 46–63. https://doi.org/10.5590/JERAP.2021.11.1.04

Bajaj, P., Khan, A., Tabash, M. I., & Anagreh, S. (2021). Teachers' intention to continue the use of online teaching tools post Covid-19. *Cogent Education, 8*(1). https://doi.org /10.1080/2331186X.2021.2002130

Barshay, J. (2018, September 10). College students predicted to fall by more than 15% after the year 2025: But high demand likely to persist for top 100 elite institutions. *The Hechinger Report.* https://hechingerreport.org/college-students-predicted-to-fall-by -more-than-15-after-the-year-2025/

Bates, T. (2021, August 26). Research showing that virtual learning is less effective than classroom teaching—right? *Online Learning and Distance Education Resources.* https://www.tonybates.ca/2021/08/26/research-showing-that-virtual-learning-is-less -effective-than-classroom-teaching-right/

Bower, M. (2011). Synchronous collaboration competencies in web-conferencing environments - their impact on the learning process. *Distance Education, 32*(1), 63–83. https://doi.org/10.1080/01587919.2011.565502

Catalano, A. J., & Phillips, S. R. (2016). Information literacy and retention: A case study of the value of the library. *Evidence Based Library and Information Practice, 11*(4). https://doi.org/10.18438/B82K7W

Center for Teaching & Learning, UMass Amherst. (n.d.). *How do I involve TAs in online learning?* https://www.umass.edu/ctl/how-do-i-involve-tas-online-learning

Chen, J. C. (2017). Nontraditional adult learners: The neglected diversity in postsecondary education. *SAGE Open, 7*(1), 1–12. https://doi.org/10.1177/2158244017697161

Council on Social Work Education. (2021). *2020 statistics on social work education in the United States: Summary of the CSWE annual survey of social work programs.* https://www.cswe.org/getattachment/726b15ce-6e63-4dcd-abd1-35d2ea9d9d40/2020-Annual-Statistics-On-Social-Work-Education-in-the-United-States.pdf?lang=en-US

Council on Social Work Education. (2022). *2022 Educational policy and accreditation standards.* https://www.cswe.org/accreditation/standards/2022-epas/

Creswell Báez, J., Marquart, M., Yae-Eun Chung, R., Ryan, D., & Garay, K. (2019). Developing and supporting faculty training for online social work education: The Columbia University School of Social Work Online Pedagogy Institute. *Journal of Teaching in Social Work, 39*(4–5), 505–518. https://doi.org/10.1080/08841233.2019.1653419

Dawson, B. A., & Fenster, J. (2015). Web-based social work courses: Guidelines for developing and implementing an online environment, *Journal of Teaching in Social Work, 35*(4), 365–377. https://doi.org/10.1080/08841233.2015.1068905

Dumont, G., Ya Ni, A., Van Wart, M., Beck, C., & Pei, H. (2021). The effect of the Covid pandemic on faculty adoption of online teaching: Reduced resistance but strong persistence concerns. *Cogent Education, 8*(1). https://doi.org/10.1080/2331186X.2021.1976928

Faulconer, E. K., Griffith, J., Wood, B., Acharyya, S., & Roberts, D. (2018). A comparison of online, video synchronous, and traditional learning modes for an introductory undergraduate physics course. *Journal of Science Education and Technology, 27*(5), 404–411. https://doi.org/10.1007/s10956-018-9732-6

Feist, L. (2003). Removing barriers to professional development. *T.H.E. Journal, 30*(11). https://www.learntechlib.org/p/97481/

Fischer, C., Baker, R., Li, Q., Orona, G. A., & Warschauer, M. (2021). *Increasing success in higher education: The relationships of online course taking with college completion and time-to-degree* (EdWorkingPaper: 21–427). Retrieved from the Annenberg Institute at Brown University. https://doi.org/10.26300/m9ra-kr67

Fountain, J. H. (2021, August 17). *The Higher Education Act (HEA): A primer.* Congressional Research Service. https://crsreports.congress.gov/product/pdf/R/R43351

Fronek, P., Briggs, L., Rondon-Jackson, R., Hay, K., Maidment, J., & Medina-Martinez, K. (2021). Responding to Covid-19 in social work field education in Australia, New Zealand and the United States. *International Social Work (20211026).* https://doi.org/10.1177/00208728211048934

Galanek, J. D., Gierdowski, D. C., & Christopher Brooks., D. (2018, October). *ECAR study of undergraduate students and information technology, 2018* [Research report]. EduCause Center for Analysis and Research. https://library.educause.edu/-/media/files/library/2018/10/studentitstudy2018.pdf?la=en&hash=C590C1F6C62B77792711BFAC1F642254A5618590

Gonzales, A. L., Calarco, J. M., & Lynch, T. (2018). Technology problems and student achievement gaps: A validation and extension of the technology maintenance construct. *Communication Research, 47*(5), 750–770. https://doi.org/10.1177/0093650218796366

Herrman, J., & Waterhouse, J. (2010). Benefits of using undergraduate teaching assistants throughout a baccalaureate nursing curriculum. *Journal of Nursing Education, 49*(2), 72–77. https://doi.org/10.3928/01484834-20090918-05

Higher Education Opportunity Act, Pub. L. No. 110-315, 122 Stat. 3078 (2008). https://www.govinfo.gov/content/pkg/PLAW-110publ315/pdf/PLAW-110publ315.pdf

Ilgaz, H., & Gulbahar, Y. (2017, July 20–22). *Why do learners choose online learning: The learners' voices* [Paper presentation]. International Association for Development of the Information Society (IADIS) International Conference on E-Learning, Lisbon, Portugal.

James, S., Swan, K., & Daston, C. (2016). Retention, progression and the taking of online courses. *Journal of Online Learning, 20*(2), 75–96. https://doi.org/10.24059/olj.v20i2.780

Jaschik, S., & Lederman, D. (Eds.). *2019 survey of faculty attitudes on technology: A study by Inside Higher Ed and Gallup.* Inside Higher Ed. https://www.insidehighered.com/system/files/media/IHE_2019_Faculty_Tech_Survey_20191030.pdf

Jones, K. R. (2013). Developing and implementing a mandatory online student orientation. *Journal of Asynchronous Learning Networks, 17*(1), 43–45. https://doi.org/10.24059/olj.v17i1.312

Knowles, A. J. (2007). Pedagogical and policy challenges in implementing e-learning in social work education. *Journal of Technology in Human Services, 25*(1/2), 17–44. https://doi.org/10.1300/J017v25n01_02

Kourgiantakis, T., & Lee, E. (2020). Social work practice education and training during the pandemic: Disruptions and discoveries. *International Social Work, 63*(6), 761–765.

Leary, H., Dopp, C., Turley, C., Cheney, M., Simmons, Z., Graham, C. R., & Hatch, R. (2020). Professional development for online teaching: A literature review. *Online Learning, 24*(4), 254–275. https://doi.org/10.24059/olj.v24i4.2198

Lederman, D. (2021, September 16). Detailing last fall's online enrollment surge. *Inside Higher Ed.* https://www.insidehighered.com/news/2021/09/16/new-data-offer-sense-how-covid-expanded-online-learning

Levin, S., Fulginiti, A., & Moore, B. (2018). The perceived effectiveness of online social work education: Insights from a national survey of social work educators. *Social Work Education, 37*(6), 775–789. https://doi.org/10.1080/02615479.2018.1482864

Lieberman, M. (2017, September 13). *Welcome aboard.* Inside Higher Ed. https://www.insidehighered.com/digital-learning/article/2017/09/13/orientation-programs-set-online-learners-success

Los, R., De Jaeger, A., & Stoesz, B. M. (2021). Development of the Online and Blended Teaching Readiness Assessment (OBTRA). *Frontiers in Education, 6,* 1–8. https://doi.org/10.3389/feduc.2021.673594

MacDonald Kuhn, M., & Wyskocil Garcia, B. (2020). Advising the online student: A breakout of advising frequency, preferences, and satisfaction of online students. *Online Journal of Distance Education Administration, 23*(3). https://www.westga.edu/~distance/ojdla/fall233/kuhn_garcia233.html

Martin, F., Budhrani, K., & Wang, C. (2019). Examining faculty perception of their readiness to teach online. *Online Learning, 23*(3), 97–119. https://doi.org/10.24059/olj.v23i3.1555

Mathes, J. (2020, April 13). A defining moment for online learning. *OLC Insights.* Online Learning Consortium. https://onlinelearningconsortium.org/a-defining-moment-for-online-learning/

Mayer, G., & Sekayi, D. (2018). Pedagogical practices of teaching assistants in polysynchronous classrooms: The role of professional autonomy. *InSight: A Journal of Scholarly Teaching, 13,* 130–149.

McGee, P., Windes, D., & Torres, M. (2017). Experienced online instructors: Beliefs and preferred supports regarding online teaching. *Journal of Computing in Higher Education, 29,* 331–352. https://doi.org/10.1007/s12528-017-9140-6

Means, B., & Neisler, J., with Langer Research Associates. (2020). *Suddenly online: A national survey of undergraduates during the Covid-19 pandemic.* Digital Promise. https://digitalpromise.org/wp-content/uploads/2020/07/ELE_CoBrand_DP_FINAL_3.pdf

Means, B., Toyama, Y., Murphy, R., & Baki, M. (2013). The effectiveness of online and blended learning: A meta-analysis of the empirical literature. *Teachers College Record, 115*(3), 1–47. https://doi.org/10.1177/016146811311500307

Miller, N., Greer, K. Cozier, L., Whitener, S., Patton, J., & Koffarnus, J. (2019). An advising initiative for online students on academic probation. *NACADA Journal, 39*(1), 5–21. https://doi.org/10.12930/NACADA-16-019

Moore, S. E., Golder, S., Sterrett, E., Faul, A. C., Yankeelov, P., Weathers Mathis, L., & Barbee, A. P. (2015). Social work online education: A model for getting started and staying connected. *Journal of Social Work Education, 51*(3), 505–518. https://doi.org/10.1080/10437797.2015.1043200

Murray, A. (2014). *Academic libraries and high-impact practices for student retention: Library deans' perspectives* (Paper 57) [Doctoral dissertation, Western Kentucky University]. TopSCHOLAR. https://digitalcommons.wku.edu/diss/57/

National Association of Social Workers. (2017). *NASW, ABSW, CSWE, & CSWA standards of technology in social work practice*. https://www.socialworkers.org/includes/newincludes/homepage/PRA-BRO-33617.TechStandards_FINAL_POSTING.pdf

National Association of Social Workers. (2021). *NASW code of ethics*. https://www.socialworkers.org/About/Ethics/Code-of-Ethics/Code-of-Ethics-English

National Center for Education Statistics. (n.d.). *Distance education in IPEDS*. https://nces.ed.gov/ipeds/use-the-data/distance-education-in-ipeds

Online Learning Consortium. (2022). *Our learning framework*. https://onlinelearningconsortium.org/about/quality-framework-five-pillars

Ortagus, J. C., & Tanner, M. J. (2019). Going to college without going to college: A case study of online student recruitment. *Innovative Higher Learning, 44*, 53–57. https://doi.org/10.1007/s10755-018-9448-9

Paul, J., & Jefferson, F. (2019). A comparative analysis of student performance in an online vs. face-to-face environmental science course from 2009 to 2016. *Frontiers in Computer Science, 1*, 1–7. https://doi.org/10.3389/fcomp.2019.00007

Pedro, N. S., & Kumar, S. (2020). Institutional support for online teaching in quality assurance frameworks. *Online Learning Journal, 24*(3), 50–66. https://doi.org/10.24059/olj.v24i3.2309

Pew Research Center. (2021, April 7). *Internet/broadband fact sheet*. https://www.pewresearch.org/internet/fact-sheet/internet-broadband/

Phillips, E. S., Wood, G. J., Yoo, J., Ward, K. J., Chen Hsiao, S., Singh, M. I., & Morris, B. (2018). A virtual field practicum: Building core competencies prior to agency placement. *Journal of Social Work Education, 54*(4), 620–640. https://doi.org/10.1080/10437797.2018.1486651

Phipps, R., & Merisotis, J. (2000, March 31). *Quality on the line: Benchmarks for success in internet-based distance education*. ERIC. https://eric.ed.gov/?id=ED444407

Quality Matters. (2022). *Quality matters*. https://www.qualitymatters.org/index.php

Reamer, F. G. (2013). Distance and online social work education: Novel ethical challenges. *Journal of Teaching in Social Work, 33*(4–5), 369–384. https://doi.org/10.1080/08841233.2013.828669

Rhode, J., Ritcher, S., & Miller, T. (2017). Designing personalized online teaching professional development through self-assessment. *Tech Trends, 61*(5), 71–86. https://doi.org/10.1007/s11528-017-0211-3

Rose, J. R. (2018). *Studying the influence of an online student orientation on students' resource awareness and utilization* [Unpublished doctoral dissertation]. University of Delaware. http://udspace.udel.edu/handle/19716/21507

Safford, K., & Stinton, J. (2016). Barriers to blended digital distance vocational learning for non-traditional students. *British Journal of Educational Technology, 47*(1), 135–150. https://doi.org/10.1111/bjet.12222

Salisbury University. (n.d.). *Bachelor of arts in social work student handbook and field manual.* https://www.salisbury.edu/academic-offices/health-and-human-services/social-work/_files /handbooks/basw-student-handbook.pdf

Salisbury University. (2022). *Certificate for online learning and teaching—social work.* https://succeed.salisbury.edu/browse/chhs/socialwork/courses/sw-colt

Sankar, S. (2012, Spring). Field learning in online social work programs. *Field Educator, 2*(1). https://fieldeducator.simmons.edu/article/field-learning-in-online-social -work-programs/

Sankey, M., Carter, H., Marshall, S., Obexer, R., Russell, C., & Lawson, R. (2014). *Benchmarks for technology enhanced learning.* ACODE. http://www.acode.edu.au

Seaman, J. (2009). Online learning as a strategic asset. Volume II: The paradox of faculty voices— Views and experiences with online learning. *ERIC.* https://eric.ed.gov/?id=ED517311

Seery, K., Barreda, A. A., & Hein, S. G. (2021). Retention strategies for online students: A systematic literature review. *Journal of Global Education and Research, 5*(1), 72–54. https://www.doi.org/10.5038/2577-509X.5.1.1105

Sheingold, B. H., Hahn, J. A., & Hofmeyer, A. (2013). Hiding in plain sight: Building community social capital in distance education graduate programs. *Contemporary Issues in Education Research, 6*(2), 265–272. https://files.eric.ed.gov/fulltext/EJ1073197.pdf

Skelcher, S., Yang, D., Trespalacios, J., & Snelson, C. (2020). Connecting online students to their higher learning institution. *Distance Education, 41*(1), 128–147. https://doi.org/10 .1080/01587919.2020.1724771

Smith, C. L., & Allen, J. M. (2014). Does contact with advisors predict judgments and attitudes consistent with student success? A multi-institutional study. *NACADA Journal, 34*(1), 50–63. https://doi.org/10.12930/NACADA-13-019

Southern Association of Colleges and Schools Commission on Colleges. (2020). *Distance education and correspondence courses: Policy statement.* https://sacscoc.org/app/uploads /2019/07/DistanceCorrespondenceEducation.pdf

Stoebe, A. (2020). The effect of new student orientations on the retention of online students. *Online Journal of Distance Learning Administration, 23*(2). https://www.westga.edu /~distance/ojdla/summer232/stoebe232.html

Talbot, R., Hartley, L, Marzetta, K., & Wee, B. (2015). Transforming undergraduate science education with learning assistants: Student satisfaction in large-enrollment courses. *Journal of College Science Teaching, 44*(5), 24–30. http://www.jstor.org/stable/43631844

Tzavara, D., & Wilczek, B. (2019). Online: A new "geography" of learning that supports female access to higher education. In J. Hoffman, P. Blessinger, & M. Makhanya (Eds.), *Strategies for fostering inclusive classrooms in higher education: International perspectives on equity and inclusion* (pp. 213–231). Innovations in Higher Education Teaching and Learning.

U.S. Department of Education, National Center for Education Statistics. (2018, May). *Table 311.22. Number and percentage of undergraduate students enrolled in distance education or online classes and degree programs, by selected characteristics: Selected years, 2003–04 through 2015–16.* https://nces.ed.gov/programs/digest/d19/tables/dt19_311.22.asp

U.S. Department of Education, National Center for Education Statistics, Integrated Postsecondary Education Data System (IPEDS). (2020). *Table 9. Unduplicated headcount enrollment at Title IV institutions, by control of institution, student level, level of institution, and distance education status of student: United States, 2019–20.* https://nces.ed.gov

/ipeds/Search?query=&query2=&resultType=all&page=1&sortBy=date_desc&overlayTableId =28465

Venable, M. (2012, November 29). Working with online teaching assistants. *Faculty Focus: Higher Education Teaching & Learning.* https://www.facultyfocus.com/articles /online-education/working-with-online-teaching-assistants/

Washburn, M., & Zhou, S. (2018). Teaching note—Technology-enhanced clinical simulations: Tools for practicing clinical skills in online social work programs. *Journal of Social Work Education, 54*(3), 554–560. https://doi.org/10.1080/10437797.2017 .1404519

Wingo, N. P., Ivankova, N. V., & Moss, J. A. (2017). Faculty perceptions about teaching online: Exploring the literature using the technology acceptance model as an organizing framework. *Online Learning, 21*(1), 263–276. https://doi.org/10.10.24059/olj.v21i1.761

Xu, D., & Jaggars, S. S. (2014). Performance gaps between online and face-to-face courses: Differences across types of students and academic subject areas. *Journal of Higher Education, 85*(5), 633–659. https://doi.org/10.1080/00221546.2014.11777343

Yang, D., Baldwin, S., & Snelson, C. (2017). Persistence factors revealed: Students' reflections on completing a fully online program. *Distance Education, 38*(1), 23–36. https://doi.org/10.1080/01587919.2017.1299561

CHAPTER 8

Overcoming the Challenges

Tips for Surviving and Thriving as a Program Director in a Small BSW Program

Heather Kanenberg
Stephen "Arch" Erich

When considering becoming a program director of a small BSW program, it is easy to bemoan the challenges of limited financial and faculty resources. However, serving in leadership in a small BSW program with only two full-time faculty, the minimum as outlined by the Council on Social Work Education (CSWE, 2022), may have many advantages and benefits. Leadership and administration in higher education require a skill set that partners well with social work training and practice. In confronting some of the typical struggles as opportunities, it is possible to develop a leadership style that promotes a thriving program and develops faculty who embrace diversity and inclusion. Communication, flexibility, and strong positive working relationships are identified as key components to healthy, synergistic, small BSW programs.

Research has indicated that access to resources and autonomy of programs can cultivate program health and well-being (Drumm et al., 2002). Viable small programs with access to resources and autonomy are perhaps better positioned to weather the storm of economic challenges that face higher education today. As conceptualized by Drumm et al., resources are conceptualized as assets, such as financial allotments or budgets provided to programs, faculty, support staff, and equipment, needed for a program to operate effectively. Autonomy within programs is identified as the program's level of control over income and expenditures, curriculum, faculty hiring and promotion processes, and the existence of a clear reporting line and open communication with a dean or higher education administrator (Aguilar & Aigner, 1997; Drumm et al., 2002). Having constrained resources in terms of faculty and finances does not mean that small BSW programs cannot thrive; a small program, however, might require additional creativity, closer partnerships, and increased transparency in communication within and external to the program.

It is true that the issue of limited resources affects role functioning, assessment, accreditation and reaccreditation, working with students, external supports, and responding to crises (CSWE, 2022). Yet, shared understandings and intentions among the faculty of the small BSW program can mitigate these effects.

Program History and Context

The University of Houston-Clear Lake (UHCL) BSW program was granted initial candidacy in 2001 and initial accreditation in 2004. At the time, the university was an upper-level institution, and since then, it has become a traditional, regional, comprehensive university enrolling first-time students all the way from the freshman year through doctoral degrees. Institutional structural changes have certainly affected the BSW program. In 2020, the university comprised approximately 85% transfer students and 99% nonresidential students. The program has seen enrollment growth over the past decade, even amid all of the challenges of the past few years.

The program is historically small, consisting of two faculty members, a program director, and a director of field education. In fall 2020, the number of fully admitted students was 53, and the total number of students served (those intending to apply to the major and those enrolled) was 105. The CSWE 2020 Annual Survey of Programs indicates that the average number of degree conferrals per year in a BSW program is 39, and the average student enrollment is 129 (CSWE, 2021). The UHCL BSW program has conferred an average of 19 degrees per year over the past 5 years. These are the contexts that inform our perspective.

One last important note: It is impossible to run a program without a solid team, all of whom validate the importance of diversity and inclusion. As coauthors, we share insights and lessons learned, having served in both required administrative roles—program director and field director—that exist within an accredited BSW program, and are informed by the partnership of our work for more than 12 years. Again, it is our assertion that it is impossible to run a successful BSW program when one person (the program director) is shouldering the majority of the work, and if it does happen in this way, burnout and resentment may occur.

Servant Leadership in a Small BSW Program

Servant leadership, as a construct, is centrally focused on the attitudes, behaviors, and approaches of the leader in such a way that the leader ultimately empowers and serves their team, organization, or society (Spain, 2014; see Chapter 2 for more information on servant leadership). Although the servant leadership model may well serve BSW programs of all sizes, it can be particularly useful for small programs. The BSW program director who uses a servant leadership approach is motivated by a desire to help meet the needs of those with whom they work, as well as to promote the well-being or betterment of the program and institution (Northouse, 2016; Spain, 2014). The servant leadership model promotes a sense of shared program ownership and opportunity for growth and development in the BSW program (Northouse, 2016; Spain, 2014). It has been asserted that the servant leadership model is enhanced and influenced by context (mts5386, 2020). This means that, in a small BSW program, the impact of variables (e.g., the personality of the program director) on other faculty within the program are amplified.

Additionally, the program's culture, policies, and procedures can be affected positively to a significant degree when the program director is wholly committed to being a servant leader. Although higher education is often considered political and bureaucratic, being able to shape and guide the functioning of the program at the "local level" is an opportunity that cannot be underestimated (Parris & Peachey, 2013; Spain, 2014). By validating faculty concerns and ideas, the program director then facilitates each faculty member, staff member, adjunct instructor, and student worker in moving toward their full potential, while being empowered to take ownership of their role and impact on the program.

In a small BSW program, communication dyads and triads can have a significantly deeper impact on functioning than when there are many more faculty to help defuse those alliances or any tensions that might arise from them. An authentic sense of shared responsibility, a true team approach, and the empowering of others that comes with servant leadership can help to defuse or prevent these potential challenges in a small program. The nature of small programs with limited faculty resources often requires a flexibility in roles and responsibilities. Servant leadership, with its focus on shared power, parallels and supports this flexibility well.

The *ecological perspective* suggests that the actors within a system influence one another as well as the functioning of the system as a whole (Kirst-Ashman & Hull, 2018). With this in mind, servant leaders must ensure that they are acting in ways that encourage appropriate faculty behavior and discourage inappropriate behavior (Fields et al., 2015). This includes fostering an environment that emboldens faculty participation, including sharing novel and honest ideas and feedback, even if different from the ideas of the servant leader. Further, it is critical that the servant leader models desired behaviors to faculty—for example, ensuring inclusion and diverse perspectives, and managing criticism. Social work conflict-resolution skills, authentic communication, and openness partner perfectly with a servant leadership approach, in valuing disagreement, discourse, and openness about one's own mistakes (Northouse, 2016). Using these skills in a program with few faculty can help to maintain rapport and positive working relationships, which will, in turn, increase efficacy. Ultimately, creating an environment that fosters critical thinking and active brainstorming enhances opportunities for program growth with few faculty and limited financial resources.

Additionally, reliance upon the servant leadership approach helps to support inclusion among a diverse faculty group. The qualities that servant leaders demonstrate, including humility, gratitude, and selflessness, can help facilitate trust among the faculty (Sims, 2018). This mutual trust empowers all to engage in the free and open communication needed to address conflict productively, which will help to ensure more beneficial and positive interactions among diverse faculty members. A program director can promote inclusion by embodying the shared constructs of the servant leadership model and the social work profession itself: empowerment, authenticity, and fidelity to support a diverse team of faculty (Sims, 2018).

Staffing and Role Functioning

Although a small BSW program may include more than two full-time faculty, the two roles that must exist within any program, regardless of size, are program director and director of field education (CSWE, 2022). The role of program director typically exists within the university context for any number of disciplines and is a partial administrative role between department chair and program faculty. This role within the university may also include collecting and submitting teaching schedules, assisting with institutional assessment work, communicating with adjuncts, and more. The role of program director often does not come with additional compensation. In many colleges and universities, one does not formally apply for the role; typically, it is taken on as a service by a faculty member in each program, and in some programs, it rotates every few years (Mapp & Boutté-Queen, 2020). So, while the conceptualization of the role of program director in most institutions is not nearly as complex or as much work as the expectations for program directors within an accredited social work program, the latter is still a generally understood role.

The director of field education role, however, is often something unique to professional or accredited programs and not often replicated within institutions. Thus that role requires a good bit of educating institutional administration and colleagues. The role of the director of field education within a small BSW program may benefit from being intentionally crafted as a tenure-track position. Research has indicated that being tenure track helps to confer some status to the director of field education (Wertheimer & Sodhi, 2014). When a two-person program must function within a larger department, college, or university, barriers common to the politics of higher education should be minimized to the largest extent possible. Then, the director of field education will be able to engage in institutional discussions, respond to concerns, and speak with some authority in the eyes of colleagues and administration.

Note that given the significant workload and duties of a director of field education, the tenure-track nature of the position only adds responsibility and pressure (Wertheimer & Sodhi, 2014). The person who fulfills this role should do so with a clear understanding of tenure expectations, and be given the support and mentoring needed to help balance the responsibilities of the role and being a tenure-track faculty member.

The program director using a servant leadership approach to their work with the director of field education can assist in navigating and making meaning of the challenges and potential barriers. This is even more impactful in a small program. Given that small-program faculty must work closely together, empowerment, inclusion, and modeling, as well as vision and listening (Russell & Stone, 2002), can enhance a feeling of support and sense of partnership between the program director and director of field education, thus making politics and institutional nuances more manageable.

PRACTICE TIP: States, regions, and local communities frequently have their own program director and field director networks. It would be difficult to list them all here, but they can have a wealth of helpful information and we encourage you to seek out these organizations online and to connect with any active listserves or networks in your state or region.

Supports for the Small Program

With the ecological perspective as a guiding principle, staffing and role functioning are particularly important in small BSW programs with limited resources. They include consideration of all persons assigned directly or indirectly to the program, including full- and part-time faculty, adjunct faculty, administrative assistants, and student workers. In addition, there are various other employees whose functions are to serve the BSW program as well as several other programs, and each are vital to the program's functioning. Implementation of the servant leader model should be emphasized to all staff regardless of position, status, or role (Fields et al., 2015). All persons assigned to the BSW program should see high levels of consistency from those in positions of authority and/or who are responsible for decision making.

Most important, staffing and role functioning should serve to optimally meet the needs of small BSW programs' functioning and maintenance of accreditation. In small programs, especially two-person programs, involved parties must strive for as much clarity as possible regarding individual and collective role functioning. On one hand, fewer faculty may decrease the chances of miscommunication but, on the other hand, complicate the roles involved with each person's duties. Clarity and transparency about role functioning allow faculty the greatest opportunity to meet program and student needs through maximizing individual faculty strengths and flexibility in addressing needs. Members of the faculty of a small BSW program with limited resources will benefit from being open to the idea that roles can be flexible or altered when considering individual talents, skills, and interests. To develop a well-functioning partnership, roles may need to be altered and expectations adjusted, and most certainly, communication about any of these changes is essential.

Working Relationships

Clarity and transparency are best achieved through safe, ongoing, reciprocal interactions among faculty in small BSW programs with limited resources. Communication must flow freely for the faculty to feel that their messages are heard and valued. In larger programs, there are additional colleagues who can help faculty deal with conflict or process interpersonal differences. However, in a small program, it is essential that the confidence and trust of all parties are upheld in communication patterns and processes. Intentional application of these foundational social work skills in faculty interactions for a small program can advance healthy homeostasis and functioning. These communication approaches support small program success more than the antiquated, primarily unidirectional, top-down model where the program director, acting as boss, tells others what their respective roles are going to be and how problems are going to be solved. This is not to suggest that there are no formal supervisory, administrative, and/or evaluative roles that the program director must undertake. There are clearly situations that will involve the program director responding, based on their role, to administrative requests, CSWE inquiries, and evaluation-related activities.

However, with that said, a primary role of any leader is to encourage and model healthy problem-solving skills among group members, in keeping with the servant leader model. This includes brainstorming and asking powerful questions of faculty who submit ideas for group discussion (see Chapter 2 for a discussion of "powerful questions"). It is also worth saying explicitly that faculty in small programs who are willing to be vulnerable with one another as a result of building trust and respect and utilization of open communication practices means that it is possible to admit mistakes and work together to move toward solutions or corrections. When working to address challenges or problems, the servant leader and strong team, operating as a unit, can swiftly move toward resolution. The purpose of a well-functioning partnership within a small BSW program is both altruistic and self-serving. Maximizing individual efforts and recognizing the power of the group to develop problem-solving skills and use creative ways of addressing issues ultimately supports all members and helps to get the work done.

Communication

When there is consistent and frequent communication between the program director and director of field education, it becomes much easier to function as a partnership. Each party can then excel in their areas as well as the domains that represent opportunities for growth and development. Truthfully, when both faculty members are able to identify with and embody the servant leadership model, the partnership approach to running the program, responding to students, meeting administrative needs, and supporting adjunct faculty becomes much easier (mts5386, 2020; Parris & Peachey, 2013). We found that it was not uncommon to discuss significant issues or programmatic decisions (e.g., admission issues, probationary issues, hiring of adjuncts, etc.) two or three times in a relatively short span of time to ensure that each person's perspectives were heard, alternatives were considered, and, ultimately, collaborative decision making could be reached.

PRACTICE TIP: It can be helpful when working with just two or three faculty to have a meeting to discuss a program issue or programmatic response to an institutional issue (e.g., course caps are being raised by administration). At the end of the meeting, schedule a brief check-in the following day after all parties have had an opportunity to think through the response, assertion, and plan of action of the program. This allows for the benefit of time and reflection. A small program does not have multiple perspectives in a program meeting simply because of its size, and thus the time for consideration and reflection can benefit the few faculty who might have to make a decision of significance in a short period of time. It is also possible that a final check-in and review immediately before responding to the situation or individuals may be helpful (e.g., all reviewing the email response to administration, all reviewing key talking points prior to a meeting with a student, etc.).

It really goes without saying, but to say it anyway: As a program director of a small BSW program, frequent communication with your full-time and adjunct faculty, staff, and student workers is of vital importance. It is helpful to have a discussion early during the onboarding of a director of field education, any other full-time faculty, and student workers to review the expectations and hopes for communication. Discussing each person's preference for type of communication—text, email, office visit, phone call, and so on—will ensure that all parties are comfortable with the frequency and method of communication. Additionally, a frank conversation about how everyone prefers to approach communication can help to set the tone of how the program will function, how the day-to-day work will get done, and what to do when issues arise.

You will find that as a faculty team, you will learn the schedule of your colleagues: teaching days, standing meetings, grading times, family times, and so forth. This helps to plan and coordinate program work and tasks that require the team to work together, in a manner that is respectful of boundaries and work-life balance. This type of flexibility and shared decision making around meeting times, communication preferences, and more may be challenging to achieve. In such instances, having open discussions about what works best for all faculty in the program can help minimize frustrations and enhance collegiality.

Talking with your colleagues about significant tasks on the horizon is helpful for determining who will be responsible and what working deadlines are feasible. It is preferable and perhaps essential in small BSW programs to engage in program assessment or program review with all full-time faculty contributing. So, discussions about the work that needs to be done, who will be responsible for which components, and the required timeline are very beneficial. Additionally, in small BSW programs, routine conversations at the outset of the semester regarding classes, student performance, and other matters will ensure that all are fully informed and facilitate consistent and transparent communication with other constituents (other faculty, students, adjuncts, etc.). These interactions, in the vein of servant leadership, will contribute to empowering those who are on the team, as the program director is being transparent, valuing their faculty members' contributions, and working to honor the day-to-day work of the other faculty (Fields et al., 2015; Northouse, 2016).

Adjunct Faculty

An underaddressed issue in many programs with limited resources is the role(s) of adjunct faculty. Small programs often have to rely on several adjunct faculty to teach the curriculum and to function within the CSWE Accreditation Standards. Small BSW programs may use several adjuncts, depending upon the semester and the course offerings. Seek individuals who represent diversity along many variables to teach within the program, and make a concerted effort to develop a group of adjunct faculty who have a variety of experience in the field of social work. Ultimately, personal and professional diversity of adjunct faculty will enrich the program and the students' classroom experience. Given the prevalence of low pay to adjunct faculty across most disciplines and institutions of higher education (Murray, 2019), full-time social work faculty may want to advocate for increases in salary and consider nominating adjuncts for institution-wide annual awards whenever appropriate.

In small BSW programs with limited resources for hiring additional tenure-track faculty, adjunct faculty become essential and may play an important role in overall program functioning. With this in mind, adjuncts should be consulted on course structure, content, and texts and resources for the courses they teach. Additionally, encouraging adjunct faculty as they develop new courses helps support their autonomy and ownership over the courses they teach. Remain ever mindful that adjunct faculty may have a full-time job in addition to their work as adjuncts, so these discussions about courses and curriculum should always begin with a check-in to assess their capacity and depth of interest in participating in this level of work. Working to ensure that adjunct faculty are included, engaged to the degree that they are interested and able, as well as acknowledged for their important work should be an intentional effort of the program director and the director of field education.

These activities can be beneficial in recruiting and retaining a skilled group of diverse adjuncts to help support the development of your BSW students and the BSW program. While involving and engaging adjunct faculty in this way is certainly best practice for any BSW program, it is essential in a small BSW program that the students spend much more time with adjunct faculty than they do in programs with more full-time faculty. Additionally, when there are very few faculty in a BSW program, it is easy for any number of other activities or responsibilities to take precedence or require your attention. Overlooking adjunct faculty input can lead to reduced consistency and inadvertent curriculum or course changes, and thus perhaps lead an adjunct to decline future work with the program.

Adjunct faculty provide invaluable assistance to programs that often lack sufficient financial support to hire additional full-time faculty. However, if left out of faculty discussions and decision making as well as being undersupported, they may not be fully aligned with program goals and accreditation requirements, or at worst subvert those goals. Keeping them abreast of programmatic happenings, asking for their opinion, rendering feedback, and encouraging participation in faculty meetings and decision making will support their inherent worth to the program, encourage continuity across semesters when able, and ultimately improve the program's ability to meet student learning objectives.

Other Staff and Support Services

Developing clarity about the roles of administrative assistants and supporting their valuable work further enhances the overall functioning of a small BSW program with limited resources. Ensure that their roles are appreciated and that each individual is viewed as an integral part of the program. This can often be accomplished with clear and transparent communication with administration and the support staff as well. Being treated with respect, advised of their responsibilities to the program, and asked how they prefer to then accomplish that work will facilitate positive and proactive work efforts. This nurturing of relationships often does not take an inordinate amount of time, but reaps rewards when support is needed to process program applications, prepare for reaccreditation, and more.

Universities, colleges, schools, and programs are complex systems with many interconnected parts. For instance, student learning centers, fundraising, faculty senate, student recruitment programs, and centers that provide services for students with mental, physical, or educational needs all have administrators who play important roles as external partners with the overall functioning of small BSW programs. It is critical for small-program BSW faculty to develop strong working relationships with these parties to facilitate a thorough understanding of one another's role and function. Investing a portion of the limited time available in relationship building with these essential components of the university can reap rewards as student needs are identified, programmatic support is needed, and institutional barriers are encountered. Ensuring that the BSW program faculty fulfill their role and function with respect to these entities will help to ensure that the reciprocal, supportive relationship is healthy and well balanced.

> **PRACTICE TIP:** Establishing a relationship with your student accessibility center or the entity responsible for coordinating a variety of services for students who live with disabilities can be helpful for all BSW programs, but it might prove to be especially helpful for a BSW program with few faculty. The relationship can help facilitate understanding of the supports needed in the classroom and the demands of the social work curriculum, including the skills coursework and field placement. A preexisting partnership and intentional investment in this relationship will aid the program by reducing time and energy needed to explain situations, concerns, or constraints that might come up with the program or the support center. It can also aid in ensuring that plans can be made to support students' success in the program with open communication and forestall the need for special meetings, time-consuming back-and-forth emails, and a significant investment of time when the program and support service need to connect.

Hiring

As has been emphasized multiple times, it is essential to have positive and supportive working relationships. Ideally, the strengths, skills, and assets of each team member complement the others'. While important in any program, hiring new faculty can be even more impactful on a small BSW program because the team must work so closely together. Before any adjunct, student worker, or new full-time faculty member is hired, consider and discuss what characteristics are important and why they are important.

Also, ensure that the entire search committee has engaged in implicit bias training before a search begins, so that the search will be fair and inclusive. Key questions might include: Is there a need to bring on a new member who has a particular disposition? Can diversity of demographics and perspectives be assessed in the interview? What is the potential impact of a new person on a well-functioning but small team?

These considerations are of utmost importance as new faculty and staff are hired. This might require advocacy within the institution to department chairs, deans, or provosts so that the search is focused on the essential elements that are needed and it targets the right audience. Consider whether you need a faculty member to assist with field placement. Perhaps a robust local search would benefit the program more than a national search. Or perhaps a faculty member could be hired who has expertise teaching in a particular area of the curriculum or area of specialty. In these cases, the advertisement and recruitment materials should articulate this clearly.

Additionally, communicate to each applicant the importance of being a faculty member who is engaged and participatory, with an understanding of the value of diversity and inclusion. If your small program is structured as a partnership and there is an expectation of shared responsibility as well as ownership, every job candidate needs to know this. This might include sharing expected schedules; for example, if physical presence in the office or at the university is expected, that should be said up front.

PRACTICE TIP: If a program has a preexisting, well-functioning approach that requires people to be on campus several days a week, then a faculty member who does their research off-site with a community partner, has a part-time private practice, or engages in service to the community (e.g., by being on community advisory boards) may not be the right fit for the program. In a BSW program with few faculty and limited resources for supports, hiring a person who is not a good fit can be felt in deep and impactful ways. Adding someone to a two- or three-person team will certainly affect communication patterns, the roles of each program faculty member, and working relationships. These changes are not always negative or detrimental to program functioning. Perhaps the program leaders and members decide to adjust in order to welcome and accommodate a new focus or approach or to help ensure there is good fit with a new person. However, if the person hired creates added strain or difficulties because they do not fulfill needed roles, the program can suffer greatly, especially when there are only two or three other faculty.

Know where you and your program are willing to be flexible and creative, and willing to adjust to support your new hires. There are times when an applicant's teaching expertise may be more important than another applicant's particular or productive research agenda, and vice versa. Be reflective and transparent internally about what is needed, be specific about that in the job ad, and be forthcoming with candidates. This level of honesty and effort will pay dividends in the future. Although getting to know the candidates or new hires can be challenging, frank conversations and questions that elicit insights will help to advance the team and support the program.

Assessment

The importance of assessment cannot be overstated. With small programs, in particular, assessment serves as the main tool to justify the existence and growth of the program. Assessment includes examining program goals and objectives, student learning outcomes, criteria for student admission, and faculty evaluation. For internal constituencies, assessment must often be framed as student enrollment, semester credit hours, and student recruitment and retention.

There are many avenues to develop assessment strategies and tools. Participation of all faculty to the greatest degree possible is highly desired in small BSW programs. Encouraging faculty participation, including adjunct faculty, enhances creativity and fosters a strong faculty learning environment. Time, however, is always an issue in small BSW programs, and when developing an assessment strategy, consider the amount of time required to execute the assessment plan. Keeping in mind that adjunct faculty likely have a primary full-time job or might be piecing together adjunct work from multiple institutions, assessment of student learning outcomes is best when it is informed by or includes program adjuncts. Assessment of student learning outcomes as well as program utilization of artifacts from courses taught by adjuncts can lead to robust assessments while not burdening adjuncts with sole responsibility for these tasks. Given the generally low pay to adjunct faculty on a per-class basis, in addition to their other work and life constraints, it is a significant request to ask an adjunct to play a critical role in data collection for assessment purposes. If there is not enough time to execute the best assessment plan, it may come back to haunt you in the form of useless partial data and concerns from CSWE.

Program assessment and assessment of student learning outcomes must be deeply rooted in CSWE standards. Beyond that, how a program goes about measuring achievement can vary greatly but should provide meaningful information to the program. Programs may use qualitative and/or quantitative forms of data and may consider various sources for data. Although qualitative data provide depth and richness, it may be too time-consuming for small programs to collect and analyze. An alternative is a series of questions using Likert scale response options, which are likely easier to compile and aggregate according to program needs. The downside, of course, is less richness in the data.

Another consideration within the constraints of time is that multiple sources of data are required by the Educational Policy and Accreditation Standards (EPAS). Sources may include student responses on assessment measures (like those used in the Social Work Education Assessment Project, or SWEAP), a rubric assessing key student assignments, or final field evaluations by field instructors. An additional data source might be a final field internship assignment (e.g., capstone assignment, field portfolio, etc.), which can be evaluated not only by the director of field education but also by members of a program's advisory board, which, aside from offering another perspective, saves program faculty from yet one more assessment task. In addition, developing routines for this data collection is essential in small programs. Given that the task requirements are the same for all programs, when completing them with only two or perhaps three faculty, it can seem like an insurmountable amount of work.

Setting a schedule and collecting the necessary data each year can help tremendously when institutions and CSWE come calling. Honestly, while it seems obvious, putting the dates for assessment activities in your e-calendar to remind you each year when the data should be collected and when to engage in the data collection process is a simple strategy. In a small BSW program, there will always be tasks that must be done or items that get inserted on the to-do list. Scheduling time for these important tasks is both necessary and advantageous. Developing this muscle memory for the task of assessment and building the databases of necessary information saves immeasurable time when preparing for an institutional program review or the self-study process for reaccreditation.

Accreditation and Reaffirmation

There is no doubt that the work of initial accreditation and reaffirmation is one of the most important kinds of work done by faculty in any social work program. It is not possible to do this work or facilitate the development of new professionals if the program is not accredited or does not maintain accreditation. A small program may experience pressure because of the added workload, undermining work-life balance for those who are tenure-track and who are already experiencing pressures to continue to teach, produce research, and contribute service beyond the program. A thoughtful and intentional approach to the process will help moderate these challenges.

Process

With limited faculty and financial resources, it is particularly important for small BSW programs to plan in advance for any and all milestones, due dates, and process requirements for CSWE. Given the previous discussion about sharing the workload and working as a team, it will not surprise the reader to learn that the approach taken by our program is to work as a team to write the self-studies and reaffirmation documents. With a full-time faculty of two, each with administrative responsibilities in the program as well as teaching responsibilities in the regular academic semester, it was imperative to begin the work of culling program assessment data and drafting the program self-study a full 2 years in advance of the due date of the documents. We recommend that 2 years prior to the submission date of the program self-study, faculty refresh themselves collectively on what is due, distribute the work among the full-time faculty, identify tentative due dates, and begin the work.

One process that can work in a BSW program with few faculty is for each person to write their assigned portion in accordance with the CSWE guidelines and expectations and then share all drafts with the other colleague(s) to add, edit, and refine. The bulk of our writing happens during the two summers preceding our self-study due date, as well as during winter breaks and spring breaks. Some work happens during the traditional semester, but with teaching, service, and program administrative responsibilities, the available time to write and edit is significantly diminished. The collective approach to writing and tandem timing of work ensures a consistency of voice and approach to discussion of the program. Furthermore, this shared approach and longer timeline benefits a small program as it reduces the pressure of deadlines (slightly) and allows for time to share work generated, discuss approaches, decide how to describe and accurately express all of the accomplishments, and more. Small programs also benefit from the reality that all members are likely intimately familiar with the curriculum, policies, processes, and more, and this helps ease the process of drafting the self-study.

Additionally, having both (or all) members of the BSW program participate in the drafting of all documents can prove to be beneficial toward ensuring that everyone is clear and in agreement on understanding how and why the program functions as it does; it ensures that there are discussions about curricular consistency, learning outcomes, goals for students, and uniformity of policy interpretation and implementation.

Student Involvement

We also find that it is important to involve the students in the reaffirmation process as well as to communicate consistently about our accreditation expectations and timeline with students. It has proven to be a wonderful learning opportunity to repeatedly, throughout the years, discuss the expectations of accreditation with our students in the classroom and during program orientations. We find that discussing the context for the competencies and behaviors that translate into learning objectives in the classroom sparks myriad conversations about the goals of the curriculum, the purpose of the content, and the way those translate to professional development goals for our students. These have been mutually beneficial classroom and student conversations. We find that just as the students understand the goals of the program and their own learning goals with more depth, the program is also made more rigorous and robust by having to justify and explain routinely, in each class, how and why we engage in the work that we do.

External Supports

As directors of small programs, we have also found that it has been most beneficial to communicate frequently with our accreditation specialist. Having a relationship with these individuals has ensured that we can get clarity on questions, that we are aware of any and all expectations, and that our timeline for our work is accurate. Additionally, locating and building a working relationship with a skilled and well-informed consultant has been most beneficial in our reaffirmation processes. We have used the Association of Baccalaureate Social Work Program Directors (BPD) listserv, as well as the BPD and CSWE conferences to attend trainings and seminars about reaccreditation and the new EPAS, and to identify people who might serve as an accreditation consultant. We have used our consultants to review and edit our self-study documents, discuss approaches to describing and explaining our program, and review our assessment results. These third-party supporters have proven to be invaluable in our reaffirmation process as a small BSW program, as they provide additional perspective and help expand our capacity for such a considerable endeavor.

Students: Admission Reviews and Advising

Having clearly articulated admission criteria to assess students serves the small program well. Many small programs are afforded a more personal admissions process because they are able to get to know students well while teaching, advising, and orienting those interested in the major. One beneficial requirement for small BSW programs that might have challenges with full-time faulty interacting with all students prior to application is to require prerequisites for the BSW program that include courses taught within the BSW program. An example is to have students take initial social work courses such as "Introduction to Social Work" or "Issues and Ethics in Social Work Practice" as opportunities to assess students' openness and readiness to engage in the social work curriculum and process of developing a professional identity. A small BSW program with limited faculty and financial resources might find that having one of these courses taught by a full-time faculty member or a well-established adjunct would support the capacity to perform required gatekeeping functions at the admission stage.

Students frequently must complete an application packet that includes transcripts, letters of recommendation, and a personal statement of sorts. Once students have completed these requirements, typically full-time faculty evaluate the application packets and must come to consensus regarding all students' admission status. Assessing the key variables required for admission—academic performance, openness to the social work values and ethics, writing skills, and the student's capacity to accept and integrate feedback—can be made much easier with consideration of items required in the application packet. Ultimately, if the full-time faculty have had limited opportunity for direct interaction with the student applicants, the letters of recommendation, the personal statement, and documentation of academic performance can facilitate a thorough assessment. In a small BSW program, each student is likely assessed individually by both/all full-time faculty, and then scores can be compared and contrasted, along with a discussion with any adjuncts who teach the prerequisite courses. It has been our experience that this communication regarding the application packet and the assessment of the student prove to be relatively quick yet essential for consensus building regarding the secondary admission process for all student applicants.

Advisement

It is true that advising is one key way to reach students and socialize them into higher education and to the profession. As Negroni-Rodríguez et al. (2006) emphasize, it is important to stay grounded in the ecological systems model while considering advising. Students in higher education are interacting and engaging in transactions with a multitude of new and different systems, structures, and groups as they integrate into the university setting. Experiences with these other systems and within the institution can influence a student's motivation, view of the institution (e.g., positive or negative, supportive or challenging, etc.), and self-confidence in being a student learner. We found it imperative to keep in mind these theoretical underpinnings while engaging and establishing rapport with our students. Be cognizant that advising students helps to socialize them not only into the profession of social work but also into higher education and the university setting. The strength of these relationships built through advising contributes to student retention; we found that students were more willing to reach out and communicate when they needed to slow down to attend to personal or family issues or wanted to adjust their curriculum plan for future semesters (Hessenauer & D'Amico Guthrie, 2018). Additionally, open communication and frequency of engagement make space for students to share their concerns so that faculty can offer perspective and supports, if needed.

PRACTICE TIP: Advising is one additional place to support and empower diverse students and those who have been and/or are oppressed. Our institution is a Hispanic-serving institution, with numbers of first-generation students and veteran-affiliated students that are higher than the national higher education averages for these groups. Ensuring that advising conversations always start from a place of genuine interest in the students' lived experience, honoring their current reality, and making space for conversations to assess what strengths exist are all valuable in meeting the needs of diverse students. Ensuring that no matter the reason for the meeting, a deficit perspective is not what frames your engagement, will help students to feel seen, heard, and valued. We have been asked to explain the profession to parents of students from countries where social work is stigmatized. We have had the joy of being the first person in a student's life to accept their identity and authentic selves. We have also had the opportunity to brainstorm with students ways to help them advocate for their rights within and outside of the university system. Each of these discussions, during advising appointments, help to support the student's sense of belonging at the university and in social work just as they also help them to be able to thrive in the classroom.

Institutional Advising Partners

If there is an undergraduate advising office within the university, college, school, or department to which all students are connected upon enrollment, it can be fruitful to develop a strong working relationship with the staff, given the particulars associated with matriculating through the BSW program. A small BSW program may be the only accredited undergraduate degree at the institution and the only undergraduate program that requires secondary admission and its own advising structure, so nurturing and then working to maintain a relationship with these more general academic advisors can be helpful.

Ultimately, when rapport and strong working relationships have been established with the institutional advising staff, these relationships can serve to expand the advising capacity of the program and availability of advising supports for potential BSW students. Any small program can benefit from making time at the end of each academic year to meet with the full team of advisors to answer questions about the BSW program, discuss any issues or questions that surfaced during advising in the past year, and ensure that any new staff are trained or educated and view themselves as an important part of the extended BSW program team.

Make it clear that your program advisors do not seek to replace the university advisors, but rather seek to partner with them. One result of cultivating this kind of relationship is that students interested in social work are encouraged by their general advisors to begin advisement with BSW faculty as soon as possible, and students who make their way directly to BSW faculty are encouraged to check in with the general advisors to make sure that all of their institutional requirements are addressed.

Early Advisement

The beauty of beginning advising as soon as students start taking social work courses (or prerequisites) in a small program is that students and faculty will begin the process of building a healthy professional relationship. These early interactions with students also help to set expectations and standards for the future. Strong, healthy, professional advising focusing on professional comportment, establishment of boundaries, and development of key skills and abilities, early in the student's engagement with the program, often reduces misunderstandings and problems in the future.

Because early advisement also includes reinforming students of processes for managing behavioral and/or academic issues, we have ensured that students have been fully informed of their rights and the program expectations, thus promoting open communication and modeling transparency for the students. Utilizing this process for advising with its shared vision or approach is one that also helps when it is time to respond to the CSWE requirements regarding "policies for academic and professional advising" and demonstrating "professional advising is provided by social work program faculty or staff" (CSWE, 2022, p. 26).

> **PRACTICE TIP:** Establishing a BSW program orientation that all students must attend as they are engaged in their early coursework of the program may prove to be particularly helpful to a small BSW program. Structure the experience such that all students must attend an orientation once throughout their time in the BSW program; this can be done anytime prior to or during the semester immediately following their secondary admission to the BSW program. In this half-day orientation, you might consider reviewing the student handbook, all important and relevant policies that affect students, how to apply to the program (for those who have not yet done so), the field placement process, and expectations for behaviors. An orientation such as this can be a wonderful opportunity to help socialize the students into the profession, as conversations about the connection of the curriculum and degree to the profession and practice of social work, behavioral expectations for social work students and professionals, and more can be covered in the time together as a group. Orientations such as this can also help to identify a student with a challenge or concern, allowing faculty to reach out individually to support or address the issue when and if it surfaces. An activity such as this maximizes the reach of the program faculty in a small BSW program, given that one session includes many students at multiple points early in the curriculum. Implementing this practice also ensures consistency of message delivery, as the students can benefit from hearing from all full-time faculty in one session.

In a small program, it can be beneficial to encourage students to initiate advising on their own to ask for feedback from faculty about their strengths and weaknesses, rather than wait for faculty to initiate contact with them about a specific issue or problem. Although personal advising can be time-consuming, it can help a program with few faculty to establish a reputation for supporting students and helping to develop well-trained professionals, because students feel supported and challenged simultaneously on their path toward developing their professional identity and degree completion.

External Supports: An Advisory Board

Small BSW programs with limited faculty and resources may find particularly helpful an advisory board that reflects the community at large. Whether forming the advisory board when program faculty are first hired or reinitiating or adding a person as a new program support, the composition of membership and mission is an important consideration. Identifying and inviting social work leaders in various areas of expertise within the area or region of the program is ideal. The advisory board can be convened at a frequency that best helps meet the programmatic needs. In a small program, it might be that twice per year and with all program faculty present is the most inclusive and sustainable approach.

The purposes of an advisory board may include supporting the BSW program's goals and objectives, promoting a new program to the surrounding communities, providing feedback or suggestions about issues relevant to program functioning, advocating for the program with the university or college administration, reviewing annual performance measures or outcomes, reviewing accreditation documents, participating in reviewing field student final assignment evaluations, and assisting with the discussion and formulation of financial issues.

There are a few iterations of an advisory board that can support the functioning of the small program with limited resources. For instance, a field advisory board can assist with some of the intense work of the field director, like suggesting and recruiting new field placement partners, assessing needed services in the community, and even assisting with assessment of field internship success. Some board members might also serve as adjunct faculty, thus giving the board direct information about program functioning as well as strengths and weaknesses while also serving as a staffing resource for BSW program faculty. The advisory board can be quite valuable overall and can serve a program well when there are only a few faculty to share perspectives or offer considerations of the important areas of program functioning. Consideration regarding advisory board composition is vitally important and should be based on program needs.

PRACTICE TIP: The advisory board has been mentioned in the "Assessment" section of this chapter, but we'd like to include a special note regarding how valuable members can be during the process of accreditation and/or reaffirmation. As an example, in our program the Field Advisory Board (a subcommittee of the Advisory Board) served as a small group to review field student portfolios and assess student mastery of the competencies expected of them. This engagement was simple to orchestrate, as it required very little of program faculty to schedule and yielded a valuable and significant portion of program assessment data. This activity happened only once a year, asked those involved for half a day of their time, and required only a quiet room on campus and some snacks. Using advisory board members to assist with program assessment can maximize their utility for programs with few faculty but all the same required tasks of accreditation and reaffirmation.

Upon reflection, in our program, we wish we had brought in board members with specific expertise in fundraising to facilitate the development of needed resources. When it came time to discuss budgets and limited resources to support the program, the members of our Advisory Board were solid advocates and engaged with university administration. However, we view our failure to attend to this element of membership selection as a missed opportunity to raise funds for student scholarships, support for students to attend conferences, and more, as has been done successfully in other programs.

Make sure that the following have been articulated before they are needed: procedures for board functioning to assist with the facilitation of meetings, how to bring new members aboard, and how to remove a board member if necessary. As is good social work practice, all meetings should have an agenda developed by program faculty. One nice additional element is to invite a current "student of the year," students who have received acknowledgment for special projects or work, and similar, with each providing a 5-minute presentation on their experiences or goals within the profession. Additionally, if your small program has a social work student organization, invite the student leaders to facilitate their voice and involvement in setting policies, addressing curricular changes, and influencing the direction of the program. This gives board members firsthand experience with some of your excellent BSW students while also allowing students to mingle with social work leaders in the surrounding communities.

Responding to Crises

As higher education continues to go through a dynamic and changing period, so do individual institutions. Times of crises, including budget austerity, changes in mission, shifts in enrollment, and changing student demographics, all require the institution, college, or department to make timely yet well-thought-out adjustments to its functioning. As in any system seeking a new level of optimal homeostatic functioning, when one variable changes, other areas will also be affected. Attending to the needs of all affected areas will help the system remain synergistic (Kirst-Ashman & Hull, 2018).

Achieving an optimal level of synergy can be facilitated through leadership based on the servant leadership practices emphasizing humility, gratitude, selflessness, modeling, and empowerment in service to maximizing trust, inclusion, and active participation among key players (Sims, 2018). Often the small BSW program may need to respond to a crisis, which may be an area of relative strength given its small size. Indeed, the program director of a small BSW program who uses a servant leadership approach might find that developing a consistent response, ensuring that all are in agreement, and communicating in a clear and timely fashion are all easier to facilitate partly because of the program's small size.

Crises can manifest in any form and might mean responding to the tragic loss of a student or an alumnus, responding to an ill or impaired student in the classroom, responding to calls from administration to shut down the program because of costs or budget constraints, supporting students in the middle of a natural disaster that closes the university for an extended period of time, responding to social and political unrest, or maintaining program functioning during a global pandemic. We do not choose these examples to sound dramatic. Indeed, each of these scenarios has transpired during our time as program directors. However, when the program functions as a healthy system and a solid team, each crisis can be attended to appropriately.

Key lessons learned during and after a crisis include the following:

- ensure that you are processing your thoughts and feelings with the faculty and students who have a reason and right to know;

- work to ensure that there are consistent messages communicated from the program director, the director of field education, and any or all faculty within the program; and

- take your time to formulate a thoughtful response (do not be rushed into decision making by people external to your program).

Although having a larger faculty brings many benefits, a small program faculty can often mean a more agile response to crisis. With two or three faculty, it is often much easier to connect and communicate with faculty to explain the situation, consider responses, and implement a plan.

As crises arise, inform those who have a need to know or a vested interest in the situation. Ensuring that all are informed can prevent surprises, miscommunication, and conflicting messages going out from faculty. Clearly, no matter the situation, everyone will have thoughts, feelings, and reactions, and using conversations with the director of field education or other full-time faculty to allow for processing these feelings and emotions will help to develop a consensus when responses are needed and ensure that all feel included and supported. In truth, you are a team when responding as a program, and you want to operate as one. No one should feel forced into responding to a crisis alone, if it can be avoided.

Additionally, in times of crisis, make sure that messages are clear and consistent from each member of the program. This can be easier in small programs, given that with few faculty, less time and effort are needed to align on messaging, there are fewer people to connect with, and there is reduced repetition of communication within the program. For instance, during hurricanes, times of social or political unrest, or significant community changes, it is important for the program to send messages that represent a shared voice of the program director, the director of field education, the full-time faculty, and the adjuncts, if possible. Notes that share important information, supportive messaging, and necessary details can be crafted together or with feedback from all and distributed widely. Although it is true that there are times when the program director is ultimately responsible or the lead on tasks, the more effort that can be made to facilitate the crisis response as inclusive, the better for the maintenance of a healthy functioning relationship.

Universities are notorious for bureaucratic processes and slow decision making or efforts toward change. That is until it is time for a program or faculty to respond to a crisis; in those moments, faculty are given mere days to respond and sometimes only hours. Do not let yourself be pressured into providing an answer to a situation of program structure, funding, or functioning with an arbitrary or unreasonable time frame. It is more than acceptable to indicate that conversations need to be had among the program faculty. It is acceptable to ask for an explanation of unreasonable time frames if they are placed upon you. It is important to process the situation, come to a programmatic decision, and then communicate with administrators in a timely fashion.

Last, there is no way to predict what kinds of crises will arise. The key is knowing that they will arise and that as a program director, you are not alone in bearing the burden of responding to them. You have a team, even if just one other person, to assist you and to serve as a supportive contributor to the problem solving. If functioning as a servant leader, consulting and trusting your director of field education and other full-time faculty will reinforce that their voices are valuable and necessary for the program to thrive (Fields et al., 2015).

One additional important note: Be sure to communicate any and all decisions or concerns to your adjunct faculty and, when possible, include them in decision making. They should feel fully informed, which will reinforce their role as important members of the program. This will also help to ensure that there is diversity of perspective and approach as possible solutions or responses to crises are considered. It is not their responsibility to assist with all crisis response; however, at the very least, ensuring that they have copies of communications shared with students, emails to summarize situations, or updates on challenges facing the program will help them to educate and support students.

Conclusion

Leadership in a small BSW program is not so different from leadership in midsize or large programs. However, differences in financial and faculty resources pose challenges and, on occasion, recognizable benefits. We believe that the servant leader model and the ecological perspective provide a strong base for our work and growth. Each of these perspectives is reflected in the energy and time required for adaptation, flexibility, and communication within our program. Ultimately, theory-based, high-quality communication practices have supported our best work over the years, allowing us to not only survive but also thrive and grow as a program and as social work educators, and we welcome our readers to consider these thoughts.

Suggested Readings and Resources

Association of Baccalaureate Social Work Program Directors Conference: https://www.bswpdonline.org/the-conference

Council on Social Work Education Annual Program Meeting: https://www.cswe.org/events-meetings

CSWE trainings regarding accreditation or reaffirmation: https://cswe.org/Accreditation/Training

North American Network of Field Educators & Directors: https://www.nanfed.org/

van Dierendonck, D. (2011). Servant leadership: A review and synthesis. *Journal of Management, 37*, 1228–1261. doi:10.1177/0149206310380462

References

Aguilar, G. D., & Aigner, S. (1997, March). *Autonomy, grievances, and resources in baccalaureate programs.* Paper presented at the CSWE Annual Program Meeting. Chicago, IL.

Council on Social Work Education. (2021). *2020 statistics on social work education in the United States.* https://www.cswe.org/Research-Statistics/Research-Briefs-and-Publications/2019-Annual-Statistics-on-Social-Work-Education

Council on Social Work Education. (2022). 2022 *Educational policy and accreditation standards.* https://www.cswe.org/accreditation/standards/2022-epas/

Drumm, R., Suppes, M., & Kersting, R. (2002). Autonomy and resources in small baccalaureate social work programs. *Journal of Baccalaureate Social Work, 8*(1), 51–67.

Fields, J., Thompson, K., & Hawkins, J. (2015). Servant leadership: Teaching the helping professional. *Journal of Leadership Education, 14*(4), 92–105. https://doi.org/10.12806/V14/I4/R2

Hessenauer, G., & D'Amico Guthrie, D. (2018). Advising in social work education: Student and faculty perceptions. *The Journal of Baccalaureate Social Work, 23*(1), 11–30. https://doi.org/10.18084/1084-7219.23.1.11

Kirst-Ashman, K., & Hull, G. (2018). *Understanding generalist practice* (7th ed.). Nelson-Hall.

Mapp, S., & Boutté-Queen, N. (2020). The role of the US baccalaureate social work program director: A national survey. *Social Work Education, 40*(7), 843–860. https://doi.org/10.1080/02615479.2020.1729720

mts5386. (2020). The benefits of servant leadership. *Leadership: PSYCH 485 blog.* PennState. https://sites.psu.edu/leadership/2020/11/04/the-benefits-of-servant-leadership/

Murray, D. S. (2019). The precarious new faculty majority: Communication and instruction research and contingent labor in higher education. *Communication Education, 68*(2), 235–245. https://doi.org/10.1080/03634523.2019.1568512

Negroni-Rodríguez, D., Dicks, B. A., & Morales, J. (2006). Cultural considerations in advising Latino/a students. *Journal of Teaching in Social Work, 26*(1–2), 201–221. https://doi.org/10.1300/J067v26n01_12

Northouse, P. G. (2016). *Leadership: Theory and practice* (7th ed.). Sage.

Parris, D. L., & Peachey, J. W. (2013). A systematic literature review of servant leadership theory in organizational contexts. *Journal of Business Ethics, 113*(3), 377–393. https://doi.org/10.1007/s10551-012-1322-6

Russell, R. F., & Stone, A. G. (2002). A review of servant leadership attributes: Developing a practical model. *Leadership & Organization Development Journal, 23*(3), 145–157.

Sims, C. M. (2018). The diversity intelligent servant leader: Developing leaders to meet the needs of a diverse workforce. *Advances in Developing Human Resources, 20*(3), 313–330.

Spain, M. A. (2014). *Changing the world through servant leadership* (Publication No. 15903) [Doctoral dissertation, Pepperdine University]. Pepperdine Libraries Digital Collections.

Wertheimer, M. R., & Sodhi, M. (2014). Beyond field education: Leadership of field directors. *Journal of Social Work Education, 50*(1), 48–68. https://doi.org/10.1080/10437797.2014.856230

CHAPTER 9

Leading and Managing a Large BSW Program

DuWayne Battle
Cathryn C. Potter

Although many of the aspects of leading a large baccalaureate social work (BSW) program are similar to those of smaller programs, there are unique demands on time and resources, as well as opportunities for improvement. This chapter examines these challenges and opportunities through an anti-racism, diversity, equity, and inclusion (ADEI) lens (CSWE, 2022b). We address matters directly involving large BSW programs and program leadership, the organizational structure of large programs, and curriculum essentials including course scheduling and faculty deployment, field education, and expanding electives. We examine the available BSW program data and emphasize the importance of knowing, advising, instructing, and resourcing BSW students throughout the chapter. We take a brief look at expanding electives and program opportunities, as well as accreditation and assessment. Large BSW programs are likely to exist in schools where a MSW program is also offered, and thus the BSW program director works within a larger, perhaps more complex, administrative structure. A case study is provided at the end of the chapter as a way of describing how leading a large BSW program might be experienced in a real-life setting.

Approximately a quarter of all BSW programs are considered large, according to Council on Social Work Education (CSWE) criteria, defined as more than 71 graduates a year, and these programs have particular challenges and opportunities. The focus of this chapter is on the special issues encountered by these programs, which can affect experiences through the student life cycle. There are additional program director and faculty issues, including program leadership and management, teaching and advising, and mentoring and support. Because large programs are located in different areas of the country, it is critically important that BSW program directors examine available student and program data from CSWE, as well as scholarly articles, albeit limited, on large BSW programs. These resources can provide relevant geographical, organizational, and demographic contexts for these programs. The importance of using an ADEI lens is stressed throughout the chapter and focuses on students, maximizing your organizational structure, working with other departments, and keeping in view of the surrounding community, student advising, curricula essentials, course scheduling, and field education.

BSW Program Leadership

Chapter 1 provided an overview of the existing literature on BSW program leadership. The director's understanding of personal, structural, and institutional power influences their perception of power for midlevel management in academia (Harper et al., 1991). The areas where BSW program directors need to be most empowered to manage their programs are related to "budget/resource management, program/curriculum management, and faculty administration" (Harper et al., 1991, p. 183). This may be especially true for leaders in large programs, which are often embedded in larger universities and more complex organizational structures.

Mapp and Boutté-Queen (2021a, 2021b) found that challenges related to the role and responsibilities of BSW program directors include accreditation, the lack of preparation and leadership training to step into the program director role, unrealistic time demands, and the high expectations that came along with limited resources. BSW program directors were most pleased with the opportunity to work with students and colleagues and to advance undergraduate social work education. Together, Harper et al. (1991) and Mapp and Boutté-Queen (2021a, 2021b) drew attention to some of the challenges of leading and managing BSW programs. Therefore, BSW program directors should seek opportunities to engage in leadership development training that are provided through their academic institutions, other schools and universities, and professional organizations, such as CSWE and the National Association of Social Workers (NASW), both regional and national. Rutgers School of Social Work (SSW) and other schools of social work provide excellent continuing education opportunities that can strengthen the leadership and management skills of BSW program directors.

Large BSW Programs

There is a dearth of literature on BSW programs in general, and none of those studies focuses directly on the size of programs. Therefore, we worked with colleagues to conduct secondary analyses with a special focus on program size, using data from the Mapp and Boutté-Queen (2021b) survey of BSW program directors, and data from the 2019 Council on Social Work Education program survey (CSWE, 2019). Mapp and Boutté-Queen generously provided us with data for our analysis, and a CSWE data analyst ran follow-up analyses on CSWE data.

Mapp and Boutté-Queen (2021b) surveyed program directors of the 528 accredited BSW programs, asking 65 questions related to the program directors' roles, responsibilities, preparation, and support, as well as general program information. In all, 268 responses were received, for a response rate of 48.6%. The additional analysis involved using CSWE billing categories related to size, with 56 programs designated as large (22% of programs with more than 71 graduates per year, corresponding to an overall program size of more than 142 students) as compared with the remaining programs.

There were no significant associations between program size and BSW director characteristics, including current director rank, director tenure status, and highest degree earned. There were no significant associations between program size and characteristics of a director's appointment, such as appointment length (9- or 12-month appointments), teaching responsibilities onload, or additional stipend compensation. Nor were there differences related to whether the department was interdisciplinary. Similarly, there were no significant differences between program size and any of the director workload variables: average hours worked per week, work-life balance, and time spent on specific program responsibilities, such as faculty personnel issues, student conduct issues, accreditation and administrative tasks, loss of scholarship time, and need for time management.

Program directors from large programs were significantly less likely to have been appointed to their role from within the social work program faculty and more likely to be in a public institution. They were almost twice as likely to be colocated with a MSW program and were less likely to be serving as chair of their academic department (See Table 9.1). Because BSW program directors from large programs are less likely to head the unit, their autonomy to lead as they might prefer may be limited.

TABLE 9.1

Significant Differences Between Large and Small Programs
(data from Mapp & Boutté-Queen, 2021b)

	Large Programs	All Other Programs	Chi Square
BSW leader appointed from within the program	25.3%	74.7%	X^2 (1, N = 253) = 4.798, p = .030
Colocated with MSW program	60.7%	31.8%	X^2 (1, N = 253) = 15 442, p < .001
Serving as chair of department	23.6%	41.6%	X^2 (1, N = 252) = 5.923, p = .015
Located in a public institution	83.3%	44.7%	X^2 (1, N = 253) = 26.219, p < .001

The CSWE survey data came from the 2019 annual survey of all accredited social work programs. This survey differs from the Mapp and Boutté-Queen study, in that the CSWE data came from almost all accredited BSW programs, whereas the Mapp and Boutté-Queen study represents a smaller, more voluntary subgroup. In addition, the CSWE survey data also focus more on the structural variables of the programs rather than on the experiences of program directors.

For the CSWE 2019 survey, of 531 baccalaureate programs, 469 responded, for a response rate of 88.3%. Programs ranged in size from 10 to 798 students. For these analyses, CSWE constructed a variable with three levels of program size, based on natural data breaks, rather than its standard categories. For this variable, small programs (N = 187) have fewer than 74 total students, medium programs (N = 139) have between 75 and 149 students, and large programs (N = 124) have more than 150 students. Note that these variables are based on the number of students rather than graduates, and there are variations in the previously mentioned variables for program size.

There were significant differences between program size and most variables related to program structure. Large programs are more likely to be in institutions with a Carnegie classification of Doctoral Research University/Very High (RU/VH) and equally likely with medium-sized programs to be at a Doctoral Research University/High (RU/H). Programs of all three sizes are equally likely to be found at Master's College/University Large size and less likely to be at all other Carnegie classification universities.

Both large and medium BSW programs are more likely to be found at public institutions, and 87% of large baccalaureate programs are colocated. Large programs are more likely to be found in minority-serving institutions (all types together), though the differences are not large. Large and medium programs were more likely than small programs to offer multiple modes of course delivery (in-person, hybrid, and online. See Table 9.2.) There was no significant association between program size and region of the United States.

TABLE 9.2

Significant Differences According to Program Sizes (CSWE 2019 Data)

	Large	Medium	Small	Chi Square
Carnegie classification Doctoral Research University/Very High	62.3%	28.9%	8.9%	$X^2 (14, N = 450) = 122.58$, $p =< .001$
Doctoral Research University (RU/H)	47.4%	42.1%	10.5%	
Master's College or University	36.1%	31.9%	31.9%	
Public Institution	45.0%	40.8%	14.2%	$X^2 (2, N = 450) = 168.079$, $p < .001$
Minority-Serving Institution	37.2%	33.0%	29.8%	$X^2 (2, N = 450) = 7.606$, $p = .022$
Multiple Program Delivery Options (in-person, hybrid, online)	47.0%	37.6%	15.4%	$X^2 (8, N = 450) = 69.681$, $p < .001$

From these two data sources, we see that large social work baccalaureate programs, as defined by number of graduates or number of students enrolled, are most likely to be found in large, public institutions of the master's large-institution type and both doctoral-granting research classifications. Thus, they are more likely to be embedded in complex organizational structures. They are more likely to serve in institutions designated as minority serving and may be more likely to serve a diverse student body.

Large BSW programs are more likely to be colocated with MSW programs, and their directors are more likely to be embedded in a larger social work administrative structure. They are more likely than leaders in smaller-sized programs to have come into leadership from outside the institution. Therefore, they may face a period of acclimatization following hire that requires quickly assessing the organization, building relationships, and learning institutional history. Program directors from large programs are similarly situated to those in smaller programs in terms of personal characteristics and most features of their appointments, including specific areas of work responsibility. Note that there are no additional release requirements for directors of large BSW programs compared with those of small programs.

> **REFLECTION QUESTIONS:**
> - Do your greatest challenges to lead and manage a large BSW program in your setting align with these findings?
> - How empowered do you feel to lead as you choose in your program in the areas of budget or resource management, program or curriculum management, and faculty administration?
> - What would improve your ability to lead your large BSW program in the areas mentioned above or other areas?
> - What are the leadership development and management opportunities available to you at your university or in your area?
> - How can you balance the fulfilling and challenging aspects of managing a large BSW program, such as working with students and advancing BSW education versus challenging time demands, elevated expectations, and limited resources?
> - Given some of the similarities between large and medium-sized programs mentioned previously, how can medium programs improve leadership, empowerment, and management of budgets, resources, curriculum, and faculty administration in their current size or during anticipated growth of the program?

Using an Anti-Racism, Diversity, Equity, and Inclusion Lens

Any consideration of what it takes to lead and manage a BSW program must begin with an ADEI lens (CSWE, 2022). Addressing ADEI in a large program has particular challenges, opportunities, and complexities as a result of more complex administrative structures and larger numbers of people. In addition, the previous analysis found that these programs are more likely to be at institutions designated as serving traditionally oppressed populations.

Although all social work programs must attend to ADEI concerns, as mentioned previously, large BSW programs are more likely to be in minority-serving institutions and may have greater diversity among their students. The same could be said of their faculty and staff, making the ADEI perspective essential to the program's mission, vision, and values.

When considering ADEI, these terms often overlap as they deal with people, opportunities, and environments. Anti-racism is the practice of actively opposing racism. Diversity here is about difference in representation of perspectives, people, and ideas. Equity has to do with treating all people with fairness, including students, faculty, staff, the community where the university is located, and the people it seeks to serve. Inclusion involves creating communities that are open and supportive of diversity and difference. Therefore, it is important to understand, frame, and celebrate diversity, while also challenging disparities in programs.

It is essential to have historical and current knowledge of ADEI among the student body. What has been the history of the school regarding available student demographic data? How have these demographics changed and shifted over time? What populations are students being prepared to serve? And relatedly, how do the student data compare with the community and client population data? While social work programs have historically celebrated diversity and inclusion, they are not immune to histories of bad behavior. It is important that BSW leaders of large programs be prepared to engage those histories, and their resonance in local communities, even as they strengthen ADEI initiatives going forward.

Universities are also likely to have recruitment officers, admissions counselors, academic advisors, and transfer deans who will work closely with BSW program directors when advising students in their majors. It is important to take the ADEI perspective in recruitment and student advising, both explicitly and implicitly. Policies and procedures should reflect ADEI. Directors of large BSW programs may find this more challenging as they work with more university partners and larger numbers of students, staff, and faculty. Therefore, program directors should work with administration, faculty, staff, and students to encourage, facilitate, and help create a climate and culture reflecting ADEI.

Again, celebrating diversity and challenging disparities must go hand in hand. Students need to see this messaging when considering admission into your school, but it is even more important that they have this experience once they are matriculated in your program. Involving a variety of students from different demographics in planning and programing is crucial at this point. Provide students with opportunities to evaluate their ADEI experience at your school, which can be accomplished through surveys, open forums, focus groups, and the like.

Pay attention to minoritized students, making sure that their representation and voices are included and concerns are addressed through committee appointments, curriculum content, student government, and so forth. Leading from an ADEI perspective means allowing for and managing a diversity of opinion, as well as supporting and advising for student activism. BSW program directors can be creative about how they go about this. You can create an ADEI committee or workgroup; plan activities, such as a speaker series, book clubs, and discussion groups; or embark upon advocacy and community organizing efforts. You can reflect ADEI in all of your marketing and messaging, on your program website, and in your social media presence.

While ensuring that your ADEI messaging is not performative, having images that represent the students served can help to create a sense of belonging that affects retention (Beadlescomb, 2019; Davis et al., 2021). The important thing, though, is to include others who integrate the ADEI lens in the policies, planning, programming, and administration of these ADEI efforts. This will help to ensure that your efforts are substantive, rather than mere window dressing.

Leaders of large BSW programs may also want to consider opportunities for special partnerships with 2-year schools. One pathway to a 4-year school is through local community colleges that offer associate's degrees in a range of majors in liberal arts, sciences, human services, and social work. Large BSW programs may attract larger numbers of students needing to focus on their liberal arts foundation, especially if their first 2 years of college were more narrowly focused on a natural science or professional degree program such as nursing. The community college entry point also provides an opportunity for building close relationships aimed at creating a seamless pathway for students. Community colleges are also an affordable option for students and provide an important entry point for diverse students as well. Rutgers has one BSW site that is colocated at a remote southern New Jersey community college and has strong affiliations and memorandums of understanding with many other community college partners.

For example, the Latino/a Initiatives for Service, Training, and Assessment (LISTA) initiative at Rutgers illustrates how to recruit, train, and prepare students to serve their communities (Sanchez Mayers et al.,

2020). This program resulted from research on demographic changes and a shortage of social workers to provide services in the Hispanic community. Remembering that large BSW programs are more likely to be housed in public institutions that serve minoritized students, it is reasonable to assume that these students represent the diverse communities where they live. It is vitally important, then, that culturally relevant community engagement be a priority. The LISTA program is an example of how BSW program directors can respond to the ADEI needs mentioned previously, especially as they relate to preparing students to engage in culturally relevant, equitable, and inclusive social work practice to meet the needs of minoritized communities.

However, programs need to be focused on their implicit curriculum as well. Historically, organizations addressed ADEI concerns through implicit bias training. While important, this has done little to bring about the desired changes (Onyeador et al., 2021). It is not enough to become aware of implicit bias without establishing the strategic initiatives to support equity and inclusion within organizations. Therefore, BSW program directors should work collaboratively within their organizations to improve their ADEI efforts by educating organization members both on bias within the organization and the organization's responses to the bias, such as creating safe spaces for affinity group development, providing creative opportunities for intergroup interaction, and establishing inclusive messaging that is welcoming and affirming. There may be more opportunities in large BSW programs to offer a range of affinity groups and networks because specific identities are more likely to be represented in a large number of students. Similarly, larger programs with large numbers of faculty can take on the faculty advising roles of student groups in their own areas of identity, interest, and research.

Leaders of large BSW programs should anticipate, but not accommodate, resistance to ADEI initiatives. Given the larger numbers of faculty, staff, and students, a broader range of diversity is possible, in terms of both demographics and different points of view. These larger numbers may also create greater special interests, competing concerns, and the need to work harder at reaching compromise and consensus. Program directors should work collaboratively with administration, faculty, students, and staff to make the necessary changes to the organization's structure to frame, focus, and facilitate the organization's ADEI goals and strategies.

At Rutgers, this approach is embedded in the strategic plan and is guided through the leadership of the dean and associate dean for diversity, equity, and inclusion (DEI) and operationalized throughout all policies, programs, and procedures with the involvement of faculty, staff, and students. An advantage of large programs is that they may be embedded in structures that have the resources to hire or designate staff to lead the ADEI initiatives, rather than enfolding them into someone else's existing duties and responsibilities.

PRACTICE TIPS AND REFLECTION QUESTIONS:
- Identify your school's and program's history of ADEI regarding students, faculty, staff, and community. If your program is medium-sized, think about the impact of ADEI on barriers and facilitators to program growth.
- How can you work with your university's and program's efforts to develop and implement an ADEI perspective? Ask how you can contribute to efforts to include ADEI as a part of your university-, college-, and program-level strategic planning processes.
- Remember that the goals and strategies in the strategic plan can help to operationalize ADEI in recruiting and admitting a diverse and inclusive student body, recruiting and hiring faculty and staff, and creating a culture of equity and inclusion throughout the program.
- Determine how you can increase community engagement. Build relationships with local disenfranchised communities, and be prepared to hear both good and bad news from them.
- Ask yourself, "What do anti-racism, diversity, equity, and inclusion look like to me? Who's included? Who's missing?" Determine if there are opportunities and options you wish to pursue.
- Provide open forums, surveys, focus groups, and other opportunities for students to give feedback on how they experience your program's implicit and explicit ADEI initiatives.

Maximizing Your Organizational Structure

It is hard to overstate the importance of BSW program directors knowing their organizational structure and developing strategies for working with other departments within the university or, quite possibly, other units within their department or school. Given the findings discussed earlier, leaders of large programs should reflect on their organization's type and structure. Is the program part of a larger school of social work? If so, does the school offer both undergraduate and graduate degrees? Does it offer doctoral degrees: DSW or PhD? Is the social work program freestanding or part of a larger school? Who are the players in the larger organization?

It may be helpful to use some basic social work tools, such as an eco-map to visualize the organization of the entities and relationships surrounding the BSW program. As with all areas of this important work, program directors of large BSW programs should consider ways to work with administration to identify and address organizational and structural barriers to achieving DEI within their institutions. This should be an inclusive effort involving administration, faculty, staff, students, and possibly community partners to engage in an ongoing process to raise awareness and take action.

Because large BSW programs are more likely to be housed with MSW programs, it is particularly important to develop collegial relationships, partnerships, and strategies for working within your school and with other departments at your university. Be prepared to articulate a clear vision for baccalaureate education as distinctly different from graduate-level education, including emphasizing the liberal arts perspective (Educational Policy and Accreditation Standards [EPAS] Standard 3.1; CSWE, 2022b). Many large BSW programs are also likely to be more visible within the university. This may attract more students to the social work major, allow for more engagement between faculty and students, and present opportunities for more interdisciplinary collaborations and activities.

Large social work programs with both undergraduate and graduate programs will have separate program directors and may have separate faculty, field staff, administrative support, and other resources to effectively deliver the BSW curriculum and administer the BSW program. Many large BSW programs are housed in large public universities with regional and state associations and connections. Therefore, BSW program directors need to map their program's social network in the larger community and develop key relationships. BSW program directors managing large programs need to think about the geographical realities that are built into their organizational structure. Operating with an ADEI lens means the program director seeks to ensure student access to the BSW program, and thus large programs may have on- and off-campus locations, as well as in-person and online program options, that are spread throughout the state, region, or country. Large BSW programs may have to address other geographical differences, such as urban and suburban, inner city and rural, and national and global. The national and global concerns are related to international students, as well as online, synchronous remote, study away, and learning abroad opportunities.

Eco-Map: Other Departments

All program directors work with other units on campus, but those in large programs may have more of these relationships through serving jointly on university-wide committees; sharing in joint curriculum opportunities; attending recruitment events; and engaging with students across other programs, departments, and majors. This relates to BSW students participating in opportunities sponsored by other departments, as well as allowing other undergraduate students to join in opportunities designed to address the interests and concerns of both social work students and students from other majors.

In addition, large BSW programs will have to work with other departments in every possible area, from recruitment and admissions, to advising and retention, to graduation certifications and convocations. Very often, BSW program directors will also have to work with departments that specialize in meeting specific student needs, such as undergraduate admissions, the registrar's office, libraries, computer labs, student housing, financial aid, accommodations for students with disabilities, student counseling services, hospital and health care facilities, and so forth.

Clearly, benefits and challenges will arise. Working with other departments may lead to expanded research opportunities, internships, employment, and university career services. Units can work together to sponsor speakers or initiatives to serve the campus or the community. However, there are downsides as well. More involvement with other departments will place greater demands on your time and energy. It may cause fear that you are going to take their students. There are often budget concerns, and more resources may be expended. The benefits may include more exposure, networking opportunities, and partnerships. Thus, laying out the pattern and network of these relationships can help to illustrate these benefits and challenges.

Eco-Map: Community Networks and Program Offerings

It is equally important for BSW program directors to map their program's organizational social network in the larger community to illustrate key relationships. Large BSW programs are likely to have a greater presence in the community, often because they have more alumni, faculty, and staff with wider community and agency connections. There are likely to be more field education placements and adjunct faculty, which expand links back into the community. Developing these community networks relates to marketing and communication directors, agency leaders, alumni, and other schools and social work programs, especially feeder programs that may be housed in nearby community colleges.

Additionally, many large BSW programs have regional and state associations and connections. Rutgers, for instance, is connected to the New Jersey Baccalaureate Social Work Education Association, which sponsors an Annual Policy Symposium. This is done in partnership with the National Association of Social Workers New Jersey Chapter (NASW-NJ), which also offers opportunities for undergraduate student representation on the board of directors, a student conference during the annual professional conference, and the Legislative Education and Advocacy Day at the state capital, Trenton. The Baccalaureate Child Welfare Education Program Consortium is also an important organization that strengthens social and professional networks.

Many other regions have similar organizations that BSW program directors can join. Program directors of large BSW programs should use their expanded opportunities and resources to promote student and faculty engagement with the broader community. They should also lead the way in strengthening community networks and partnering with other schools and agencies to expand the social work presence in the larger community through service, research, advocacy, and other forms of civic engagement. Given their program's size and resources, they are often in a better position to lead such efforts as a result of greater numbers of staff and students, campus resources, and budget.

PRACTICE TIPS AND REFLECTION QUESTIONS:

- Identify your organizational structure. Large BSW programs may exist in more complex organizational structures. Therefore, identify, clarify, and share your organizational structure with students, faculty, staff, other departments, and community partners.
- It may be more challenging to identify and address structural and organizational oppression in large organizations. Brainstorm the areas where you need to address organizational ADEI issues.
- How can you, as the director of a large or medium-sized BSW program, specifically work to promote ADEI within your organizational structure?
- Determine what your community, social, and virtual networks look like. Are there are any partners missing from your network?

- How can you, as the director of a large or medium-sized BSW program, specifically work to eliminate barriers and promote ADEI within your community, social, and virtual networks?
- Analyze how well you work with other departments and programs in your school or university.

Students in Large BSW Programs

Because large BSW programs have more students, directors may find it more challenging to get to know students on an individual basis. It is critical, then, to have a student-centered approach, create opportunities for students and faculty to meet on a regular basis, and design opportunities for student involvement. Large BSW programs may have more program-level opportunities in addition to those offered on the larger campus.

For example, here at Rutgers, in addition to our fall orientations and spring graduation receptions, we have Undergraduate Social Work Organizations (USWOs) on our two main campuses, where students organize and create events and opportunities for peer support and community engagement. We involve BSW students in our research and curriculum assistantships, study abroad and study away programs, conference presentations, and student-faculty committees, such as the curriculum committee and our committee focused on ADEI initiatives. We make use of social media, student forums, and our communication team's efforts to keep students connected, informed, and engaged. BSW students are featured regularly in our communication efforts through our website, marketing materials, infographics, and BSW newsletter.

Having a student-centered approach contributes to student retention, academic success, and degree completion. Although all social work programs should pay attention to ADEI concerns, large programs may have greater diversity among their students. They may have, for instance, more nontraditional (older) students who are seeking second careers or people finally beginning or returning to school to complete their undergraduate degrees. Again, this may be related to the fact that large BSW programs are more likely to be located at institutions serving historically minoritized populations or able to offer multiple course sections, including evenings and online. Think about the students enrolled in your program and the demographics of the communities they are being prepared to serve. Operating out of a cultural humility framework can help program directors of large BSW programs recruit and support diverse students to succeed in their academic programs and social work careers.

Unrau et al. (2020) identified the financial challenges faced by social work students. They noted that many students do not receive adequate information about the cost of their education and end up with considerable student loan debt. In fact, there was a 10% increase in student loan debt among BSW graduates over the 10-year period from 2010 to 2020 (CSWE, 2021a). This rise in student loan debt has been increasing for several decades (Fry, 2014). Perry et al. (2021) identified the disproportionate impact of student loan debt on Black students, who owe nearly twice as much as White students 4 years after graduation. This is important for large BSW programs because they may have more Black students than smaller programs with less racial diversity among the student body.

Although student loan debt is not uncommon among students pursuing degrees leading to many careers, social work students are engaged in a lower-wage helping profession that promotes social justice and equity for the common good. Moreover, analysts and scholars alike identify student loan debt as a problem in the United States, and they believe that some portion of this debt needs to be forgiven (Perry et al., 2021). As such, BSW program directors should ensure that students talk with their institution's financial aid office to understand their choices regarding debt and the implications of student loan debt. Program directors must also lead and join the effort for policies and the allocation of resources to promote the affordability of higher education and student loan forgiveness.

Title IV-E programs can help to combat this. Broad partnerships and the use of funds to provide trained social workers for employment in child welfare, as well as a return to school for those already employed, are important elements (Konrady & Battle, 2020; Zlotnik & Pryce, 2013). Large BSW programs can contribute to a consortium of schools of social work and partner with the state child welfare agency (Konrady & Battle, 2020). Such initiatives can improve child welfare, reduce student debt, and support returning to school.

Gatekeeping in Large BSW Programs

Another important challenge is the gatekeeping role of BSW program directors. In any program, there are some students who are better suited for a different career path, and BSW program directors have an important role to play in this regard. Just as people fishing with larger nets may have an increased number of fish to pull ashore, larger BSW programs will have a larger number of students, some of whom may need to be advised out of the social work major (see Chapter 17 for more information on gatekeeping). In smaller programs, there may be the opportunity to interview students during the admission process. This may not be the case with larger BSW programs, and program directors may have to rely on other ways to assess new students, such as well-designed reference forms, reflective essays, and a dedicated committee or staff to review admission applications.

The same is true when preparing to place a student in the field. Additional care may be taken, for instance, when doing background checks and onboarding for students to engage in field education. Field education directors may need to do more-thorough assessments of a student's mental, emotional, and ethical fitness to advance in social work education, in much the same way that we evaluate a student's academic and intellectual preparedness to advance toward graduation and careers in social work.

Utilizing the ADEI lens, reexamine the things that determine how and why you may restrict some students from entering the profession to ensure that you are not seeking merely to replicate the profession, but are providing equitable paths to success. Also think about the interests and rights of a more diverse body of students, as well as the interests and needs of a diverse client population, the interests of the BSW program, and the interests of the social work profession (Blakely & Gibbs, 2000).

Holley et al. (2020) suggested identifying other resources that can be useful in gatekeeping with students with mental health issues, such as referrals to student counseling services, obtaining legal counsel, and developing important connections with offices of disability services. They also argued that "it is important for social work program administrators to have frank conversations about these complex and often competing roles and reflect on their policies and practices. In doing so, program administrators can identify strategies to be fully inclusive of students with mental health conditions while also ensuring a sound educational journey in which students develop social work competencies that prepare them for professional practice" (Holley et al., 2020, p. 18).

PRACTICE TIPS:
- Identify creative ways to get to know your students by using social media, featuring students in communications, offering student forums, and so on.
- Program directors and faculty in large programs may find it difficult to get to know students individually. Therefore, having reliable demographic student data is crucial.

- Program directors and faculty in medium-sized programs should work hard to manage growth in a way that does not weaken the students' sense of belonging, community, or engagement.
- Ask yourself, "Who are the students we are trying to reach? Who are the students missing from our program?"
- Determine how effective you are at reaching, resourcing, and retaining minoritized students, from admission into our program through degree completion.
- Ascertain your gatekeeping role and how you examine that role through an ADEI lens. This is especially important for large BSW programs, where more students will need to determine if social work is the best major and career option available to them.
- How can you as a BSW program director work collaboratively at every level (program, university, state, and national) to advocate for an increase in the affordability of higher education and student loan forgiveness?

Student Advising

One of the key areas where BSW program directors must dedicate their time and energy is overseeing student advising, which runs through every part of the program. There is an aspect of student advising that takes place during recruitment and admission to the institution, especially for those students who express an interest in the social work major or enter into a pre–social work major. Large universities are likely to have marketing managers, branding staff, and communication directors who influence how large BSW programs market, brand, and communicate their own mission, vision, and values.

The school or department housing the large BSW program may have its own employees dedicated to these specialized areas, but the BSW program director will be called upon to work collaboratively with department, school, and university staff in these important areas. An example is providing content for the build-out of the BSW program's portion of the website and the development of promotional resources and brochures.

Steingass and Sykes (2008) suggested that student advising is one of the most important aspects of a college student's experience and is invaluable to student success. Therefore, they make the case for centralizing student advising. This is true for both large universities and large undergraduate social work programs. The availability of a full-service, centralized advising team enables students to consistently receive the correct information and to have their advising needs met systematically. Social work faculty and staff can then focus on professional advising to fulfill EPAS 4.1.6, which states: "The program has policies for academic advising and professional advising. Professional advising is provided by social work program faculty or staff" (CSWE, 2022, p. 26).

Large BSW programs can create centralized advising, with program directors, faculty, and staff sharing the responsibility for academic and professional advising. Realistically, though, large BSW programs will likely increase the advising loads for BSW directors. Academic advising and career services may be centralized in larger universities, and professional advising done at the program level. Still, students will seek some degree of academic advising and career planning from those who provide professional advising. In some cases, the program director is responsible for all or most student advising, and even when others are involved in student advising, the program director has to ensure that such advising takes place, as well as the accuracy and quality of the student-advising experience.

To do this well for a large number of students, think about the macro level and how to structure it. Applegate and Hartleroad (2011) made several important suggestions for high-quality advising, such as knowing your student demographics, making use of technology, providing group advising, and expanding staff to deal with increased demands for student advising. Looking at student demographics, large programs are likely to have a wide diversity of students, such as pre–social work majors, continuing students, transfer students, nontraditional students, international students, students with learning accommodations, honors students, and students struggling both academically and personally, such as those on academic probation.

In a large program, you may have difficulty ascertaining that the support needs of different student groups are consistently recognized, and thus you should consider utilizing technology to record these needs. It could be useful to provide general coding for these student groupings to make it easier to recognize their status and provide them with the most effective advising, especially if multiple people are providing student advising. This can help with challenges such as the decline in advisor availability, the increase in nonresident students, the impact of budget cuts on the number of advisors, inexperienced advisors, and students' increased use of smart phones for information, which requires websites to have responsive designs (University of California San Diego, 2010).

Large programs face challenges to communicating consistently with all students, and a more diverse student body may necessitate diversity in preferred modes of communication. Broadly speaking, students are likely to use technology as a primary means of accessing information. Therefore, advisors can use email, text messaging, websites, blogs, podcasts, vlogs, learning management systems (such as Canvas and Blackboard), and social media (e.g., Facebook, LinkedIn, Twitter). We have also found it useful to have a mix of individual and group advising when working with large numbers of students. We provide general information and advising sessions, for instance, on the child welfare and study abroad options we offer. All interested students are invited to attend. We then offer individual advising for students with additional questions or those who want to apply for these programs.

Endeavor to make good use of your social work training when providing advising and support to social work students. More students represent more needs. Lambert and Siegel (2018) suggested that social workers can enhance student success by seeking social justice in higher education by reducing stigma, increasing available support at times that are known to be challenging during any particular semester, being available to students, and helping students with problem solving. This may include developing individualized action plans for students, from a social work or social justice perspective. It may also include knowing when to refer students to others for counseling and other services (Lambert & Siegel, 2018). Lambert and Siegel (2018) offered suggestions for improving students' sense of connection with social work programs through the use of advising resources, such as:

- utilizing doctoral students to assist with advising,

- implementing same-day appointments to limit advising no-shows,

- creating a new job title for professional academic advisors,

- standardizing the training of advisors,

- centralizing advising,

- promoting professional development opportunities,

- offering student-centered advising, and

- providing administrative support staff to increase advising effectiveness.

In addition to developing a centralized advising center, get student feedback to determine if the advising system is working. All of this is to underscore the need for directors of large BSW programs to give serious attention to quality improvement in the area of student advising.

Student Organizations

Other issues related to organizational structure and student engagement, especially as it relates to our work with other departments, involves student activities and student groups. This may create additional opportunities and challenges for directors of large BSW programs, where similar student organizations exist in other areas. In the authors' setting, as mentioned earlier, we have a USWO on each of the two main campuses with student leaders from all locations. Students across the campuses seek to share ideas and support one another's efforts where possible. These organizations must be open to all undergraduate students, including those from other university departments.

The program director and assistant director serve as faculty advisors for the USWO groups. This requires a considerable amount of time in recruiting, advising, and meeting with student leaders and participating in their events. Program directors of large programs can work with other campus partners who focus on supporting student groups. You might also be able to work collaboratively with other faculty responsible for advising their student groups. It may also be helpful to provide training for student leaders, establish regular times to meet with student leaders, and maintain open lines of communication between you and these student leaders.

PRACTICE TIPS:

- Identify and implement ways to improve student advising. Large programs require additional advisors, creative approaches, and resources to improve student advising.
- Be sure to meet with campus partners, community colleges, and other sending schools so that they will have the most recent information about your program, because they advise students who are interested in pursuing the social work major at your institution.
- Identify the ways that you can use technology to improve your student advising. Who are the people in your school who can assist you in these efforts? This is important for both medium and large BSW programs.

- Examine how effective you are at supporting your student organizations, especially if they meet at different locations. This may be another area where you can use technology—perhaps by meeting remotely rather than traveling long distances.

- Meet with new student leaders early and regularly to make sure that they are organized, have reasonable and inclusive plans, have open communication with all students, and feel supported.

- Consider how you can leverage your program or university resources to improve student advising and support student organizations in both the short and long term.

Curricula Essentials

BSW program directors must have a handle on curricula essentials, including any prerequisites, meeting the required CSWE competencies, additional departmental or university requirements, and other curricula opportunities. Although this is true of all BSW programs, it is likely more complex for large and medium programs due to more program options, sections, and so on. Dynamic curriculum opportunities may include social work electives, curriculum assistantships, honors programs, certificate programs, study away and study abroad or global learning, and child welfare stipend programs, such as through Title IV.

Other curriculum issues relate to balancing the breadth and depth of the curriculum; managing the horizontal and vertical integration of curriculum content; responding to current events, issues, and special topics; and managing the interface between the BSW and MSW programs. To do this well, engage in ongoing review and revision of the curriculum, with regular meetings, workgroups, and task forces.

In addition to involving faculty with expertise in their areas of research, teaching, and practice, it is vitally important to include students in curriculum revisions and development. Students should be elected or appointed to serve on curriculum committees. Course evaluations should have questions that directly relate to the curriculum, and opportunities should be provided so that students can offer valuable insights on their experience with the curriculum, as well as what they perceive to be gaps and opportunities to improve the curriculum.

BSW program directors are familiar with the advanced standing option available to students who successfully complete their BSW degrees and apply for admission into MSW programs. However, prospective students may be thinking about how long it will take to earn their MSW, such as through a 2+1 or 4+1 option for transfer students with an associate's degree and continuing students at a 4-year school, respectively. This is particularly important to large BSW programs because, as previously indicated, many of these programs are situated within institutions that also offer an MSW, typically with advanced standing.

Students likely think of this when they make their decisions about where they want to apply for their undergraduate social work education. Similarly, directors of large BSW programs need to remember the CSWE (2022) EPAS requirement for a program to provide "its policy for ensuring that students from CSWE-accredited baccalaureate social work programs do not repeat generalist content at the master's level that has been achieved at the baccalaureate level" (p. 26).

It is vitally important to work with the BSW's curriculum committee and faculty for curriculum mapping, especially when revising the curriculum, and coordinate with the MSW program, if applicable. Provide easy-to-follow curriculum summaries, such as a curriculum at-a-glance, which is extremely helpful for students in large programs, so that students can map their progress toward degree completion. Curriculum summaries are also helpful when different advisors are attempting to explain the BSW program's curriculum requirements and options.

There is so much that has to be accomplished in the short time that we have to prepare our students for professional graduate study and careers in social work. Remember that the focus is not just on content and knowledge, but also on values, competencies, and skills. Identify the horizontal movement from fall and spring semesters, as well as junior and senior years. Programs can choose how they accomplish this horizontal and vertical integration. Some will identify prerequisites and corequisites to establish the curriculum grids for the required social work classes. Others may begin the major before the junior year. Keep in mind that the horizontal and vertical integration at the undergraduate level must relate well to the curriculum at the graduate level.

The integration of the curriculum is well served when intentional interaction occurs between the BSW and MSW program directors, as well as among field directors, faculty, and staff serving each program. This can be accomplished through committee appointments, such as curriculum committees, task forces, and other ad hoc committees. The key here is to make sure that committee members—including student representatives from different groups—are fully engaged, empowered, and committed to doing the important work of the committee, so that it does not fall on a select few.

Depending upon the organizational structure, large BSW programs may have an associate dean of academic affairs in the school to help facilitate faculty participation in the curriculum development and revisions for the required social work classes, as well as the social work electives. Beyond this, large social work programs will need to work collaboratively within the larger university structure to bring about curriculum revisions and changes.

BSW programs must tend not only to what is taught through the explicit curriculum but also to the student's learning experience and the program environment—or implicit curriculum (CSWE, 2022). This includes "student development, admissions, advising, retention, and termination; student participation in governance; faculty; administrative and governance structure; and resources. All elements of the implicit curriculum are expected to demonstrate the program's commitment to anti-racism, diversity, equity, and inclusion (ADEI)" (p. 24).

Similarly, Bogo and Wayne (2013) argued that there must be consistency between what is taught in the classroom and what the student experiences in the implicit curriculum, which they refer to as the "culture of human interchange." This involves everything that affects the student experience and the potential for professional development, such as policies and procedures, student governance, transparency, the field education experience, respect for both academic freedom and difference of opinion, effective communication, conflict resolution, and so forth. Again, the goal is to reinforce implicitly what is explicitly taught in the classroom.

For more detail, read Holosko et al. (2010) for insights from a large BSW program that developed an organized approach to focusing on the implicit curriculum, including a glossary of terms for students, frequently asked questions (FAQs) for advisors, and FAQs for field students, all of which are related to their five steps of building a BSW implicit curriculum. This process includes "developing key values and assumptions, student glossary of terms for BSW curriculum, BSW advising FAQs, field problems and resources FAQs, and assessment" (Holosko et al., 2010, p. 417).

Course Scheduling and Faculty Assignments

In addition to the aforesaid organizational and curricula matters, BSW program directors must focus on the operational issues and challenges of managing large numbers of class sections, as well as partnering with and supporting larger numbers of faculty dedicated to the development and delivery of courses within the program. This will most likely include a combination of tenured and tenure-track faculty, non-tenure-track contingent faculty, and adjunct faculty or part-time lecturers. Course scheduling for large BSW programs requires a lot of advance planning to determine the courses needed, the required number of sections, when and through what course delivery method they will be taught, and who will teach them. Obviously, there are budget concerns that affect this, and the dean and unit financial officer will project and monitor budgets.

The BSW program director is likely working together with others, such as an associate dean for academic affairs, an assistant BSW program director, a program coordinator, and administrative staff. Projected admission numbers are used to determine enrollment estimates for new and continuing students. Required and elective courses are identified, and the number of sections and mode(s) of delivery (in person, synchronous remote, and asynchronous online) are determined. This information is put into the university's course scheduling system, paying attention to the specific campus, days and times needed, and available classroom spaces. Once the full-time instructors are assigned, then part-time faculty must be recruited and assigned to ensure that all sections are aptly covered.

As our analyses found, large BSW programs are more likely to offer a full range of program delivery options, including on-the-ground, hybrid, and fully online programs. Although there are substantially fewer online-only BSW programs than MSW programs (CSWE, 2022a), that number has been growing and may increase because of experiences gained as a result of the COVID-19 pandemic as well as other factors. The pandemic taught us many things, including that humans create community in many ways. Whatever location and program options you provide your students, directors of large BSW programs must work hard to ensure the same educational quality in the different program offerings, while striving for regional and cultural relevance and providing an equitable distribution of resources.

Large BSW programs must also work to ensure the commitment of faculty resources and the quality of course instruction within the BSW program. This is very challenging, given the myriad demands of faculty—for example, those wanting to teach only evenings or no evenings, only online or only in person, only on specific days, or only on certain campuses. All of this must be woven together in an equitable manner. Pay attention to faculty preferences, students' needs, and the program requirements. If possible, work with the dean to establish a policy that all faculty be available to teach as the program requires.

Rutgers SSW requires that faculty teach across campuses and program offerings, meaning both BSW and MSW programs, as well as in person, online, and synchronous remote. Full-time faculty should identify their course preferences well in advance of the academic year or at the start of the previous semester for a subsequent semester. This should include several options that will be matched to the needs of the program.

Many adjunct faculty are employed elsewhere and may be available only on certain days or times of day for in-person instruction. Other faculty may be better suited for online teaching or in-person instruction, or on certain campuses. Keep a record of what works best from previous assignments. Again, establish a policy of faculty preference and flexibility. In our program, all faculty are screened and vetted before hiring, of course, and evaluated during and after teaching each course. Faculty are given a great deal of support, and numerous professional development and teaching excellence opportunities are provided through the SSW and the university.

PRACTICE TIPS:

- Explain the curriculum to larger numbers of people within and beyond the program. Use a curriculum at-a-glance to make it easy for students, faculty, university partners, sending schools, and other constituents to understand your curriculum.

- Identify the areas where and ways that you can improve your curriculum. For instance, use assessments to seek to understand the gaps between your explicit and implicit curriculum, and determine how to fill those gaps.

- Clarify for students and faculty what makes your curriculum different from what other BSW programs offer, especially programs in your area. What are the unique needs and challenges you face or options and opportunities available to you?

- Evaluate the process for reviewing and revising your curriculum. This may be more challenging for large and medium BSW programs. Program directors should lead this effort but should not do it alone. Consider who should be a part of this process, such as a curriculum committee, students, faculty, and community partners. Collaborate with the associate dean for academic affairs, faculty teaching in the program, and students.

- Examine the process used to schedule classes and assign faculty. Are there ways that this process can be improved? Identify ways to promote and expand ADEI efforts in both faculty assignments and the students' experience with faculty.
- Examine how effective you are at providing a consistently high-quality learning experience through your various program offerings and at different locations. What needs to change to ensure an equitable program delivery?

Field Education

Given the prominent role that field education plays in social work programs, BSW program directors have to address the opportunities and challenges that large programs have with identifying suitable placements for field education, as well as nurture and sustain partnerships among the school, agencies, and the broader community. This will most likely require supporting the director of field education through a sufficient complement of faculty, staff, field instructors, field liaisons, and agency partners to provide students with the integration of classroom and field practice experience.

Large BSW programs will likely face special challenges in the area of field education. More students with competing interests require more field placements. At Rutgers, our field office works each academic year with nearly 1,000 agencies assigning more than 1,500 students in field placements in both the undergraduate and graduate programs. This makes it challenging to match students with agencies serving desired populations in preferred arenas of practice. Additionally, because large BSW programs tend to be colocated with MSW programs, there may be competition between the programs for field placements. There may also be competition for highly desired field placements among schools of social work in a particular state or region. The same can be said of medium programs, especially if they are experiencing growth and anticipate future expansion.

Therefore, BSW program directors must work closely with field directors to clearly identify the sites best able to provide a generalist undergraduate experience. It is vitally important to acknowledge and appreciate agencies and field supervisors for the opportunities they provide to students. Given that large programs may have more offerings, invite field supervisors to attend continuing education classes, webinars, professional trainings, and networking events. It is especially considerate if you are able to offer these opportunities without cost and occasionally provide free continuing education credits.

To serve large numbers of students well, consider a required BSW orientation at the start of the fall semester or at a time that works best for their setting, which can be in person and/or online. The BSW director can give students an overview of the curriculum requirements, and the field director can make a presentation about fieldwork and invite students to join in a question-and-answer session or follow up later with additional questions.

It may also be useful for large programs to offer group field supervision and make effective use of technology to improve the field education experience (see Chapter 11 for further discussion of using technology to support field education). The BSW director, assistant director, program coordinators, and field staff should routinely monitor each BSW student's progress in the field and confer immediately when special concerns, issues, or needs arise. This is particularly important in those unfortunate cases where field placements are disrupted or students are terminated from the field.

Integrating ADEI Into the Curricula

Confronting racial injustice must be addressed by all social work programs (Battle et al., 2022; CSWE, 2022; Grand Challenges for Social Work, 2021; NASW, 2021), and those responsible for leading and managing large BSW programs should do their part to lead in this effort. Although speaking mainly about MSW programs, Bodenheimer (2016) suggested that social work programs should do a better job of integrating racial justice content throughout the curriculum. Curran et al. (2022), noting the legacy of Black social work leaders in the anti-racist tradition, argued that social work educators should challenge anti-Black racism across the social work curriculum. Large BSW programs are well placed to offer a larger number of courses and can provide student access to a wide diversity of instructors, including contingent or adjunct faculty. Although guided by CSWE accreditation requirements, individual programs have an opportunity to establish an ADEI curriculum framework that is overarching to all school programs.

The Rutgers 2020 strategic plan, *Toward a More Just Future*, has a central overarching goal to promote inclusion, intersectionality, diversity, equity, and advancement. As part of that goal, we have adopted a libera-tory consciousness (Love, 2000) framework across the BSW program and our broader efforts. This framework allows much room for diversity in our course offerings, while providing an important framework for revis-ing and aligning curriculum. Additionally, in keeping with our school's strategic plan, the undergraduate, graduate, and doctoral programs have engaged in a curriculum audit to see where we are in terms of addressing anti-racism, leadership development, and the use of technology in social work. Large BSW programs can explore opportunities to expand curricula and program options that will operationalize and reinforce the vision and strategic plan in their settings.

Many large baccalaureate programs have the capacity to offer multi-ple courses, including electives and additional competencies, sometimes organized into certificates, as well as partnerships with other majors to create interesting major and minor combinations to better serve stu-dents, prepare them for practice in a variety of contexts, and achieve social justice aims. Rutgers established a Social Work and Social Justice Minor, for example.

In addition, large programs may have more bandwidth to create con-nections to university honors and study abroad programs. Large programs may also have multiple gateway courses for recruitment into the social work major that meet the university's undergraduate core requirements, such as the Rutgers "Introduction to Social Work & Social Justice," "Understanding Violence: Causes, Consequences and Social Justice Change," and "Childhood Inequalities" courses, all of which are in the general education program for all undergraduate students in the School of Arts and Sciences. Cross-listed classes are another way to work with other departments. We were successful in doing this with the development of an elective on "Global Health Perspectives."

Given the likelihood that a large program is embedded in a research-oriented university, larger programs have cocurricular opportunities, such as research and curricula assistantships between students and individual faculty and with research centers. This may create special opportunities for large-program directors to obtain assistance with their research and curricula agendas, while offering valued experience and faculty mentoring to students. These could also be paid assistantships, which would provide much-needed income for students.

REFLECTION QUESTIONS:

- Identify the challenges you face to prepare and place BSW students in appropriate field placements. Who leads this effort? How can you support those efforts?

- How does your school recruit and support field supervisors? What training do you provide? How do you recognize their service?

- Are there opportunities for your program to offer relevant electives, especially those that will promote racial justice?

Accreditation, Assessment, and Large BSW Programs

The mission and goals of the BSW program are designed to equip students to empower and serve individuals, families, and communities through generalist practice within a variety of agency and community settings and with diverse populations, including minoritized and vulnerable groups, in the program's region and elsewhere. To ensure the quality of this effort, all BSW programs are required to undergo the accreditation review process, which "provides professional judgments on the quality of social work education programs in institutions and encourages continuous improvement. These findings are based on the Educational Policy and Accreditation Standards (EPAS) developed by the Commission on Accreditation (COA) and the Commission on Educational Policy (COEP)" (CSWE, 2022b, p. 5).

This is a dauting task for any BSW program, and it is especially challenging for large programs that must organize large numbers of program-level, university, and community partners in preparation for writing the self-study and arranging the site visit (see Chapters 3 and 4 for more information on accreditation and assessment). Given the complexity of large BSW programs, start early and be sure to include administrators, faculty, staff, students, agency leaders, alumni, consultants, and others in various trainings, retreats, information sessions, focus groups, and extended periods of writing.

All of this is aimed at getting an accurate review of the program's implicit and explicit curriculum to identify strengths and areas of ongoing improvement in helping students to gain knowledge, values, and skills related to the EPAS competencies. Directors of large BSW programs should coordinate their efforts with the school's lead on outcomes and assessments, because these institutions are more likely to have additional resources and requirements because of their complexity. At Rutgers, the BSW director works with the associate dean of academic affairs, the director of assessments and outcomes, and the school's committee on assessments and outcomes to develop and train faculty on the use of rubrics, design and implement surveys, ensure the distribution and collection of survey data, and examine and disseminate results.

Embedded assignments are selected to assess student attainment of the competencies, as the students meet the criteria for assessment of the competencies, which is done by program-designated faculty. These embedded assignments and field evaluations are used across all program options and at the generalist level. In this way, large BSW programs can ensure consistent ratings across faculty, including fulltime and adjunct. It also helps to keep everyone up to date on accreditation requirements.

REFLECTION QUESTIONS:

- Examine your school's vision and strategic plan and identify creative ways with which you can support this effort.
- What strategies have you developed to prepare your program for the accreditation process, especially the self-study and site visit?
- Who leads the assessments and outcomes efforts at your school? How are you able to contribute to these efforts?

Conclusion

In the previous sections, we have discussed a number of important issues that are particularly relevant to large BSW programs. BSW program directors seeking to lead and manage large programs will face challenges and opportunities involved in course scheduling, managing large numbers of class sections, and recruiting the faculty needed to teach a large number of students. The makeup of the faculty will likely include a mix of full-time faculty, tenured and tenure-track faculty, and nontenured faculty. Further, program directors will be collaborating with and supporting large numbers of part-time lecturers and adjunct faculty. Additionally, an ongoing challenge and opportunity that large BSW programs face has to do with identifying suitable placements for field education and nurturing and sustaining partnerships among the school, agencies, and larger community to provide important support for and essential civic engagement within the community.

Leading and managing a large BSW program can be both challenging and fulfilling. BSW program directors serving in this role must face important responsibilities and discover unique opportunities to prepare students for careers in social work. Program directors from large programs are more likely to be in a large public institution with a colocated MSW program, with a doctoral-granting research classification, and may have been appointed to their role from outside the social work program faculty. It is extremely important for BSW programs to operate with an ADEI lens. Program directors of large BSW programs should work from an ADEI perspective in all matters related to students, organizational structure, curricula essentials, and the unique opportunities and challenges they face in their unique settings. We encourage you to think about what we have covered in this chapter as you consider the following case study.

A BSW Case Study: Dr. Piper Groverton

Dr. Piper Groverton is in her mid-40s and is new to her school's social work program, which is housed in a large public university in the Northeast. In addition to the BSW program, her school also offers an MSW degree and both DSW and PhD degrees. Dr. Groverton, known to her students as Dr. G, was recruited to serve as the BSW program director, joining the faculty from a smaller BSW program in a neighboring state. Her previous program did not have an accompanying MSW program at the institution. Her new BSW program has grown a great deal over the past decade; it is now serving nearly 350 majors and is among the largest majors at her university. Housed in the School of Social Work, the BSW program is offered as a major in the College of Arts and Sciences (CAS), with the BSW program functioning much like a department in CAS in terms of processes. Her new school has a very large MSW program (more than 1,800 students) and a robust advanced standing option.

Dr. G's previous teaching assignments were in the BSW program, and her research focus was in the child welfare arena. She also had limited experience on the BSW curriculum committee at her previous institution. Dr. G. will now teach in both the BSW and MSW programs. In an effort to prepare for her new assignment, she attends sessions at both the CSWE and the Association of Baccalaureate Social Work Program Directors (BPD) conferences.

It occurs to Dr. Groverton that she needs to learn all she can about leading and managing a large BSW program. She needs to learn more about reaching and teaching undergraduate students. She wants to know about recruitment, marketing, and admissions to determine what has contributed to the growth of the program. In making the shift to leading the BSW program, she wants to think more about the organizational structure of the BSW program in her school in relationship to the CAS and within the larger university. She is giving a lot of thought to the curricula essentials in undergraduate social work education and how they relate to the required classes in the MSW program. She is beginning to understand just how important this is to students who will apply as advanced standing students to the MSW program.

Dr. G is genuinely excited about this opportunity, but is feeling a bit overwhelmed as she thinks about all she needs to do. She wonders about meeting the expectations and having the resources to make her work successful. She is also pondering the possible challenges and opportunities of the BSW program. The previous program director offered initial support, but is now on sabbatical teaching abroad as a visiting professor and doing research. Dr. Groverton has met with the dean of her school and the associate dean of academic affairs, both of whom offered their support and broad expectations. She is charged with working with the faculty, staff, and students to create a 3-year strategic plan that advances the BSW program and makes it distinctive from other BSW programs in the area. Dr. Groverton is encouraged and excited about the possibilities of her new assignment, after hearing your presentation on "Leading and Managing a Large BSW Program." She raised several questions both during the Q&A and when she spoke with you after the session. Below are Dr. G's questions. How might you respond to her questions and offer her your support?

CASE STUDY QUESTIONS:

1. What should Dr. G. put on her "first 100 days" list to learn and to do?

2. What does she need to do to learn about the students in her program?

3. What should she learn about her organizational structure and the implications for her work?

4. How can she promote student engagement and build a strong sense of community?

5. What does she need to know about the core BSW curriculum?

6. What can she do to help her school distinguish its BSW program from other programs in the area?

7. Thinking about the content covered in this chapter, what are some of the challenges and opportunities that she might find in her new role?

Suggested Readings

Holley, L. C., Charles, J. L. K., Kondrat, D. C., & Walter-McCabe, H. A. (2020). Supports and gatekeeping: Experiences of schools of social work with students with mental health conditions, *Journal of Social Work Education*. https://doi.org/10.1080/10437797.2020.1798312

Holosko, M., Skinner, J., MacCaughelty, C., & Stahl, K. (2010). Building the implicit BSW curriculum at a large southern state university. *Journal of Social Work Education, 46*(3), 411–423. https://doi.org/10.5175/JSWE.2010.200900068

Love, B. J. (2000). Developing a liberatory consciousness. In M. Adams (Ed.), *Readings for diversity & social justice*, (pp. 470–474). Routledge.

Onyeador, I. N., Hudson, S. T. J., & Lewis, Jr., N. A. (2021). Moving beyond implicit bias training: Policy insights for increasing organizational diversity. *Policy Insights From the Behavioral and Brain Sciences, 8*(1), 19–26. https://doi.org/10.1177/2372732220983840

Special Issue of *The Journal of Teaching in Social Work, 42*(2/3). Challenging anti-Black racism across the social work curriculum.

Steingass, S., & Sykes, S. (2008, Winter). Centralizing advising to improve student outcomes. *Peer Review: Emerging Trends and Key Debates in Undergraduate Education, 10*(1), 18–20.

Unrau, Y., Sherwood, D., & Postema, C. (2020). Financial and educational hardships experienced by BSW and MSW students during their programs of study. *Journal of Social Work Education, 56*(3), 456–473. https://doi.org/10.1080/10437797.2019.1656687

References

Applegate, D. Y., & Hartleroad, G. (2011, March). Effective ways to deal with large advising loads. *Academic Advising Today, 34*(1). https://www.nacada.ksu.edu/Resources/Academic-Advising-Today/ViewArticles/Effective-Ways-to-Deal-with-Large-Advising-Loads.aspx

Battle, D., Curran, L., & Jones, S. (Guest Eds.). (2022). Challenging anti-Black racism across the social work curriculum [Special issue]. *The Journal of Teaching in Social Work, 42*(2/3). https://www.tandfonline.com/toc/wtsw20/42/2-3?nav=tocList

Beadlescomb, T. L. (2019). BSW students of color: Principle factors influencing intent to persist through completion of degree. *Journal of Social Work Education, 55*(2), 215–223. https://doi.org/10.1080/10437797.2018.1544522

Blakely, E., & Gibbs, P. (2000). *Gatekeeping in BSW programs*. Columbia University Press. https://doi.org/10.7312/gibb11050

Bodenheimer, D. (2016, August 25). What's so wrong with social work school? (And how to make it more right). *The New Social Worker*. https://www.socialworker.com/feature-articles/real-world-clinical-sw/whats-so-wrong-with-social-work-school-and-how-to-make-it-more-right/

Bogo, M., & Wayne, J. (2013). The implicit curriculum in social work education: The culture of human interchange, *Journal of Teaching in Social Work, 33*(1), 2–14. https://doi.org/10.1080/08841233.2012.746951

Council on Social Work Education. (2019). *2019 statistics on social work education in the United States: Summary of the CSWE annual survey of social work programs*. https://www.cswe.org/about-cswe/governance/commissions-and-councils/commission-on-research/research-statistics/research-briefs-and-publications/2019-annual-statistics-on-social-work-education-in-the-united-states/

Council on Social Work Education. (2021). *2020 statistics on social work educational programs in the United States: Summary of the CSWE annual survey of social work programs*.

https://www.cswe.org/getattachment/726b15ce-6e63-4dcd-abd1-35d2ea9d9d40/2020
-Annual-Statistics-On-Social-Work-Education-in-the-United-States.pdf?lang=en-US

Council on Social Work Education. (2022a). *Current number of social work programs.*
https://www.cswe.org/Accreditation

Council on Social Work Education. (2022b). *2022 Educational policy and accreditation
standards.* https://www.cswe.org/accreditation/standards/2022-epas/

Curran, L., Battle, D., & Jones, S. (2022). Challenging anti-Black racism across the
curriculum: Situating the social work legacy and moving forward. *Journal of Teaching in
Social Work, 42*(2–3), 102–119. https://doi.org/10.1080/08841233.2022.2074766

Davis, D., Barrick, A., & Talley, K. (2021). "What does this have to do with me?" Black
student perspectives of image-based PowerPoints in BSW classes. *Journal of Social Work
Education, 57*(4), 666–675. https://doi:10.1080/10437797.2020.1713946

Fry, R. (2014, October 7). Cumulative student debt among recent college graduates. *Pew
Research Center.* https://www.pewresearch.org/social-trends/2014/10/07/cumulative-student
-debt-among-recent-college-graduates/

Grand Challenges for Social Work. (2021). *Eliminate racism.* https://grandchallengesforsocialwork
.org/eliminate-racism/

Harper, K. V., Emeritus, J. H. R., & Zook, L. J. (1991). BSW program administration:
Directors' perceptions of their power to manage. *Journal of Social Work Education, 27*(2),
176–186. https://doi.org/10.1080/10437797.1991.10672187

Holley, L. C., Charles, J. L. K., Kondrat., D. C., & Walter-McCabe, H. A. (2020). Supports
and gatekeeping: Experiences of schools of social work with students with mental health
conditions, *Journal of Social Work Education.* https://doi.org/10.1080/10437797.2020
.1798312

Holosko, M., Skinner, J., MacCaughelty, C., & Stahl, K. (2010). Building the implicit BSW
curriculum at a large southern state university. *Journal of Social Work Education, 46*(3),
411–423. https://doi.org/10.5175/JSWE.2010.200900068

Konrady, D., & Battle, D. (2020). Partnering to improve child welfare in New Jersey.
Children's Voice, 29(2), 33–35.

Lambert, C. P., & Siegel, D. H. (2018, September/October). Social workers in higher
education—New roles, new opportunities. *Social Work Today, 18*(5). https://www
.socialworktoday.com/archive/SO18p16.shtml

Love, B. J. (2000). Developing a liberatory consciousness. In M. Adams (Ed.), *Readings for
diversity & social justice* (pp. 470–474). Routledge.

Mapp, S., & Boutté-Queen, N. (2021a). The role of the baccalaureate social work program
director: A qualitative understanding. *Journal of Social Work Education, 57*(1), 127–137.
https://doi.org/10.1080/10437797.2019.1661922

Mapp, S., & Boutté-Queen, N. (2021b). The role of the US baccalaureate social work
program director: A national survey. *Social Work Education, 40*(7), 843–860. https://doi
.org/10.1080/02615479.2020.1729720

National Association of Social Workers. (2007). *Institutional racism & the social work
profession: A call to action.* https://www.socialworkers.org/LinkClick.aspx?fileticket
=SWK1aR53FAk%3D&portalid=0

National Association of Social Workers. (2021). *Code of ethics* (Revised). https://www
.socialworkers.org/About/Ethics/Code-of-Ethics/Code-of-Ethics-English

Onyeador, I. N., Hudson, S. T. J., & Lewis, Jr., N. A. (2021). Moving beyond implicit bias
training: Policy insights for increasing organizational diversity. *Policy Insights From the
Behavioral and Brain Sciences, 8*(1), 19–26. https://doi.org/10.1177/2372732220983840

Perry, A. M., Steinbaum, M., & Romer, C. (2021, June 23). *Student loans, the racial wealth
divide, and why we need full student debt cancellation.* Brookings. https://www.brookings.edu

/research/student-loans-the-racial-wealth-divide-and-why-we-need-full-student-debt
-cancellation/

Rutgers University School of Social Work. (2020). *Toward a more just future: A five-year strategic plan.* https://socialwork.rutgers.edu/about/toward-more-just-future-five-year-strategic-plan

Sanchez Mayers, R., Cuesta, L., Davis, R., & Curran, L. (2020). Developing a program for social work with Latino populations: A case study. *Social Work Education, 39*(4), 445–461. https://doi.org/10.1080/02615479.2019.1660315

Steingass, S., & Sykes, S. (2008, Winter). Centralizing advising to improve student outcomes. *Peer Review: Emerging Trends and Key Debates in Undergraduate Education, 10*(1), 18–20.

University of California San Diego. (2010). *Student academic advising inquiry.* https://academicaffairs.ucsd.edu/_files/ug-ed/uaac/uaac_uc-saai.pdf

Unrau, Y., Sherwood, D., & Postema, C. (2020). Financial and educational hardships experienced by BSW and MSW students during their programs of study. *Journal of Social Work Education, 56*(3), 456–473. https://doi.org/10.1080/10437797.2019.1656687

Zlotnik, J., & Pryce, J. (2013). Status of the use of Title IV-E funding in BSW and MSW programs. *Journal of Public Child Welfare, 7*(4), 430–446. https://doi.org/10.1080/15548732.2013.806278

CHAPTER 10

Windows and Mirrors

Creating a Culture of Inclusivity in Undergraduate Social Work Programs

Tanya Greathouse
Lori Darnel
Consuelo Elizabeth Mendez-Shannon
Judith Kay Nelson

"Human behavior is the product of an endless stream of perceptions, feelings, and thoughts, at both the conscious and unconscious levels. The idea that we are not aware of the cause of much of our behavior can be difficult to accept" (Mlodinow, 2013, p. 16). However, that is exactly the premise with which a reflective leader must start as they provide effective and impactful guidance to a social work program. When leadership is reiterative and culturally driven, the social work program can reflect a system that frames its operations as inclusive and deepens the awareness of collective behavior. Creating a social work program that is inclusive means that educators mirror this process with students through curriculum, teaching, advising, research, and practice, particularly when serving our marginalized populations and vulnerable communities.

Introduction

Emily Style understood that there is more than one way to see the world and that a balanced program requires looking at reality through various window frames. She referred to her mirrors and windows metaphor as "the great conversation between various frames of reference" (Style, 1988,

p. 1). A mirror reflects one's own culture while also helping to form an individual identity; a window is a resource that offers an individual a view into someone else's experience (Style, 1988). This metaphor represents an important process in the foundational work of inclusion because it provides a scaffold for building successful equity-minded programming. The strategies discussed here are not a definitive or exhaustive list of directions but rather provide a framework for a social work program and its director to start the intentional process by assessing an institution's commitment to supporting an inclusive environment in which programmatic leadership models cultural consciousness.

Creating and maintaining an inclusive social work program must involve all aspects of the program, from recruiting and retaining diverse staff to creating program dynamics that focus on anti-oppressive, inclusive policies, operations, and curriculum. Equally important is to ensure that your social work program's vision is aligned with your college or university. Programs should not operate in silos; aligning programs' diversity and inclusivity initiatives with university-wide strategic planning commitments will provide a web of support that can acknowledge and sustain structures for administrators, faculty, and staff. Comprehensive equity and inclusion commitments are often found in institutional strategic plans, and broader organizational assessments are widely available (Racial Equity Tools, 2021).

The foundation of social work education is based on the tenets that reform is necessary within most social systems, making the social work discipline uniquely qualified to understand and implement both incremental and significant changes across the micro, mezzo, and macro levels. According to the 2022 Educational Policy and Accreditation Standards (EPAS) of the Council on Social Work Education (CSWE), "Social workers understand how racism and oppression shape human experiences and how these two constructs influence practice at the individual, family, group, organizational, and community levels and in policy and research. Social workers understand the pervasive impact of White supremacy and privilege and use their knowledge, awareness, and skills to engage in anti-racist practice" (CSWE, 2022, p. 9).

Learning about power, privilege, and oppression is part of the educational fabric within social work programs, and intersecting this knowledge with practice creates an inclusive anti-oppressive discipline. For example, the clinical skills that are the focus of much of the curriculum within social work programs emphasize the important union of understanding the individual while conceptualizing the bigger picture of change. Social workers are trained to understand an individual's motivations for behaviors and capacity for change by extrapolating core principles across multiple theories and paradigms and interpreting their adaptations across social environmental systems and generational history. The social work program, which adopts an inclusive culture that moves social work content fluidly across the micro or macro spectrum, will prepare students for consciously minded, evidence-based practice, seamlessly moving into an anti-oppressive professional practice.

Understanding Historical Context and Cultural Consciousness

> The United States Government does not discriminate in employment on the basis of race, color, religion, sex (including pregnancy, gender identity, and sexual orientation), parental status, national origin, age, disability, genetic information (including family medical history), political affiliation, military service, or other non-merit-based factors. (U.S. Equal Employment Opportunity Commission, 2021)

Title VII of the Civil Rights Act, specifically Section 703, identifies unlawful employment practices that discriminate against an individual for a recognized identity (Civil Rights Act of 1964). Most employers, therefore, adopt an equal employer opportunity statement like the U.S. government's, which explicitly informs applicants, as well as current and future employees, of the employer's efforts to create an inclusive work environment. However, employers still struggle with the meaning of inclusivity and how it can be truly obtained within the workplace.

For years, those in power structures of employment organizations have held on to the idea of being "color-blind" to implement fair-minded practices of hiring, promotion, and termination, as well as daily protocols within the workplace. When membership is assigned based on a race-designated group, it traditionally results in advantages, such as access to citizenship and rights to education and property, or it results in marginalization through enslavement, economic immobility, and segregation (Varghese, 2016).

Openly racist beliefs about White superiority have been replaced by a much more subtle message of color blindness. The ideology of being color-blind, however, maintains a racial hierarchy that has presented itself as much more slippery to define, thereby allowing for justification of the status quo (Bonilla-Silva, 2018). According to Bonilla-Silva (2018), racism is a structure; that is, a network of social relations at social, political, economic, and ideological levels that shapes the life chances of the various races. Color blindness, on the other hand, is a false belief contending that race does not matter and does not play a role in shaping outcomes, thus perpetuating racism and White privilege by not acknowledging and addressing the very real disparities that exist between White people and people of color (Constance-Huggins et al., 2020).

Not only should those practices be called into question, but also the entire notion of being a color-blind society is insulting and dismissive of one's unique, authentic identity; it defeats the intention of treating individuals within a group environment in an equitable manner. The absence of mindful and intentional understanding of an employee's race, ethnicity, religion, gender, sexual orientation, culture, and so on only serves to perpetuate the status quo of the dominant identity within an organization. U.S. Supreme Court Justice Neil Gorsuch stated in the recent ruling of *Bostock v. Clayton County*, 590 U.S. ___ (2020):

> Sometimes small gestures can have unexpected consequences. Major initiatives practically guarantee them. In our time, few pieces of federal legislation rank in significance with the Civil Rights Act of 1964. There, in Title VII, Congress outlawed discrimination in the workplace on the basis of race, color, religion, sex, or national origin. Today, we must decide whether an employer can fire someone simply for being homosexual or transgender. The answer is clear. An employer who fires an individual for being homosexual or transgender fires that person for traits or actions it would not have questioned in members of a different sex. Sex plays a necessary and undisguisable role in the decision; exactly what Title VII forbids.

Extending the notion of civil rights as the law of the land for the first time in decades, arguably, the U.S. Supreme Court is emphasizing the importance of establishing a workplace for a multicultural society.

Truly understanding an organization's culture and norms is key to dismantling hidden assumptions and beliefs that perpetuate the status quo and work against creating an inclusive work environment. Unfortunately, in spite of our aims and values, the history of social work is one that has perpetuated the status quo, and social workers have been collaborators within the organizations and institutions around them, maintaining racism without necessarily realizing it or making an active contribution

(Kivel, 2017). Social work programs need to move past the idea of "not being racist" to actively work with an anti-racism/discrimination agenda that can flourish in the very culture of the program, true to its mission. This is a key concept added to the newest version of EPAS (CSWE, 2022), especially in Standard 2.0, but present through the document.

Assessing Cultural Consciousness

In many ways, organizational culture is invisible—although it can be both conscious and unconscious—even though at the same time, it serves as the glue that binds and builds a sense of cohesion within schools (Teasley, 2016). Preliminary assessment reveals that many social work programs are well aware of the need to address an anti-oppressive culture, as evidenced through examples of mission statements. Consider the following examples:

- *Columbia School of Social Work*—At the Columbia School of Social Work, we believe that systems of racial oppression that impact our engagement across all sectors of society must be studied and challenged in order to dismantle these systems and address inequities across social identities. We are committed to centering race in our pursuit of social justice and anti-oppressive practice. We view this as a guiding principle for our community—using a power, race, oppression and privilege (PROP) framework across our curriculum, administrative practices, operations and personal interactions. Through the PROP lens, we aim to foster brave spaces where students, faculty and staff can engage in critically analyzing and addressing institutionalized racism, multi-systemic inequities and various forms of oppression, thus creating an environment where diversity, equity and inclusion are at the center of our research, scholarship and all interactions with individuals, organizations and communities that we serve. (Columbia School of Social Work, 2020, para. 1)

- *University of Michigan School of Social Work*—Advancing the social work profession's vision and values, the University of Michigan School of Social Work seeks to develop a more equitable, caring, and socially just society. Such a society meets basic human needs, eliminates social and economic inequities, and empowers individuals, their communities, and institutions to reach their aspirations and potential. Drawing on an interdisciplinary faculty within a public university seated in a region of enormous need and promise, the school is dedicated to education, research, and service that fosters progressive change at local, national, and global levels. (University of Michigan School of Social Work, 2021b, para. 2)

Promoting an equitable society, as seen in these mission statement examples from social work programs, demonstrates the widely accepted commitment to inclusion. However, implementing the ideals of equity and inclusion is an ongoing and difficult endeavor, and one that requires intentional action. Undeniably, starting with a strong mission statement is important, and some may even say the process of getting to a strong mission statement is a labor-intensive process. The intensity, however, cannot subside and must focus on the enactment of values, goals, and real-time evaluation of the efforts. In other words, how does a BSW program director answer the following question over and over again: How did we advance our mission of equity, inclusion, and belonging in this task?

A department can answer this question in different ways, though one effective way is by understanding the rituals it develops to promote equity. Rather than thinking of agency—the power to influence and make decisions—as something only individuals possess, the ideal is to have communal rituals that take on the force or power to shape their communicative practices (Driskell et al., 2018). For example, as a program deliberately develops policies and procedures to promote equity and belonging, the shared program culture will eventually expect and reflect such changes. This process of creating strategies to promote this type of cultural organizational change is best appreciated as a reflexive, nonlinear process. While this chapter introduces a few ideas around reflexive exercises and programmatic ideas, it is not an exhaustive list by any means. Therefore, as a program director, it is important to remain current on research, literature, and exercises. Proprietary curriculum and assessments can be helpful but promoting equity in social work programs should not be cost-prohibitive.

The responsibility of social work programs to teach and model the value of social justice and seek to promote sensitivity to and knowledge about oppression and cultural and ethnic diversity (National Association of Social Workers [NASW], 2021) demands thoughtful attention to the culture of a social work program itself. CSWE supports this belief as an ethical principle in its 2022 EPAS, specifically requiring social work education to include advancing human rights and social, racial, economic, and environmental justice (Competency 2). Therefore, social work students must learn how to advocate for human rights at the individual and system levels and engage in practices that advance social, racial, economic, and environmental justice (CSWE, 2015, 2022).

Social work programs are gaining momentum toward a more diverse student body, as enrollment in CSWE-accredited social work programs in 2020 included 49.1% White students, 21.7% African American/Black students, 17% Hispanic/Latinx students, 2.6% Asian American/Pacific Islander students, and 1.1% American Indian/Alaska Native students (CSWE, 2021, p. 3). However, anecdotally, within the profession, many social workers hold a similar intersectionality of being White women, often with some economic means. As of 2015, 83% of social workers were women and almost 70% were White. So, fewer than 20% are not female and fewer than 30% are non-White (Salsberg et al., 2017). Therefore, it becomes even more critical to intentionally assess a social work program from a structural perspective and endorse a culturally inclusive curriculum across its micro, mezzo, and macro aspects to prepare the next generation of social work professionals. Inviting diversity of both social identities and thought requires attention to inclusivity within the program.

BOX 10.1

Preparing Your Program for Diversity, Equity, and Inclusion Work

Following the preliminary stage of establishing/revising a mission statement that is intentionally inclusive, it is important to assess the program's starting stage. To express the intention to engage in diversity, equity, and inclusion work with the entire BSW program, start by asking key reflective questions:

- Is this a value within the university?
- Is this a value within the program?
- What does a more inclusive program look like?
- What theories, definitions, and terminology guide us as a program?
- What resources do we have within the program to start this process?
- What resources do we need from the university to start this process?
- Are there other areas we need to pursue before moving forward?

These discussions create collective experiences as the group shares individual interpretations about the topic of diversity, equity, and inclusion at a programmatic level alongside an examination of how to achieve an internal sense of belonging.

Inclusion as a Sense of Belonging

Inclusion stands apart from diversity and equity in that those precepts are concrete; they can be set in policy, quantified, and measured. An inclusive environment, as defined by the University of Michigan School of Social Work, however, represents more than its quantifiable aspects. An inclusive environment:

> fosters a culture of belonging by bringing and empowering traditionally excluded voices into decision-making processes. Inclusion mandates the establishment of a balance of power and shared rights.... . Inclusive spaces are empowering environments where each voice is valued and supported to actively participate through purposeful, deliberate, and authentic efforts. (University of Michigan School of Social Work, 2021a, para. 6)

The quality of "belonging," which anchors this definition, represents a more fragile and elusive dimension of inclusion. It is an interpersonal one that comes to the heart of the entire trinity; that is, inclusion in the sense of how comfortable and welcoming the seat at the organizational table feels to marginalized individuals. In other words, how valued and respected does each person feel (Ohio State University Center for the Advancement of Teaching, 2020)?

One newly emerging method for programs to recognize the distinction between administrative inclusion and a subjective sense of belonging, and to prioritize the latter, is by creating an administrative position that focuses on "belonging." For example, Pepperdine University recently appointed an assistant dean of student life, diversity, and belonging, and Harvard has a newly appointed associate dean of students for inclusion and belonging. The University of California at Berkeley established an Othering and Belonging Institute (2012), which brings together a multidisciplinary team of faculty from diverse fields committed to a vision "centered on realizing a world where all people belong" and to celebrating our "inherent interconnectedness" aimed at "building an Ecosystem of Belonging" (para. 2).

The opposite of belonging is exclusion. In a study of exclusion in Canadian schools, Dei and James (2002) wrote, "It isn't just the responsibility of institutions to merely name those who are different," but rather to seek "to understand their everyday lived social and cultural reality" (pp. 64–65). The hurt caused by exclusion is well understood and shared by all going back to the pain of being excluded from a kindergarten birthday party or of not being picked for a baseball team. Studies in the neurosciences have found that the pain of exclusion is similar to physical pain. In one such study, participants were scanned while playing a virtual balltossing game from which they were eventually excluded. During social exclusion, brain scans revealed a "pattern of activations similar to those found in studies of physical pain ... providing evidence that the experience and regulation of social and physical pain share a common neuroanatomical basis" (Eisenberger et al., 2003, p. 291). Pain, they articulated, "acts as a neural 'alarm system'" and serves as the "most primitive signal that something is wrong" (Eisenberger et al., 2003, p. 291).

Focusing on the institutional- and program-level culture of inclusion underpins the more basic concept of how individuals, at all levels within the program, experience belonging or exclusion. As a social work program director leads the unit to making the intentional commitment to being more welcoming and ensuring belonging, basic models of program development should be followed, beginning with an assessment of the program as a whole as well as individual administration, faculty, and staff.

What to Assess

Equity work requires a thoughtful approach, especially when laying the groundwork for a program and inviting individuals to be vulnerable in the process. Therefore, it is important to determine the level of cultural consciousness or awareness of the entire program as well as individual participants. There are a number of assessment tools that can help measure cultural consciousness and ensure that a social work program is proceeding in an evidence-based manner. Be sure to address several aspects, including but not limited to the following:

- *Common language of equity*—Social work program faculty should agree on definitions of terms for equity work. The language of diversity, equity, and inclusion is fluid and rapidly changing, thus the need to identify the relevant terminology.

- *Create ground rules*—Social work program directors and faculty need to create an environment that enables individuals to practice their reflexive muscles without shame or blame.

Assessment Tools

The following tools can help you gain an understanding of the level of cultural consciousness or awareness within your unit.

THE INTERCULTURAL DEVELOPMENT INVENTORY

Kruse et al. (2014) suggested that program directors committed to supporting their program's development in building culturally conscious policies, programming, curriculum, faculty, staff, and students may choose to invest in an inventory assessment to help individuals understand how they want to demonstrate cultural consciousness and how they are interacting across cultural differences. The Intercultural Development Inventory (IDI) is an assessment tool that is not a stand-alone intervention but rather designed to be used in conjunction with other activities to promote cultural consciousness (DeJaeghere & Cao, 2009; Fitzgerald & Marzalik, 2018; IDI, 2019; Kruse et al., 2014; Paige et al., 2003).

The IDI is designed to support and facilitate interventions to improve cultural consciousness, as well as provide quantitative evidence of the effectiveness of various interventions. The IDI assesses the ability to engage with cultural differences and give individualized or group feedback. The feedback is given by trained and licensed "Qualified Administrators," who attend 15 hours of training over 3 days. As of August 2022, the website for the IDI lists the cost for training as $2,000, with a discount for educational institutes of $400.

The inventory is built on Bennett's five-stage continuum of cultural development from denial to adaptation, proposing the process of learning and self-awareness for participants (Organizing Engagement, 2021). Individuals in the first stage—denial—are those whose understanding of cultural differences is limited and who support a worldview of denying cultural differences. As individuals begin to have more experiences with differences, in the second stage—polarization—they may either overvalue their own culture while devaluing others or devalue their own culture while overvaluing others.

The third stage of cultural development on the IDI continuum is minimization, which is marked by individuals recognizing cultural differences while minimizing the impact of history, power, oppression, and privilege on various populations. The fourth stage is acceptance, wherein individuals recognize cultural differences and appreciate the complexity of how one's social identities inform their cultural experiences. Adaptation is the fifth stage, representing a worldview that allows the individual to engage differentially with others in appreciation of one's cultural identification.

The IDI has been a valuable tool when used in conjunction with interventions intended to facilitate critical discussions that engage in self-reflection. Programs vested in promoting organizational or programmatic cultural inclusivity should emphasize the importance of increasing "cultural self-understanding, including awareness around power and privilege as well as other patterns of cultural difference (e.g., conflict resolution styles), culture-general frameworks (e.g., individualism/collectivism), and culture-specific patterns" (IDI, 2019, p. 12). The next step in this process is developing shared culturally conscious language, which is necessary when engaging in critical discussions around race, immigration status, gender, sexual orientation, religion, class, and other social identities.

HARVARD IMPLICIT ATTITUDE TESTS

When program leadership, faculty, and staff take two or three Harvard Implicit Attitude Tests (Lehr & Banaji, 2001), conversations can ensue on the detrimental effects of unprocessed implicit biases. After everyone has taken the tests and had an opportunity to reflect on the results, they should engage in critical discussions about how implicit stereotypes affect individuals' lives. It is essential that people whose intersectional identities provide them with a more privileged positionality understand that their privilege allows them to be unaware of the effects of implicit stereotypes that develop from unprocessed implicit biases.

Style's concept of windows and mirrors helps explain the utility of this activity by allowing individuals to identify and understand the implications of their biases, moving from a *window* perspective to appreciating their *mirror* involvement: "How is it a 'mirror' of something familiar? How is it a 'window' into something new?" (Style, 1996, p. 1). Broadening this view to include all intersectional identities—privileged and marginalized—provides a foundation for faculty, staff, and leadership to begin engaging in program initiatives that encourage cultural consciousness building.

Developing a Culturally Conscious Social Work Program

The EPAS contains nine competencies that guide social work education (CSWE, 2022). As noted, Competency 3 describes the need for social workers to engage in "how racism and oppression shape human experiences and how these two constructs influence practice at the individual, family, group, organizational, and community levels and policy and research" (p. 9). Understanding how discrimination characterizes and shapes the human experience on a micro, mezzo, and macro level informs cultural humility, self-awareness, and self-regulation when engaging in work with diverse populations. Competency 3 stresses the importance of understanding the multiple dimensions of diversity as defined by intersectionality (the diverse dimensions of self based on a multiplicity of factors including but not limited to age, class, race/ethnicity, ability, gender, sex, sexual orientation, immigration status, and veteran status) viewed through a lens that incorporates privilege, oppression, and marginalized dynamics (Crenshaw, 2017).

The social work profession is built on a set of core values that recognize the "dignity and worth of the person," "the importance of human relationships," and "social justice" (NASW, 2021). These values are supported by required competencies through the CSWE. To promote the best application of social workers in the helping process and to recognize the necessity for advocacy on behalf of clients, BSW program directors need to ensure that their programs are infused with these core values, which acknowledge the individual's right to self-determination and encourage a nonjudgmental stance of others. These core values undergird the entire social work curriculum, whether the content relates to policy, human development, or working with organizations or social systems. Program leaders play a central role in guiding and supporting organizational development. They need to reflect the values and behaviors they want to see demonstrated in their programs.

When envisioning an inclusive environment, programs sometimes focus on diversifying the faculty and staff by hiring individuals who look different from the majority race. More broadly, however, inclusion acknowledges and encompasses intersectionality across the identity spectrum and requires cultural adaptation that acknowledges, accepts, and practices culturally conscious leadership and communication styles. Diversity does not automatically produce inclusion, and fostering each within a program requires deliberate strategies (Tienda, 2013).

A social work program director is primed to focus on organizational culture and its capacity to be inclusive. Even though the term *inclusion* tends to create an image of equity and diversity, it requires a closer look at the systemic experiences within the organization as well as intentional action to create inclusivity. "Social workers have to examine how their personal stories affect meaning construction when interacting with clients and be curious about the assumptions behind formal and practice theories" (Leung, et al. 2012, p. 57). Therefore, in addition to the theories and paradigms mentioned, a key focus is to evaluate how a social work program's collective culture and guiding principles incorporate the myriad evidence-based theories of equity, inclusion, and belonging for faculty and administration. Social work programs need to be built on a framework that scaffolds organizationally inclusive initiatives, allowing for reflecting on and revising strategies to actively promote cultural consciousness.

"Critical racial and cultural consciousness should be coupled with self-reflection in both … teacher education and in-service staff development" (Gay & Kirkland, 2003, p. 181) to encourage inclusive institutional cultures. Inclusive program cultures adapt and form anti-oppressive strategies such as reframing communication styles and organizational artifacts. These outcomes reflect inclusivity that weaves in and represents collective diverse social identities. Working toward a culture of inclusivity calls on program leaders to adapt their approach to activate anti-racist and anti-oppressive strategies. Infusing anti-oppressive leadership, which reflects a collective organizational structure, with anti-oppressive pedagogical content across the curriculum ultimately demonstrates a social work program's commitment to social, racial, and economic justice (Constance-Huggins et al., 2020).

Implementing Plans

Emily Style used her windows and mirrors to demonstrate a balancing of self-reflection with a multiculturally inclusive view. She recognized:

> the common sense of needing to provide both windows and mirrors … may seem unnecessary to emphasize, and yet recent scholarship on women and men of color attests abundantly to the copious blind spots … white males find … many mirrors to look in, and few windows which frame others' lives. Women and men of color, on the other hand, find almost no mirrors of themselves …; for them it is often all windows (Style, 1988, p. 4).

As noted above, many change processes are nonlinear. Addressing organizational growth is "an ongoing and dynamic developmental process with no endpoint—one that requires active, critical, and purposeful engagement on the part of the social worker entering the helping relationship" (Azzopardi & McNeill, 2016, p. 289). The first stage of this process involves introspection, building on individual awareness and self-reflection. The second stage focuses on supporting a culturally conscious program environment. The third stage involves building inclusive programming that demonstrates the intentional infusion of culturally aware initiatives to support a culture of inclusivity including programmatic policies and curriculum.

Each stage is dynamic, and reflexive reworking is based on assessing the effective strategies, listening to feedback, and redesigning programming as needed. This process is informed by continual organizational growth, critical conversations, the accrual of knowledge, and critical individual reflection that promote cultural shifts and structural changes, bringing into focus the constantly changing larger society within which the program is situated.

A culturally conscious, inclusive social work program begins with introspection by everyone involved in developing the program. As Ibram X. Kendi (2019) explained, to promote inclusivity and dismantle oppressive policies, one must engage in ongoing self-reflection: "Like fighting an addiction, being an antiracist requires persistent self-awareness, constant self-criticism, and regular self-examination" (p. 23). A key step is individual introspection that encourages critical self-reflection of how one is taught to recognize and respond to differences. Individuals need to work on recognizing how their implicit biases may produce negative stereotypes and/or reactions to cultural differences.

Individual Awareness and Self-Reflection

Individual introspection involves a scaffolded approach, starting with identifying and articulating one's intersectional identity. Having all program members identify, articulate, and share their intersectionality will build a foundation for appreciating how privilege dynamics and oppressive dynamics shape an individual's identity. For example, individuals can start seeing how their race may carry privilege, but their ability status has exposed them to oppressive or discriminatory practices. Table 10.1 provides a chart of social identities. This is not an exhaustive list of social identities but simply a starting place for each program to begin thinking about what diversity looks like in their community.

Once individuals have filled out their chart, it is important to engage them in conversations about what they learned regarding their intersectional selves. As they identify their privileged and marginalized statuses, an exercise that is useful in this process is called practicing intersectional introductions (Greathouse, 2020). Program directors may encourage individuals to identify their social identities while reflecting on how these identities hold privileged and/or marginalized statuses, though this should be framed in a way that people do not feel pressured to share more than they are comfortable. Sharing these insights with one another might be a community-building exercise. The program director may find value in identifying commonalities and differences among individuals as the director builds a diverse program that appreciates the sense of belonging commonalities may create and valuing creativity that diversity may promote.

TABLE 10.1

Social Identities Chart

Social Identity Categories	Privileged Status	Marginalized Status
Race		
Class		
Gender		
Sexual orientation		
Ability		
Religion		
Age		
Immigration status		
Primary language		
Education		
Other		

Windows and Mirrors Exercise

Using Style's (1988) framework, this exercise promotes group reflection and perspective. Begin by offering items for participants to examine. The items can be photographs of cultural experiences or life events, or cultural artifacts reflecting global meanings (not just local references), for example. After providing time to consider all the items, ask the participants to choose one item and to consider these questions reflectively: Using the metaphor of the window, what do you see looking in? Using the metaphor of the mirror, how does the item relate to you? In this exercise, the item will prompt reflection to function as both a window and a mirror, to "reflect and reveal" both a multicultural world and the individual—to look through window frames to see the realities of others and into mirrors to see the individual's own reality reflected (p. 1).

You can devise additional reflective prompts to expand the window and mirror metaphors. This exercise can be done in pairs, too. Encourage the participants to delve deeply about how the item relates to each person or what they have newly learned. For example, participants might be reminded of memories while processing the initial reflective questions. Debriefing as a larger group, faculty and staff are encouraged to share in a manner comfortable for the participants. Likewise, program directors who create this type of welcoming environment can continue to support, mentor, and coach participants as they anchor and build their reflection and personal examination.

Culturally Conscious Programming

Having all program employees—administrators, faculty, and staff—engage in cultural consciousness training builds the groundwork for developing individual cultural integrity and consciousness. These trainings need to be developed and agreed on by your faculty, staff, and leadership. The following are examples of activities to help frame programmatic trainings: book clubs, current events discussions, pedagogy and diversity workshops, and affinity groups.

Book clubs: Create a book club where individuals can read books about the history of racism (e.g., Kendi, 2016), white privilege (e.g., DiAngelo, 2018), understanding the social construct of race and ethnicity (e.g., Gomez, 2020), or dismantling oppression (e.g., Kivel, 2017). If program dollars permit, purchase the books for members. Members should set a meeting schedule to discuss what they have learned and they will do as a result of this new knowledge. Discussions can also be centered around videos, documentaries, and pictures, which participants can process through discussions.

Current events discussions: Bring in accounts of current events and discuss using a critical conversation framework (Kang & O'Neill, 2018), where group members co-create group norms. All members of culturally inclusive social work programs must know how to facilitate critical discussions related to oppressive, discriminatory interactions and behaviors. These discussions should be grounded in call-in cultural values (see next paragraph) that support brave space conversations. As Brené Brown (2012) explained, it is important to create brave, courageous spaces that encourage vulnerability.

To create these types of spaces, practice being curious while asking clarifying questions, withholding judgment, and calling in instead of calling out. "Call-out culture [is] the act of publicly shaming another person for behavior deemed unacceptable. Calling out may be described as a sister to dragging, cousin to problematic, and one of the many things that can add up to cancellation" (Bennett, 2020, para. 5). Dismissing and silencing those who do not agree with the majority view or one's personal view is another example of calling out.

Pedagogy and diversity workshops: These workshops are meant to give faculty a "facilitated space to discuss how issues of diversity, social identity, and oppression influence their teaching, the classroom environment, student interactions, and the overall campus climate" (Garran et al., 2014, p. 564). These facilitated workshops encourage faculty to share using a group format that invites varying perspectives, sharing tools of the trade, and valuable peer support.

Affinity groups: Affinity groups are "formed around a shared identity or common goal to build community among members of non-dominant groups and to foster inclusion and awareness in the broader university" (Loyola University Maryland Office of Academic Affairs, 2020, para. 2). Affinity groups are one way to provide a secure base for underrepresented, diverse faculty; this base is also a place for them to return to as they navigate challenges in their programs. Underrepresented faculty may experience feelings of isolation, imposter syndrome, and differential treatment as they work toward tenure and leadership positions. To combat these issues, affinity groups are a way for these faculty members to raise a collective voice about program, college, and university concerns.

Regardless of activity, when creating an inclusive programmatic culture, prioritize cultural consciousness building among all members of the program. Cultural consciousness reflects individuals' critical awareness and analysis of the world, and their willingness and ability to take action against oppressive practices. Additionally, there exists a positive and dynamic correlation between leaders' and followers' levels of intercultural sensitivity in organizational change. An individual's level of intercultural sensitivity is reflected in their ability to work with different cultures. Matkin and Barbuto (2012) found that increasing supervisors' intercultural sensitivity predicted positive changes in supervisee intercultural sensitivity. Hence, as stated earlier, program directors are in a unique position to take the lead and frame this process.

Maintaining and Sustaining Cultural Consciousness

Equity work is challenging and collectively humbling. Therefore, a program director should be well prepared when stepping into this space. Any effort to implement programming needs to be intentional and sustained; there is no "one and done" in equity work. Equally important is the system of resources and support available and accessible on and around campus. Remember to focus on the brave space created to have these difficult conversations, leaning into the uncomfortable.

Program directors should set aside time at the beginning and end of each semester to set and assess inclusivity goals. Formal and informal evaluations at the end of each semester should be done to determine if the goals have been met. The feedback should then inform goals for the next semester (Box 10.2).

BOX 10.2

Example of Measurable Goals Supporting Sustainability

1. Structural or programmatic
   a. Develop spaces for staff and faculty to discuss what inclusivity looks like in your program.
   b. Develop a book club or movie club to read books or watch movies about diversity and equity.
2. Pedagogical
   a. Organize and hold regular pedagogy and diversity spaces.
   b. Develop a resource library with diverse authors.
3. Interpersonal growth and self-growth
   a. Research cultural assessments for staff and faculty to take.
   b. Invest in staff and faculty taking cultural assessments.

Conclusion

The social work profession and social work schools exist in a racist, capitalist, and classist society. Social work training institutions are almost exclusively in predominantly White educational systems. As social work educators, we have long known about the need to reach out and broaden social work programs' identification with marginalized cultures by recognizing the need for and working toward diversity in faculty and administration to reflect the communities served. We have stood up for social justice and equity against the forces of institutional racism within social work schools, community agencies, communities served, and the government. We have taught and shown by example that social workers are allies, accomplices, advocates, and partners in the social and economic struggles of clients, students, and the communities that social workers serve. Social work programs must therefore work diligently at developing an inclusive work setting where all people are represented; all voices have power; differences are recognized and valued; and students, faculty, and staff are not only included in the educational culture and process but also feel that they belong to a community that welcomes and values them.

Suggested Readings

Dee, T., & Gershenson, S. (2017). Unconscious bias in the classroom: Evidence and opportunities. *Google's Computer Science Education Research*. https://services.google.com/fh/files/misc/unconscious-bias-in-the-classroom-report.pdf

Gómez, L. E. (2022). *Inventing Latinos: A new story of American racism*. The New Press.

Kendi, I. X. (2019). *How to be an antiracist*. One World.

Kivel, P. (2017). *Uprooting racism: How white people can work for racial justice*. New Society Publishers.

McGhee, H. (2021). *Sum of us: What racism costs everyone and how we can prosper together*. One World.

Strayhorn, T. L. (2012). *College students' sense of belonging: A key to educational success for all students*. Routledge.

References

Azzopardi, C., & McNeill, T. (2016). From cultural competence to cultural consciousness: Transitioning to a critical approach to working across differences in social work. *Journal of Ethnic & Cultural Diversity in Social Work*, *25*(4), 282–299. https://doi.org/10.1080/15313204.2016.1206494

Bennett, J. (2020, November 19). What if instead of calling people out, we called them in? *The New York Times*. https://www.nytimes.com/2020/11/19/style/loretta-ross-smith-college-cancel-culture.html

Bonilla-Silva, E. (2018). *Racism without racists: And the persistence of racial inequality in America*. Rowman & Littlefield.

Bostock v. Clayton County, 590 U.S. ___ (2020);140 S. Ct. 1731; 207 L. Ed. 2d 218; 2020 WL 3146686; 2020 U.S. LEXIS3252.

Brown, B. (2012). *Daring greatly: How the courage to be vulnerable transforms the way we live, love, parent, and lead*. Gotham Books.

Civil Rights Act of 1964 § 7, 42 U.S.C. § 2000e et seq (1964).

Columbia School of Social Work. (2020). *Social work mission statement*. https://socialwork.columbia.edu/about/dei/dei-mission-statement/

Constance-Huggins, M., Davis, A., & Yang, J. (2020). Race still matters. *Advances in Social Work*, *20*(1), 132–151. https://doi.org/10.18060/22933

Council on Social Work Education. (2015). *Educational and policy accreditation standards*. https://www.cswe.org/getattachment/Accreditation/Accreditation-Process/2015-EPAS/2015EPAS_Web_FINAL.pdf.aspx

Council on Social Work Education. (2021). *2020 statistics on social work education in the United States*. https://www.cswe.org/getattachment/726b15ce-6e63-4dcd-abd1-35d2ea9d9d40/2020-Annual-Statistics-On-Social-Work-Education-in-the-United-States.pdf?lang=en-US

Council on Social Work Education. (2022). *Educational and policy accreditation standards*. https://www.cswe.org/accreditation/standards/2022-epas/

Crenshaw, K. (2017). *On intersectionality: Essential writings*. The New Press.

Dei, G. J. S., & James, I. M. (2002). Beyond the rhetoric: Moving from exclusion, reaching for inclusion in Canadian schools. *The Alberta Journal of Educational Research*, *48*(1), 61–87.

DiAngelo, R. J. (2018). *White fragility: Why it's so hard for White people to talk about racism*. Beacon Press.

DeJaeghere, J., & Cao, Y. (2009). Developing U.S. teachers' intercultural competence: Does professional development matter? *International Journal of Intercultural Relations, 33*(5), 437–447. https://doi.org/10.1016/j.ijintrel.2009.06.004

Driskell, G., Chatham-Carpenter, A., & McIntyre, K. (2018). The power of a mission: Transformations of a program culture through social constructionist principles. *Innovative Higher Education, 44*(1), 69–83. https://doi.org/10.1007/s10755-018-9449-8

Eisenberger, N. I., Lieberman, M. D., & Williams, K. D. (2003). Does rejection hurt? An fMRI study of social exclusion. *Science, 302*(2003), 290–292. https://doi.org/10.1126/science.1089134

Fitzgerald, E., & Marzalik, P. (2018). Assessing intercultural development pre- and post-education abroad. *Journal of Nursing Education, 57*(12), 747–750. https://doi.org/10.3928/01484834-20181119-08

Garran, A. M., Kang, H., & Fraser, E. (2014). Pedagogy and diversity: Enrichment and support for social work instructors engaged in social justice education. *Journal of Teaching in Social Work, 34*(5), 564–574.

Gay, G., & Kirkland, K. (2003). Developing cultural critical consciousness and self-reflection in preservice teacher education. *Theory Into Practice, 42*(3), 181–187.

Gómez, L. E. (2022). *Inventing Latinos: A new story of American racism*. The New Press.

Greathouse, T. (2020). Promoting multicultural humility: A strategy for building a foundational building block for multiculturally informed supervision. *Reflections: Narratives of Professional Helping, 26*(2), 101–106.

The Intercultural Development Inventory (IDI). (2019). *IDI general information: The Intercultural Development Inventory® (IDI®)*. https://idiinventory.com/generalinformation/the-intercultural-development-inventory-idi/

Kang, H. K., & O'Neill, P. (2018). Teaching note—Constructing critical conversations: A model for facilitating classroom dialogue for critical learning. *Journal of Social Work Education, 54*(1), 187–193.

Kendi, I. X. (2017). *Stamped from the beginning*. Avalon.

Kendi, I. X. (2019). *How to be an antiracist*. One World.

Kivel, P. (2017). *Uprooting racism: How White people can work for racial justice* (4th ed.). New Society.

Kruse, J., Didion, J., & Perzynski, K. (2014). Utilizing the Intercultural Development Inventory® to develop intercultural competence. *SpringerPlus, 3*(1), 1–8. https://doi.org/10.1186/2193-1801-3-334

Lehr, S., & Banaji, M. (2001). *Implicit Association Test (IAT)*. http://oxfordbibliographiesonline.com/view/document/obo-9780199828340/obo-9780199828340-0033.xml

Leung, G., Lam, D., Chow, A., Wong, D., Chung, C., & Chan, B. (2012). Cultivating reflexivity in social work students: A course-based experience. *Journal of Practice Teaching & Learning, 11*, 54–74.

Loyola University Maryland Office of Academic Affairs. (2020). *Affinity groups*. https://www.loyola.edu/program/academic-affairs/equity-inclusion/affinity

Matkin, G., & Barbuto, J. (2012). Demographic similarity/difference, intercultural sensitivity, and leader–member exchange: A multilevel analysis. *Journal of Leadership & Organizational Studies, 19*(3), 294–302. https://doi.org/10.1177/1548051812442748

Mlodinow, L. (2013). *Subliminal: How your unconscious mind rules your behavior*. Vintage.

National Association of Social Workers. (2021). *Preamble to the NASW Code of Ethics*. https://www.socialworkers.org/About/Ethics/Code-of-Ethics/Code-of-Ethics-English

Ohio State University Center for the Advancement of Teaching. (2020). *Sense of belonging in the college classroom*. https://ucat.osu.edu/bookshelf/teaching-topics/shaping-a-positive-learning-environment/sense-of-belonging-in-the-college-classroom/

Organizing Engagement. (2021). *Developmental model of intercultural sensitivity.* https://organizingengagement.org/models/developmental-model-of-intercultural-sensitivity/

Othering and Belonging Institute. (2012). *Vision statement.* https://belonging.berkeley.edu/vision

Paige, R., Jacobs-Cassuto, M., Yeshiva, Y., & DeJaeghere, J. (2003). Assessing intercultural sensitivity: An empirical analysis of the Hammer and Bennett Intercultural Development Inventory. *International Journal of Intercultural Relations, 27*(4), 467–486. https://doi.org/10.1016/S0147-1767(03)00034-8

Racial Equity Tools. (2021). *Organizational assessment tools and resources.* https://www.racialequitytools.org/resources/plan/informing-the-plan/organizational-assessment-tools-and-resources

Salsberg, E., Quigley, L., Mehfoud, N., Acquaviva, K., Wyche, K., & Sliwa, S. (2017). *Profile of the social work workforce.* https://www.socialworkers.org/LinkClick.aspx?fileticket=wCttjrHq0gE%3d&portalid=0

Style, E. (1988). Curriculum as a window and mirror. *Nationalseedproject.org.* https://nationalseedproject.org/Key-SEED-Texts/curriculum-as-window-and-mirror

Style, E. (1996). Resources and strategies for doing window and mirror curriculum work. *Nationalseedproject.org.* https://nationalseedproject.org/Key-SEED-Texts/resources-and-strategies-for-doing-window-and-mirror-curriculum-work

Teasley, M. L. (2016). Organizational culture and schools: A call for leadership and collaboration. *Children & Schools, 39*(1), 3–6. https://doi.org/10.1093/cs/cdw048

Tienda, M. (2013). Diversity ≠ inclusion: Promoting integration in higher education. *Educational Researcher, 42*(9), 467–475. https://doi.org/10.3102/0013189X13516164

U.S. Equal Opportunity Commission. (2021). *Equal employment opportunity policy.* https://www.eeoc.gov/eeo-policy-statement

University of Michigan School of Social Work. (2021a). *Diversity, equity, and inclusion.* https://ssw.umich.edu/offices/diversity-equity-inclusion

University of Michigan School of Social Work. (2021b). *Mission.* https://ssw.umich.edu/about/ssw-advantage/mission

Varghese, R. (2016). Teaching to transform? Addressing race and racism in the teaching of clinical social work practice. *Journal of Social Work Education, 52(Sup 1)*, S134–S147. https://doi.org/10.1080/10437797.2016.1174646

CHAPTER 11

Technology for the Effective Management of BSW Programs

Laurel Iverson Hitchcock

This chapter provides a big picture view of educational technology in social work education, focusing what a baccalaureate program director needs to know about the purposes of, and reasons to use, different types of digital technology to support administrative and educational functions in higher education. This chapter will also offer a framework by which to understand the role of technology in BSW programs as well as practical approaches to implementation. Finally, the chapter is organized in relation to the Educational Policies and Accreditation Standards (EPAS) of the Council on Social Work Education (CSWE, 2022), offering examples of how technology can be used to support the explicit and implicit curricula as well as program assessment for the BSW program. While the possibilities are almost endless, attention will be given to the most relevant and available digital and social technologies for educational programs.

Because technology is now ubiquitous in higher education, there are more potential topics than space in this chapter, which means that some topics will not be covered here. For example, ethical concerns and inclusive practices will be mentioned, but an in-depth review of ethics and technology in social work education is beyond the scope of this chapter. Readers interested in learning more about developing and managing an online BSW program should refer to Chapter 7 in this book. Last, although the inclusion of technology as a content area to be taught in BSW programs is essential (e.g., how to conduct a telehealth session), this content could fill an entire book or, minimally, an entire chapter on its own.

Readers interested in the development of course content specific to the use of technology in social work practice should start with the Technology Standards of the National Association of Social Workers (NASW, 2017) and expand their inquiry from there. Finally, this chapter is not a guide on how to use the different types of technology covered; software and hardware are constantly being updated, and any user of a specific type of digital or social technology needs time and training to fully and effectively engage with that product.

Why Does the BSW Program Director Need to Understand Technology?

Briefly, BSW program directors need to make decisions about technology integration in their programs, and these decisions should be practical, pedagogically sound, fiscally responsible, and ethical (Hitchcock et al., 2019). To be clear, these decisions are not about if or even when to bring technology into a BSW program, but why and how a BSW program director would make these decisions. There is more than 10 years of research in the social work literature supporting the use of online delivery systems for social work content and skills (Cummings et al., 2013; Forgey & Ortega-Williams, 2016; Vernon et al., 2009). Many social work educators and administrators acknowledge the role of technology in the design and delivery of competency-based social work education. The profession's major professional organizations—CSWE, NASW, and the Association of Social Work Boards (ASWB)—all have updated their standards and regulations to include guidance for the ethical and competent use of technology in social work education (ASWB, 2015; CSWE, 2022; NASW, 2017, 2021).

Further, the upheavals from the COVID-19 pandemic show the need for social work educators to be able to shift from seated classrooms to emergency remote teaching to maintain the learning gains and professional development of individual students (CSWE, 2020). With awareness and careful planning, BSW directors can indeed integrate technology into their programs in ways that meet the educational and administrative needs of students, faculty, and staff.

BSW directors should also consider how digital technologies provide opportunities for networking and leadership. To make decisions about technology, today's BSW program director needs to keep up to date on trends and research related to the use of digital and social technologies for instructional and administrative purposes as well as the educational, practice, and regulatory standards in social work education about the effective and ethical use of technology, a monumental task with the fast-paced change of technology in today's world (CSWE, 2022; NASW, 2017). Data from student learning outcomes can also inform these technology integration decisions, and through the use of digital technology itself, social work education now has the opportunity to use big data sets to inform what to teach when and for how long (Robbins et al., 2016).

Because many digital and social technologies require significant financial and human capital costs, such as annual software subscriptions and training of faculty on how to design effective online learning modules within a specific platform, having a network of other BSW program directors to ask questions and from whom one can get practical advice is invaluable. Finally, recent scholarship shows that a digital presence is essential for leaders of all types (Cortellazzo et al., 2019; Sage et al., 2021). This is known as digital leadership, and BSW program directors can use digital platforms such as Twitter or LinkedIn to communicate with stakeholders, model ethical social work practice with technology, and even advocate for institutional or systemic changes (Ahlquist, 2020).

Frameworks for Technology Integration

Now that the question of why BSW program directors need to understand technology has been addressed, the next essential topic is how to successfully integrate technology into a BSW program. Again, the answer to this question could fill a book, and there is no one right way to do it, as many factors affect implementation plans, such as institutional support; quantity and quality of software and hardware programs; and capacity of students, faculty, and staff. What can be helpful is to adopt an integration framework that informs and guides one's approach to making decisions about the role of technology in an undergraduate social work program.

It should go without saying that the NASW Code of Ethics (NASW, 2021) and the NASW, ABSW, CSWE, & CSWA Standards for Technology in Social Work Practice (hereafter, referred to as the Practice Standards for Technology; NASW, 2017) offer ethical frameworks to guide technology integration. For example, the profession's value of social justice requires that BSW program directors work to ensure that all students have access to the hardware and software needed for their education. This is also supported by Standard 4.0.8 of the Practice Standards for Technology, which states that social work educators who use technology should make sure that students have access to the technical support needed to effectively use the hardware and software (NASW, 2017).

Figure 11.1 lists all 12 standards from the Practice Standards for Technology on the use of technology for social work education and supervision. These standards provide an ethical framework for BSW program directors when considering the role of technology in their programs. For example, Standard 4.0.6 focuses on the importance of managing technological disruptions that may impede the educational process, such as software viruses, power outages, or the theft of hardware. Thus, when implementing a new web-based software program to help students in the field track their hours, a BSW program director should also consider what will be done if the program is offline for any period of time, and even ask questions about technological disruptions of the developers before purchasing the software. These standards can also be used in conjunction with any institutional policies or procedures or federal policies such as the Federal Educational Rights and Privacy Act (FERPA). For more information about ethics and technology, please review additional resources in the suggested readings list at the end of the chapter.

FIGURE 11.1

Framework for Ethical and Inclusive Practices When Using Technology in Social Work Education

---

Excerpts from Section 4: Social Work Education and Supervision of the NASW Standards for Technology in Social Work Practice (NASW, 2017):

- *Standard 4.01. Use of Technology in Social Work Education*: Social workers who use technology to design and deliver education and training shall develop competence in the ethical use of the technology in a manner appropriate for the particular context.

- *Standard 4.02. Training Social Workers About the Use of Technology in Practice*: Social workers who provide education to students and practitioners concerning the use of technology in social work practice shall provide them with knowledge about the ethical use of technology, including potential benefits and risks.

- *Standard 4.03. Continuing Education*: Social work educators who use technology in their teaching and instruct students on the use of technology in social work practice shall examine and keep current with relevant emerging knowledge.

- *Standard 4.04. Social Media Policies*: When using online social media for educational purposes, social work educators shall provide students with social media policies to provide them with guidance about ethical considerations.

- *Standard 4.05. Evaluation*: When evaluating students on their use of technology in social work practice, social work educators shall provide clear guidance on professional expectations and how online tests, discussions, or other assignments will be graded.

(continued)

Figure 11.1 (cont.)

- *Standard 4.06. Technological Disruptions*: Social work educators shall provide students with information about how to manage technological problems that may be caused by loss of power, viruses, hardware failures, lost or stolen devices, or other issues that may disrupt the educational process.
- *Standard 4.07. Distance Education*: When teaching social work practitioners or students in remote locations, social work educators shall ensure that they have sufficient understanding of the cultural, social, and legal contexts of the other locations where the practitioners or students are located.
- *Standard 4.08. Support*: Social work educators who use technology shall ensure that students have sufficient access to technological support to assist with technological questions or problems that may arise during the educational process.
- *Standard 4.09. Maintenance of Academic Standards*: When social work educators use technology to facilitate assignments or tests, they shall take appropriate measures to promote academic standards related to honesty, integrity, freedom of expression, and respect for the dignity and worth of all people.
- *Standard 4.10. Educator–Student Boundaries*: Social work educators who use technology shall take precautions to ensure maintenance of appropriate educator–student boundaries.
- *Standard 4.11. Field Instruction*: Social workers who provide field instruction to students shall address the use of technology in organizational settings.
- *Standard 4.12. Social Work Supervision*: Social workers who use technology to provide supervision shall ensure that they are able to assess students' and supervisees' learning and professional competence.

Beyond the profession's ethical code and standards, there are two theoretical models specifically designed around technology that offer the BSW program director a framework for integration of the technology itself, as well as helping faculty, staff, and students to effectively use the technology. The first is Puentedura's substitution, augmentation, modification, redefinition (SAMR) model for technology integration, and the second is Rogers's diffusion of innovation.

Puentedura's SAMR Model for Technology Integration
Originally designed to help individual educators, Ruben Puentedura's (2013a; 2013b) SAMR model for technology integration offers a guide for adapting traditional assignments to a technology-mediated approach regardless of the curricular content. The model can easily be applied to other educational contexts and this section offers such an expansion by discussing the SAMR model for the use of technology in program administration.

First, the SAMR model identifies a spectrum of technology adaptation, starting with the use of technology to enhance an administrative task at the lowest end of the spectrum, to the incorporation of technology that transforms a task into something different at the highest end of the spectrum. Next, although an administrative task can be adapted by technology at any level of the SAMR model, some technology-mediated substitutions only replace a traditional tool, such as the use of an email for a paper letter sent through the postal service in response to a potential student's inquiry. Other technology substitutions can change the administrative or educational task entirely, such as the use of social media to post student-created videos about their field placement experiences as a way to recruit new students. BSW program directors can use the SAMR model to reflect on and evaluate how they are incorporating technology into the program across a range of administrative and educational functions.

Table 11.1 shows the levels of the SAMR model, defines each level, and offers examples of common administrative and educational functions in BSW programs. The dotted line in the middle of the table represents a function that has been transformed by the integration of technology and offers the BSW program director an opportunity to reflect on how technology serves to improve the efficacy and quality of the program.

To explain the SAMR model, it is helpful to use the example of how technology can be employed to communicate with an important stakeholder of any BSW program—the prospective student. Briefly, the first stage in the SAMR model is *substitution*, when technology works as a direct tool substitute, with no practical change to the communication task. So rather than sending a paper letter to a prospective student, the BSW program director sends an email with information about the program. At the stage of *augmentation*, the BSW program director now includes hyperlinks (connections between two digital documents) in the email, which direct the reader to important information on the university's website or to the BSW student handbook, which is stored in Dropbox, a cloud storage program, or on the program's website. In both situations, the email is just a direct substitution for a paper letter, but the hyperlinks improve the quality of the communication, what Puentedura (2013a, 2013b) would call *improved functionality*.

At the stage of *modification*, the BSW program director could create a social media account on a platform such as Facebook or Instagram to share information about the BSW program to prospective students. This transforms the communication process as the BSW director is actively

TABLE 11.1

SAMR Model for Technology Integration Adapted Administrative Functions

	Level of Technology Integration	Video Example
Transforming	**Redefinition** Technology allows for the creation of a new task, previously inconceivable.	Creates how-to videos about interviewing technique, incorporating editing, and annotation software, to be posted on public video-sharing website.
	Modification Technology allows for a significant redesign of the task.	Social media account is created to share written information with prospective students.
Enhancing	**Augmentation** Technology acts as a direct tool substitution with functional change in the task.	Email includes hyperlinks to content on a website or documents shared via a cloud storage service.
	Substitution Technology acts as a direct tool substitution with no functional change in the task.	Email to prospective student rather than paper letter sent through the mail.

Adapted with permission from Hitchcock et al. (2019).

providing content in virtual spaces where prospective students are scrolling through content, rather than passively waiting for email inquiries to arrive in their inboxes. Finally, at the *redefinition* stage, the BSW program director works with current students to create short videos about their learning experiences and then shares these videos on the program's social media accounts. By sharing student videos, the communication has been transformed from an email response to visual information from an engaging source—the current students.

By using the SAMR model as a framework, BSW program directors can systematically integrate technology into a BSW program by starting with a *substitution* for the administrative task, and then progressing over time to a *redefinition* of the task. This process has several advantages. First, the BSW program director takes measured steps toward technology integration, identifying clear reasons for using different types of technology while also mapping out a plan. Second, this model helps a BSW program director determine their comfort level, knowledge, and skills with different types of digital and social technology, also known as digital literacy. By recognizing their digital literacy, a BSW program director can identify their own knowledge gaps, begin to ask questions, and then learn to assess the digital literacy of important stakeholders of the BSW program such as students, faculty, and staff. Another theory, Rogers's (2003) diffusion of innovation, can help provide insight on where various stakeholders are in their understanding of and comfort with digital and social technologies.

Rogers's Innovation Adoption Curve

Rogers's (2003) diffusion of innovation theory offers the BSW program director a way to understand the actual adoption and embrace of technology by stakeholders of the program through an understanding of the reasons individuals may be more or less inclined to adopt technology in their professional life. Rogers defined adoption of new technologies as a social process influenced by five factors:

1. the technological innovation such as the specific hardware or software;

2. the adopters such as students compared with faculty members;

3. the communication patterns between the adopters such as how the field director trains new field supervisors;

4. how long the technology has been available; and

5. the larger social system of the adopter such as the institutional and regional contexts of the educational program.

Based on these five factors, Rogers contended that individuals fit into one of five types of technology adopters that fall along what he called an innovation adoption life cycle, as illustrated in Figure 11.2. *Innovators* adopt the technology because it is novel, and they are willing to risk failure to see how the technology applies in their work environment. Innovators are typically small in number within an organization and often do not exert a lot of social influence with the other adopters. *Early adopters* embrace new technology before others, but are more risk-averse, preferring to learn more about the technology before committing to its use. Innovators influence early adopters only when it comes to adopting a new technology, but early adopters have more social influence with other types of stakeholders.

Next are the *majority adopters,* who are the critical mass of stakeholders needed to ensure that technology is adopted. There are two types of majority adopter: (1) *early majority adopters,* who value the practical benefits of technology with a proven track record, and (2) *late majority adopters,* who will use the technology out of necessity rather than personal interest. These stakeholders expect assistance in learning and applying the technology to their work environment. Last, the *laggards* are individuals who seem resistant to technology and will be among the last to use technology in the work environment.

FIGURE 11.2

Rogers's Innovation Adoption Life Cycle

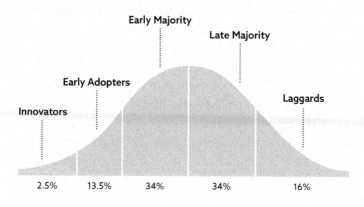

Similar to understanding the SAMR model, BSW program directors can use the innovation adoption life cycle to systematically engage and educate various stakeholders around technology and its integration. By starting where stakeholders are with their comfort and preference for technology, a program director can better plan for when, with whom, and how to implement a new software program for data collection or a new digital camera system in the classroom. Additionally, understanding where you fall on this adoption curve will give you insight on your technology preferences and how your preferences affect others in your environment.

Technology for the Explicit Curriculum

In BSW education, the explicit curriculum refers to the courses and field experiences that prepare students for their future generalist-level social work practice (CSWE, 2022). Both CSWE and NASW support the use of technology in the design and delivery of the explicit curriculum for BSW programs (CSWE, 2022; NASW, 2017). In this section, two commonly used technologies in BSW programs will be discussed: learning management systems (LMS) and their integrated eLearning tools and field placement software. Most educators in higher education use some type of LMS to communicate and share course content with students (Allen & Seaman, 2016), from supporting a traditional seated course to delivering a fully online course. Although the number of BSW programs using field placement software is unknown, recent scholarship suggests that the process of selecting this type of software is complex, involving the review of numerous products and input from many stakeholders (Samuels et al., 2020).

Learning Management Systems and eLearning Tools

There are numerous LMS platforms being used in higher education today, including proprietary and open-source platforms as well as systems developed by institutions to meet the needs of their organization. This section focuses on the functionality of these software systems rather than specific brands such as Canvas or Moodle. The reasons for this approach are because (1) LMS brands frequently change as the companies who created them update or develop new systems, and (2) universities typically purchase an LMS from a company and may change systems or contract for different services within one system. Thus, BSW program directors need to understand the purpose and features of LMS generally, rather than focusing on one specific brand. This is the same for eLearning tools (e.g., videoconferencing software); these programs or applications (apps) are different from LMS but integrate with systems so that the user will have a seamless experience.

Specifically, LMS are software platforms that serve as a repository for course content and allow for the delivery of a course through a web-based interface. These systems offer numerous features for the design of content for learners, and they also track what tasks and content learners review within the system. Instructors can use the multiple features to design how the content will be delivered, such as via web pages, discussion boards, and/or hyperlinks.

The following are some other features of LMS: (1) multiple users can interface with an LMS at the same time; (2) different user roles provide a comprehensive learning environment for the students, instructors, and instructional support staff; and (3) built-in features for assessment allow instructors and administrators to certify completion and levels of content mastery. Other variations of learning systems include learning content management systems (LCMS) and content management systems (CMS), which offer different options for the delivery of educational content, from serving more as a repository for the learning content to allowing course content to be displayed on any website. LCMS and CMS are also valuable to BSW program directors because these systems are often used for the delivery of professional development content within an organization or continuing education for professionals.

As previously noted, eLearning tools are programs or apps that are separate from LMS and typically offer features not available in LMS. For example, apps such as Zoom, VoiceThread, or Kaltura offer tools for capturing lectures through video or audio recordings that are often not available from LMS. Table 11.2 covers several of the most common eLearning tools with definitions and examples of software brands. Most LMS are designed to accommodate eLearning tools within their systems, but a BSW program director should always ask to make sure that this integration is possible within their institution's LMS before adopting a new tool.

TABLE 11.2

Types of eLearning Tools in Learning Management Systems

Type of eLearning Tool	Purpose
Content capturing	Instructors can create content for courses such as videorecorded lectures, audio directions, or written formulas from a whiteboard. Examples include VoiceThread, Kaltura, and lightboards. Sometimes referred to as video or screen capturing.
Collaboration tools	These tools are often third-party apps that allow learners and instructors to work on projects in online environments at the same time in one location such as wikis, Google Documents, and cloud-sharing services.
ePortfolios	An ePortfolio is a digital collection of a student's completed work that is organized to demonstrate learning over time and can be created in a variety of platforms, from a blog to proprietary apps such as TaskStream and TK20 by Watermark.
Content repositories	These repositories are digital databases that allow instructors to store, search, and retrieve digital content for inclusion in a course.
Academic integrity	Academic integrity software enables instructors and institutions to determine the identity of students and help to prevent cheating and plagiarism through proctoring, assessing writing, and locking down web browsers on computers. Examples include ProctorU, SafeAssign, Turnitin, and Respondus Lock Down Browser.

(continued)

Table 11.2 (cont.)

Type of eLearning Tools	Purpose
Video- or audio-conferencing	These services allow for communication between persons in different locations via video and/or audio and are typically for synchronous classes or office hour meetings. Examples include Adobe Connect, Zoom, Google Hangouts Meet, and GoTo Meeting.
Streaming services	These services offer digital media content for use in the classroom. Content can come from textbook publishers, news outlets, and governmental agencies. Some institutions purchase subscriptions for direct upload into LMS.
Audience response tools	These tools enable instructors to poll a classroom for responses to comments or questions and can help with assessment. Examples include iClickers and Poll Everywhere.

Reprinted with permission from Hitchcock et al. (2019).

With respect to LMS and eLearning tools, the role of the BSW program director is to ensure that both full-time and adjunct instructors are able to effectively deliver course content and engage with students using the institution's LMS and that students understand how to access and navigate the LMS. Although this seems like a monumental task, most higher education institutions offer assistance and training through separate units, such as a center for teaching and learning, which can provide training opportunities for full-time and adjunct faculty members about best practices for online education, or an academic technology support office, such as an eLearning office that manages LMS for the institution and provides services and support directly to faculty and students. Additionally, many universities have an office dedicated to technology support such as an information technology (IT) unit that provides help with hardware and software integration across multiple platforms. BSW program directors should be aware of the equivalent offices at their institutions, understand the services provided by these units, and be prepared to refer faculty and students to the appropriate service based on need.

Finally, there are two approaches that support the ethical and inclusive use of LMS and eLearning tools in social work education. First is the universal design for learning (UDL). The principles of UDL help to increase accessibility of digital content for people with disabilities within LMS and eLearning tools as well as the approaches used by educators when delivering content (Burgstahler, 2020). For example, LMS will often have alternative text boxes for photos or images where an instructor can describe the image, and this description would be read by a screen reader for someone with a vision impairment. Additionally, an instructor should always verbally describe an image used during a class lecture to be inclusive of people with vision impairments. Another example would be to provide closed captions for videos and transcripts for podcasts used within a course. Program directors should partner with their institution's office for disability services to make sure that they are aware of current best practices for UDL.

Second is the professional Practice Standards for Technology in social work education. These standards are outlined in NASW (2017) and further developed in the publication *Technology in Social Work Education: Educators' Perspectives on the NASW Technology Standards for Social Work Education and Supervision*, a curated booklet offering practical suggestions for how to implement the NASW standards (Hitchcock et al., 2018). For example, the NASW standards encourage social work educators and administrators to develop competency in the ethical and inclusive use of technology to design and delivery social work education. As a BSW program director, applying this standard would include developing one's own knowledge and skills using LMS by participating in training and professional development opportunities, attending presentations at social work education conferences, and connecting with other BSW program directors who are also using LMS.

Field Placement Software

In addition to the technology required for coursework (e.g., LMS, video-conferencing software), many BSW programs rely on a well-defined system of recordkeeping to document activities for field education, from attendance at field orientations to the selection and placement of students in community-based agencies. Many BSW field programs use some form of digital technology to catalog or track this essential information. Some common recordkeeping needs for BSW field programs include (1) managing field applications and learning plans; (2) tracking learning outcomes; and (3) keeping lists of student cohorts, placement sites, instructors, and liaisons. To meet these needs (e.g., cost or institutional requirements), a range of software options are available to BSW programs. Some of the software programs are free, and other programs are proprietary and are not free. Some BSW field programs use just one software package for all their needs, and other programs use several systems to monitor the field placement process. Features of field placement software vary and may include basic data storage and retrieval, document tracking, electronic survey forms, bulk emailing and email merges, and automated matching of student and field placement attributes (Samuels et al., 2020). See Box 11.1 for a detailed list of features.

BOX 11.1

A Sample of Field Software Features

• Data storage and retrieval	• Electronic forms
• Document tracking	• Bulk emailing, email merging
• Filtering and matching student and agency attributes	• Automatically generated email for placement interviews
• Assessment of learning outcomes	• Data and outcome reporting
• Off-site (nonuniversity) login	• Dashboards
• Interoperability with other software or databases	• Import and export features

Reprinted with permission from Hitchcock et al. (2019).

Generally, the use of technology to support BSW field education ranges from the integration of multiple single-use software programs to one specialized software program that integrates all functions into one platform, with other options in between. Here are some different kinds of approaches:

- *Using multiple software programs*—This approach uses multiple programs that serve one function each, creating a system when used in conjunction. For example, spreadsheet software to keep up with lists of students and field instructors, an email system to support the tracking and communication functions, and a cloud storage system to share information between users.

- *In-house software system*—This approach involves working with technical support such as the IT department at your institution, which develops, implements, and monitors the software. Advantages of this approach are the ability to design the software system specifically to meet the needs of the particular BSW field program.

- *Single software system with add-on features*—This approach involves working with a vendor to purchase a packaged software solution and then supplementing the program with add-on features, either from the vendor or through another software program. For example, DocuSign is a web-based program for collecting authenticated signatures. You may wish to add DocuSign to an existing field placement program for field agreements with community-based agencies so that everyone can sign online. Ideally, the field placement software can directly interface with other software programs through connected databases.

- *Single software system*—This approach requires program directors to purchase a highly customizable web-based software program, which may include ePortfolio tools, accreditation data tracking tools, and field placement databases. With user-friendly dashboards, data about field students and placement demographics are easy to share, but these software systems come with fees, such as setup costs, student access fees, and/or monthly maintenance dues.

Although there are many advantages to using field placement software, BSW program directors should be aware of the challenges and risks of these systems. For example, it takes time to set up technology-mediated systems for field education, such as time for faculty and staff to learn how to use the features as well as training students and field instructors. Among the disadvantages are that systems from third-party providers can go offline, the company may go out of business, or the program may not control the database. Further, some institutions are wary of external, noncontracted platforms holding student data, and the state system that oversees higher education may even have a policy prohibiting this practice.

Last, the IT support at an institution may not provide support for software that is not licensed through the university system. Because of these potential risks, it is recommended that, before embarking on the process, BSW program directors consult with institution stakeholders, such as an IT or eLearning office, about policies and options. Another best practice is to create an ad hoc committee to help with the decision process that includes representatives from the faculty, the field office, agency settings, and your campus IT department (Hitchcock et al., 2019). See Box 11.2 for sample questions to consider before adopting field placement software, and read Case Example 11.1 for an example of how one BSW program director got started with the process of adopting field placement software.

BOX 11.2

Questions to Ask When Planning to Adopt Field Tracking Software

1. Do you need a system that can connect to key software and databases; that is, university enrollment systems, an agency database, and a student database?

2. Does your program retain ownership of the data? Who else has access?

3. Are the data stored locally on a university server, or stored remotely?

4. Is storage on a secure server, or is storage cloud-based?

5. What are the costs of implementation, ongoing fees, and updates?

6. What level of support is provided?

Adapted from Samuels et al. (2020).

CASE EXAMPLE 11.1

Armon Researches Field Placement Software

Armon, the BSW director for a growing program, sits at his desk, staring at his computer monitor and feeling a bit overwhelmed. Recently, the BSW field coordinator met with him to request help with tracking placements for field students because of the increased number of students in the field. The field coordinator asked that Armon look at field placement software programs that they could recommend to the chair. Armon's quick Google search came up with more than 20 different choices, and he has no idea how to narrow down the options. He quickly types into the search box, "How to select student placement software for the social work field office?" The third item down on the search page is a blog post by Dr. Kristen Samuels about her experience with selecting software for her program. He opens up the blog post and starts reading.

The first thing Armon notices is a table with different questions to consider when selecting a software program, ranging from cost and functionality to integration with other software programs used at the institution. He takes quick note of all the different categories of questions, realizing that he does not have answers for many of them. He thinks: "How will I figure all of this out?"

As Armon continues reading, the next paragraph mentions the importance of working with others from different stakeholder groups throughout the decision-making process. "What a relief," he thinks; "I don't have to make this decision on my own." His next thought is to recommend an ad hoc committee be formed to vet the software programs and decide. He opens his email program and types up a short note to the BSW field coordinator with his idea and a link to the blog post: Samuels, K. (2018, September 7). Student Placement Software for the Social Work Field Office: Goodbye Post-it Notes! *Teaching and Learning in Social Work*. https://laureliversonhitchcock.org/2018/09/07/student-place-ment-software-for-the-social-work-field-office-goodbye-post-it-notes/.

Technology for Implicit Curriculum

In social work education, the implicit curriculum refers to the broader learning environment of social work programs (CSWE, 2022). The typical learning environment of a BSW program is vast and complex, ranging from administrative functions that support the development of students and faculty all the way to the hardware and software used by an institution to support workflow. Keeping up with an ever-changing work environment and new digital technologies is a herculean task, and BSW program directors are better off focusing on the administrative need or function of the implicit curriculum first and then identifying their technology needs. For example, a BSW program director may want to offer training to newly hired adjuncts, and finding a time and location is challenging because of work schedules and campus parking. Instead, the director could use the university's LMS to offer an online, asynchronous workshop for new hires. Applying the SAMR model, LMS could also be used as an online group for all of the program's adjuncts, where announcements could be posted and questions answered, thus transforming the administrative task beyond a workshop to an online learning community.

This section focuses on technology that can support four essential administrative functions within the implicit curriculum of most BSW programs: admission, retention, advisement, and communication with stakeholders. Although there are many more administrative tasks that support the implicit curriculum of a BSW program, these four functions are easily and routinely supported by digital and social technologies. For example, Young (2020) found that several social work programs were using the social media platform Twitter to share information and build community among key stakeholders. Additionally, some software applications can serve multiple functions. For example, a cloud-based document storage system can be a repository for all of the digital documents of a BSW program, such as a list of advisees, applications to the program, and minutes from key meetings of faculty and other stakeholders.

Admissions

Like most professional education programs, undergraduate social work programs require an admissions process beyond being admitted to the institution (Standard 4.1, CSWE, 2022). Steps in the admission process include dissemination of the admission criteria, collection of applications, review of applications, and evaluation of applications to determine the students' fit with the values of the social work profession (Macy et al., 2000). Technology can be applied in each step of the admissions process to create a digital workflow from start to finish.

Further, BSW programs can implement field placement software to manage the application process to the BSW professional program. As previously noted, in Box 11.1, many of the features available in field placement software, such as digital forms to collect information from students and the document storage features, provide faculty reviewers with access to the applications for review. Further, the student applications can be matched with field applications and data in the future, linking data across the entire program. BSW program directors interested in field placement software should consider how the software could be used across the entire program from admission to a student's final assessment in field placement.

Other technology-mediated options for the BSW program admissions process include online survey software and ePortfolios. There are a variety of online survey software platforms such as Qualtrics, Survey Monkey, and Google Forms. As with a lot of software, there are free and paid versions, each with different features. Minimally, a BSW program director will want the ability to collect different types of data from students as part of their applications and then download those data for review purposes. Most survey software allows for collected information to be downloaded into a spreadsheet where data can be sorted and then shared with others. Additionally, the BSW program director can use the survey software to create a rubric for faculty reviews of the applications.

Another option is to use an ePortfolio program, which is designed so that students can showcase their accomplishments or learning with a variety of digital tools (Fitch et al., 2008). Examples include uploading an assignment that demonstrates their level of competency for social work practice across learning outcomes or completing a project that showcases a holistic view of their knowledge and skills. Many LMS have ePortfolio features already built in or have add-on products such as Portfolium for the Canvas LMS. Other options include freestanding programs such as FolioSpaces, or social networking platforms such as LinkedIn, or even asking each student to create their own blog, which offers the benefit of public-facing profiles that students can share with future employers. However, ePortfolio programs are not designed to be systems for gathering the traditional application materials for a BSW program admissions process, and therefore they must be adapted for this purpose. One advantage of using a freestanding ePortfolio program is that individuals from outside of the institution, such as practitioners or field instructors, can easily be given access to the program so that they can offer feedback about students' applications.

Use of Technology Policies That Support Retention in the BSW Program

With respect to retention of students in a BSW program, policies about the use of technology play a more important role than the technology itself. Many problems related to the retention of social work students fall into one of two categories—academic performance or demonstration of professional behavior—and it is the latter category where a BSW program needs policies about the ethical, inclusive, and professional use of technology in social work education. The two common technology-driven policies needed by a BSW program are a social media policy targeted toward student use and the use of technology to manage online academic integrity.

Social Media Policies

Many BSW programs have established social media policies for students, which is considered a best practice in social work education (Hitchcock et al., 2019; NASW, 2017). The goal of a social media policy is to provide students with guidance on the ethical and professional use of social media, both personally and professionally. There is no one right way to draft a social media policy; some policies are very general, with a focus on professional social work ethics, and others are very detailed and prescriptive (Karpman & Drisko, 2016). Additionally, BSW program leaders need to align their policies with anti-racist, diversity, equity, and inclusion (ADEI) approaches and the values of the social work profession (CSWE, 2022; NASW, 2021). A general social media policy makes students aware that professional ethics apply within digital environments, but it does not inform students about specific ways that professional roles and ethics can play out on social media. However, many prescriptive social media policies, while providing specific details about dos and don'ts on social media, leave out situations or require frequent updates as technology changes.

The function of social media platforms can vary widely and change over time, making it difficult to stay current on behavior online while ensuring that the social media policy will encompass all of the roles of BSW students. For those BSW program leaders interested in a more detailed social media policy, Karpman and Drisko (2016, p. 1) recommend six domains within the policy: (1) understanding social media; (2) legal obligations; (3) the implications of personal and professional online presence; (4) institutional obligations to the social work program; (5) productivity implications; and (6) possible consequences for violations of the policy. Box 11.3 shows an example of a more general social media policy. Either way, the social media policy should be discussed with students to help them think critically about ethics related to digital practice.

BOX 11.3

Sample Social Media Policy

Students are expected to follow the BSW program's professional standards, the NASW Code of Ethics, and the University of Alabama at Birmingham's Student Code of Conduct always, including but not limited to classes, field placements, volunteer work, and digital contexts. Digital contexts include but are not limited to social networking sites (Facebook, LinkedIn, Twitter, Instagram, etc.), text messaging, apps, blogging, virtual worlds, and email. For more information about social work standards in digital contexts, students are invited to review the *NASW, ABSW, CSWE, & CSWA Standards for Technology in Social Work Practice* (NASW, 2017), available on the NASW website.

Adapted from Samuels et al. (2020).

Finally, a BSW program director should encourage all BSW faculty to develop their own individualized social media and technology policies or guidelines for classroom and other professional settings. The program director can model this practice by developing their own social media policy (Brady, et al., 2015; Curington & Hitchcock, 2017; NASW, 2017). These guidelines can be shared on a course syllabus or verbally and are meant to be unique to the individual educator or program director. Common points addressed by this type of social media policy are expectations for professional email communications and when and how the BSW program director will engage with stakeholders via social media. See Case Example 11.2 about one director's personalized social media policy.

CASE EXAMPLE 11.2

Jameka Creates Her Social Media Guidelines

Jameka, a brand new BSW program director, attended a session about ethical social media use in social work education at a national social work conference. She learned about creating social media policies for the BSW program as well as the need to create one for herself to use with students and colleagues. Using the worksheet provided at the conference session, she spends the time on her return flight home planning out her policy.

The first question on the worksheet is, "What sources do you need to review and/or incorporate into your social media policy?" Jameka starts to list them out: NASW Code of Ethics, the NASW Technology Standards, and the Federal Educational Rights and Policy Act (FERPA). Then she adds her institution's social media policy. "That's a good start," she thinks. The facilitators of the session said that social media policy could be updated as needed, so she can identify other sources later as needed. She makes a note to search for other examples of individualized social media policies by other social workers.

The next question asks, "Whom do I need to target with my social media policy?" Jameka writes down "students" and "colleagues," and then she pauses. As she sits for a minute, she realizes that as the new BSW program director, there are many other stakeholders that she needs to think about such as alumni, field instructors, and community-based learning partners. She starts writing again.

Jameka pauses again as she looks over the third question on the worksheet, "What ethical concerns do you need to address in your social media policy?" As a social work educator, she knows that avoiding dual relationships is important, and she realizes that she wants to maintain and model boundaries in virtual spaces as well as in real life. She also thinks that integrity has always been an important core social work value for her, which she operationalizes through accountability and accessibility with others.

The next two questions of the worksheet take her through a series of questions about different types of online activities that are common with social media use. She uses the questions to document her use and then responds to the prompt, "Do you need to change your social media practices, and if so, how?" Jameka realizes that she has good boundaries on social media with students and others because she uses LinkedIn and Twitter for professional connections and Facebook for personal connections only. While she tells this to students and colleagues, she acknowledges that this could go into her social media policy. She writes down the following bullet points on the worksheet:

"I will work to maintain and model virtual boundaries by:

- Accepting requests to connect or follow students and colleagues only on Twitter and LinkedIn, my professional social media accounts.
- Not connecting with students and colleagues on Facebook, Instagram, and other social media accounts that I use for socializing."

Jameka smiles to herself as she thinks, "This is a good start." The final question on the worksheet asks the user to commit to writing their own professional social media policy by a specified date. Jameka writes down a date for two weeks in the future and smiles as she puts the worksheet into her computer bag.

Technology and Academic Integrity

For the BSW program, academic integrity involves maintaining high standards of honesty in education and professionalism. Unfortunately, digital technology has made it easier for students to cheat (Fishman, 2014). Common examples include purchasing prewritten papers, hiring someone to take an online exam, sharing questions from online exams, using artificial intelligence programs like ChatGPT to author papers, or simply copying and pasting content from websites and documents on the internet. BSW program directors need to manage violations of academic integrity with technology in two ways: enforcement and prevention (Lee-Post & Hapke, 2017).

Enforcement focuses on detecting violations of academic dishonesty with digital features that are often built into software programs or products that can be added on to other systems. The following are some examples of these features and products:

- user authentication methods that verify user identity upon logging in to the software system, such as limiting course access to registered students with a photo ID or biometric methods (i.e., fingerprints)

- lockdown browsers that block printing or screenshots of exam questions

- software, such as SafeAssign or Turnitin, with large repositories of text that screen for plagiarized text

- proctoring services delivered via video-based technology that require a webcam to be on while the student is logged in to an online course or an exam

BSW programs using these technologies should have established policies that inform students and guide faculty about when and how these digital tools will be used. In conjunction with these digital tools, BSW program directors should work to create an environment where academic integrity is highly valued and clearly defined, which leads to a more preventive approach to addressing academic dishonesty. This approach can involve developing social work–specific honor codes and processes to address and monitor violations, educating students and faculty about academic integrity, and ensuring that faculty members prioritize academic integrity in their courses (Lee-Post & Hapke, 2017).

Advisement

In BSW programs, advising includes disseminating both academic and professional information, which requires that the BSW program director and faculty members meet with students. There are a few essential software programs that can help manage this process: (1) appointment-scheduling software; (2) calendar software; and (3) videoconferencing software. Individually or combined, these programs enable a social work educator to book an appointment with a student and then hold a virtual meeting with the student from almost any location.

This section will offer a brief overview of each software platform with some example brand-name products—but no recommendations of any particular products. These programs can also be used to manage other types of work processes, making them valuable products for social work educators. Thus, as a BSW program director, consider the administrative needs of your program and the purpose of the software when making the decision about one digital platform over another. Finally, consult with the institution's IT office to see if the software or app you are planning to use is compatible with or supported by the institution's other systems or if the institution provides access to a similar program at no cost and with training.

Advising typically requires meetings with students to discuss their progress in the BSW curriculum and future career options (Macy et al., 2000). Appointment-scheduling software allows the user to set up appointment slots, eliminating back-and-forth email and automating the process of booking appointments. Among the advantages of this type of software are sharing one's availability with others, options for rescheduling appointments, and syncing with a digital calendar. Disadvantages include cost, as these types of programs are subscription based, and there is a learning curve for using the system. Examples of appointment-scheduling software include Acuity, Calendly, and YouCanBook.Me.

Calendar software typically includes a digital calendar and other features such as an appointment book for scheduling events and a contact or address list. Advantages of using calendar software include the ability to sync appointments across one's calendar on multiple devices, allowing others to access and manage one's calendar for consensus scheduling, and setting up alerts and reminders for upcoming events. Disadvantages to calendar software include problems with compatibility with computer operating systems and mobile devices that are unable to access a calendar because of a technology glitch or perhaps a drained battery. Brands of calendar software include Google Calendar, iCloud Calendar, as well as the calendar features that come with email software such as Microsoft's Outlook or Apple's Mac Mail. Also, LMS frequently include a calendar tool for course management that can be synced with the educator's calendar.

Finally, videoconferencing software offers a platform for real-time meetings through a computer using internet access, web cameras, and microphone headsets to transmit images and sound. Advantages of videoconferencing software include the ability to meet with other individuals regardless of geography and the option of recording the meeting for later use. Disadvantages include the costs associated with the hardware and software needed to use these types of platforms as well as high-quality internet access. Brands of videoconferencing software include AdobeConnect, Google Meet, Skype, and Zoom. Again, these software programs require training for effective use, and BSW program directors should provide students and faculty with information on how to professionally present oneself on video and/or over audio.

Communication With Stakeholders

Stakeholders of BSW programs include, but are not limited to, students, faculty, staff, institutional administrators and services, community-based agencies, alumni, and local professional organizations. Each of these stakeholders requires different types of information from the BSW program director. Digital and social technologies have shaped 21st-century communication in many ways, each presenting advantages and disadvantages. Advantages include the ability to communicate quickly and easily via email, text messaging, and videoconference calls; disadvantages include managing higher volumes of digital information across multiple programs and the need to understand new tools and technologies. This section reviews common technology tools for communicating with a variety of stakeholders.

Email is one of the most common forms of technology-based communication in higher education (Pignata et al., 2015). This technology allows for a message, with or without attachments, to be sent to one person, several people, or a group of people, such as an online discussion group. BSW program directors can have different lists of email addresses for different types of stakeholders such as students, faculty, and alumni. Over the past decade, research studies have reported that email communication improves organizational productivity because of the ease of sending an email, but it can also decrease an individual's productivity because of the large quantity of email messages and because the sender is always favored in the communication process, as the receiver spends more time decoding the meaning of an email than does the sender (Mark et al., 2016). Additionally, email can be sent and received at any time during the day or evening, and some individuals or organizations expect rapid responses to email, creating a culture that requires individuals to constantly read and respond to email. To successfully manage the use of email within a BSW program, the director should incorporate practices such as setting a schedule for checking email, using automatic reply features to inform others when to expect a response, and sending email only during traditional work hours (Pignata et al., 2015).

Social media, also known as social networking sites, is composed of web-based software applications designed for the purposes of communication and sharing digital content (e.g., photos, video clips, and memes) (Westwood, 2014). Examples of social media apps are Facebook, Twitter, LinkedIn, and Instagram. In higher education, social media apps are frequently used to inform internal and external stakeholders about events and news, recruit prospective students, and maintain relationships with alumni—all important tasks for a BSW program director (Nyangau & Bado, 2012). Using social media for a BSW program requires establishing a user account for the program, creating digital content to share, and consistent posting of content along with responding to stakeholder posts. Because of the plethora of social media apps, there are many possibilities available to the BSW program director about which apps to use and the different types of digital content that can be created and shared. Here are some examples:

- Twitter account where the BSW program directors, administrative staff, or field directors announce important due dates and reminders for students and answers questions

- Facebook or LinkedIn group for alumni that the program uses to recruit and engage with field supervisors

- digital newsletter created using MailChimp that is emailed to subscribers on a quarterly basis

- YouTube channel in which the BSW program shares student-created videos about their field experiences

Regardless of the type of social media account used, BSW program directors should implement best practices when using social media to communicate with stakeholders. These practices comprise consistent publishing of posts and responding to other users' comments, maintaining a positive tone, and sharing content that is research-informed and grounded in the core values of the social work profession (Kimball & Kim, 2013; Young, 2020). BSW program directors will also want to draft messages and model communication that is anti-racist and respects the diversity, equity, and inclusion of all students, faculty, and other constituents (CSWE, 2022; NASW, 2021). Finally, program directors will want to follow any relevant policies and practices from their institution, such as the use of media release forms for publishing student photos.

Technology for Program Assessment and Ongoing Feedback

Accredited BSW programs in the United States are required to collect and report program assessment data related to student learning outcomes to stakeholders, including the general public (CSWE, 2022). This has prompted many BSW program directors to employ technology-mediated options for the collection, analysis, and dissemination of these data. A brief review of options is covered in this section.

For data collection, the type of data collected varies by program, but often includes learning outcomes related to the program's competency-based curriculum and student feedback on the implicit curriculum. Depending on available resources and program size, a BSW program director may want to choose a software system that simultaneously helps to manage the process of field placements and collects program assessment data. As discussed earlier in this chapter, field placement software can assist in the collection and storage of student learning outcome data (as previously discussed). Another option for data collection is online survey software, also discussed earlier in this chapter.

Finally, a proprietary and fee-based option for BSW program directors is the Social Work Education Assessment Project (SWEAP), which offers a variety of web-based instruments for program assessment from knowledge exams to field practicum assessments (SWEAP, 2020). Its instruments can be administered through a hyperlink or integrated into LMS. All three of these collection options offer the ability to download the data into spreadsheet or statistical analysis software. Using spreadsheet software programs such as Microsoft Excel or Google Sheets, a BSW program director can sort, analyze, and aggregate data for needed reporting purposes. Statistical analysis software programs such as SPSS and SAS offer similar options, although these programs are more complex to use and significantly more expensive.

To disseminate data related to student learning in BSW programs, a director is required to post information on the program's website using preformatted forms from CSWE (2022). A hyperlink to these forms can be shared with stakeholders. Additionally, a BSW program director may want to create other digital products for sharing relevant program assessment information. One way to do this is by designing an infographic, which is a visual display of information and data around a theme in a single page or poster. Although it is possible to create an infographic in a single slide in a program like Microsoft PowerPoint, there are many apps designed for creating infographics, such as Canva and Piktochart, which offer discounts to educational programs. Other ways to share assessment data are the BSW program's digital newsletter and digital slide presentation software such as Microsoft PowerPoint or Google Slides.

Conclusion

This chapter has offered an overview of digital and social technologies that support the most common administrative functions in a BSW program. By the time this chapter is printed and read, some of these technologies may be obsolete, or newer and improved software programs will have been developed. Either way, a BSW program director needs to stay on top of current news, the latest research, and trends related to educational technologies, engaging in lifelong learning practices (NASW, 2017). Although there are many strategies for lifelong learning, two robust approaches involve the use of technology: creating one's own professional learning network (PLN) or professional collaboration network (PCN) and participating in a virtual community of practice (VCoP).

First, a PLN involves the use of social media to collect information related to professional interests, share this information with others, and collaborate with others in their professional networks on projects (Richardson & Mancabelli, 2011). For example, a BSW program director might use their PLN to collect email alerts from news sources about higher education or social work practice and then share them with colleagues or students via Twitter or Facebook. Prior to the explosion in online content and tools, a PLN might have included an article from a trusted daily newspaper or a print version of a journal, which a BSW program director could have photocopied for colleagues.

Like a PLN, a PCN is unique to its user but encourages active engagement with other individuals and groups to develop professional relationships, identify networking opportunities, and disseminate one's own work (Sage et al., 2021). One advantage of a PCN is that it offers a BSW program director a systematic way to stay on top of ever-changing trends in educational technology by following leaders in the field and monitoring online conversations with specialized hashtags such as #EdTech or #Elearning.

Second, a VCoP is an online group connected by a common interest for the purposes of sharing information and shifting learning from an individual process to a community effort (Christson & Adedoyin, 2016). One of the best known VCoPs in social work education in the United States was the email discussion group from the Association of Baccalaureate Social Work Program Directors (BPD). This group created connections between its subscribers and the organization by providing a digital venue where people can share ideas and consult one another about issues related to social work education (BPD, n.d.).

Along with these lifelong learning practices, a BSW program director can draw on the frameworks discussed earlier in the chapter to determine how to best enhance one's own learning with digital and social technologies. Given the speed of change, time to learn new technology tools, ethical considerations, and the financial costs of technology, this learning may be the most important step to integrating technology into a BSW program. Knowledge about the program's goals as well as obligations will help a program director make the best decisions for effectively incorporating technology into their BSW program.

Suggested Readings and Resources

This list provides resources on the use of technology in social work education and represents starting points for staying current on the ethical and practical use of technology for effective education.

- *Harness Technology for Social Good.* Grand Challenges for Social Work. https://grandchallengesforsocialwork.org/. This effort focuses on how digital and social technologies can address social and educational problems.

- The Council on Social Work Education (https://www.cswe.org/) has many resources, including:

  - *Teaching With and Teaching About Technology Initiative,* led by the Technology Advisory Group, includes technology-based resources for social work educators.

- *Technology in Social Work Education and Practice Track* for CSWE's annual program meetings encourages and supports presentations on a broad use of digital and social technologies in social work education and practice.

- *Teaching Social Work With Digital Technology,* published in 2019, by Laurel Iverson Hitchcock, Melanie Sage, and Nancy J. Smyth, provides a comprehensive overview of using technology in social work education. Chapter 8 focuses on ethical considerations and inclusive practices for technology-mediated teaching and learning.

• EDUCAUSE (http://www.educause.edu/) is a nonprofit association with the mission of advancing higher education through IT. EDUCAUSE reports on trends about the ethics, innovation, and use of technology in higher education, both domestically and globally.

• The Social Work Distance Education Conference (https://www.ollusa.edu/worden-school /swde/index.html) was established in 2015 by the University of Indiana and CSWE and is now sponsored by Our Lady of the Lake University. This conference focuses on the use of information and communication technologies for curriculum and administration in social work education.

• The University of Buffalo School of Social Work's *Social Worker's Guide to Social Media* (http://socialwork.buffalo.edu/resources/social-media-guide.html) is a free infographic with videos designed to help social workers navigate the ethical dilemma related to the professional use of social media.

• *Open Social Work* (https://opensocialwork.org/) is a collaborative project designed to support open and free access to affordable educational materials for social work.

• *Social Work Futures* (https://socialworkfutures.com/) is a blog written by Dr. Laura Nissen about how social workers can apply futures thinking and forecasting to shape the profession of social work, including the use of technology.

References

Ahlquist, J. (2020). *Digital leadership in higher education: Purposeful social media in a connected world.* Stylus Publishing.

Allen, I. E., & Seaman, J. (2016). *Online report card: Tracking online education in the United States.* Babson Survey Research Group. http://onlinelearningsurvey.com/reports /onlinereportcard.pdf

Association of Baccalaureate Social Work Program Directors. (n.d.). *BPD home page.* http://www.bpdonline.org/

Association of Social Work Boards. (2015). *Model regulatory standards for technology and social work practice: ASWB international technology task force, 2013–2014.* https://www.aswb.org/wp-content/uploads/2015/03/ASWB-Model-Regulatory -Standards-for-Technology-and-Social-Work-Practice.pdf

Brady, S. R., McLeod, D. A., & Young, J. A. (2015). Developing ethical guidelines for creating social media technology policy in social work classrooms. *Advances in Social Work, 16*(1), 43–54.

Burgstahler, S. (2017, January 30). *ADA compliance for online course design.* EDUCAUSE Review. https://er.educause.edu/articles/2017/1/ada-compliance-for-online-course-design

Christson, A., & Adedoyin, A. (2016). Deploying virtual communities of practice as a digital tool in social work: A rapid review and critique of the literature. *Social Work Education, 35*(3), 357–370. https://doi.org/10.1080/02615479.2016.1154660

Cortellazzo, L., Bruni, E., & Zampieri, R. (2019). The role of leadership in a digitalized world: A review. *Frontiers in Psychology, 10.* https://doi.org/10.3389/fpsyg.2019.01938

Council on Social Work Education. (2020). *Social work student perceptions: Impact of Covid-19 pandemic on educational experience and goals.* https://cswe.org/getattachment/ResearchStatistics/Social-Work-Student-Perceptions.pdf.aspx

Council on Social Work Education. (2022). *2022 Educational policy and accreditation standards for baccalaureate and master's social work programs.* https://www.cswe.org/accreditation/standards/2022-epas/

Cummings, S. M., Foels, L., & Chaffin, K. M. (2013). Comparative analysis of distance education and classroom-based formats for a clinical social work practice course. *Social Work Education, 32*(1), 68–80. https://doi.org/10.1080/02615479.2011.648179

Curington, A., & Hitchcock, L. I. (2017, July 28). Social media toolkit for social work field educators—Get your free copy! *Teaching & Learning in Social Work.* http://www.laureliversonhitchcock.org/2017/07/28/social-media-toolkit-for-social-work-field-educators-get-your-free-copy/

Fishman, T. (2014). *The fundamental values of academic integrity* (2nd ed.). Clemson University. http://www.academicintegrity.org/icai/assets/Revised_FV_2014.pdf

Fitch, D., Peet, M., Reed, B. G., & Tolman, R. (2008). The use of ePortfolios in evaluating the curriculum and student learning. *Journal of Social Work Education, 44*(3), 37–54. https://doi.org/10.5175/JSWE.2008.200700010

Forgey, M. A., & Ortega-Williams, A. (2016). Effectively teaching social work practice online: Moving beyond can to how. *Advances in Social Work, 17*(1), 59–77.

Hitchcock, L. I., Sage, M., & Smyth, N. J. (Eds.). (2018). *Technology in social work education: Educators' perspectives on the NASW technology standards for social work education and supervision.* University at Buffalo School of Social Work, State University of New York.

Hitchcock, L. I., Sage, M., & Smyth, N. J. (2019). *Teaching social work with digital technology.* Council on Social Work Education Press.

Karpman, H. E., & Drisko, J. (2016). Social media policy in social work education: A review and recommendations. *Journal of Social Work Education, 52*(4), 398–408. https://doi.org/10.1080/10437797.2016.1202164

Kimball, E., & Kim, J. (2013). Virtual boundaries: Ethical considerations for use of social media in social work. *Social Work, 58*(2), 185–188. https://doi.org/10.1093/sw/swt005

Lee-Post, A., & Hapke, H. (2017). Online learning integrity approaches: Current practices and future solutions. *Online Learning, 21*(1), 135–145.

Macy, H. J., Turner, R., & Wilson, S. (2000). *Directing the baccalaureate social work education program.* Eddie Bowers Publishing Company.

Mark, G., Iqbal, S. T., Czerwinski, M., Johns, P., Sano, A., & Lutchyn, Y. (2016). Email duration, batching and self-interruption: Patterns of mail use on productivity and stress. *Proceedings of the 2016 CHI Conference on Human Factors in Computing Systems,* 1717–1728. https://doi.org/10.1145/2858036.2858262

National Association of Social Workers. (2017). *NASW, ABSW, CSWE, & CSWA standards for technology in social work practice.* http://www.socialworkers.org/includes/newIncludes/homepage/PRA-BRO-33617.TechStandards_FINAL_POSTING.pdf

National Association of Social Workers. (2021). *Code of ethics.* https://www.socialworkers.org/About/Ethics/Code-of-Ethics/Code-of-Ethics-English

Nyangau, J., & Bado, N. (2012). Social media and marketing of higher education: A review of the literature. *Journal of the Research Center for Educational Technology, 8*(1), 38–51.

Pignata, S., Lushington, K., Sloan, J., & Buchanan, F. (2015). Employees' perceptions of email communication, volume and management strategies in an Australian university.

Journal of Higher Education Policy and Management, 37(2), 159–171. https://doi.org /10.1080/1360080X.2015.1019121

Puentedura, R. (2013a). *SAMR: A contextualized introduction.* http://hippasus.com/rrpweblog /archives/2014/01/15/SAMRABriefContextualizedIntroduction.pdf

Puentedura, R. (2013b). *The SAMR ladder: Questions and transitions.* http://www.hippasus .com/rrpweblog/archives/2013/10/26/SAMRLadder_Questions.pdf

Richardson, W., & Mancabelli, R. (2011). *Personal learning networks: Using the power of connections to transform education* (3rd ed.). Solution Tree Press.

Robbins, S. P., Regan, J. A. R. C., Williams, J. H., Smyth, N. J., & Bogo, M. (2016). From the editor—The future of social work education. *Journal of Social Work Education, 52*(4), 387–397. https://doi.org/10.1080/10437797.2016.1218222

Rogers, E. M. (2003). *Diffusion of innovations* (5th ed.). Free Press.

Samuels, K., Hitchcock, L. I., & Sage, M. (2020). Selection of field education management software in social work: The field educator. *Field Educator Journal, 10*(1). https://fieldeducator .simmons.edu

Sage, M., Hitchcock, L. I., Bakk, L., Young, J., Michaeli, D., Jones, A. S., & Smyth, N. J. (2021). Professional collaboration networks as a social work research practice innovation: Preparing DSW students for knowledge dissemination roles in a digital society. *Research on Social Work Practice, 31*(1), 42–52. https://doi.org/10.1177/1049731520961163

Social Work Education Assessment Project. (2020). *Social work education assessment project home page.* https://www.sweapinstruments.org/

Vernon, R., Vakalahi, H., Pierce, D., Pittman-Munke, P., & Adkins, L. F. (2009). Distance education programs in social work: Current and emerging trends. *Journal of Social Work Education, 45*(2), 263–276. https://doi.org/10.5175/JSWE.2009.200700081

Westwood, J. (Ed.). (2014). *Social media in social work education.* Critical Publishing.

Young, J. A. (2020). #SocialWorkEducation: A computational analysis of social work programs on Twitter. *Journal of Social Work Education, 58*(2), 215–222. https://doi.org /10.1080/10437797.2020.1817821

Section Three

Faculty Issues

CHAPTER 12

Recruitment of Social Work Faculty With a Commitment to Diversity

Candyce S. Berger

Recruitment of faculty is a systematic process to identify and secure the best faculty available in the marketplace to meet institutional needs. The recruitment process is defined as "the steps that organizations use when identifying job vacancies, analyzing requirements for a position, reviewing applications, short-listing candidates, and choosing the new hire" (van Maanen, 2019, p. 3). It is institution-specific, with academic administration assuming "overall approval" to recruit and hire, and "process oversight" typically resides within human resources (HR) with attention to Equal Opportunity and Affirmative Action (EOAA) requirements.

Although many commonalities exist across university settings, the process often differs in unique ways. Organizational values, policies, priorities, procedures, financial situations, and workforce needs will shape decision making. Social work chairs and program directors must adhere to the Council on Social Work Education (CSWE) accreditation guidelines that set the requirements for faculty, as well as the commitment to recruiting diverse faculty who reflect local, regional, and national demographics. The goal is to create a diverse, equitable, and inclusive workforce and to ensure the success of all faculty.

Before launching into the discussion of recruitment, I recognize that many higher education institutions use different terminology for the same activity, role, or function. The following terms are used in this chapter to avoid confusion or wordiness:

- university or college: academic institutions
- chair: Search Committee leader

- director: department or program leader

- department: BSW program

- hiring official(s): those with final decision-making authority (e.g., department director, dean, provost)

- HR: institutional departments that encompass personnel and affirmative action

- announcement: the position announcement document specifically linked to recruitment and used for advertising the position

- committee: the Search Committee

- short list: applicants selected for preliminary interviews by phone or videoconferencing from which finalists for campus visits are chosen

- finalists or final list: those invited for campus visits

The focus of this chapter is recruitment controlled by the university, not a search firm. The chapter provides practical strategies to achieve a successful recruitment of new faculty. It is not a cookbook. It is a guide to evaluate the necessary phases, steps, and strategies to achieve a successful search. Much of the content draws from the literature, as well from my practical experience of more than 40 years of recruiting social work faculty and staff in both academic and practice settings. Leadership by the BSW administrator is essential to providing guidance to shape the process by clearly articulating program goals and objectives and the decision-making process. Transparency is also critical to encourage input from a broad and diverse constituency. This input will enrich decision making by infusing different perspectives. Leadership should strive for the highest level of transparency within the confines of strict confidentiality.

This chapter addresses the first three phases of recruitment: preparatory, recruitment, and selection. Within each phase, review by HR and hiring officials may occur to ensure compliance with federal, state, and university regulations and policies. Space limitations prohibit inclusion of two additional phases: negotiating the contract and onboarding, which are essential to hiring and retaining faculty (for some guidance on contract negotiation, see the recruitment guides for University of Michigan, 2018, pp. 26–27). The ultimate goal of recruitment is to employ an individual who is the best fit for your program rather than one who has the most impressive credentials.

CASE EXAMPLE

A BSW program at a college in the Midwest noted an increasing rate of turnover among faculty. Teaching was the highest priority for the program, with faculty typically assigned five courses per semester. The BSW director hired a consultant to assess the recruitment process. She noted that those applicants receiving the highest scores based on the recruitment assessment form graduated from research-intensive universities with a strong record of research and scholarship. From a review of the faculty who resigned, the majority reported "inability to maintain an active research agenda" as leading to their decision.

The consultant's report pointed to the rating form that favored scholarship (e.g., publications, research, and grants). While such applicants may be fantastic candidates for some programs, they may not be the best fit for a program that prioritizes teaching. The consultant recommended reviewing the rating form to align criteria effectively with program goals and priorities. The BSW director organized a full-day retreat to review the recruitment process and then revised the rating form to align weighted criteria to activities related to teaching.

Poor hiring decisions can have a devastating effect on a program, including loss of students or staff, and fiscal resources. van Maanen's (2018) study of 278 employers found that employers lost money related to poor hiring decisions: 21% reported loss of clients or staff, and 17% reported personnel disruptions related to interpersonal conflicts.

Social work values emphasize a commitment to justice, equity, and inclusivity. This commitment undergirds an emphasis to create and maintain a diverse faculty. The profession's commitment to diversity results in an emphasis in the demographic characteristics of applicants, their areas of scholarship or research, areas of service, and effective work with diverse students and faculty, particularly those from traditionally oppressed groups (University of Michigan, 2018).

Achieving departmental diversity, equity, and inclusion requires a long-term vision and commitment. It cannot rely solely on an individual recruitment process. It requires proactive search strategies that actively reflect the pursuit of potential faculty prior to an official recruitment process. Faculty can nurture these relationships over time with potential applicants (e.g., informal contacts at annual conferences and meetings, inviting potential applicants to participate in local conference planning committees, sending invitations to present workshops at local conferences, etc.) (Fine & Handelsman, 2012).

CASE EXAMPLE

Leaders of a BSW program set a long-range goal to expand their focus in the health care arena with an emphasis on health care disparities and to increase representation of faculty from minoritized groups. After a failed search, the BSW director encouraged faculty to attend conferences and meetings to reach out to colleagues with health specializations. Faculty members on a local planning committee invited two individuals identified at these conferences to be speakers at a conference addressing health care and health disparities. The faculty met with them during breaks and meals to learn about their areas of interest and expertise. The invited speakers were able to learn about the institution and community. Some of the BSW faculty maintained collegial relationships with these individuals while attending conferences. These contacts helped the program to delineate essential criteria and qualifications to shape the job announcement to target faculty of interest as well as instituting curricular changes to incorporate health and health disparities.

Two years later, the college approved a second faculty search, expanding it to include a joint appointment with the public health program. The second search produced a larger applicant pool based on revisions made to the job description and the expansion to a joint appointment. Two of the earlier speakers applied for the position. Both were from minoritized groups with expertise in health disparities of racially oppressed populations. These two speakers were among the finalists; the hiring official offered the appointment to one of these individuals, who accepted the appointment. Of note, neither of these two applicants applied during the earlier search.

Building a relationship over time fostered a stronger interest in employment. Proactive recruitment strengthened the process by setting criteria that were more specific to recruitment goals, and improved recruitment efforts to reach those from minoritized racial groups.

As illustrated, program directors cannot post a job and passively assume that well-suited candidates will apply. Hiring a well-qualified candidate and retaining that person require ongoing work to cultivate candidates. This chapter focuses on the first three phases in the recruitment process to identify, recruit, and hire faculty. It includes a delineation of the activities and strategies common to each phase. I provide a brief overview of steps, with more detail in the relevant sections.

The preparatory phase focuses on determining the priorities that will shape the profile of a potential candidate for the position. It culminates in the development of the job description to market the position. The steps involve:

- development and implementation of an environmental analysis that informs the profile of the desirable applicant;

- identifying members to serve on the search committee and working with HR to ensure that the committee adheres to compliance with national and institutional equal opportunity policies and guidelines;

- effectively managing the committee working relationships to achieve defined objectives and goals;

- development of the job announcement and job specifications to effectively reach desired applicants; and

- development of standardized interview and evaluation forms.

The recruitment phase begins once the hiring officials approve posting the announcement. The process focuses on the strategies that will be used to reach and identify potential applicants and concludes with a list of recommended applicants to be considered for interviews. The steps involve:

- development of the recruitment plan that delineates the passive and proactive strategies to identify applicants and encourage submission of applications;

- examination of resources and effective strategies for recruitment of underrepresented groups among your faculty;

- identifying the roles and responsibilities of committee members and departmental faculty in the recruitment process;

- articulating the various marketing strategies to reach potential applicants;

- analysis of the budgetary requirements for recruitment and determination of responsibility to assume the costs;

- using monitoring systems to support and document the recruitment process, including the development of a timeline; and

- preparation of recommendations of applicants to move to the selection phase.

The selection phase initiates the interview process for applicants identified in recruitment. It involves sequential steps beginning with a thorough review of submitted application materials that determines if the applicant receives an interview and ending with a list of finalists to receive a campus visit. The steps involve:

- examining and deciding on what process will be adopted for review and decision making to identify which applicants move forward in the interview process;

- creating structured interview forms and processes for scoring of the interviews;

- ensuring compliance with EOAA guidelines during all interviews (e.g., what can and cannot be asked during an interview);

- documentation of the decision-making process in selecting applicants to be interviewed;

- selecting the first set of applicants for preliminary interviews (i.e., short list);

- selecting the next set of applicants for final interviews (i.e., campus visits) and designing the event using strategies from the hospitality industry;

- gathering information from the finalist's list of references; and

- preparation by the chair of the final report submitted to the hiring officials with hiring recommendations.

Preparatory Phase

The preparatory phase focuses on determining the priorities that will shape the profile of a potential candidate for the position. In the phase, the hiring needs of the BSW program are determined, culminating in a profile for a successful candidate captured in the position announcement. A common error is to use a generic job description or copy the position announcement used to recruit a previous faculty member. This approach is not likely to incorporate present and future departmental priorities into the job description and can negatively affect the recruitment of targeted faculty groups. This first step for an environmental analysis prevents the development of an announcement that will be insufficient to recruit desirable applicants.

Environmental Analysis

The purpose of an environmental analysis is to determine the criteria needed to move the program forward. If recruitment is for a newly developed position, the environmental analysis is integral to the approval process, eliminating the need for additional analysis. If recruiting for a vacancy, some universities prohibit initiating recruitment until the existing position becomes vacant. However, the department can initiate an environmental analysis to gather information and delineate specific criteria essential to the development of an announcement that aligns with departmental priorities.

The environmental analysis requires input from a variety of potential stakeholders, including the department, the school, the college, other campus educational units, the university, faculty, students, and community agencies. Another essential element is a critical review of state and national policies and trends as well as economic developments in the community. The following are some examples of questions to guide the analysis:

- Are faculty needed to address specific standards in the Educational Policy and Accreditation Standards (EPAS)? The BSW program captures these in its accreditation documents and in the standards for accreditation at CSWE (2022).

- Where are the gaps in the curriculum to address cutting-edge and innovative practices (e.g., trauma-informed care, new evidence-based interventions) to promote best practice?

- Will this position address the needs of the classroom and/or field education priorities?

- How will this position serve as a bridge to these components of the curriculum?

- Are there university initiatives that require BSW representation (e.g., institutional committees and task forces)?

- Are there fiscal issues within the department or institution that will influence the decisions regarding faculty rank, breadth of recruitment strategies, and financial support for campus visits?

- What are the most pressing issues or gaps within the community that the curriculum does not sufficiently address?

- How have economic factors influenced community-based education and research, employment of social work graduates, and availability of practicum sites?

- Are there exceptions that allow for greater flexibility in the recruitment of faculty? (For examples, refer to the recruitment phase.)

- Are there priorities that emphasize the need to enhance inclusivity among faculty in order to provide a learning environment that promotes understanding of difference?

- Is the composition of the faculty congruent with student and community demographics?

Examples of data elements that evolve in response to these questions include the following:

- mission, values, and strategic plans from campus sources, including the department, school, and university (if appropriate);

- department and institution financial records and priorities;

- present and future community priorities, issues, and challenges;

- innovative and cutting-edge interventions;

- student evaluations of the program and faculty;

- external funding priorities and opportunities;

- accreditation or licensure requirements;

- faculty and student demographics; and

- evaluation data from previous searches (e.g., number of applicants, demographics of applicants, strategies used to identify applicants).

The outcome of the environmental analysis is a profile of a desired applicant by prioritizing criteria to be included in the announcement.

Developing the Search Committee

Institutions use different approaches to assemble search committees. A common approach has the hiring official (e.g., dean or provost) responsible for identifying the search committee chair; they may also appoint committee members with input from the chair. Some institutions split these functions, allowing the hiring official to appoint the chair and the department to identify the committee members. Alternatively, the department can select the committee members, and then the members select the chair. At the initial meeting of the committee, the hiring official may meet with the committee to clarify their charge, tasks, and responsibilities and to establish upfront the committee's role in decision making, which is typically advisory to the hiring official or the director.

Membership on the committee should also represent diversity and a demonstrated commitment to inclusivity. Whenever possible, avoid reliance on members of traditionally oppressed groups to be the only champions for diversity; all members must be committed to ensuring a fair and inclusive search process (Fine & Handelsman, 2012). Although student representation on the committee could provide additional perspectives, institutions may not allow it for legal reasons. Drawing on members from the whole campus and the community can also enrich the process (Abrams, 2018; Columbia University, 2016). A diverse membership has the potential to increase diversity in the applicant pool by infusing new ideas and strategies for recruitment, bringing experience in recruiting underrepresented applicants to expand the recruitment plan, and accessing additional networks for marketing the announcement.

Prior to initiating the work of recruitment, HR should meet with the committee to provide an overview of federal, state, and university policies and procedural guidelines for recruitment. It may be wise to involve all program faculty to participate in this training because they will be involved in many activities in the selection phase.

Academic institutions typically have manuals and tools available that will assist the committee in identifying regulatory requirements, providing examples of standardized interview schedules, defining what questions can be asked and what is not allowed in interviews, and establishing the timing of reporting requirements for approval from hiring officials and HR. Please refer to the manuals from universities listed in the "Suggested Readings" section in this chapter; all have excellent information and tools in their appendices.

A thorough discussion of federal and state legislation is not feasible in this chapter, though some important and pertinent pieces are integrated here. HR typically has excellent resources that address policies and how they affect the recruitment processes (refer to the recruitment and selection phases for how these affect recruitment processes and strategies to avoid violations). These policies are the following:

- The Civil Rights Act of 1964 opened the door to prohibiting discrimination in hiring practices of federal employers or subcontractors based on race, color, religion, sex, or national origin; and to recruit and advance qualified minorities, women, persons with disabilities, and covered veterans. It is central to affirmative action.

- The Equal Employment and Opportunity Act of 1972 introduced four major concepts related to discriminatory hiring practices:
  - Civil rights (see Civil Rights Act of 1964, see previous)
  - Blind to differences: views all applicants for employment as equal
  - Affirmative action (see previous)
  - Protected class (i.e., prohibits discrimination in hiring practices based on sex, race, religion, color, national origin, age [40 and older], and physical or mental disabilities)

Task, Roles, and Responsibilities of the Committee

Another important step in the preparatory phase is for the chair to facilitate discussion on how the committee will work together to accomplish its tasks. The chair should emphasize an appreciation of the value and importance of each member's contribution to the search process. Early in the process, the chair should lead a discussion addressing tasks, roles, and responsibilities of the committee, but this alone is insufficient. The chair must also possess excellent group process skills to address challenges that emanate from group dynamics related to power differentials and interpersonal conflicts. As with all groups, identifying and managing conflict is essential to group success.

There is a tendency for most groups to jump into discussion of the work, without first addressing group processes. The problem is one of "pay now or pay later." If time is not set aside in the beginning to address how the group will work together, greater challenges and time demands will emerge when addressing the conflicts that can derail the efficiency and effectiveness of the group. This entails the development of ground rules with committee members to promote collaboration. The discussion might include how the group will work together, how decisions will be made (e.g., consensus or majority vote), expectations for meeting attendance and participation, and decorum (e.g., phones off, criticize ideas not people, promote open discussion that welcomes all points of view, and respectful communication) (Harvard University, 2016). The chair should address the need for confidentiality until finalists are chosen; violations could subject the university to lawsuits and members could experience sanctions by state licensing boards or professional bodies.

The chair must also facilitate discussion of the tasks and timelines in the process. These include review of the environmental analysis report in developing the announcement, creation of the evaluation form(s), development and implementation of the recruitment plan, and active participation in most steps in the selection process (e.g., preliminary and final interviews, scheduled group meetings such as the search committee, and attendance at the finalists' presentations). Clarification of the tasks of the chair versus the committee members helps to clarify understanding and promotes effective working relationships. Some task-related examples for the chair include (Fine & Handelsman, 2012; Harvard University, 2016):

- scheduling meetings;
- preparing and distributing the agenda prior to meeting;
- assigning tasks to members and holding them accountable;
- managing group dynamics;
- clarifying and enforcing group ground rules;
- respecting members' time commitments through frequency and timing of meetings;
- maintaining records of all meetings, discussions, and voting;
- timely completion of all required reports; and
- contacting only those references identified by the applicants, or others with applicants' permission.

Examples of members' tasks include (Fine & Handelsman, 2012; Harvard University, 2016):

- regular attendance at committee meetings;
- participating in proactive recruitment activities;
- timely completion of assigned tasks;
- thoroughly reviewing applications;
- actively participating in decision making;
- completing and submitting evaluation forms to the chair at each step of the process;
- participating in every opportunity to meet with or attend the meetings or presentations of the applicants during the selection phase; and

- committing to diversity in recruitment by strategic outreach to potential applicants, and promoting a fair and equitable evaluation of applicants.

Position Announcement and Position Specification

The announcement is the primary outcome of the preparatory phase. Creation of the announcement builds from the findings of the environmental analysis. It typically provides the following types of information:

- job description: Include a brief description of the role, work-specific activities, and reporting relationships.

- academic rank: The announcement may include single or multiple acceptable ranks (e.g., assistant, associate, full professor). If all possible ranks are considered, the announcement calls for an "open" recruitment. Multiple ranks typically increase applicant pools.

- educational attainment: According to CSWE (2022), the majority of faculty in the BSW program must hold an MSW degree from a CSWE-accredited program (Accreditation Standard B4.2.1). To expand the applicant pool, a doctoral degree might be listed as a "preferred" criterion, or note that either a PhD or a DSW is acceptable, depending on the requirements of the position and tenure expectations of the institution. To meet accreditation standards, the BSW program must have no fewer than two full-time faculty primarily assigned to the program and the BSW director must have an MSW degree from an accredited program (Accreditation Standard B4.3.4 (b)).

- desired qualifications: Identify the experience, skills, and expertise desired for the position. Is the faculty member expected to assume any leadership positions (director, coordinator, committee leadership)? Will they be responsible for advising and mentoring students? Will they be required to engage in community-based practice, teaching, and scholarship? Will they address the needs of the classroom and/or field education priorities; will they be a bridge to these components of the curriculum? Are faculty needed to address specific competencies or hold the requisite social work degree (MSW) to be the BSW director as defined by the EPAS (CSWE, 2022)? In terms of experience, it helps to quantify evidence by years and months, and describe the relevance of this experience to BSW practice.

- Behavioral specifications: Seek an individual who will work effectively with diverse students, faculty, and staff. Are they able to work effectively as a member of an intra- or interdisciplinary team?

Many announcements include information about the organization and the community. This is particularly important for recruitment of underrepresented groups and women. One goal of recruitment is to entice an applicant to apply, even if they're not necessarily searching for a new position. For example, characterizing the organization as "family-friendly" has been associated with successful recruitment and retention. The literature spans more than three decades, but still lacks consensus on this information's influence on recruitment in comparison to other benefit packages (Baranczyk, 2013).

Catanzaro et al. (2010) examined the issue with a broader lens, focusing on the effect of organizational culture on application intention (i.e., the congruence between personal needs and organizational culture). They examined the interest of men and women applicants with examples of a competitive culture ("masculine") versus a supportive culture ("feminine"). Men were more likely to pursue employment in a competitive culture, but the majority of men and women preferred a supportive culture even when the salary was lower. Wagner and Scott (2019) emphasized that the announcement should have information or expectations related to social justice, equity, and inclusion throughout the document, not just in a general statement at the end.

The reality is that family-friendly policies are not the purview of a BSW director; they reside in HR or institutional administration and are mandated by federal or state legislation. However, the director can influence a family-friendly or supportive culture within the program through work flexibility, resource lists of dependent care resources, and encouraging faculty to access Family and Medical Leave Act (FMLA) resources through HR. Though this would be unlikely to arise for an applicant during recruitment, a supportive culture will be evident to applicants during interviews.

HR officials may encourage including in the announcement a statement that resonates with those who are not a traditional applicant, an upper-middle class White man. For example, "We welcome applications from dual-career couples" may encourage more women to apply because women are more likely to have a partner in academia (Zhang et al., 2019). "Ranked #1 for the social mobility of students" may speak to an applicant's commitment to working with disadvantaged students, just as reporting the university's classification as a "minority-serving institution" could attract faculty from these demographic groups. If the institution has a vision or mission statement that includes indicators of work-life balance, these should be included in the announcement.

Visuals should include pictures that capture diversity to entice potential applicants to apply when they see themselves in marketing and informational materials. If your goal is to diversify your faculty, you may need to go beyond a generic statement that encourages applications from underrepresented groups. At a minimum, the announcement should affirm the institution's commitment as an EOAA employer that does not discriminate based on defined protected classes (i.e., race, color, national origin, sex, religion, age, disability, genetic information, and veteran status; some states include sexual orientation). However, adding additional comments characterizing a work and learning environment that promotes understanding of difference and inclusivity makes a stronger appeal to underrepresented populations. It is also possible to include a statement that encourages submission of applications from those belonging to specific groups (e.g., women, LGBTQ+); Harvard University's (2016) manual provides several examples.

Diversity priorities often require alternative recruitment strategies to more effectively facilitate recruitment, including:

- dual-career recruitment and hiring,
- provost initiatives that fund specific recruiting priorities,
- grant funding that requires hiring faculty before funds are released,
- identifying an outstanding diversity hire, and
- approval of a "cluster hire" that specifies interprofessional specializations to create the core grouping (Columbia University, 2016).

Here are other types of content that may be included in an announcement:

- a generic statement about salary and benefits (i.e., competitive salary based on rank, qualifications, and experience, with an excellent start-up package and fringe benefits); and

- instructions on how to apply, with a clear time period to submit applications (e.g., provide a defined deadline or state "open until the position is filled" to allow more flexibility to generate applications). The downside of greater flexibility is the need to continue reviewing applications until at least the campus interviews.

The announcement should capture the elements identified in the profile of the ideal candidate. The committee must discuss and agree on the specifications and receive approval from HR and the hiring officials before posting. The efficiency of recruitment may be compromised, which opens the door to increased bias in the process, if approval is not received (Fine & Handelsman, 2012). Once posted, it becomes a binding document throughout the recruitment process.

CASE EXAMPLE

A BSW program posted an announcement for an assistant professor. The top finalist requested an appointment as an associate professor without tenure with the understanding of an early tenure review. When the chair sought approval for this request, HR denied the request. The reasoning was that this violated equal opportunity because other associate professors might not have applied because of the lower posted faculty rank. HR and the hiring officials advised the committee to explore another finalist or withdraw the announcement and start the process again with revision to faculty rank.

There is an art to creating announcements. It entails balancing a detailed description of the specifications while framing the description to attract the applicants you are seeking. If the specifications are too broad, the number of applications submitted can overwhelm the committee; if the specification are too narrowly focused, qualified applicants may not apply (Abrams, 2018; Harvard University, 2016). Size, geographic location, and reputation of the program can also influence the number of applications. If the program is well known or desirable, it may typically receive a greater number of applications, which would support increased specificity; a small or less known program may routinely use less specificity as a strategy to increase applications. The strong indicator for balance is to review past recruitment efforts.

The announcement requires an effective balance of *required* versus *preferred* qualifications. All required qualifications *must* be met even to be considered. Preferred qualifications do not eliminate applicants, but only increase an applicant's score. If recruitment produced too many applications in the past, increase *required* criteria; if there are too few applicants, decrease *required* and expand *preferred* criteria.

Another consideration is to avoid using "superlatives" in the criteria, especially if recruiting non-tenure-track faculty. For example, "exceptional leadership" may prevent a potential applicant from applying because they interpret this to mean a national recognition (Harvard University, 2016); "strong record of teaching" fails to define what constitutes *strong*. Is it teaching courses at a university level? Not clarifying what the superlatives mean could prevent qualified applicants from applying through self-elimination.

An important determination in developing the announcement is what faculty rank is required. The determination of rank is dependent on the definition for a "terminal degree" (i.e., defined by the regional institutional accrediting body and the university as the highest degree required) to be considered for a specific rank. There are three primary groupings of faculty positions: (1) tenured or tenure-track, (2) non-tenure-track, and (3) adjunct or part-time. Tenure/tenure-track typically require a doctoral degree and applies to full, associate, and assistant professors. However, this could limit the potential pool, given that 29% of full-time BSW faculty hold a master's degree as their highest earned degree (CSWE, 2021).

Non-tenure-track faculty include full-time lecturers and visiting, research, and clinical faculty. These positions also could range from assistant to full professors, with renewable contracts but no tenure commitment. Lecturers and clinical appointments typically require a BSW or an MSW from a CSWE-accredited program; doctorates may be required at senior levels. Recruitment often occurs in the local community, where experience and expertise relevant to program priorities are the defining criteria. The work assignments for clinical faculty prioritize teaching, and these faculty members tend to carry larger course loads than tenured/tenure-track faculty.

At some institutions, the announcement can be posted with a specific rank (e.g., tenure-track assistant professor) or include multiple ranks (tenure-track assistant or associate professor). If all rankings are considered, the announcement lists the position as an "open recruitment" that accepts applications from all three levels (i.e., assistant, associate, or full). Even if hiring at a senior level (i.e., associate or full), the institution may hire an individual without tenure; a tenure review is typically required within 1 to

3 years of appointment. This allows a department or program to evaluate the person's productivity and compatibility before making a commitment to tenure. Leaders must be cautious that unconscious bias does not cause discrimination, wherein institutions may be more likely to hire women and non-White individuals into senior levels without tenure. To hire with tenure typically requires the vote of tenured faculty at the same or higher rank as the applicant. The HR department will have guidelines describing this process.

CASE EXAMPLE

A BSW program was recruiting a new director. Hiring officials approved the department's request to initiate the search immediately. For the Search Committee, a chair was selected from the department (a White, male, tenured full professor) and three department members, who were all women. One was a clinical instructor (non-tenure-track), one a tenure-track assistant professor, and one a tenured associate professor; all were non-White. The outside member was a White male, tenured full professor from another department.

The first recruitment had few applicants and lacked any diversity; the dean declared it as failed search. The postevaluation of the recruitment revealed that power differentials within the committee had had an adverse effect. The announcement had a very long list of 15 required recruitment criteria that the chair insisted were necessary. The members described the chair as overriding input of committee members and said that the chair became angry when challenged. They described the outside member as passive, and said that he rarely attended meetings and often deferred to the chair's opinions. The chair consistently reminded members that he had held this role as director 8 years ago and that he was more qualified to guide the criteria for the announcement. The other members described deferring to his opinion to avoid conflict and for fear that challenging him could potentially create problems, especially around issues of future promotion. This inhibited open exploration of issues and led to an inability to engage in constructive conflict.

When hiring officials approved a second search, the dean initiated changes to the committee membership, including expanding the committee to include faculty from other programs and colleges and increasing membership that represented diversity. The dean appointed a tenured full professor (Hispanic woman) from outside the department to serve as chair of the search committee; this individual had a history of collaboration with social work through research projects, co-teaching, and serving on the university's undergraduate council, where she worked directly with the BSW director on various projects. She brought an understanding of many of the professional goals and objectives of the department, the BSW curriculum, and social work's values and commitment to inclusivity from her work on the undergraduate council. She also had experience serving as a committee chair for other faculty searches outside her own department.

(continued)

The restructuring of the committee with expanded and diverse membership led to more innovative recruitment strategies such as advertising on a broader list of online discussion forums that focused on minority and professional leadership groups, reviewing faculty rosters and lists of editorial boards of journals, and engaging in personal outreach to encourage submission of applications.

Another strategy was to move several of the required criteria to the preferred section on the announcement based on the recruitment conducted by outside members. They also recommended deleting the use of superlatives. For example, when "strong evidence of leadership experience" was required, does *strong* mean a national reputation? In addition, what does *leadership* mean? Is it having a formal administrative title such as director or chair? However, other titles such as coordinator, team leader, principal investigator, or supervisor might also meet the criteria.

The outcome of these expansive strategies resulted in a fourfold increase in completed applications, with a 50% increase in diversity of the applicant pool. Meeting minutes captured evidence of more open discussions with varying opinions, and the majority of decisions were by consensus versus majority vote.

Chairs and committee members need to be cognizant of the barriers to recruitment that can hamper successful outcomes. Fiscal constraints were the most common barriers in the recruitment of full-time faculty (CSWE, 2021) and included budget constraints that affect salary (34.5%) and lack of funds to conduct recruitment (36.1%). Competition from other programs was the second highest reported barrier (38.5%). Other reported barriers included geographic location of the program (20.9%) and not enough candidates with the necessary degree (22.1%) or experience (10.9%).

As discussed earlier, competition for applicants is more difficult for smaller programs or those in "less desirable" locations. However, these programs can reduce the negative impact by including in their announcements positive attributes, such as a smaller number of faculty members, which can promote collegial relationships; lower crime rates; lower cost of living; stronger community cohesion to support community-engaged teaching opportunities; excellent public schools; and easy access to recreational activities.

Developing Evaluation Forms

The last activity in the preparatory phase is the development of a standardized evaluation tool used in the selection phase. At some institutions, these may already exist and be required by HR, whereas in other institutions, evaluation forms may be created at the department level. Form development begins when HR and hiring officials approve the announcement for posting.

Once the selection phase begins, changing the evaluation criteria can introduce challenges, requiring the committee to rereview applicants and reach out to screened-out candidates to gather information on new criteria.

Linking the evaluation tool to the required and preferred criteria increases the likelihood of identifying a successful applicant. (See the "Suggested Readings" section for sample forms.) It is equally important to identify who will participate in rating candidates throughout the process (e.g., faculty, administrators, and community members) and in which activities (e.g., individual meetings, group meetings, presentations, meals, or social events, or limited to reviewing only the application materials) to ensure that the forms capture this information.

The structure of rating forms typically includes both fixed-response and open-ended questions. The heading should include the position title, the name of the applicant, the name of the reviewer and their role (e.g., search committee member, faculty, staff, administrator, or student), and the date of the review. The name of the reviewer is typically required for search committee members. It is usually optional for others who want to maintain anonymity, which can increase response rates.

Fixed-response rating scales are often 5-point scales, ranging from 1 = *strongly disagree* to 5 = *strongly agree* as the anchors. An alternative is a 3-point scale with *not met, met,* and *exceeded* as the anchors. This has the potential to reduce rater bias with a person's usual tendency in assigning scores (i.e., use or avoidance of the extreme rating based on the reviewer's tendency). For example, using a 5-point scale, some people are naturally reluctant to give an extreme rating (e.g., 1 or 5) except in very rare situations, and others are more inclined to assign these extreme ratings. The raters' propensities account for the difference among raters rather than a true measure of the criteria. Whichever rating scale is used, the committee must discuss and agree on what evidence is required to assign each anchor. For example, in a 3-point scale, if a criterion is a doctoral degree, 1 (*not met*) means doctorate in progress or no evidence of a completed doctorate, 2 (*met*) means a recent graduate up to 1 year postgraduation, and 3 (*exceeds*) means 2 or more years postgraduation.

All involved in the selection process could use one form, or the committee could develop multiple forms depending on the specificity of the form. For example, one department used two forms. The committee used a more detailed form that gathered information through multiple contacts with the applicant, using a 3-point scale as described previously. All data elements linked directly to the rating of each required and preferred criterion. The form included space for comments, and committee members were strongly encouraged to provide evidence and rationales for their rating scores. All other participants involved in the selection phase used a form with more general questions and a 5-point scale from *strongly agree* to *strongly disagree*. An additional rating of 0 = *unable to answer* was added because many of these individuals were limited to one or two encounters and did not have enough information to answer the question. Examples of topics covered in the questions included "evidence of strong teaching skills," "evidence of ability to work with a diverse student population," and "evidence of good citizenship and teamwork." Open-ended questions were included to increase depth in key areas such as teaching, scholarship, commitment to diversity, community service, and engaged practice.

The committee must also decide whether required and preferred criteria should have a weight factor when scored. For example, if the BSW program prioritizes teaching, the scoring of "evidence of relevant teaching experience" or "evidence of community-engaged teaching activities" might have a weight factor. If the program serves a large Hispanic student and community population, a preferred criterion might be "bilingual in Spanish" and assigned a weighted score. When using any language criteria, the committee should establish benchmarks for assessing competency, such as a conversation in the desired language, a standardized assessment, and so forth. For example, if an applicant indicates fluency in Spanish, a bilingual committee member could ask a question in Spanish and request that the applicant respond in Spanish to evaluate competency.

Recruitment Phase
Following the preparatory phase activities, including receipt of institutional approval to post the announcement, the next step entails refinement of the recruitment plan developed during the preparatory stage. The plan details a comprehensive strategy to recruit applicants. The primary goal is to identify potential applicants, especially those from a desired demographic pool, and encourage their application submission. The number of applications is not necessarily indicative of a successful search. The goal is to identify applicants who meet the criteria and align with established priorities. The plan should include an examination of the various strategies to identify applicants; the marketing strategies used to distribute the announcement; how the committee distributes responsibility for the delineated activities, HR, and faculty roles and responsibilities; and the fiscal requirements to implement the plan and who assumes these costs.

Analysis of budgetary requirements for recruitment is essential to a successful process. The director and chair must identify the budgetary requirements, establish priorities, and clarify which expenses the university, department, or HR will assume. There are several common sources of costs to consider (Bates, 2019). For example, advertising the announcement on job boards may involve a fee based on length. If the costs for advertising are excessive, an alternative is to post a more abbreviated notice with a URL link that directs interested applicants to the whole announcement.

Recruiting venues include local job fairs or professional conferences. Committee members who already received approval and are supported financially to attend a conference can conduct recruitment activities to reduce expenditures. If no one is attending, the committee chair should attend or send a senior committee member to recruit, but this will add to the costs. Other faculty members who attend can help by distributing the job announcements, but they should not be responsible for formally meeting with potential applicants if they have never participated in the various trainings for and steps in the recruitment process. Another expense may be covering a course release for the committee chair to acknowledge the workload demands of their responsibilities.

Campus interviews present one of the largest expenditures, including travel, housing, and entertainment costs, especially if the applicant lives out of the area. Recognizing and ensuring what financial resources are needed increases the likelihood that the plan is realistic and achievable.

The recruitment phase often involves additional meetings with HR to reconfirm expectations and processes for both the recruitment and selection phases. HR departments have guidelines for how to identify potential applicants; HR may also assume responsibility for posting the announcement through several venues. For example, the HR department at a public university may post position announcements internally as well as post them on job boards and websites from a long list of minority-serving institutions (e.g., historically Black colleges and universities [HBCUs] and Hispanic-serving institutions [HSIs]) and other organizations that are congruent with affirmative action initiatives.

The committee chair must clearly articulate monitoring and evaluation requirements so that all committee members understand their expectations. Reviewing HR's standardized forms will facilitate the monitoring process and establish the timelines for approval of hiring officials. It is imperative that the chair maintains documentation of every step in the process and stores it for a defined period to allow for postrecruitment evaluations or challenges to the recruitment process.

Many HR departments use an applicant tracking system (ATS) to monitor the application processes efficiently and effectively. The chair should meet with the HR representative to identify the steps and tools for the review and processing of applications. The committee may also be able to complete evaluation forms electronically and store them in the ATS, eliminating the need for paper documents and storage (Russell, 2020).

The ATS can be set up to receive and log applications into the system, notify applicants of incomplete applications, and apprise them when HR forwards the completed application to the committee for review. The system can determine if an applicant has met the required criteria and notify applicants to provide additional documentation to complete the evaluation process. Finally, the ATS can inform applicants that they do not qualify for further consideration if they have not met the required criteria.

If an ATS does not exist, most of this work will fall on the chair and committee members. Once the committee receives the application for review, the chair assumes responsibility for all communication with applicants. Russell (2020) emphasized that a candidate's first impression of the university and the program is the efficiency of the recruitment process, including the timeliness of communications. When the chair responds to questions in a timely manner, the applicant is likely to form a positive impression of the institution.

An effective strategy is to develop a timeline for recruitment and then work backward from the anticipated hiring date to delineate critical steps and timing of these activities. Committee members may perceive committee assignments as adding to their workload and thus assign lower priority to them because of competing demands. The timeline enables the committee to anticipate their responsibilities and timelines so that they can more effectively balance recruitment activities against other academic demands. The timeline can also help the chair to manage the recruitment process by quickly identifying breakdowns in processes and intervening to resolve the barriers to get the group back on track.

The next critical task is to identify the recruitment strategies that the plan comprises. The committee begins development of the plan in the preparatory phase, but the plan needs to be refined and finalized either before or by the beginning of the recruitment phase. The committee articulates the strategies incorporated in the plan and used in marketing the announcement and reaching potential applicants. The final step is to obtain HR approval, if required, before implementation of the plan.

Recruitment strategies are broken into passive and proactive approaches. *Passive* strategies target individuals who are actively searching for faculty positions (Deutsch, 2016; "The Recruitment Process," n.d.). As discussed earlier, it is a mistake to assume that if you merely post the announcement, all desired applicants will apply. *Proactive* recruitment is a stronger approach, in which the committee develops additional strategies by actively pursuing applicants. This may focus on those who are not necessarily looking for a new position or are unaware of the announcement, but may be enticed to consider applying. Proactive strategies are especially important in recruiting faculty from underrepresented groups. Harvard University (2016) reported on a recent study where two-thirds of non-White faculty versus only one-third of White faculty reported applying because someone contacted them directly to encourage submission of an application.

Faculty searches use a variety of passive and proactive strategies. The following are some passive strategies for recruitment:

- Post the announcement on job boards and websites with professional and social work organizations (e.g., the CSWE, National Association of Social Workers, Society of Social Work Research, American Psychological Association, and HigherEd.com). The National Association of Deans and Directors of Schools of Social Work is an additional resource if the position includes responsibilities in the BSW and MSW programs.

- Post on websites and newsletters of underrepresented groups (e.g., National Association of Black Social Workers, Association of Latina/Latino Social Work Educators, and American Association of University Women [AAUW]).

- Post on recruitment websites targeted to the academic employment sector, including the *Chronicle of Higher Education* and the Higher Education Recruitment Consortium, if your institution is a member.

- Post on public social media sites, which is an effective strategy for those not actively seeking employment (e.g., Facebook, LinkedIn, Twitter). Please refer to the "Selection Phase" section, which examines the pros and cons of using social media to identify and recruit faculty.

- Send announcements to administrators of doctoral programs, particularly when recruiting assistant professors.

- Post announcements on online discussion groups, particularly those associated with national, state, and local social work and field instructor groups. Professional online groups specifically for women and minoritized groups can also be of assistance.

Proactive strategies are more labor intensive, but effective in reaching members of traditionally underserved groups and those not currently seeking employment. Proactive approaches are especially beneficial if previous searches did not yield enough qualified applicants or large enough pools of applicants. Proactive strategies include the following:

- Make direct contacts with academic colleagues across the country, especially to reach senior-level and minoritized groups. If the contact is not interested, they may become a good referral source to identify other potential applicants.

- Review faculty rosters at peer universities and targeted minority-serving institutions to identify and contact potential applicants.

- Scan editorial board members of journals that focus on areas of interest (e.g., racial equity, substance abuse, administration, and community organizing).

- Conduct literature reviews on priority recruitment topics.

Attend professional conferences to observe and assess potential applicants' teaching skills and scholarly pursuits. Follow up with an informal conversation to share the announcement and highlight *only* the advantages of your department, your university, and the community. This conversation is not an interview to assess the applicant's qualifications if the individual has not already submitted an application; this would be a violation of an equitable recruitment process because not all potential applicants were informed of the opportunity to be interviewed.

As the recruitment plan rolls out, all members of the committee, as well as other department faculty members, should participate in identifying potential applicants. Fine and Handelsman (2012) recommended that each member of the committee be responsible for at least 10 outreach efforts; department faculty can also participate with direct contacts in their networks and distribute the announcement in their online discussion groups. The chair must keep a detailed record of all outreach efforts: contacted individuals, the date, type of outreach (e.g., direct contact, email, text), who made the outreach, and the outcome. This captures evidence of the extent of outreach, particularly when reaching out to members of underrepresented groups. HR often requests this type of information, and it is useful in postrecruitment evaluations.

The social work profession is committed to social justice, which applies to achieving inclusivity in faculty and staff recruitment. The goal is to identify a broad group of candidates, and the committee needs to be thoughtful about posting the announcement at sites that attract underrepresented faculty. Three excellent resources found in the "Suggested Readings" section are Columbia University (2016), University of Michigan (2018, p. 30), and Fine and Handelsman (2012, pp. 25–33), all of which provide a comprehensive list of resources to promote recruitment of those from traditionally underrepresented groups and include examples of forms and tools that assist with recruitment, evaluation, and regulatory compliance.

Over the past decade, the use of social media sites has expanded, particularly in relation to identifying applicants and evaluating their qualifications. While the use of social media in identifying and evaluating applicants has some advantages, it also has disadvantages that create concern about its usefulness. Advantages include reaching a wider audience, especially marginalized populations who do not have the resources to attend professional conferences or job fairs outside of their local geographic areas (Wagner & Scott, 2019). However, use of social media can raise ethical and legal issues, including the validity of the information obtained. Additionally, serious legal risks can occur that are associated with the right to privacy (Lam, 2016; Kroeze, 2015). Committees must weigh the advantages of social media against the disadvantages; refer to Kroeze (2015) and Lam (2016) for detailed discussions.

Selection Phase

After completion of application reviews, the process moves to the selection phase. The selection process involves sequential steps to identify the applicants who will move forward in the review process. Fine and Handelsman (2012) encouraged focusing discussions on whom to include rather than whom to exclude. Search committees tend to be more careful in their review of criteria when selecting who moves forward, rather than determining whom to eliminate.

Research by Hugenberg et al. (2006) supports the use of inclusion strategies (i.e., selecting suitable individuals) versus exclusion strategies (i.e., selecting unsuitable individuals) to reduce bias in decision making; they referred to this as "inclusion-exclusion discrepancy." The researchers found that individuals have greater depth of analysis and discussion when using inclusionary mindsets; exclusionary mindsets produce less depth, making such individuals more susceptible to social stereotypical factors in eliminating applicants (e.g., women, ethnic minorities).

In some universities, HR and the hiring officials must approve the list of interviewees before the committee moves to the selection phase. If the pool lacks sufficient diversity, HR may direct the committee to expand the list of interviewees or extend recruitment to increase diversity representation before the committee begins scheduling interviews. This presents challenges because most committees do not receive applicants' demographic information. A deeper review of submitted materials may provide hints of diversity, such as areas of interest, universities attended, research and scholarship, practice experience, and professional affiliations, but these may not be sufficient or accurate. If recruitment materials encourage applications from women and other minoritized groups, cover letters may include self-identification. HR can also provide guidance regarding target areas for additional recruitment of diverse candidates.

Prior to reviewing applications, the committee must agree to the process for review using the developed standardized forms (see the "Developing Evaluation Forms" section earlier in this chapter). As discussed previously, the first step in the process is for HR or the committee to determine if the applicant has met the required criteria, based only on information contained in the submitted application documents. The applicant legally cannot move forward regardless of their other qualifications if there are any required criteria missing. Either HR or the chair then informs the applicant of this decision.

CASE EXAMPLE

Dr. Jackson is the chair of a search committee for an assistant professor in their BSW program. Required criteria for this position include having completed a PhD in social work (or be within 1 year of completion) and have experience teaching social work classes. Ideally, the candidate would have expertise related to health care and be able to teach the policy course. While completing the initial review of applicants, the committee is very impressed by the cover letter of Candidate A, who was a medical social worker before returning to earn a PhD with a focus on health care policy. However, a closer reading revealed that Candidate A is just completing the coursework portion of the program and thus is not expected to graduate for several years. Based on the review, Dr. Jackson and the committee cannot recommend advancing this candidate.

All remaining applicants who meet the required criteria must undergo a thorough process of review to determine which applicants will move forward to interviews. The most common approach is for each member independently to review applications using the standardized evaluation form. Each member commits to thoroughly reviewing all elements in the application packet (e.g., curriculum vitae, cover letter, letters of support, and examples of writing if requested). At a meeting of the committee, each member participates in a discussion of the assessment of each applicant.

Committee members are encouraged to set a time when the review process will receive their undivided attention (e.g., with no interruptions from phones, colleagues, students, or other disturbances) to effectively and efficiently complete the review. Fine and Handelsman (2012) suggested that reviews should take 15–20 minutes per application. The amount of time will vary depending on the academic rank of the applicant given their years of experience (i.e., those applying for higher ranks typically submit larger application packets). The experience of the committee member in serving on other recruitment committees can also influence the time required. Rather than emphasize time, the priority should be to complete a thorough assessment that includes documentation of elements that validate the ratings.

When discussing the reviews as a group, the chair must ensure that members hear everyone's opinion. The committee members record individual ratings on the standardized form(s) and submit them to the chair for collation. Individual assessments prior to discussion prevents pressure on members to assign ratings that align with more vocal or senior faculty members. Group discussions are valuable because they allow members to provide factual evidence supporting a rating that others may have missed. However, the chair should caution members against revising their individual ratings without evidence of *factual* data, rather than merely opinion.

CASE EXAMPLE

A senior faculty member on a committee rejected an applicant on the criterion of "potential for research and grant development" because of their recent doctoral dissertation, stating that the dissertation did not represent rigorous research. Several members challenged this rating as biased toward quantitative, experimental designs, noting that the applicant's qualitative designs met rigorous methodological and analytical standards for this research method, and that the applicant's work should be measured against those standards.

Another potential bias to decision making occurs when "goodness of fit" becomes a qualifier in the review process. Harvard University (2016) cautioned against relying on "fit" without factual evidence that substantiates this claim, particularly in the review of those from underrepresented groups. The following quote from Harvard University (2016, p. 11) illustrates this point: "If 'fit' were the best driver of decision making, the Harvard of today would be identical to the Harvard of the past." There is a tendency for individuals to show preference for those who have similar characteristics and to assign goodness of fit to support their preferences. This has contributed to the underrepresentation of traditionally oppressed groups in a White-male-dominated workforce.

Each member computes their total score assigned to each applicant and submits the form to the chair, who then collates the "average total score" for each applicant and then ranks the applicants from highest to lowest total score. At the next meeting, the list is distributed, and the committee engages in group discussion with the goal of selecting those who will move forward to a short list for phone or video interviews.

Fine and Handelsman (2012) recommended another method that is especially effective when receiving large numbers of applications. First, all committee members briefly review all applications. Second, the chair assigns a limited number of applications to two-member groups to review, ensuring equal distribution among member pairs. If the pairs cannot reach agreement, the chair can request an additional member to review the application. Third, the pairs present their review at a committee meeting for group discussion, culminating in a group decision in the selection of applicants who will move forward.

Although score rank provides an important source for decision making, it is not necessarily the only source. When scores are close, consideration of other factors may influence decisions. For example, when scores are the same or extremely close, achieving inclusivity may advance an applicant forward over another applicant. If one's specialty area is a high priority for the department, university, or community, this may also sway decision making beyond just the score rank. It is also possible that the workload expectations of an applicant could sway decision making.

It is imperative that every step in the process be documented (e.g., application documents, evaluation forms, documentation of ratings, and notes on committee discussions and decision making), to be stored for a defined time to allow for postrecruitment evaluations or to address complaints about the recruitment process. It is important to clearly articulate why the committee moves an applicant forward versus eliminating them from further consideration, with data to support decision making. This validates that a fair recruiting and evaluation process occurred.

HR may also require completion of a summative form that captures this information for all applicants, including tracking the progress of the applicant from submission through selection of the finalists. If HR does not provide these forms, the chair should create a spreadsheet to summarize the same information. Once the evaluation of those submitting applications is completed, the committee discusses all applicants and the rankings to produce a list of recommendations; HR and hiring officials may again require approval of the list before contacting applicants to participate in the selection phase.

Although this process may provide strong evidence for decision making, be cautious about potential bias within individual ratings that may negatively affect consideration of underrepresented populations. If concerns exist regarding the lack of diversity, HR may ask the committee to reevaluate selections or expand the list to ensure representatives from underrepresented groups. The following steps provide a framework for the interview process.

Step 1: Preparation for Interviews

The first step is for the committee to create a structured interview format for both the short and final interviews. Although standardization is the goal for the interview stage, complete standardization is difficult, especially during campus visits, which involve unstructured conversations and interviews, such as meals, receptions, individual interviews by non–committee members, and questions and answers following presentations.

Interview schedules should be prepared in advance and vetted by HR to ensure that questions do not violate federal and state laws or university policies. The committee members must be familiar with EOAA policies so that they do not ask questions regarding the applicant's personal life or attempt to gather other protected information. This includes questions regarding race, sex, disability, age, religion, national origin or citizenship, sexual orientation, political affiliations, marital or family status, pregnancy, child care arrangements, weight or height, military or veteran status, arrest records, and credit status (University of Texas-El Paso, n.d.).

Committee members must agree upon a consistent process for the interview and evaluation of applicants. A common approach for structured interviews is for each member to use a standardized, structured interview form approved by HR. Each member rates applicants independently. The chair collects and ranks the applicants and distributes the rankings to the committee for group discussion and the selection of the final list of candidates invited for a campus visit. HR or hiring officials must review and approve the list before the committee extends invitations. Some universities may require fewer steps in the review process, but the processes tend to be very similar.

Step 2: Conducting the Preliminary Interview

The preliminary interview involves those selected for the short list. HR and hiring officials must approve the list before notifying the candidates and setting up the interviews. The committee members are the only ones present for the interviews by phone or videoconference call (e.g., Zoom or Microsoft Teams) with typically no more than 10 finalists. The purpose is to gather additional information not captured in paper documents.

The preliminary interview is the first step in examining what Abrams (2018) described as "hard skills" (e.g., knowledge and techniques) and "soft skills" (e.g., attributes such as being a good communicator, interacting well with others, having rapport with students, and being a team player). Hard skills produce a more reliable assessment, whereas soft skills are often difficult to measure and lack predictive accuracy, particularly when the interview is unstructured.

Preliminary interviews may still be advantageous even when the applicant pool is relatively small. For example, if the committee receives five applications, the committee members could go straight to recommending applicants for campus interviews. But campus visits are expensive, requiring a large commitment of faculty and staff time. A preliminary interview could shorten the list to preferred applicants (e.g., two or three applicants) for the campus visit. Another option is to conduct preliminary interviews at professional conferences. However, unless the whole group has been selected at this stage, such interviews could violate requirements for an equitable recruitment process because some applicants perform better face-to-face and may struggle with phone or video interviews. This creates inequity for those unable to attend the conference and participate in a face-to-face preliminary interview.

Upon completion of the preliminary interviews, the committee meets again to determine its recommendations for finalists invited for campus visits.

Step 3: Final Interview for a Campus Visit

The next interview is the campus visit. This visit is the strongest tool to market the BSW program, the campus, and the community. Remember that the interview is a two-way process. Fine and Handelsman (2012) emphasized that the interview is a dual process in which the department and institution are evaluating the applicant, and the applicant is evaluating potential colleagues, campus assets, and the community. The following is a limited list of suggestions for the campus visit (see Columbia University, 2016; Fine & Handelsman, 2012; University of Michigan, 2018). Universities would be wise to draw on practices from the hospitality industry to achieve the most welcoming experience:

- Arrange all travel plans, including transportation from and to the airport. It is more welcoming for a committee member to pick up the candidate.

- Ensure that hotel accommodations are close to campus or in an area that is walking distance to locations that capture the culture and appeal of the community.

- Leave a gift basket in the hotel room including water, snacks, and brochures showcasing the campus and community.

- Identify restaurants for meals that highlight local cuisine. Prior to the visit, ask the candidate if they have any food preferences or restrictions. Make reservations, if possible.

- Choose faculty members to host meals who will highlight the assets of the campus and community.

- Prepare an agenda reflective of program priorities and with input from the candidate regarding special needs and specific interests. List all meetings and events, including the date, time, location, and attendee(s) with their titles.

- Identify one or two faculty or students who will escort the candidate to and from meetings. Do not expect the candidate to find their own way around campus.

- Because the focus of BSW programs is the students, schedule a meeting with students that does not include faculty to promote open discussion; this is advantageous for both the candidate and the students. Be certain to invite students to the candidate's presentation(s), especially the teaching demonstration.

- Include a tour of the campus and community.

- The agenda should include small breaks during the day and a space where the candidate can retrieve emails.

The following example illustrates the importance of hospitality.

CASE EXAMPLE

The committee chair contacted an applicant for a campus visit. The university arranged flight and hotel accommodations. The administrative assistant instructed the applicant to arrange their own transportation from the airport to the hotel and to walk to the university where the social work program was located. A few selected faculty members met with the applicant individually and then the applicant met with the whole faculty to give their presentation. Only faculty attended the presentation, no contact occurred with students or other administrators in the university, and they provided no informational materials about the campus or community. During the presentation, the faculty and social work director got into an argument in response to content from the presentation. After the presentation, the applicant thanked the director and walked alone back to the hotel. No meals occurred with faculty, students, or university administrators. The applicant arranged their own transportation to the airport the following day. The next day, the applicant withdrew their name from consideration.

Prior to the visit, the chair needs to make sure that an equivalent agenda is distributed to all finalists and those involved in interviewing. Anyone involved in scheduled activities should receive the finalists' CVs and cover letters. Meetings may be scheduled with the search committee, department faculty, college faculty (if relevant), students or student association leadership, and community groups. Other group meetings may include members of interdisciplinary teams and research centers or groups relevant to the applicant's scholarly interests, as well as a visit to a community agency, if requested. Individual meetings with the chair, dean, provost, and president as well as other key institutional leaders are encouraged. Although faculty may request individual interviews, these can have limitations related to inefficiency and unstructured interviews.

CASE EXAMPLE

A finalist interviewed at a university where they sat in a room for most of the day and faculty signed up for 30-minute individual interviews. These were not structured interviews, resulting in a great deal of repetition in questions, less content depth, and less time for the applicant to ask questions. A group interview with faculty may have been more productive, especially if using a structured interview schedule. This would ensure that all necessary topics and the applicant's questions are addressed.

The chair should schedule the same social events; if these include meals, ideally the same individuals should attend, if possible. All contacts related to support services should be consistent, such as the campus tour, HR, benefits, library, Office of Research, and departments or programs related to campus life (e.g., Office of Student Affairs, student and faculty disability services, Title IX office, and family support resources). Finally, the chair and HR should prepare information and activities in relation to onboarding, including documents (e.g., maps, listing and ratings of school districts) and tours of the community. Scheduling a meeting with a Realtor may also be important, regardless of whether the candidate is local or from out of town. This would support equity in the process and considers that a change in position for a local finalist might enable the purchase of a new home.

A common practice is to require a presentation by finalists. BSW programs set a high priority on excellence in teaching and may ask applicants to do one or two presentations. It is typical for a candidate to demonstrate teaching skills and philosophy, so student attendance should be encouraged. There may also be another presentation on scholarly interests, depending on the program. The chair arranges distribution of the announcement of the applicant's presentation(s) to all faculty using institutional distribution lists or postings on communication boards across campus so faculty can attend the presentation(s). This promotes future collaborative partnerships if the finalist is hired. Every finalist should have the same number of presentations, and to standardize the process as much as possible, use the same location, if possible; allow the same amount of time; distribute the same documents; have the same individual introduce the candidate; and use sign-in sheets.

CASE EXAMPLE

The chair potentially introduced bias when the first of two finalists asked the chair to make copies of a few of their selected publications; the chair agreed and distributed the copies at the colloquium. After the colloquium, the director questioned if the chair offered this to the second finalist; the chair said no, indicating that the applicant did not request it. The director instructed the chair to immediately contact the second finalist and offer the same service. The second finalist accepted the offer to distribute a few copies of their publications. If this had not occurred, HR could have nullified the entire recruitment based on an inequitable recruitment process.

A last step in the campus visit is a final meeting with the committee; the director or hiring official may also choose to attend or request individual meetings. This is the opportunity for the applicant to ask additional questions or clarify information. It also creates an opportunity for the chair and committee members to question the applicant to clarify information presented during the interview. The chair should inform applicants that if they have more questions after the interview, they are free to contact the chair or director.

As described earlier (see the "Developing Evaluation Forms" section), the chair is responsible for ensuring the distribution, collection, data entry, and analysis for all evaluation forms. The committee uses these data to support decision making and recommendations submitted at the end of the interview process. Analysis across subgroups (e.g., department faculty, other faculty, students, and staff) can provide evidence to support decisions as well as the evaluation of the recruitment process.

At this point, the chair contacts references only for the candidate(s) recommended for appointment. Using a standardized interview form, the chair interviews the references. Rather than using broad, generic questions, such as "What are the applicant's strengths and weaknesses?," gather information specific to the required and preferred criteria delineated in the announcement. Use the same interview process described earlier in this section and in the preliminary interviews. The committee meets to decide whom they will recommend to the hiring officials based on all the information gathered.

The chair typically produces a detailed report on the recruitment and selection process, the results of the evaluations from stakeholders, feedback from references, and the committee vote on those finalists recommended to the hiring official for appointment. If this is an appointment on the tenure track or with tenure, the university typically requires tenured faculty within the program at the same faculty rank or above to vote on whether they support the appointment.

Some committees feel that more than one candidate could be considered for hiring. In this situation, the university may require the committee to rank their recommended candidates. Other departments or programs instruct the committee to submit the recommended applicants without any ranking. The hiring official will make the decision as to who receives an offer. If the first-choice candidate declines the position, the hiring official can offer it to the alternate candidate or declare a failed search.

If the committee does not recommend any of the finalists after the campus visit, the committee could return to the short list to recommend additional finalists for a campus visit, assuming that the chair or HR did not send letters of rejection to these individuals. Even if the committee ranks the recommended candidates for employment, typically the decision ultimately rests with the hiring official regardless of the committee's ranking. Exercise caution before notifying any finalist, should the first choice and the hiring official not reach agreement on a contract. The hiring official would have three options: (1) offer the position to the alternate candidate, (2) repost the announcement as it exists, or (3) delay further recruitment to allow the committee to evaluate the search in order to redesign and improve the recruitment processes (Bates, 2019). When the search process has reached its conclusion, notify all applicants that the search has been completed and thank them for their interest in your program. While not selected this time, they may be strong applicants for future opportunities.

Several strategies can help guide the evaluation of the recent recruitment efforts. To encourage honest feedback, it is best if HR participates in this evaluation. Reach out to recent hires to obtain feedback on their experiences with recruitment. Create a climate where critical feedback, both positive and negative, is encouraged along with recommendations for improvement. Evaluate each step from the preparatory phase to the selection phase to identify where improvements can make the process more efficient, increase applications, and improve the rate of success in hiring. If HR keeps hiring analytics on past searches, review the data on past recruitment (Russell, 2020), examining conversion rates (i.e., hits on the announcement on the university website compared with the number of completed applications). Review data on the time from posting the announcement to completion of the hiring process to identify barriers and slippage in the process that contributed to delays. Other metrics to include in the evaluation are the number of early turnover rates of new hires and costs per hire. If reposting the position, the committee should review the previous announcement to determine any changes that have the potential to reach a broader audience through more effective marketing strategies.

In terms of diversity, a review of the previous recruitment should occur, focusing on minoritized groups. The chair should review the application patterns among these groups to examine the number of applications received and the count of those selected for campus interviews. If previous searches in the program or from other programs were successful in recruiting those from underrepresented groups, the chair can talk to members of these search committees to identify what strategies contributed to their success. They should also examine how many minoritized finalists turned down offers and obtain data on why, if available (University of Michigan, 2018).

Conclusion

Recruitment of faculty is a systematic process that entails three sequential phases: preparatory, recruitment, and selection. The preparatory phase is to determine hiring needs, culminating in a profile that identifies the characteristics of a successful applicant. It entails conducting an environmental analysis, developing a search committee with diverse membership, constructing the position announcement, and creating and analyzing evaluation forms. The recruitment phase entails the development of a recruitment plan that produces a comprehensive list of strategies to reach potential applicants. Committee members and departmental faculty must play an active role in identifying and encouraging applicants, especially among underrepresented groups.

The selection phase involves the evaluation of applications, leading to the development of the short list for phone or videoconferencing interviews and then producing a recommended finalist list for a campus visit. Remember that the campus visit is a two-way process in which members of the campus community interview applicants, and the applicant learns about the department, campus, and community. Therefore, strategies borrowed from the hospitality sector are encouraged to promote a welcoming environment that demonstrates the many assets of the campus and community. The entire process involves collaboration with hiring officials and HR, who are responsible for monitoring and evaluating each phase in the process. The chapter does not pretend to be a cookbook, but offers suggestions and strategies that will strengthen the process.

The department grounds its recruitment process in a commitment to create and maintain a diverse faculty, congruent with the social work values of justice, equity, and inclusivity. This translates into identifying applicants from minoritized backgrounds through passive and proactive recruitment strategies. The hiring officials must set the tone for an equitable and inclusive search process, as well as demonstrate vigilance in identifying unconscious bias that can negatively influence the evaluation of minority applicants. If social media sites are used in identifying and assessing applicants, be aware of the challenges associated with this recruitment strategy. Membership on the Search Committee should reflect inclusivity, which can increase diversity in the applicant pool. Finally, achieving diversity requires a long-term commitment. A single recruitment cannot resolve the inequality. It requires proactive recruitment strategies to identify outstanding minority applicants and nurturing the relationship to achieve successful recruitment.

Suggested Readings

Catanzaro, D., Moore, H., & Marshall, T. R. (2010). The impact of organizational culture on attraction and recruitment of job applicants. *Journal of Business Psychology, 25,* 649–662. https://doi.org/10.1007/s10869-010-9179-0

Clark, H. G., Moore, B. A., Johnston, L. B., & Openshaw, L. (2011). Using adjuncts in social work education: Challenges and rewards. *Social Work Education, 30*(8), 1012–1021. https://doi.org/10.1080/02615479.2010.534450

Columbia University. (2016, July). *Guide to best practices in faculty search and hiring.* https://provost.columbia.edu/sites/default/files/content/BestPracticesFacultySearchHiring.pdf

Fine, E., & Handelsman, J. (2012). *Excellence & diversity: A guide for search committees.* University of Wisconsin-Madison.

Harvard University. (2016). *Best practices for conducting faculty searches.* https://faculty.harvard.edu/files/fdd/files/best_practices_for_conducting_faculty_searches_v1.2.pdf

Hugenberg, K., Bodenhausen, G. V., & McLain, M. (2006). Framing discrimination: Effects of inclusion versus exclusion mind-sets on stereotypic judgments. *Journal of Personality and Social Psychology, 91*(6), 1020–1031. https://doi.org/10.1037/0022-3514.91.6.1020

Kroeze, R. (2015). *5th IVA Bachelor Thesis Conference, November 5th, 2015, Enschede, The Netherlands.* University of Twente, the Faculty of Behavioural, Management and Social Sciences.

Lam, H. (2015). Social media dilemmas in the employment context. *Employee Relations, 38*(3), 420–437. DOI 10.1108/ER-04-2015-0072

References

Abrams, Z. (2018). Academic careers: 8 steps for hiring the faculty of your dreams. *Monitor on Psychology, 49*(8), 70–75. https://www.apa.org/monitor/2018/09/academic-hiring

Baranczyk, M. C. (2013). Are family-friendly policies an effective recruitment strategy? *International Journal of Business and Social Science, 4*(16), 1–8. http://ijbssnet.com/journals/Vol_4_No_16_December_2013/1.pdf

Bates, H. (2019, March 28). *11 steps to develop a 21st century recruitment plan.* https://harver.com/blog/recruitment-plan/

Catanzaro, D., Moore, H., & Marshall, T. R. (2010). The impact of organizational culture on attraction and recruitment of job applicants. *Journal of Business Psychology, 25,* 649–662. https://doi.org/10.1007/s10869-010-9179-0

Clark, H. G., Moore, B. A., Johnston, L. B., & Openshaw, L. (2011). Using adjuncts in social work education: Challenges and rewards, *Social Work Education, 30*(8), 1012–1021. https://doi.org/10.1080/02615479.2010.534450

Columbia University. (2016, July). *Guide to best practices in faculty search and hiring.* https://provost.columbia.edu/sites/default/files/content/BestPracticesFacultySearchHiring.pdf

Council on Social Work Education. (2021). *2020 Statistics on social work education in the United States.* https://www.cswe.org/getattachment/726b15ce-6e63-4dcd-abd1-35d2ea9d9d40/2020-Annual-Statistics-On-Social-Work-Education-in-the-United-States.pdf?lang=en-US

Council on Social Work Education (2022). *2022 Educational policy and accreditation standards.* https://www.cswe.org/getmedia/94471c42-13b8-493b-9041-b30f48533d64/2022-EPAS.pdf

Deutsch, M. (2016). *The 10 most critical recruitment process steps.* https://www.topechelon.com/blog/placement-process/10-critical-recruitment-process-steps/

Fine, E., & Handelsman, J. (2012). *Excellence & diversity: A guide for search committees.* University of Wisconsin-Madison.

Harvard University. (2016). *Best practices for conducting faculty searches.* https://faculty .harvard.edu/files/fdd/files/best_practices_for_conducting_faculty_searches_v1.2.pdf

Hugenberg, K., Bodenhausen, G. V., & McLain, M. (2006). Framing discrimination: Effects of inclusion versus exclusion mind-sets on stereotypic judgments. *Journal of Personality and Social Psychology, 91*(6), 1020–1031. https://doi.org/10.1037/0022-3514.91.6.1020

Indeed. (n.d.). *The recruitment process from start to finish.* https://www.indeed.com/hire/c /info/the-recruitment-process?aceid=&gclid=CjwKCAiAjeSABhAPEiwAqfxURT JWy_AIDjv-CNCt-lQr9IVVME2r0ZXLiiQtcrP1ilj2Poy3FZm-fxoCnuAQAvD_BwE

Kroeze, R. (2015, November 5). *Recruitment via social media sites: A critical review and research agenda* [Paper]. 5th IBA Bachelor Thesis Conference, Enschede, The Netherlands. https://essay.utwente.nl/68499/1/Kroeze_BA_BMS.pdf

Lam, H. (2016). Social media dilemmas in the employment context. *Employee Relations, 38*(3), 420–437. https://doi.org/10.1108/ER-04-2015-0072

Russell, C. (2020, March 19). *What are the 7 stages of recruitment?* https://www.emissary.ai /what-are-the-7-stages-of-recruitment/

University of Michigan. (2018). *Handbook for faculty searches and hiring.* https://advance. umich.edu/wp-content/uploads/2018/10/Handbook-for-Faculty-Searches -and-Hiring.pdf

University of Texas-El Paso. (n.d.). *Hiring manager resource guide.* University of Texas-El Paso Human Resources. https://www.utep.edu/human-resources/services/employment/hiring -manager-toolkit.html

van Maanen, V. (2018). The human resources employment cycle: Finding the right fit, and keeping them. *BusiDate, 26*(4), 12–14. https://library.parker.edu/eds?query= %22AUSTRALIA%22&type=DE&searchfield=SU&ff[]=Publisher:warringal %20publications

Wagner, R., & Scott, K. M. (2019, Winter). Socially just hiring practices. *New Directions for Student Services,* (168), 29–39. https://doi.org/10.1002/ss.20329

Zhang, H., Kmec, J. A., & Byington, T. (2019). Gendered career decisions in the academy: Job refusal and job departure intentions among academic dual-career couples. *The Review of Higher Education, 42*(4), 1723–1754. https://doi.org/10.1353/rhe.2019.0081

Promoting Success and Retention Among Social Work Faculty Through Effective Supervision, Mentoring, and Professional Development

Jennifer R. Jewell
Susan C. Mapp

After successfully recruiting a new faculty member, as described in Chapter 12, program directors must then help them to become successful in their position. More experienced faculty also need support throughout their careers. Appropriately crafted supervision will help to foster the success and retention of social work faculty, and thus program directors must make sure that programs and practices are provided for professional growth, such as effective supervision, mentoring, and professional development, especially for those from traditionally oppressed groups.

This chapter describes some methods to support professional development for both new and experienced faculty members through differential supervision, mentoring, and professional development opportunities across the program. Investing in initiatives to attract, retain, and develop a talented and diverse faculty body reaps a multitude of benefits for faculty, students, and the institution. This chapter includes a description of processes, practical information, and strategies for administrators, such as advocacy on the institutional level for equitable standards. This chapter focuses on supporting full-time tenure-track faculty members, while Chapter 15 focuses on contingent and adjunct faculty, but many of the same issues and supports will apply to both groups.

The Role of the Program Director

The position and authority of the BSW program director in overseeing faculty can vary significantly depending on the institution and often on whether the program director is also the head of the department or resides within a colocated program or interdisciplinary department. Whether their power is formal or informal, undergraduate program directors are in a position to either make decisions or, at least, influence decisions, based on their proximity to the dean or chair. Program directors can take action to make or influence decisions through individual supervision, on a group level through developing effective mentoring and professional development programs, or through advocating to the larger institution to ensure that the needs and priorities of social work faculty are included in institutional policies and practices.

While effective faculty are the key to an effective institution, attention and resources for faculty support and development vary widely from one institution to another and even within the same institution, depending on the investment in individual units. Yet, in many cases, faculty supports in the form of supervision, mentoring, and professional development are nonexistent or insufficient (Pesce, 2015). Specifically, investments in supervision, mentoring, and professional development all help to support faculty as they transition into new roles. They may include new faculty just joining the institution, current faculty moving through the ranks of tenure and promotion, or those moving into leadership roles. A combination of career development mechanisms throughout all the career stages can help faculty to thrive.

Creating a supportive culture can have particular benefit for traditionally marginalized groups in academia, such as women and people of color. This supportive culture can also aid in the skills development of future leaders in the department or program. A national survey of BSW program directors found that the modal years of experience was one, selected by 20% of respondents (Mapp & Boutté-Queen, 2020). Given that most program directors are new, leadership development is paramount. Faculty members who are people of color and women experience pipeline issues, thus the supports provided in academic units must also include leadership development opportunities because academic leaders are often promoted from within. As academic leadership is vital to university well-being, program directors need to implement mechanisms to identify faculty with administrative potential and provide the development needed for budding leaders to build the skills and confidence to take on leadership, whether as facilitators of committees, department or program chairs, or unit representatives on the faculty senate.

Even if the wider university may not prioritize faculty supports, social work academic leaders can lead the way in cultivating a culture of support within their units and advocate on a larger level for more opportunities. Social workers understand that the importance of human relationships and building a supportive and collaborative community aligns with the profession's ethics of strengthening relationships among individuals, groups, and organizations, with the goal of enhancing well-being (National Association of Social Workers [NASW], 2021).

Although attention often centers on tenure-track faculty in terms of the importance of supports to navigate academia, contingent faculty members—which include full-time, non-tenure-track faculty; part-time faculty; and graduate student employees—typically do not receive the same amount of attention. Social work academia relies increasingly on the use of these important colleagues, with more than 60% of social work faculty being part-time instructors (Council on Social Work Education [CSWE], 2021a). With the increased use of part-time instructors within social work education, it is necessary to develop supports that include or specifically target adjunct faculty. These faculty are discussed in more detail in Chapter 15, but we note them here because including them in development programs and opportunities can pay off for the program and its students. Investing in supports for part-time instructors can lead to enhanced teaching performance, increased student learning, and decreased time needed from academic leaders to address issues.

The Need for Attention to Mindful Support

Like other workplaces, academic institutions have a thick organizational culture, with written and unwritten procedures, creating both flexibility and ambiguity. Learning all of these nuances can put new faculty in a challenging position to learn how to survive and thrive. Although supports should be in place throughout the career span, new faculty transitioning into academia typically need additional support. Learning how to balance the competing demands of an academic role and adapting to academic culture and organizational structure can be overwhelming. New faculty have indicated their needs for guidance in teaching, and in how to advise students, apply for grants, publish, and develop a professional development plan that will lead to tenure and promotion. They have stated that being a new faculty member, especially for those from marginalized backgrounds, was a constant stressor because of work-life balance, student loans, racial stressors, and other factors (Sun & Simon-Roberts, 2020).

Helping faculty achieve successful careers means providing support beyond the initial years of their careers. Faculty members in general experience high levels of stress and occupational burnout (Weimer, 2010), which have been exponentially exacerbated by the COVID-19 pandemic (*Chronicle of Higher Education*, 2020). Although multiple factors contribute to faculty burnout, such as workload, role ambiguity, and lack of attention to professional development, supports that spur professional growth and development stave off burnout (Weimer, 2010). Thus, ensuring that all faculty have access to support and professional development for continual renewal is imperative to increase retention, maintain work-life balance, and decrease burnout.

Although all faculty must navigate these challenges, faculty of color may face additional barriers. Lack of support and mentoring makes it more difficult for any new faculty member to be successful, but additional barriers exist for faculty from minoritized identities, as they will often encounter microaggressions and overt discrimination, as well as structural discrimination (Weng & Gray, 2017). They are more likely to experience a chilly work environment in which they lack support networks, feel more isolated, feel less respected and supported, and experience lower job satisfaction than their White counterparts (Castro, 2010; Davis, 1985). This unsupportive environment is even more prominent for women of color (Gutiérrez y Muhs et al., 2012). They are often asked to take on additional teaching or service responsibilities related to diversity and inclusion that their peers avoid, or they are sought out for support by students from similar backgrounds, diverting their time away from other activities (Griffin et al., 2020; Neale-McFall et al., 2020; Weng & Gray, 2017). This can then negatively affect research productivity and ultimately the ability to secure tenure and promotion (Griffin et al., 2020; Neale-McFall et al., 2020).

Women also face additional barriers within academic institutions. Women have greater higher educational attainment levels than men, with women earning more than 50% of all degrees, from bachelor's to doctoral degrees (Johnson, 2016). While the number of women available for academic leadership positions exceeds that of men, women are less likely to be found in these roles. For women of color, that discrepancy is even more pronounced

(Johnson, 2016). These same dynamics play out in the social work realm. Despite being a female-dominated profession, academic leadership within social work mimics the representation issues exhibited in society. Almost three quarters of all full-time social work faculty members are female (CSWE, 2021a), yet proportionally there are fewer women in leadership roles, particularly as deans and directors, and women are less likely to be full professors in social work and in academia in general (Johnson, 2016; Tower et al., 2019).

Women have reported working more hours than men, having to work harder to be taken seriously, and feeling less supported, all of which led to them being more likely to consider quitting (Neale-McFall et al., 2020). Almost 20% of female social work faculty experienced bullying and incivility at work so severe that it affected their physical and mental health on a daily or weekly basis (Brocksen, as cited in McClendon et al., 2021). Black female faculty reported common experiences of isolation and bullying, and an overall lack of support (Frazier, 2011; Parker, 2017).

LGBTQ+ faculty also have reported a limiting of opportunities based on their identity: They have been denied experiences because they "would not represent the university very well" or were not able to teach the course they desired because of their social identity (Prock et al., 2019, p. 191). They reported needing to self-monitor at all times: "There are always multiple dialogues, the one in my head and the one that comes out of my mouth" (Prock et al., 2019, p. 192).

Thus, all faculty will need support from their leaders, including the program director, but additional barriers will be faced by those from traditionally oppressed groups, which may be invisible to others. BSW program directors must keep this in mind when developing a supportive culture with the procedures and programs to help all of their faculty become successful educators and scholars.

Developing Effective Educators

The most common rank by far at which social work programs hire is the assistant professor level (Barsky et al., 2014), indicating a likely low level of experience in the academy. Because many social work PhD programs do not provide education in effective pedagogy (Maynard et al., 2017), many graduates are ill-prepared to enter the academy, particularly in BSW programs with their teaching focus, though DSW programs that include a focus on teaching may help address this. Regardless, the program director needs to ensure that new hires are oriented not just to the institution but also to the expectations and abilities of the academic role.

When surveying hiring programs about areas of expertise that were lacking in the pool of applicants, the most commonly mentioned was teaching, with 40% of respondents noting this as a concern (Barsky et al., 2014). Many PhD programs prioritize developing the research skills of their students over their pedagogical skills—and some do not teach the latter skills at all. This balance seems to have improved slightly since the survey by Valentine et al. (1998), which found that few social work doctoral programs offered coursework or experiential learning opportunities that prepared students for their teaching responsibilities. The Group for the Advancement of Doctoral Education in Social Work (GADE) revised its program guidelines in 2013 to include the expectation that programs will help to develop students' teaching skills, noting that most PhD candidates want a job in which they are able to both teach and conduct research (GADE, 2013). This combination has continued to be rated highly as a student goal in both PhD and DSW programs (CSWE, 2021b).

However, the preparation required to achieve this goal continues to lag. The content analysis by Maynard et al. (2017) found that 90% of social work doctoral programs had an outcome related to developing effective educators, but only 50% required a course related to teaching, and an additional 10% had one as an elective. This leaves a mismatch of 40% where programs had preparation for teaching as a goal but did not offer a related course. This finding is supported by Franklin et al. (2021) in a survey that found that about half of social work PhD programs offered a course on teaching, but only 29% offered a practical experience; this is in contrast to the average six classes offered on research and statistics per program.

When looking at the ability to develop these skills, Maynard et al. (2017) found that 18% of programs required a teaching practicum and that 17% had an elective opportunity. However, even when students have taught, they may still lack supervision by an experienced faculty member, the ability to develop a philosophy of teaching, or receive formal training in an evidence-based pedagogy (Pryce et al., 2011). Thus, it is likely that new doctoral graduates will be starting their jobs with little to no training in effective teaching methods. This is particularly important for BSW program directors, given the concentrated focus on teaching in baccalaureate social work. Social work programs have recognized the need for faculty members, ideally in their doctoral programs, to develop an understanding of social work pedagogy, including how to teach, educational theories, and curriculum development, as well as hands-on experience, which should include mentoring by senior faculty (Barsky et al., 2014).

In a qualitative study of doctoral students' teaching experiences, Oktay et al. (2013) found that classroom skills were developed in three areas. The first was learning to establish authority, where participants reported developing classroom management skills and how to handle grading issues. In the second area—developing an effective teaching style—respondents discussed establishing an effective teaching persona that met the needs of their students through trial and error and learning to accept critical feedback and adapt their teaching in response. Last, these new educators integrated the broader context of social work education through learning to assess not just academic skills, but also the professional development needs of their students and to teach them to succeed in their future professional roles (Oktay et al., 2013). Thus, practical experience helps to expand a multitude of skills, which, if not developed before being hired, will need to be developed within the new role.

Developing Successful Scholars

Similar to the discussion of the overall challenges faced by faculty from traditionally marginalized groups, these barriers can play out in the area of scholarship as well. Settles et al. (2021, 2022) examined "epistemic exclusion" and "scholarly devaluation" in which the work of those from marginalized backgrounds is devalued because of rigid, traditional views about what is "good" scholarship, as well as who creates it. This is then replicated outside of the institution through what is deemed publishable in a "top-tier" journal, as well as "worthy" of receiving grant funding, especially through the sought-after federal grants. Much like social workers, who experience stigmatization because they work with those who are stigmatized, scholars who study marginalized populations or topics are likely to themselves be marginalized.

Scholars of color at predominately White, research-intensive institutions who researched topics related to race, ethnicity, and/or gender are more likely to feel that their work is devalued by their peers (Settles et al., 2021). In addition, those who used nontraditional methods, worked in in nontraditional spaces (such as internationally), or worked in applied research, reported that they were perceived as engaging in lower-quality scholarship. This is then compounded by the social position of those from marginalized groups who are deemed to be less credible and/or lacking in skill and intelligence compared with those from privileged social groups. Men from backgrounds other than White or Asian, as well as women from all backgrounds (as compared with all men), are significantly more likely to report experiencing this devaluation (Settles et al., 2021).

In investigating the experiences of LGBTQ+ social work faculty, Prock et al. (2019) found that some would avoid researching topics related to their identity because the topic would not be regarded as a "legitimate" research topic or one that would lead to funding opportunities. Some noted that these areas of scholarship were derided as "me-search" (Settles et al., 2021). Given that such topics are deemed less valuable or scholarly, they are less likely to be funded or published in top-tier journals, which could then lead to lower merit raises and a lower likelihood of tenure and promotion, if these factors are important to the institution. These are all significant considerations for social work leaders, including BSW program directors, who seek to foster supportive environments for all faculty members.

Onboarding

To help curtail such challenges and to develop and support quality faculty and thus retain them, an array of supports is needed. These may range from providing effective supervision and linking that to ongoing professional development to ensuring a nurturing culture in the department and establishing effective mentoring programs to advocating at the institutional level for equitable policies that allow for a diversity of successful faculty members. One of the first steps is ensuring that there is a productive onboarding process for new faculty members. Beyond a onetime event, the onboarding process can include orientation and other trainings or workshops to help the employee integrate into the program and institution.

Although program directors may have little interaction with new faculty members between when new hires sign the contract and when they arrive on campus, program directors can welcome their new colleagues, answer any questions they may have pertaining to their role within the unit, and help troubleshoot any issues with the transition. These initial interactions can help to assuage some of the likely stress of transitioning to a new job and will begin the process of building a supportive working relationship.

Once the person arrives on campus, having an effective orientation program that extends past explanation of human resource policies is an important tool to onboard new hires and help them successfully integrate into the program and institution. Intentional effort on the part of the program director to build community from the beginning can help to ease any feelings of isolation that may be present. If the BSW program is not big enough to provide its own program, it can be coordinated together with the larger school, college, or university. Faculty work is often seen as individual—teaching, scholarship—so taking deliberative steps to build a welcoming community from the very beginning will assist all new faculty and especially those from minoritized groups (Griffin et al., 2020; Howard, 2017).

Although an inclusive approach is always important, recognizing the different needs of different types of faculty is important. One school that developed a mentorship program for all new instructors—new tenure-track faculty, new contingent faculty, and new doctoral student instructors—found that these groups had different needs and goals, even down to preferred meeting times. While they overall liked having a go-to person for their questions, their identification of program strengths and challenges varied (Brady & Spencer, 2018). Therefore, the program director does need to be mindful of how to establish an onboarding process that not only welcomes those from different roles and identities, but also meets their specific needs.

When thinking about how to develop an effective orientation that goes beyond the initial few weeks and human resources' policies, Clochesy et al. (2019) described a program for faculty with four components: academic citizenship, open-forum scientific discourse, writing for publication, and evidence base for educational practice. The academic citizenship portion extends over the first 2 years of a faculty member's employment and coaches them in developing a balance among teaching, scholarship, and service appropriate to the institution; developing a professional development plan with short- and long-term goals; developing work-life balance; and learning what not to do (an area often overlooked). Academic citizenship can be explored through a comprehensive group onboarding process and/or as a component of mentoring and supervision.

Open-forum scientific discourse is for faculty of all levels of experience to share ideas and get feedback on proposed research, which may be planned topics or spontaneous. These discussions can also lead to collaborative research projects. Writing for publication includes writing circles, writing retreats, and "write your journal article in 12 weeks" seminars. Other options can include a writing circle, with faculty across years, so that newer faculty can be working alongside and learning from experienced faculty (Howard, 2017). The "evidence base for educational practice" provides a series of seminars on current research in best pedagogical practice. The social work competencies require practitioners to base their work on an evidence-informed approach—we should ask no less from their instructors. Teaching-discussion sessions could be another option for mutual sharing of ideas, as newer faculty may bring innovative methods from which experienced faculty can benefit. Discussions on the development or enhancement of the faculty member's teaching philosophy, which serves as a guide for competent teaching practice, can also take place. Part-time instructors should be invited to participate in these efforts where appropriate.

PRACTICE TIP: Don't limit these discussions to only new faculty. The interchange between new and experienced faculty can benefit everyone.

Supervision

The program director is often the first point of contact for new faculty members. As the leader for the program, the director must know how to provide substantive and meaningful supervision. The director needs to not only provide the previously discussed support for all faculty, but also create cohesion within the program and maintain a productive environment. However, a national survey found that only 12% of BSW program directors reported any formal training before assuming the position, and only about half (55%) reported any training afterward. Accreditation was the most common topic on which they were trained at either point (Mapp & Boutté-Queen, 2020). This lack of training leaves some leaders ill-equipped to provide effective and meaningful supervision, the first of which is establishing trust.

Despite an inherent hierarchy between the supervisor and supervisee, or chair/director and faculty member, establishing trust and a collegial relationship should be a priority, especially when moving into a leadership position and when a new faculty member is hired. There are multiple ways in which supervisors can develop trust, such as providing consistent and effective communication and establishing clear and consistent expectations and priorities (Buller, 2012). Borrowing from the business sector, "management by walking around" is a management style that encourages managers to wander around the workplace in an unstructured manner to build relationships with others in the unit, boost morale, and identify problems that might otherwise go unmentioned until they had grown larger (Mallard, 1999).

PRACTICE TIP: Do not wait until the annual evaluation process to have the first substantive conversation with a direct report. Schedule periodic check-ins with new faculty over the first year. These check-ins can be short but are invaluable in building relationships, demonstrating support, and mitigating feelings of isolation.

Supervision Models

Within the academy, a one-size-fits-all model of supervision does not work given the many and varied idiosyncratic needs of a diverse group of tenured, tenure-track, and clinical faculty, as well as part-time instructors. Each of these groups requires a differentiated model of supervision, each with its own unique goals. Not only do individuals vary, but program context and expectations also affect performance expectations. The relative weight of the importance of teaching, service, and scholarship varies from program to program, as well as what constitutes excellence in each of these areas. Within these areas, faculty members have different strengths and growth edges, which program directors can assist in further developing.

PRACTICE TIP: Don't limit supervision just to newer faculty members or tenure-track faculty. Prioritizing and maintaining relationships with all members of the program will help to ensure the dual purpose of supervision: support and evaluation.

There are several supervision models (see Gallacher, 1997, for a summary), and a differential supervision approach may be useful for BSW program directors. This approach recognizes that individuals operate at different levels of thought, skill level, and effectiveness, and therefore they require a model of supervision that is flexible and individualized based on the developmental stage of the person. The model discussed next is based on the work of Glickman et al. (2017), who developed their differential supervision model for the K–12 setting, which Rettig et al. (2000) applied to higher education.

Glickman and colleagues (2017) established four basic approaches to supervision along a continuum: directive control, directive informational, collaborative, and nondirective. On this continuum, the relative responsibility of the supervisor and supervisee will shift depending on the needs of the individual, with different behaviors incumbent on the supervisor at the different stages. While faculty typically exercise a high degree of autonomy, sometimes faculty need or require more directive supervision, such as a new faculty member with limited to no academia experience or a faculty member who is truly struggling. In those cases, the directive control approach is needed.

In such cases when directive control supervision is needed, the role of the supervisor tends to be very prescriptive and active, requiring the supervisor to schedule and focus the agenda of the meetings. With this approach, the supervisor identifies the issue, sets clear expectations for actions with a time frame, and informs the faculty members of the consequences for action or nonaction (Glickman et al., 2017). It is assumed that the supervisor has more knowledge than the faculty member and uses direct communication to share that information (Rettig et al., 2000). The intended outcome is to provide a clear plan for action that will lead to success with the support needed, typically determined by the supervisor (Rettig et al., 2000).

The next approach, directive informational supervision, is needed for many new faculty as they are learning to navigate the academic terrain (Glickman et al., 2017; Rettig et al., 2000). One step down from directive control, where the supervisor is more likely to make choices, this approach involves guiding new faculty as they explore their research and service interests and become more familiar and self-assured in their teaching skills. The supervisor still outlines options for paths to success, with standardization of timelines, but there is more flexibility for the faculty member to determine which route best suits their individual needs and talents. When this approach is coupled with mentoring and professional development opportunities, new faculty can gather needed guidance from several sources. While it is likely that new faculty will need this type of guidance in the beginning, seasoned faculty also may occasionally need more directive informational supervision as they transition into new roles or take on new responsibilities within the unit (Glickman et al., 2017; Rettig et al., 2000).

Once faculty develop more confidence about their role in the unit and university and with their own teaching, scholarship, and service, faculty will become more self-directed and will subsequently need less supervision. The majority of supervision within academic units, especially for more experienced but still nontenured faculty members, falls under collaborative supervision, in which the supervisor helps to clarify and provide focus through brainstorming and problem solving. This style is often used when the supervisor and faculty member have roughly equivalent experience, as it is more a discussion between peers who seek a mutually established plan through an honest exchange of ideas and thoughts (Glickman et al., 2017).

Last, nondirective supervision is most appropriate for seasoned faculty who are experts in their area. This approach assumes that the faculty member knows best how to craft a successful plan and the supervisor supports them by serving as a sounding board (Glickman et al., 2017). The self-directed faculty member may seek out the supervisor for another perspective and to help think through a dilemma. The supervisor reflects, encourages, clarifies, and listens, but the faculty member solely makes the decisions (Rettig et al., 2000).

The level of supervision needed changes as faculty members become more self-directed while they adjust to academic life and build other relationships within the unit and outside, requiring less direct supervision. Yet, typically, academic leaders may be in a position in which they are required to complete annual performance appraisals on all full-time faculty. Because of the hierarchy inherent in a supervisory relationship, it can be difficult to separate the evaluative role, in which the supervisor is making decisions about a faculty member's job performance, and the supportive role of promoting professional development (Gallacher, 1997). Therefore, thinking about how to conduct effective evaluation is essential.

Effective Evaluation

Providing ongoing supervision that is clearly tied to career stage and needs of the faculty member will ease the evaluation process for both the program director and faculty member. Through ongoing interaction throughout the year, rather than a once-a-year discussion, the faculty member will be more cognizant of their personal progress and the program director will more easily be able to assess progress in achieving goals.

Program directors need to ensure that professional standards are flexible enough to provide different paths to success, but are still clear. They can then consider how to help faculty achieve these standards in a manner that aligns the faculty member's individual talents and interests with institutional standards. Program directors can then help faculty members plan their professional growth through the use of a professional development plan. This plan should include short- and long-term goals and specific actions tied to the standard professional expectations for the program and the institution, which can be monitored and reviewed periodically throughout the year with the program director.

PRACTICE TIP: Ensure that yearly actions are specific with noted dates. Rather than "Improve pedagogy," a plan should state "Attend training on 'Teaching With Technology' in October and implement at least two new tools in spring courses." Rather than "Work on article," a plan should state "Complete literature review for new research by January and submit to institutional review board (IRB) by March."

With this specific plan for professional development, program directors have a tool on which to focus supervision meetings and determine if faculty are on track to achieve their goals. They can apply the differentiated supervision, discussed in the previous section, depending on how the faculty member is proceeding. This helps make it clear to everyone how work on the established goals is progressing. Some program directors may not want to be "mean" and tell a faculty member that they are not meeting standards or may not want to give an evaluation that is not 100% positive, but this will only harm the supervisee in the long run, as the faculty member needs to meet their professional goals and institutional requirements for promotion and tenure. A well-crafted professional development plan makes the path for achieving program and institutional expectations clear to everyone.

Classroom Observation

Supporting faculty in the classroom can be a difficult task. Sometimes it is limited to classroom observation, which gives only a narrow window into an individual's teaching and can be very subjective if not well designed. Structuring pedagogical expectations to be as clear and objective as possible, while allowing for differences in style and approach, will benefit the faculty member and the department as a whole. The faculty member should build a teaching portfolio utilizing different assessment methods, including substantial self-reflective materials documenting their knowledge and the theoretical base upon which they crafted their pedagogical approach. Peer evaluations should be conducted by those well positioned to assess content and pedagogy. Feedback from students should be included, but with the understanding that it is only a piece of information and that faculty from marginalized backgrounds are likely to experience bias in student evaluations (Chávez & Mitchell, 2020).

PRACTICE TIP: Have faculty begin a teaching portfolio in their first semester so they do not have to try to reconstruct one retrospectively for their tenure dossier. The portfolio should include documentation of how they have crafted their courses, feedback they have received, and how they have made changes in response to that feedback. The portfolio should contain a narrative related to how their philosophy of teaching is integrated into their work, the professional development they sought out, and examples of student work.

The teaching observation should never be conducted in isolation but should be bookended with pre- and postobservation meetings. The observation should always be mutually scheduled, with the person being observed selecting a class that they believe exemplifies their teaching or one on which they would like feedback. At the preobservation meeting, the observer should seek to gain an understanding of the broader context of the individual class to be observed within the course as a whole and the BSW curriculum, and how it demonstrates the instructor's teaching philosophy as well as how it incorporates knowledge about effective pedagogy. Areas of consideration and questions such as the following can help guide the conversation:

- Focus of the observation: What would the instructor like the observer to focus on most? Are there any challenges that they are working to surmount?

- Fit between the course and the overall curriculum: How does this class fit into the overall curriculum?

- Student learning outcomes (SLOs) for the class: How did the instructor develop them, if they did? Why were they selected? How do they relate to the overall departmental SLOs/social work competencies?

- Assignments: What are the major assignments and how do they relate to the student learning outcomes? How does the instructor scaffold student learning to build them to success on these assignments?

- Evaluation of assignments (after the instructor has shared a graded test and paper along with the rubrics for the paper and exam key):

How did the instructor establish the standards of evaluation? If the instructor did not develop the rubric, how was this discussed with students? What did the language and tone of the feedback convey to students? How clear was the feedback?

- Teaching philosophy (after reviewing the instructor's teaching philosophy): How does the instructor actualize their teaching philosophy in the course? What are examples of pedagogical decisions based on it?

- Use of different best practice teaching strategies: What strategies is the instructor using in the course? Upon what research is their effectiveness based? How does the instructor keep up to date on these strategies?

- Overall aims of the course: What are the broad aims of the class to be observed within the semester? What does the instructor want the students to achieve?

During the observation itself, the observer should be guided by specific behaviors that have been predetermined by the program as desirable. City et al. (2009) provided guidance on how to design an effective system for continual improvement of teaching and advised that the focus should be on learning rather than teaching. That is, the observer should focus on the students rather than the teacher. This does not mean that there are no important aspects of the instructor, such as command of relevant knowledge, but that since we focus on student learning outcomes in our assessment, we should similarly focus on student engagement and learning in our observations. City et al. (2009) noted three central questions at the heart of evaluation: What is the teacher saying and doing? What are the students saying and doing? What is the task? This brings our attention to "what students are doing when they are actively engaged in learning what we think they should learn" (p. 26).

Observations should be focused on a particular issue the instructor would like addressed and be as concrete and descriptive as possible to reduce subjectivity (City et al., 2009). Observers should be guided to take notes of what they explicitly observed, rather than what was not observed or their evaluation of what was observed. For example, rather than noting that the students were bored, the observer would note that three students were playing on their phone, two were staring into space rather than looking at the instructor, and one was doodling in their notebook.

Observers sometimes focus on what they do not see, which speaks to what they think an ideal classroom should look like—for example, "The instructor did not provide the learning outcomes for the class at the beginning." City et al. (2009) stated that this observation should then raise the question of whether the lack noted was actually needed if students gained a clear sense of the outcomes through another method. Maintaining the focus on student learning helps to reduce bias toward traditional teaching methods and keeps the focus on the students. At the postmeeting, the observer shares their write-up of specific observations with the instructor, and they engage in a mutual conversation about what went well to accomplish the aims of the class and where refinements can be made.

PRACTICE TIP: Although classroom observations may be used to inform yearly evaluations of teaching effectiveness, they are most helpful when they are viewed as formative evaluation. In that vein, these write-ups should not be part of an instructor's personnel file, but held only by the instructor.

Mentoring

Program directors do not need to be, and in fact should not be, the sole support for faculty in the program. Supervision and mentoring share overlapping elements and objectives in supporting faculty in achieving professional goals. Supervision tends to be broader in scope and typically entails performance evaluation, and mentoring tends to be narrower in scope and does not include an evaluative function. Many mentoring programs include getting to know the institution, including understanding the culture and navigating the unit and university politics, discussing teaching and research expectations, understanding the performance reviews and the tenure and promotion process, exploring how to create a work-life balance, and developing professional networks (Hanover Research, 2014). Despite some overlap between the aims of mentoring and supervision, without the evaluative function inherent in a supervisory relationship, mentoring has the potential to develop and strengthen relationships which help to retain faculty and lead to collaborative partnerships.

An effective mentorship program will broaden the assistance available to the faculty member as well as provide a range of benefits, including both professional development and psychosocial support (Chadiha et al., 2014). Mentorship has been found to improve job satisfaction, create a positive work-life balance, and increase institutional commitment and retention (Hanover Research, 2014; Johnson, 2015). Additional concrete benefits of academic mentorship include skill development in the areas of networking, problem solving, and time management, along with increased scholarly activities in the form of publications and grant writing (Hanover Research, 2014). It is critical to helping new faculty, especially those from historically underrepresented groups, learn the hidden culture of academia in general and their own institution in particular. This type of help can include information about how faculty reviews work; the timeline and expected benchmarks to move toward tenure and promotion; and indicators of excellence in teaching, scholarship, and service, as well as their relative weights (Griffin et al., 2020).

For early career educators in particular, effective mentoring can provide a supportive psychosocial environment that can ease the transition to academia; enhance effective teaching pedagogy, research, and grant-writing skills; increase awareness of organizational structure and policies; and heighten faculty confidence (Ellison et al., 2014; Hanover Research, 2014; Johnson, 2015; Wenocur et al., 2021). Mentorship enhances scholarship by presenting opportunities to publish through collaboration and co-authorship, providing critical feedback on ideas, and editing work (Allen et al., 2018). Helping mentors to see their role also as "coaches and sponsors" can help mentees build their skills and be offered opportunities, as well as be recognized for their work. Mentors can guide their mentees, including midcareer faculty, on which service and leadership opportunities to accept and which to decline (Freeman & Perna, 2022).

Mentoring is not only important for junior faculty but also for those from underrepresented groups at all levels, such as women (Conway et al., 2018) and people of color (Allen et al., 2018; Davis et al., 2021; Endo, 2020; Johnson, 2016; Oller et al., 2021). Often seen as a pipeline issue, Doctoral students of color face barriers to admission and completion of the program (Ghose et al., 2018), which is often seen as a pipeline issue. While many challenges exist, lack of mentoring opportunities can hinder retention efforts of students of color and further exacerbate pipeline issues (Ghose et al., 2018). Although BSW program directors do not have direct influence on doctoral programs, undergraduate program directors can advocate within their units that have doctoral programs and within the National Association of Deans and Directors of Schools of Social Work for more focused efforts on addressing pipeline issues for doctoral students of color.

Culturally responsive mentorship programs have been found to be helpful for minoritized faculty in feeling affirmed and less isolated (Griffin et al., 2020; Howard, 2017). A safe way must exist for faculty to share negative experiences and reflect on experiences of power and disempowerment, so these issues can be addressed in a structural way (Chadiha et al., 2014). One approach is relational mentoring, which is nonhierarchical and is based on mutual engagement, empathy, and empowerment, and aims to help with both personal and professional growth (Holcomb, 2021; Ross-Sheriff et al., 2017).

Despite the many advantages of mentoring programs, formal mentoring programs are not a routine part of many academic environments. In an exploratory study of BSW faculty members, of the 88 respondents surveyed, only 42% indicated that a formal mentoring program was available at their institution, and when available, only 22% participated as compared with 47% who participated in informal mentoring (Ellison et al., 2014).

PRACTICE TIP: Mentoring should continue past the first year, as many questions will not be or appear to be of primary importance until after the initial adjustment.

Types of Mentoring Programs

Traditionally, mentoring has been viewed as a top-down, one-on-one relationship between the seasoned mentor and the new or inexperienced protégé. Although those types of mentoring relationships still exist, there is a great deal of variation in both the focus and nature of academic mentorships, and other models are being developed that are broader and more flexible. Moving away from the traditional notion that one individual is responsible for supporting a new colleague, an increasing number of institutions are providing layers of supportive relationships (e.g., individual, group, and peer), each with a different or complementary purpose and specific set of skills or expertise.

Although informal mentoring relationships may develop organically, academic leaders have the influence to create formal mentoring initiatives. A formal program can ensure that all faculty, not just select faculty, are provided with needed support (Freeman & Perna, 2022). These mentoring programs can take a variety of formats: individual or group, hierarchical or peer, in person or e-mentoring (Hanover Research, 2014; Johnson, 2015). When making these choices, program directors should consider programmatic context and faculty needs—for example, how many new faculty the program has or expects to have in the next few years. If the number is small, joining together with another program or working with the institution as a whole may provide additional resources so that new faculty are supported within the individual unit.

Whatever mentoring type a university uses—traditional, peer, group, or another—successful higher education mentoring should be deliberate, structured, goal oriented, institutionally supported, and valued. Mentees should be carefully matched with mentors who can truly guide them and are committed to doing so. A poor match will not provide the desired outcomes, and it can also create other challenges. Formally matching mentors and mentees can be done by the academic leader, self-selected by the mentor and/or mentee, or a combination of the two. Data suggest that matches may be more successful when the mentors and mentees have some input in the selection process, but women and other underrepresented groups are less likely to develop high-quality mentoring relationships when self-selection is the only method of matching (Davis et al., 2021).

For more successful outcomes, the mentor and mentee should collaboratively create specific goals and deliverables and a meeting schedule. Formal mentoring initiatives have been found to be more effective than informal mentoring, especially if the relationship focuses on specific outcomes as identified by the mentee. These desired outcomes then shape the guidance, resources, and opportunities for the mentee through a clear professional development plan (Ghose et al., 2018; Griffin et al., 2020). Given that the needs and experiences of mentees differ, the frequency of mentoring meetings will vary and should be discussed between each pair.

Peer-mentoring groups can be effective in helping with socialization to the unit, support for moving through the tenure process, and support of teaching and scholarship goals. At the Salisbury University School of Social Work, the first listed author of this chapter, Jennifer Jewell, formerly the BSW program chair and director, found that peer-mentoring groups helped develop relationships, including those leading to multiple collaborative research projects. Removing the hierarchy associated with a tenured mentor can be more comfortable for everyone. One participant, who has now earned tenure, explained that the tenure-track peer-support group helped "to alleviate some of the ambiguity of tenure track. It is a much less threatening way to learn the ropes and get answers and intensive feedback that can then be translated into productive actions." These peer networks can be another way to build community, which may stretch beyond the social work program or even the institution (Griffin et al., 2020).

Having multiple mentors who can address the desired outcomes from various vantage points has potential benefits (Oller et al., 2021; Sorcinelli & Yun, 2007; Yun et al., 2016). Mentorship teams can also be an option for building a supportive community, in which the mentee does not have just one person who supports them, but a variety of individuals who can assist in different ways (Ghose et al., 2018). For example, the new faculty member might have someone within the department, but also someone from outside, which could make it safer to ask questions they fear could damage their internal reputation.

> **PRACTICE TIP:** Don't limit mentoring, including peer mentoring, to scholarship. Mentorship can be effective for teaching as well, such as creating a community for those who teach the same course or type of course—for example, direct practice.

Letting the mentee define their priorities may be more empowering as they identify their specific needs and build a robust support system. Weaving together a constellation of relationships from multiple levels tends to be more dynamic, less hierarchical, and more adaptable as needs change (Sorcinelli & Yun, 2007). Expanding the model of network-based mentoring, the "multi-level mentoring-partnership model" requires addressing equity issues inherent in institutions and decenters the dominant top-down mentoring model with a belief that multilevel relationships are collaborative partnerships based on equality and reciprocity, where individuals both teach and learn from each other (Endo, 2020). Although many mentoring programs focus on the early transition period, they can be valuable beyond this point through collaborative research and guidance on meeting tenure and promotion standards, work-life balance, and life posttenure, as well as other areas (Griffin et al., 2020; Oller et al., 2021).

Mentoring Those From Historically Minoritized Groups

Program directors must ensure that all faculty members have the necessary skills and knowledge to succeed, and mentoring is one method. Instituting effective mentorship initiatives can lead to the development and sustainment of a mentoring culture that promotes collaboration among faculty members and helps others evolve into mentors (Hanover Research, 2014). To support the development of those from traditionally oppressed groups, leaders need to address the powerful institutional mechanisms that reproduce unequal practices and be mindful that the supports implemented are not aimed at assimilating into toxic environments (Castro, 2010). If program directors are not purposeful about this, the unequal experience that some faculty may have encountered in their doctoral programs can be amplified (Ghose et al., 2018). Challenging the dominant paradigm of the traditional models of support, Endo (2020) advanced the idea of "equity-centric mentoring-partnership initiatives [that] radically shift the focus of assimilating and integrating BIPOC faculty into White-dominated organizations into a model where assumed or real differences are embraced as strengths" (p. 172).

Given the demographics of social work educators (more than 60% of whom are White; CSWE, 2021a), and the common small size of BSW programs (Mapp & Boutté-Queen, 2020), faculty of minoritized identities may be the only ones from each of their groups in their program, which increases the likelihood of cross-group mentorships. Researchers have identified potential issues that arise within cross-cultural mentoring relationships, such as the limited knowledge of White mentors regarding increased service demands, the importance of social justice values and community-based research, and other systemic barriers and challenges that affect the professional lives of faculty of color (Espino & Zambrana, 2019; Oller et al., 2021). Cross-cultural mentoring can also have benefits in that some mentees gain allies and become privy to knowledge and spaces to which faculty of color may not generally have access (Oller et al., 2021).

While a paucity of literature exists specifically discussing supporting faculty from minoritized identities, lessons can be drawn from literature relating to doctoral students. A framework used by Howard University emphasizes social justice, self-determination, racial identity and pride, and social integration in mentoring (Ross-Sheriff et al., 2017). Increasing social capital and feelings of belongingness through intentional community will help retain all faculty, especially faculty from marginalized groups, because the academy was built neither by them or for them and replicates Eurocentric cultural norms (Weng & Gray, 2017). These individuals may have ways of thinking, interacting, or conducting research that differ from that of their peers, and minority stress may affect them as they experience hidden and overt racism (Weng & Gray, 2017). Holcomb (2021) offered a formal mentorship framework for social workers underpinned by three principles: connection achieved through empathy and empowerment, responsive environment, and rebalance of power differentials, thus creating a more supportive departmental and institutional culture with the goal of "eliminating patterns of marginalization and enhancing efforts to recruit and retain underrepresented faculty" (p. 1204).

> **PRACTICE TIP:** Don't limit yourself in assigning mentors. Depending on the needs of your faculty and unit, mentors could be contingent faculty, experienced assistant professors, and those outside of social work or even your institution. For example, you can form a network with other regional schools to provide sufficient support for different groups of faculty if you don't have a critical mass at your own institution. Always be certain a mentor is willing and able to take on the responsibility.

Professional Development

Program directors should also work at the programmatic level to champion the ongoing support of learning needs for the unit, specifically exploring the learning needs of their program and developing a professional development plan to meet common needs related to scholarship and teaching, including both the implicit and explicit curricula. Much like the professional development plan discussed in the "Effective Evaluation" section, programs can have professional development plans. Program funds can be used to help achieve program development plans, and if they tie into goals of the broader institution, funds may be available on that level as well.

Universities expect faculty to engage in ongoing training and professional development activities to keep current with both emerging pedagogy and knowledge; however, this is a relatively new expectation as universities and colleges are pressured to deliver improved student learning outcomes in a more competitive higher learning market (Pesce, 2015). Professional development is crucial for ongoing enhancement of knowledge and skills for improved teaching quality and to address the continuous challenges that face higher education institutions, such as new instructional methods, changing demographics, and emerging technologies. Professional development can contribute to improving faculty members' teaching skills, based on both their own perceptions and those of their students (Chang et al., 2011; Mascher, 2016; Morris & Usher, 2011).

When programming is offered, it is often those who have evidenced the least need for it who will attend. While "if you build it, they will come" may be accurate in some universities, particularly if such efforts are already valued, in other institutions, incentives may be necessary to encourage participation and volunteers to serve as mentors or presenters for the professional development workshops. Incentives may encourage involvement in sessions that otherwise can feel like a burden. Although limited resources often constrict the ability to offer additional professional development opportunities, there are small ways to encourage faculty to lead professional development sessions as well as participate in these educational opportunities. For full-time and contingent faculty, professional development participation can be incentivized through the use of awards, free materials, and food. If the content meets state requirements for continuing education, continuing education units (CEUs) can be offered for part of or the entire training session. The incentive of CEUs, whether free or discounted, can help to justify the use of work hours, especially for part-time instructors who are likely still working in the field.

When bringing in trainers for CEU presentations to the community, negotiate a separate training for faculty. Another low- or no-cost professional development opportunity that requires little preparation is offering book or article discussion groups. If resources allow, purchase the books for participants. These book discussions can help deepen understanding through critical conversations and elevate relationships. For some events, lunch can be provided or a potluck planned. Food can help to boost attendance, promote creative thinking, and strengthen ties. Academic leaders with a focus on social justice should advocate for promotional opportunities for both full-time, non-tenure-track faculty and part-time instructors.

As an example, the Salisbury University School of Social Work has prioritized culturally responsive teaching and learning (CRTL) for several years. To support this programmatic goal, it has paid the registration fees of interested faculty to attend a CRTL conference for the last 4 years, hosted a 4-week training on CRTL with an outside organization, financially supported several faculty members to participate in a train-the-trainers workshop, held additional seminars led by current faculty, sponsored books and article discussions, and provided other supports that align with that priority. By receiving a slew of opportunities. SU SSW faculty receive a clear message that the priority is on sound and culturally responsive pedagogy.

Finding outside trainers or sponsoring faculty to attend costly trainings is not always possible. Many universities have in-house expertise that can be tapped for professional development opportunities. By providing trainings within the university led by existing staff and faculty, the cost to the unit is only the employee's time, and if that time is allowed to count toward annual reviews, they may be more willing to assist. There is cost saving with using existing talent, and this saving will be multiplied as more faculty members are trained (Alston et al., 2017). In addition, online professional development opportunities have increased exponentially. Examples include the Columbia University School of Social Work Online Pedagogy Institute (Báez et al., 2019) and the University of the District of Columbia Online Learning Academy (Alston et al., 2017).

> **PRACTICE TIP:** Think outside of your school for both presenters and audiences. Consider those in allied disciplines who have expertise or interest in common topics. By recruiting a presenter from outside of social work or sharing the cost of bringing in an outside trainer, costs can be reduced while still engaging high-quality presenters.

Advocacy on an Institutional Level

Recognizing the benefits of genuine investment in effective supervision, mentoring, and professional development, program leaders should advocate for institutional change in order to raise the level of value and support for engagement in these activities. Administrators should communicate about the value of teaching and its development on campus. Academic leaders can and should do more to actively promote and reward participation in mentoring and professional development opportunities. A strong message from administrators will communicate the value of these activities, and thus faculty will feel supported in their investment of time. In research-intensive universities, it is difficult to balance the roles of teacher and researcher with service requirements. With less focus on pedagogy and more investment in research activities, some faculty may not feel supported when attempting to dedicate time to mentoring or professional development activities unless tied directly to research endeavors, resulting in a challenging balancing act. To help with this, program directors can advocate for such activities to be included as part of the faculty workload or recognize the additional work through a stipend.

Advocacy for structural changes can include a review of promotion and tenure standards, including explicit valuing of these activities. Many of these standards are designed to be flexible to accommodate a range of disciplines, but this flexibility can lead to a lack of clarity and thus subjectivity in assessment. This can then perpetuate traditional standards that do not fit newer topics of scholarship, the very types of scholarship that may be of interest to scholars from marginalized backgrounds. It can also affect the methods to assess these scholars, or who will publish or fund them, which leads to scholarly devaluation (Settles et al. 2022). For example, traditional standards for evaluating scholarship focus on sole or first authorship, or a prioritization of quantitative research, which may not fit with those coming from communal cultures with a priority for collective efforts or knowledge based on qualitative research (Settles et al., 2022; Weng & Gray, 2017). Evaluating the number of grants received, the number of manuscripts published, or a scholar's h-index regarding publishing can privilege those who fit the traditional academic model, who are able to devote an excessive amount of time to these endeavors, often due to the support of a stay-at-home partner, which White men are more likely to have (Neale-McFall et al., 2020).

To address this inequity, program directors should encourage tenure and promotion standards for scholarship that are inclusive of a range of methods and topics, as well as differing outcomes from that scholarship. Although one scholar may disseminate their work in a "top-tier" journal, another might conduct participatory action research to the benefit of an oppressed community. To the extent this would not disadvantage the faculty member at the institutional level, program directors should also encourage scholars to publish their research in a journal that is best suited for the audience for their work, rather than the one with the highest impact factor, which may be less interested in nontraditional populations and methods. Program directors should advocate to the broader institution to follow suit so that these scholars are not hindered in the tenure and promotion process, such as through the adoption of Boyer's model of scholarship, which includes scholarship of discovery, but also integration, application, and teaching (Boyer, 1990).

Although scholarship is ranked as more important in some programs, ensuring the valuing of teaching and service can help to increase equity, especially in baccalaureate social work, where teaching is an important focus. Moreover, consider how excellent teaching is evaluated, and do not simply rely on student evaluations. A portfolio with a variety of types of evidence demonstrating growth and effectiveness will provide a fuller picture of pedagogy.

Conclusion

As social work leaders, investing in our faculty pays off in exponential dividends. While this involves both financial costs and time commitments, the professional and personal benefits for the faculty can affect and improve their teaching, providing a better learning environment for students. For the social work unit and the university, this leads to higher retention and reduced cost of faculty recruitment and training. Although not all programs have the capacity to roll out expansive training and mentoring programs, there are small and deliberate ways to bolster support for faculty as academic leaders, building a culture that values and centers faculty development through effective supervision, mentorship, and professional development activities.

Suggested Readings

City, E. A., Elmore, R. F., Fiarman, S. E., & Teitel, L. (2009). *Instructional rounds in education: A network approach to improving teaching and learning.* Harvard Education Press.

Glickman, C., Gordon, S., & Ross-Gordon, J. (2017). *SuperVision and instructional leadership: A developmental approach* (10th ed.). Pearson.

Griffin, K., Bennett, J., & York, T. (2020). Leveraging promising practices: Improving the recruitment, hiring, and retention of diverse & inclusive faculty. *Aspire.* https://osf.io/dq4rw/

Holcomb, D. (2021). Leveling the playing field: A conceptual framework for formal faculty mentorship in social work. *Advances in Social Work, 21*(4), 1193–1211. https://doi.org/10/18060/25213

Settles, I. H., Jones, M. K., Buchanan, N. T., & Dotson, K. (2021). Epistemic exclusion: Scholar(ly) devaluation that marginalizes faculty of color. *Journal of Diversity in Higher Education, 14*(4), 493–507. https://doi.org/10.1037/dhe0000174

References

Allen, J. L., Huggins-Hoyt, K. Y., Holosko, M. J., & Briggs, H. E. (2018). African American social work faculty: Overcoming existing barriers and achieving research productivity. *Research on Social Work Practice, 28*(3), 309–319. https://doi.org/10.1177/1049731517701578

Alston, S. T., Moore, C. S., & Thomas, M. (2017). Strategies for enhancing online teaching in social work education. *Journal of Human Behavior in the Social Environment, 27*(5), 412–423. https://doi.org/10.1080/10911359.2017.1311817

Báez, J. C., Marquart, M., Chung, R. Y., Ryan, D., & Garay, K. (2019). Developing and supporting faculty training for online social work education: The Columbia University School of Social Work Online Pedagogy Institute. *Journal of Teaching in Social Work, 39*(4–5), 505–518. https://doi.org/10.1080/08841233.2019.1653419

Barsky, A., Green, D., & Ayayo, M. (2014). Hiring priorities for BSW/MSW programs in the United States: Informing doctoral programs about current needs. *Journal of Social Work, 14*(1), 62–82. https://doi.org/10.1177/1468017313476772

Boyer, E. L. (1990). *Scholarship reconsidered: Priorities of the professoriate.* Princeton University Press.

Brady, S. R., & Spencer, M. S. (2018). Supporting and mentoring new social work instructors: A formative evaluation of the TEAM program. *Journal of the Scholarship of Teaching and Learning, 18*(2), 24–38. https://doi.org/10.14434/josotl.v18i2.22334

Buller, J. L. (2012). *The essential department chair: A comprehensive desk reference* (2nd ed.). Jossey-Bass.

Castro, C. (2010). In the margins of the academy: Women of color and job satisfaction. In A. J. Lemelle, R. Alexander, & S. E. Moore (Eds.), *Dilemmas of Black faculty at predominately White institutions in the United States: Issues in the post-multicultural era* (pp.135–157). Edwin Mellen Press.

Chadiha, L. A., Aranda, M. P., Biegel, D. E., & Chang, C. (2014). The importance of mentoring faculty members of color in schools of social work. *Journal of Teaching in Social Work, 34*(4), 351–362. https://doi.org/10.1080/08841233.2014.937891

Chang, T., Lin, H., & Song, M. (2011). University faculty members' perceptions of their teaching efficacy. *Innovations in Education and Teaching International, 48*(1), 49–60.

Chávez, K., & Mitchell, K. M. W. (2020). Exploring bias in student evaluations: Gender, race, and ethnicity. *PS: Political Science & Politics, 53*(2), 270–274. https://doi.org/10.101/S1049096519001744

Chronicle of Higher Education. (2020). *"On the verge of burnout": Covid-19's impact on faculty well-being and career plans.* https://connect.chronicle.com/rs/931-EKA-218/images/Covid%26FacultyCareerPaths_Fidelity_ResearchBrief_v3%20%281%29.pdf

City, E. A., Elmore, R. F., Fiarman, S. E., & Teitel, L. (2009). *Instructional rounds in education: A network approach to improving teaching and learning.* Harvard Education Press.

Clochesy, J. M., Visovsky, C., & Munro, C. (2019). Preparing nurses for faculty roles: The institute for faculty recruitment, retention and mentoring (INFORM). *Nurse Education Today, 79*, 63–66. https://doi.org/10.1016/j.nedt.2019.05.018

Conway, C. L. S., McCrary-Quarles, A., Sims, Y., Nicholson, C. S., Ethridge, G., Priester, M., & Thompson, T. (2018). Strategies to empower women in higher education positions: A global issue. In D. Chitakunye & A. Takhur (Eds.), *Examining the role of women entrepreneurs in emerging economies* (pp. 1–22). IGI Global. https://doi.org/10.4018/978-1-5225-5112-6.ch001

Council on Social Work Education (CSWE). (2021a). *2020 annual statistics on social work education in the United States.* https://www.cswe.org/getattachment/726b15ce-6e63-4dcd-abd1-35d2ea9d9d40/2020-Annual-Statistics-On-Social-Work-Education-in-the-United-States.pdf?lang=en-US

Council on Social Work Education (CSWE). (2021b). *CSWE/GADE report on the current landscape of doctoral education in social work.* https://www.cswe.org/getattachment/Research-Statistics/CSWE-GADE-Report-on-the-Current-Landscape-of-Doctoral-Education-in-Social-Work.pdf.aspx

Davis, L. E. (1985). Black and White social work faculty: Perceptions of respect, satisfaction, and job permanence. *The Journal of Sociology & Social Welfare, 12*(1), 79–94.

Davis, T. M., Jones, M. K., Settles, I. H., & Granberry Russell, P. (2021). Barriers to the successful mentoring of faculty of color. *Journal of Career Development.* Advance online publication. https://doi.org/10.1177/08948453211013375

Ellison, M., Moore, W., & Johnson, A. (2014). Mentoring experiences of undergraduate social work faculty: Navigating the academic maze. *Journal of Sociology and Social Work, 2*(2), 191–218. https://doi.org/10.15640/jssw.v2n2a12

Endo, R. (2020). Retaining and supporting faculty who are Black, Indigenous, and people of color: The promise of a multi-leveled mentoring-partnership model. *Multicultural Perspectives, 22*(4), 169–177. https://doi.org/10.1080/15210960.2020.1845178

Espino, M. M., & Zambrana, R. E. (2019). "How do you advance here? How do you survive?" An exploration of under-represented minority faculty perceptions of mentoring modalities. *The Review of Higher Education, 42*(2), 457–484. https://doi.org/10.1353/rhr.2019.0003

Franklin, C., Lightfoot, E., Nachbaur, M., & Sucher, K. (2021). A study of PhD courses and curricula across schools of social work. *Research on Social Work Practice*. Advance online publication. https://doi.org/10.1177/10497315211039187

Frazier, K. N. (2011). Academic bullying: A barrier to tenure and promotion for African-American faculty. *Florida Journal of Educational Administration & Policy, 5*(1). https://files.eric.ed.gov/fulltext/EJ961222.pdf

Freeman, S., & Perna, L. W. (2022, July 8). Enabling midcareer faculty of color to thrive. *Inside Higher Ed.* https://www.insidehighered.com/advice/2022/07/08/providing-midcareer-faculty-color-support-they-need-opinion

Gallacher, K. (1997). Supervision, mentoring, and coaching: Methods for supporting personnel development. In P. J. Winton, J. A. McCollum, & C. Catlett (Eds.), *Reforming personnel preparation in early intervention: Issues, models, and practical strategies* (pp. 191–214). Paul H. Brookes.

Ghose, T., Ali, S., & Keo-Meier, B. (2018). Diversity in social work doctoral programs: Mapping the road ahead. *Research on Social Work Practice, 28*(3), 265–271.

Glickman, C., Gordon, S., & Ross-Gordon, J. (2017). *SuperVision and instructional leadership: A developmental approach* (10th ed.). Pearson.

Griffin, K., Bennett, J., & York, T. (2020). Leveraging promising practices: Improving the recruitment, hiring, and retention of diverse & inclusive faculty. *Aspire.* https://osf.io/dq4rw/

Group for the Advancement of Doctoral Education in Social Work (GADE). (2013). *PhD quality guidelines.* http://www.gadephd.org/Guidelines

Gutiérrez y Muhs, G., Niemann, Y. F., Gonzalez, C. G., & Harris, A. P. (2012). *Presumed incompetent: The intersections of race and class for women in academia.* Utah State University Press.

Hanover Research. (2014, January). *Faculty mentoring models and effective practices.* https://www.hanoverresearch.com/media/Faculty-Mentoring-Models-and-Effectives-Practices-Hanover-Research.pdf

Holcomb, D. (2021). Leveling the playing field: A conceptual framework for formal faculty mentorship in social work. *Advances in Social Work, 21*(4), 1193–1211. https://doi.org/10/18060/25213

Howard, S. (2017). Black first-generation social work doctoral students. *Journal of Teaching in Social Work, 37*(5), 513–527. https://doi.org/10.1080/08841233.2017.1370431

Johnson, H. L. (2016). Pipelines, pathways, and institutional leadership: An update on the status of women in higher education. *American Council on Education.* https://www.acenet.edu/Documents/Higher-Ed-Spotlight-Pipelines-Pathways-and-Institutional-Leadership-Status-of-Women.pdf

Johnson, W. B. (2015). *On being a mentor: A guide for higher education faculty* (2nd ed.). Routledge.

Mallard, K. S. (1999). Management by walking around and the department chair. *The Department Chair, 10*(2), 13.

Mapp, S. C., & Boutté-Queen, N. (2020). The role of the US baccalaureate social work program director: A national survey. *Social Work Education: The International Journal, 40*(7), 843–860. https://doi.org/10.1080/02615479.2020.1729720

Mascher, E. (2016). *Factors influencing participation in professional development to promote online course excellence and the impact on faculty confidence and teaching* [Unpublished doctoral dissertation]. University of Arkansas.

Maynard, B. R., Labuzienski, E. M., Lind, K. S., Berglund, A. H., & Albright, D. L. (2017). Social work doctoral education: Are doctoral students being prepared to teach? *Journal of Social Work, 17*(1), 91–114. https://doi.org/10.1177/1468017316637226

McClendon, J., Lane, S. R., & Flowers, T. D. (2021). Faculty-to-faculty incivility in social work education. *Journal of Social Work Education, 57*(1), 100–112. https://doi.org/10.1080/10437797.2019.1671271

Morris, D. B., & Usher, E. L. (2011). Developing teaching self-efficacy in research institutions: A study of award-winning professors. *Contemporary Educational Psychology, 36*(3), 232–245. https://doi.org/10.1016/j.cedpsych.2010.10.005

National Association of Social Workers. (2021). *Code of ethics.* https://www.socialworkers.org/About/Ethics/Code-of-Ethics/Code-of-Ethics-English

Neale-McFall, C., Hermann, M. A., & Eckart, E. (2020). Predictive variables of faculty retention in the counselor education field: A gender perspective. *Journal of Education and Training Studies, 8*(10). https://doi.org/10.11114/jets.v8i10.4989

Oktay, J., Jacobson, J., & Fisher, E. (2013). Learning through experience: The transition from doctoral student to social work educator. *Journal of Social Work Education, 49*(2), 207–221. https://doi-org/10.1080/10437797.2013.768108

Oller, M. L., Lindo, N., & Li, D. (2021). Faculty of color's mentorship experiences in counselor education. *Counselor Education & Supervision, 60*(2), 112–128. https://doi.org/10.1002/ceas.12193

Parker, V. (2017). *How I got over: A study of the tenure experiences of Black female professors at predominantly White institutions* [Unpublished doctoral dissertation]. Louisiana State University.

Pesce, J. R. (2015). *Professional development for teaching in higher education: Faculty perceptions and attitudes* [Unpublished doctoral dissertation]. Boston College.

Prock, K. A., Berlin, S., Harold, R. D., & Groden, S. R. (2019). Stories from LGBTQ social work faculty: What is the impact of being "out" in academia? *Journal of Gay & Lesbian Social Services, 31*(2), 182–201. https://doi.org/10.1080/10538720.2019.1584074

Pryce, J. M., Ainbinder, A., Werner-Lin, A. V., Browne, T. A., & Smithgall, C. (2011). Teaching future teachers: A model workshop for doctoral education. *Journal of Teaching in Social Work, 31*(4), 457–469. https://doi.org/10.1080/08841233.2011.601941

Rettig, P. R., Lampe, S., & Garcia, P. (2000). Supervising your faculty with a differentiated model. *The Department Chair, 11*(2), 1–21.

Ross-Sheriff, F., Edwards, J. B., & Orme, J. (2017). Relational mentoring of doctoral social work students at historically Black colleges and universities. *Journal of Teaching in Social Work, 37*(1), 55–70. https://doi.org/10.1080/08841233.2016.1270250

Settles, I. H., Jones, M. K., Buchanan, N. T., & Brassel, S. T. (2022). Epistemic exclusion of women faculty and faculty of color: Understanding scholar(ly) devaluation as a predictor of turnover intentions. *The Journal of Higher Education, 93*(1), 31–55. https://doi.org/10.1080/00221546.2021.1914494

Settles, I. H., Jones, M. K., Buchanan, N. T., & Dotson, K. (2021). Epistemic exclusion: Scholar(ly) devaluation that marginalizes faculty of color. *Journal of Diversity in Higher Education, 14*(4), 493–507. https://doi.org/10.1037/dhe0000174

Sorcinelli, M. D., & Yun, J. (2007). From mentor to mentoring networks: Mentoring in the new academy. *Change: The Magazine of Higher Learning, 39*(6), 58–61. https://doi.org/10.3200/CHNG.39.6.58-C4

Sun, W., & Simon-Roberts, S. (2020). New faculty preparation, adaptation, and retention. *The Journal of Faculty Development, 34*(2), 81–87.

Tower, L. E., Faul, A. C., Chiarelli-Helminiak, C., & Hodge, D. M. (2019). The status of women in social work education: A follow-up study. *Affilia: Journal of Women and Social Work, 34*(3), 346–368. https://doi.org/10.1177/0886109919836105

Valentine, D. P., Edwards, S., Gohagan, D., Huff, M., Pereira, A., & Wilson, P. (1998). Preparing social work doctoral students for teaching: Report of a survey. *Journal of Social Work Education, 34*(2), 273–282. https://doi.org/10.1080/10437797.1998.10778923

Weimer, M. (2010). *Inspired college teaching.* Jossey-Bass.

Weng, S. S., & Gray, L. A. (2017). Advancement in social work education: Fostering a supportive environment for students of non-dominant racial and ethnic backgrounds. *Social Work Education, 36*(6), 662–677. https://doi.org/10.1080/02615479.2017.1335700

Wenocur, K., Page, A. P., Wampole, D., Radis, B., Masin-Moyer, M., & Crocetto, J. (2021). PLEASE be with me: Benefits of a peer-led supervision group for early career social work educators. *Social Work with Groups, 44*(2), 117–131. https://doi.org/10.1080/01609513.2020.1836548

Yun, J. H., Baldi, B., & Sorcinelli, M. D. (2016). Mutual mentoring for early-career and underrepresented faculty: Model, research, and practice. *Innovative Higher Education, 41*(5), 441–451. https://doi.org/10.1007/s10755-016-9359-6

CHAPTER 14

Cultivating and Valuing Contingent and Adjunct Faculty

Suzanne L. Velázquez
Warren K. Graham

Serving as a program director offers a myriad of opportunities and challenges for professional and leadership development. Keen leadership skills are required to face a variety of challenges within the educational environment (Kumar et al., 2019), one of which is providing leadership for the program's faculty, including those off the tenure track. Cultivating and supporting contingent and adjunct faculty can be a very rewarding aspect of academic administrative service. The program director needs to understand the unique qualities of this population and implement purposeful strategies to meet the needs of faculty, students, and the institution. A successful program director will understand the importance of these faculty members and work with them from an inclusive, human-rights-based perspective in the following areas:

- understanding their role in fulfillment of institutional and program missions,
- recruiting and orienting these faculty for their dynamic role,
- mentoring and coaching these faculty from the strengths perspective,
- mitigating challenges to engaging non-tenure-track and part-time faculty, and
- cultivating these faculty to work effectively across the BSW social work curricula.

This chapter provides information, strategies, and best practices to achieve these aims through cultivating and maintaining professional academic relationships with contingent and adjunct faculty in both new and established social work programs.

You may be asking who the contingent faculty are. Depending on the institution, different titles are used for this population. The most universally known may be *adjunct*; however, this term usually describes only the faculty members contracted each semester or term to teach a class. In contrast, the American Association of University Professors (AAUP) defines *contingent faculty* as both part- and full-time faculty at institutions of higher education who are appointed off the tenure track (2014).

Thus, contingent faculty can be adjuncts, but they can also hold clinical titles and academic ranks, from instructor through clinical professor, and are appointed for specific-length terms. Though there are many titles for these individuals, the common thread for all contingent faculty is that "their institutions make little or no long-term commitment to them or to their academic work" (AAUP, 2014, p. 171). Using the AAUP (2014) definition, the term *contingent* includes the many groups of faculty in non-tenured and short-term roles (McNaughtan et al., 2017). As the academy and educational marketplace continue to reduce the number of tenured/ tenure-track faculty, contingent faculty are being hired by every type of institution and academic department.

AAUP reported that at all U.S. institutions combined, 73% of instructional positions are off the tenure track (AAUP, 2018), and the Council on Social Work Education (CSWE) has reported that almost a third of all master's level courses and about a quarter of all baccalaureate courses are taught by part-time faculty (CSWE, 2021). To further reinforce the point:

> Non-tenure-track employees made up more than half of all faculty employees at all public and private nonprofit institutions. They made up over 70 percent of all faculty members at public associate and baccalaureate/associate colleges and private nonprofit master's institutions. They made up less than 40 percent of full-time faculty members at public master's and baccalaureate institutions and at private nonprofit baccalaureate colleges. (*Chronicle Almanac*, 2020, p. 1)

As noted previously, there are two predominant categories within the umbrella term *contingent faculty*: (1) non-tenure-track employed (NTTE) faculty and (2) adjunct faculty. As detailed in Table 14.1, NTTE faculty are usually fulltime with salaried, multiple-year contract terms with the institution; adjunct faculty are part-time faculty contracted each academic term for individual course(s) and paid per credit. Program directors need to understand how the dynamics, benefits, expectations, and assignments differ between the two types of contingent faculty, and how similar concerns (e.g., lack of job security) exist for both. For clarity in this chapter, the terms *NTTE* or *full-time* will be used when a concept pertains specifically to faculty employed for multiple-year terms by an institution; the terms *adjunct* or *part-time* will be used when a concept pertains specifically to faculty hired each academic term (semester or quarter) to teach; and the broader terms *faculty* or *contingent faculty* will be used when the concept pertains to both types of faculty.

TABLE 14.1

Categorization and Differentiation of Contingent Faculty

	NTTE Faculty	Adjunct Faculty
Typical contract and salary determination	Multiple years; salaried 10 or 12 months	Semester term; paid per credit
Responsibilities	Teaching, administration, advising, service (certain institutions also require some applied scholarship for promotion)	Teaching
Departmental roles	BSW faculty, field education faculty	BSW faculty, field liaison
Potential other employment beyond the educational institution	Sometimes part-time social work practice; often not able to teach or work for another institution per contract	Usually full-time employment or multiple part-time positions; may teach for several institutions at the same time

Regardless of the nomenclature used to describe faculty, it is integral to the process of education that all faculty support the institutional and program missions, students in their learning, other faculty, and field education. Faculty participate in the integration of implicit and explicit curricula, and thus the selection and retention of appropriate faculty members are critical to the learning and orientation to the social work profession.

The overarching themes connecting the categories of contingent faculty that a successful program director should attend to include addressing their sense of purpose and connectedness to the institution, the program, and other faculty, and managing the feelings associated with a lack of security stemming from the inherent nature of short-term appointments without the opportunity for tenure. This chapter provides direction and support for program directors to engage in relationship building to successfully address these common themes. Four areas of responsibility for the program director working with contingent faculty are delved into: (1) recruitment and selection for hiring, (2) orienting and onboarding faculty, (3) relationship development and retention, and (4) termination.

Recruiting and Selecting Contingent and Adjunct Faculty

Similar to how we prepare students to develop professional resources and referral contacts, it is helpful to use the professional networks of current faculty members, local chapters of professional organizations, and field education agencies to recruit prospective contingent faculty. The contemporary social work practice experience and knowledge that these potential faculty members possess are an asset to social work programs as they help students develop critical evidence-based practice and thinking skills in the classroom and field education settings (Santisteban & Egues, 2014).

When selecting prospective contingent faculty, program directors need to consider several factors beyond the obvious practice experience and knowledge requirements. Considerations include: (1) motivation and reasons for joining the academy, (2) fit with the institution's and program's mission and goals, (3) course expertise, (4) flexibility and scheduling, (5) teaching experience, (6) teaching level (undergraduate or graduate), and (7) expectations for the appointment or contract. Questions to guide the program director through each area of consideration during the selection process follow.

What Is Motivating This Candidate to Join Your Particular Program as a Contingent Faculty Member?

Just as students come to the social work profession for different reasons, people come to academia and accept contingent faculty appointments for different personal and professional reasons. Cognitive theorists describe motivation in two categories: intrinsic motivation, a result of performing an activity for its sake, and extrinsic motivation, a result of performing an activity to obtain an external reward (Pons, 2015; Pons et al., 2017; Smith, 2019). Gappa and Leslie's (1993) model of motivation speaks to extrinsic motivations (such as money, status, and promotion) and intrinsic motivations (such as a sense of satisfaction, a love of teaching, and the desire to "give back" or help society) as core reasons people take on contingent faculty appointments (Leslie & Gappa, 2002; Page, 2018). Leslie and Gappa (2002) studied part-time faculty at public and private institutions and categorized four general types:

- *professionals, specialists, and experts:* employed elsewhere in their primary careers

- *career enders:* in life transitions to retirement or are retired

- *freelancers:* prefer working simultaneously in a variety of positions, one of which is part-time teaching

- *aspiring academics:* aspiring to full-time, tenure-track faculty positions

The two most significant categories are the first and the last, as professionals, specialists, and experts make up the majority of contingent faculty and are motivated to teach because of their intrinsic satisfaction with the work itself and their dedication to teaching and to the constituencies they serve (Gappa, 2000). Aspiring academics "generally teach for economic reasons, sometimes at several campuses simultaneously, hoping that eventually they will achieve a tenure-track position" (Gappa & Leslie, 1993, as cited in Gappa, 2000, p. 79).

For social work education, particularly when recruiting experienced practitioners to teach, it makes sense for program directors to cultivate the intrinsic motivation of fulfilling the social worker's sense of paying it forward to further the profession. The *Code of Ethics of the National Association of Social Workers* (NASW) calls for social workers to heed their responsibility to the profession and include teaching and research as activities that advance the profession (NASW, 2021). Understanding the general reasons for a candidate wanting to join the faculty will help the program director to direct and guide the professional development of the faculty member, such as fitting in with course assignments and a mentoring career path, and beginning conversations that address the next questions of consideration.

How Does This Candidate Fit With Your Institutional and School Missions and Program Goals?

Accreditation standards require social work practice-designated courses be taught by faculty with a master's degree in social work from a CSWE-accredited program and at least 2 years of practice experience (CSWE, 2020, 2022). Accordingly, bringing embedded value as a practitioner into the classroom provides a foundation for learning across the social work curriculum. However, each institution, school or department, and social work program asserts a uniqueness of its mission and goals, which are often influenced by both internal and external factors, including public versus private institutions, the Carnegie classification (Carnegie Classification of Institutions of Higher Education, n.d.) of the institution, regional workforce development initiatives, and community needs and relationships. Similar to assessing a prospective student's understanding of and fit with your social work program, discussing the faculty candidate's understanding of and motivation to fulfill your particular mission and goals will serve to set a solid foundation for onboarding, orienting, and cultivating the candidate as a faculty member.

Are There Particular Courses or Diverse Area of Practice Niches to Which This Candidate Can Bring Expertise?

Depending on a candidate's practice experience, some courses may be a better fit than others. However, when possible, program directors should not pass on the opportunity to create an elective course or series of courses that utilize a candidate's unique set of skills and experiences while also addressing workforce development needs or regional/community and professional social work issues. Throughout the program director–faculty relationship, and particularly at the points of recruitment and hire, it is helpful to have discussions about potential areas of interest and expertise that a contingent faculty member can bring to the program. Developing courses or tracks for which part-time faculty can provide expertise or serve as a lead instructor can provide some sense of purpose, connectedness, and security for the contingent faculty member.

PRACTICE TIP: To determine special expertise areas for which you might want to actively recruit, survey your local field agencies and prospective employers to determine if there is a specific area of practice or a skill set needed to serve the clients of the area. You could also survey your students to see if there is an area of interest that is not currently included in your curriculum. Then survey your contingent faculty for their practice expertise to tap into for course development or ask if they know someone who could support these areas.

What Amount of Flexibility in Scheduling Does This Candidate Have?

As a program director, scheduling classes may seem like an ever-evolving and unending process. Based on enrollment and the need to possibly reallocate full-time faculty responsibilities, program directors may be asked to make last-minute scheduling changes. Being able to call upon a contingent faculty member with flexibility to fill a late opening is helpful. From the other perspective, having to change the meeting day or time or cancel an underenrolled course section can be difficult when working with faculty with limited flexibility.

Thus, scheduling should be a point of discussion during the recruitment or hiring stage so that there will be a clear understanding that scheduling changes and cancellations can happen each term, and should not be interpreted as a reflection on any specific faculty member. A good point of practice for program directors is to maintain communication and connection with contingent faculty who have been removed from one term's schedule, especially if the intention is to have them return for another term. Maintaining an already-fostered relationship is usually easier than having to forge a new one.

Another consideration about flexibility is keeping in contact with contingent faculty when classes are not in session or to consult about beginning- or end-of-term issues that may occur outside of the technical time frame of their contract or appointment. Continual communication between the program director and all faculty is necessary, particularly when it comes to matters of students having difficulties managing program expectations or being at risk of not completing coursework. This is especially critical for part-time faculty with other full-time obligations who are not on campus with the same frequency as full-time instructors.

A similar, corresponding challenge to communication with NTTE faculty is that some might maintain part-time practice obligations beyond the full-time faculty role, to maintain engagement in the field of practice or because of the uncertainty of continued appointment upon conclusion of their current term contract or appointment, which can inhibit their availability outside of contracted terms. Much of the advising and administrative work with students of adjuncts may often occur outside of the contracted time a contingent faculty member is expected to be on campus or associated with the contracted class. Adjunct faculty, being further removed from administrative practices, may mishandle situations because of ignorance of policies and procedures that govern grading and classroom management. Program directors should establish appropriate contact information and parameters with contingent faculty as part of their relationship development.

> **PRACTICE TIP:** Maintain communication with all of your contingent faculty, whether on or off contract for the term, through regularly scheduled emails or a newsletter. This is especially helpful in keeping contingent faculty who may be off contract for a teaching term connected to your program and feeling a sense of continued belonging.

How Much, If Any, and What Type of Teaching Experience Does This Candidate Have?

Contingent faculty members, particularly adjuncts, are typically hired because they bring up-to-date clinical practice knowledge to the academic classroom from their acquired expertise in their specific areas of practice (Santisteban & Egues, 2014). The MSW is considered the terminal practice degree in social work, but most social work practitioners are not educated about the role of academic faculty in their MSW programs and may face difficulties in role transitioning from social work practitioner to social work educator (Peters & Boylston, 2006; Santisteban & Egues, 2014).

To provide appropriate material in orientation programming and ongoing support and development, program directors need to understand what experience a candidate has in teaching students. If a candidate has teaching experience at a different institution, the program director should have a basic understanding about the former institution's mission and culture so that the program director can plan how to orient the candidate to the differences and expectations for teaching in the new institution. As a BSW program director, it is important to know if this candidate is specifically interested in teaching undergraduate students. If your institution offers both BSW and MSW programs, consider whether the candidate can articulate anticipated differences between teaching undergraduate and graduate students.

> **PRACTICE TIP:** "Social work practice ... is inherently and substantively educational — pedagogical. There is a particular pedagogy natural to social work where the social worker is in the forefront in the search for a clearer understanding in coming to know certain subject matter" (Freire & Moch, 1990, p. 5). Have the candidate describe their experience as a practitioner when in the educator role with their clients. As program director, extend the conversation to make connections and comparisons to teaching undergraduate and graduate students.

Social work educational standards and competencies, as provided by CSWE (2022), call for an equivalency for content and competency between a BSW student and a foundation year MSW student, leaving few distinctions between undergraduate and graduate students in professional social work education. The most common misconception or distinction has been that graduate students have more experience, whether in the field or general life experience, and come to the graduate classroom with an expected preparation of college-level knowledge acquisition and retention of core undergraduate content areas that the faculty can build upon. The reality is that many undergraduates come into the social work classroom with a bounding level of passion and excitement to learn the basics of the profession and gain their entry-level experience in the field. Therefore, basic, foundational content needs to be introduced and then reinforced throughout the undergraduate experience.

Engaging in this conversation with prospective faculty is significant, as a pervasive, assumed difference continues between undergraduate and graduate expectations, with the latter seen as more prestigious. The uninitiated may assume that the undergraduate student equates to inexperience, immaturity, and less exposure to the field of social work. But because the desire to earn a BSW may be influenced by economic considerations and promotion opportunities within places of employment, that is an incorrect assumption.

Level in a program does not necessarily mean less experience in the same way that teaching undergraduate students should not be seen as less glamorous. The pathway to contentment may not be predicated on status or perceived status, but rather on the fact that an opportunity to teach has presented itself. Program directors who include this conversation at the point of recruitment can gain a better understanding about the motivation and interest in teaching undergraduates for the prospective contingent faculty member.

Dr. Elizabeth Simmons (2016), vice chancellor at the University of California, San Diego, distinguishes general differences between teaching undergraduate and graduate students based on students' readiness to connect the course material to the specific career path. In social work education, there may be an assumption that students, both undergraduate and graduate, enter the program intrinsically interested in social work. However, social work educators also know that many students arrive at universities with a narrow definition of what social work entails, and thus it is the responsibility of the faculty to both instill and expand the social work students' passion, knowledge, values, skills, and professional competencies. It is helpful to include in the conversation with prospective contingent faculty their expectations and understanding of teaching at the different levels and the different content areas across the social work curriculum.

PRACTICE TIP: If your school or department offers both a BSW and an MSW program, consider whether a course can be cross-listed so that faculty members can gain experience teaching at both levels and students can benefit from experiencing and contributing to a diverse, energized, and active learning environment.

What Are Their Expectations for Accepting a Contingent Appointment?

As indicated in the earlier discussion about motivation, some prospective faculty apply for contingent faculty positions in the hope that such a position will eventually lead to a full-time (NTTE) and/or tenure-track position. Other prospective faculty may be specifically looking to supplement their professional practice and income, and all should be striving to fulfill their ethical responsibility to the social work profession, 5.01 Integrity of the Profession (NASW, 2021), by teaching part-time and preparing the next generation of social workers.

Depending on the type of institution, the hope of transitioning from contingent to a full-time appointment can be rooted in reality or have little to no chance of coming to fruition. Just as a social work practitioner serves as a sounding board and provides clients with reality checks, program directors should tell a candidate the truth about career pathways in academia. While some community colleges or teaching colleges may expect a prospective faculty member to teach on a contingent contract before qualifying for a full-time teaching position, most NTTE faculty at universities have appointments that include administrative duties and other university service in addition to an expected teaching load, so the job posting may include additional experience expectations other than teaching.

Also dependent on the type of institution are aspects such as salary compensation, contract dates, institutional exclusivity clauses, benefits eligibility, and others, which are part of the recruitment and hiring conversations. Some program directors may be empowered to have these conversations, and others may have to defer to the dean, associate dean, or institutional human resources department. Regardless of who has the responsibility of conveying this information, similar to the social work role of serving as a point of resource and referral, the program director should know the basic answers to these human resources types of inquiries, along with whom to contact for information or when something goes awry while the contingent faculty member is on contract or transitioning off or back onto contract. Clearly articulating the parameters and expectations of the contingent term appointment is a critical aspect of the program director role in the recruitment and selection process.

> **PRACTICE TIP:** Social work licensure requirements vary by state; however, most require the completion of continuing education units (CEUs). Program directors should check with their state's licensing board to determine if CEUs can be granted for preparing and teaching a social work course at their institution. This can be a helpful incentive for contingent faculty, particularly for those teaching at institutions with lower-than-desirable or contracted compensation rates or ranges lower than nearby institutions.

Onboarding and Orienting Contingent Faculty

Similar to intern or employee orientations received in field agencies and other workplaces, orientation programs in academia should assist new faculty members in making the transition to social work educator. Orientation programs should "help them become familiar with the system in which they will be working, and provide opportunities for building skills, integrating into the academic culture, networking, and mentorship"

(Suplee & Gardner, 2009, p. 514; Center for Community College Student Engagement, 2014).

Social work education is the venue for preparing and producing the next generation of social workers. To achieve this, the contingent faculty must have the required knowledge, skills, and values and disseminate, teach, and model them to the students (Teater & Lopez-Humphreys, 2019). Given their experience as social work practitioners, they can bring current policy or practice perspectives into the classroom (Fagan-Wilen et al., 2006) and are well positioned to convey practice wisdom to students.

One of the many functions of the program director is to ensure that faculty and staff understand and fit with the program mission and goals. A critical skill for a program director is being able to articulate vision and goals and make connections regarding where and how each member fits into the provision of social work education.

Tenure-track faculty, clinical or NTTE faculty, adjunct faculty, field instructors, and field liaisons all have a teaching responsibility. There should be a synergy among all of them that serves as the foundation for a comprehensive education, and that provides a comprehensive education for students. In the classroom, faculty have an obligation to teach material such as theory, practice, research, and human behavior, while field faculty teach professional practice and integration. Each has a unique role in fulfilling programmatic objectives.

Faculty members must realize that the knowledge they possess is not readily apparent to students; it must be taught, both intentionally and explicitly, in classrooms (Moor et al., 2012) and in the field. Faculty expertise in specific practice settings and with certain populations is considered an underused resource in social work departments (Mehrotra et al., 2013), and efforts need to be made to maximize opportunities for faculty members to showcase their skill set, knowledge base, research interests, and intersecting interests outside of the academy that may yield educational opportunities. It is in these areas that contingent faculty, particularly adjuncts maintaining full-time employment in the field, can pull from their vast experiences to offer content to students.

In considering a contingent faculty member's potential practice experiences as a social worker, program directors need to ensure that they know *how* to teach. There is a lack of professional preparation for faculty to learn pedagogy and adult learning theory as opposed to their ability to be practitioners. Although the ability to teach social work coursework requires that faculty hold an MSW and possibly licensure, adjunct faculty may feel isolated and struggle with their teacher identity, and they are often assumed to vary in their commitment, motivation, and ability to teach (Barbera et al., 2017; Reeder, 2020; Snook et al., 2019). MSW-level faculty likely will not have received any training in pedagogy, given that even those graduating from social work PhD programs have not received much education in effective teaching (Maynard et al., 2017; see Chapter 13 for further discussion).

All faculty, and especially new and contingent faculty, look to the program director to onboard and orient them to the academic environment and create a supportive structure with ongoing opportunities for professional development. Albeit a small slice of the directorship responsibilities, helping contingent faculty get to know campus policies, grow their instructional expertise, understand how they support a successful student experience, and contribute to the social work program is a huge responsibility for a program director. This onboarding process requires that program directors orient contingent faculty to understand the curriculum, its structure, and fit in the big picture; syllabus preparation and its effects on grading; and how to manage difficult conversations (Strom-Gottfried & Dunlap, 2004).

Social work program directors bear the responsibility of ensuring the highest quality education in social work knowledge and skills (Clark et al., 2011). Considering that the purpose of social work education is to offer students the knowledge and practical experience to become competent, effective, and ethical social work practitioners, the support adjuncts need is critical because many may never have taught in a college classroom before (Barbera et al., 2017). While institutional supports may exist for new contingent faculty by way of campuswide orientations or centers for learning, teaching, or technology, program directors may need to connect new faculty to them.

Orienting all faculty to their role begins unofficially during the recruitment process and officially once onboarded. The school's perspective, mission statement, and strategic plan should be shared so that faculty feel empowered to support students within the framework of the institution's goals. Program directors able to develop a system of support for contingent faculty can reap many benefits that strengthen the program—both the implicit and explicit curricula—and improve both faculty and student experiences.

Engaged and aware adjunct faculty are more likely to connect students to college and campus systems, connect with the overall program of study as they see their course's place in the overall program, and receive professional development in support of pedagogy and technology. Supported adjuncts are more likely to return to teach their courses, which keeps program continuity (Edwards, 2019). Developing such a supportive system takes planning and calls for the program director's attention, energy, and commitment early in the process; yet results, such as better prepared and connected faculty and retention of faculty, will mean less future recruitment and onboarding (Edwards, 2019).

> **PRACTICE TIP:** Think back to entering a field placement or your first day as a professional. What information did you need to know? What information did you learn along the way but wished that someone had told you about beforehand? Include this information in your orientation programming for new faculty. And remember the little things that can make a big difference, such as the copier code, where to find staples, or where they can refill a water bottle!

Be certain to orient contingent faculty to the institutional policies and practices for contact with students. Many require the use of an institution-provided email address or contact solely through the institution's learning management systems. Structure and language about expectations around receipt of and responses to emails, or phone calls, or text messages from students should be explicated by the program director. Some faculty, particularly those new to teaching and trying to impress, may struggle with even asking about this, so it is good practice for a program director to include the setting of boundaries in the initial conversations and again during orientation.

Once the new hires are onboarded, the program director needs to outline expectations for appropriate time frames within which the faculty is expected to respond to student or program contacts. To keep the program in compliance with institutional policies and procedures, program directors may also need to determine how they, on behalf of their contingent faculty, will complete any necessary grading or administrative paperwork, including changes from an incomplete to a letter course grade, that is required between terms.

The COVID-19 pandemic added a new dimension to recruiting, selecting, and orienting faculty to their dynamic role with the implementation of online learning platforms. The pandemic highlighted the skills necessary to teach both in a traditional classroom and in a synchronous or asynchronous online setting. However, keep in mind that not all students have access to the technology this learning entails, and not all contingent faculty have access to or the aptitude for the integration of learning in this new environment.

Training faculty in the use of technology is a necessity to adjust to how environmental issues, like poverty, class, and access, are negatively affecting the teaching and learning process. Both students and faculty can benefit from being directed to institutional resources, such as instructional technologists, to better incorporate technology into their teaching and learning. A decade later, the pandemic supported Buquoi et al.'s (2013) findings that BSW educators "did not appear to be using technology in the teaching and learning process at an advanced or even moderate level, but they were found to be more likely to incorporate technology in the process as the amount of technology available increased and their teaching philosophy strengthened" (p. 481).

> **PRACTICE TIP:** As a program director, how familiar are you with the technological resources and trainings offered by your institution? Poll your faculty regarding their expertise and comfort with using technology and learning new online learning platforms. Plan an in-service training for your contingent faculty and possibly all faculty!

To ensure high-quality online social work based on best practices, faculty must receive training on how to do so (Báez et al., 2019). This will help to compensate for the deleterious effects that extraneous variables, like the pandemic, have had on those accustomed to brick-and-mortar education. This added consideration of faculty training must inform conversations and orientation topics around familiarity and comfort with technology, online education, synchronous learning, and asynchronous models of instruction.

Cultivating Relationships and Continuing Connections

No single orientation program can cover all of the potential issues that may emerge for faculty throughout the term. It is imperative that the connections made during the recruitment and orientation process continue through both individual and group mentoring opportunities. Just as scheduling an orientation program for adjuncts is challenging, so too is creating mentorship space. Flexibility of time boundaries is necessary for a program director to be able to respond to issues that arise and provide guidance to contingent faculty. Contingent faculty, particularly adjuncts, are often allocated into the course schedule after tenured/tenure-track faculty and likely into the evening and weekend slots because many work in full-time positions elsewhere.

Having an open-door policy, whether in person or virtual (including email and videoconferencing) and particularly during times that fall between classes, is especially helpful and encourages adjunct faculty to drop in immediately before or after their classes. These drop-ins can be a time for faculty to exchange information about students or class-related material or issues, and more important, this time helps to build the relationship between program director, individual faculty members, and the school or institution. In addition, ensure that contingent faculty with similar schedules are able to connect with one another between class times or in a shared office or printer/copier room. All of these formed relationships help to motivate individual faculty members and strengthen the connection to the institution and faculty role, which in turn strengthens the teaching and learning in and outside of the classroom.

Across the educational landscape, curriculum delivery changed in the context of the COVID-19 pandemic, with many institutions having a temporary or permanent shift from the traditional face-to-face, on-campus experience to utilizing technology for online learning in a virtual classroom. This shift in course delivery also affected the relationships formed with and among faculty and called upon the program director to be intentional about continuing to cultivate the relationships with faculty and connections between the school and contingent faculty. This also upended the demarcations that professionals make to separate their professional and personal lives. Navigating between teaching in a classroom and working from home removed some of the ritualistic behaviors necessary to support professional boundaries. Even as we continue to move on from the immediate response, some of the issues linger.

In a traditional sense, there are physical activities, like walking to the car, making sure that the necessary materials are present, or driving past the local coffee shop, that are instrumental in allowing an educator to shed their personal identity and assume their role as a teacher. When working from home, these landmarks do not exist in the same way, so it may be difficult ending one mode of being and engaging another. Not only is the *doing* affected but the ways in which faculty support students are as well. Many faculty arrive early before a physical class to engage students and check in with them to support and address challenges. The artificial construct of online teaching platforms makes that difficult, though there are options to open "waiting rooms" using Zoom or use other best practices in online teaching to foster class connections.

The difference in a physical space versus an online atmosphere affects both students and faculty. Thus, program directors need to support best practices in online teaching and learning. In addition, other significant behaviors attached to the workplace that normalize workdays, like meeting at the water cooler or copier, do not exist in this virtual teaching world. The lack of socialization is a significant impediment not only for vulnerable clients, but also for professional helpers and teachers, too. These rituals that we all engage in have changed and further challenge how we cultivate relationships in a parallel process: faculty to student, and program director to faculty.

To develop the relationships to connect contingent faculty with the program, the program director needs to consider how to engage contingent faculty in ways that support collegial collaborative relationships beyond the administrative relationship between program director and faculty. Program directors should create forums, without administrative oversight, for faculty members to connect about teaching virtually, as well as offer a space to address feelings of uncertainty and changing expectations of contingent faculty and encourage the formation of friendships that lead to strengthened work relationships (McMurtrie, 2020; Seck et al., 2013).

PRACTICE TIP: Create a collegial space for contingent faculty to meet and connect with an agenda-free opportunity to share resources, thoughts, ideas, and strategies. Schedule different days of the week and times so contingent faculty can participate based on their availability. At the State University of New York Stony Brook University School of Social Welfare program, the first author listed for this chapter, Suzanne Velázquez, introduced such "virtual water cooler" sessions with resounding success. The "BSW Faculty Fun 'n Fuss" sessions have faculty, some of whom may not have met one another in the hallways of the school, drop in when their schedules allow. In this virtual space, they can connect with one another and share resources and stories; some have even developed referral relationships with one another for their private practices. The program director attends as a faculty colleague instead of as an administrator, and all faculty teaching in the BSW program are invited, even if they may be off contract for the current semester. These sessions have strengthened a collaborative esprit de corps throughout the faculty team that has resulted in maintained connectedness and an improved sense of belonging, trust, and safety among contingent faculty.

Challenges Engaging Part-Time Faculty

As previously discussed, the fulfillment of institutional and program missions relies on the institution's ability to engage adjunct faculty. Aside from their commitment to the institution, these professionals may carry full-time responsibilities outside of the school. Thus, they may feel disconnected from the full-time educational culture, not being in the rhythm of the day-to-day activities. The risk of emotional detachment from an academic institution is what adjuncts may face if they are excluded from participating in faculty meetings, attending professional development sessions and special events, or having their presence felt at workshops. This can lead to feeling disconnected from the corresponding educational institution (Pettit, 2020; Santisteban & Egues, 2014). The lack of physical proximity and almost transient nature of the assignment requires due diligence that may include hosting an adjunct orientation at the beginning of an academic semester.

Program directors must develop sound policies of engagement to ensure parity in the ways part-time faculty engage with students, how school-based initiatives are understood, and how connected to the mission of the school part-time faculty feel. Contingent faculty, particularly adjuncts, often experience a sense of isolation from social work programs, feeling invisible because of the lack of contact with other faculty members (Fagan-Wilen et al., 2006), so policies should be aimed at bridging the gap to use more experienced faculty as mentors to strengthen the connection adjuncts feel toward the academy. Mentoring programs, especially collaborative peer models as opposed to traditional top-down mentoring, are helpful in providing a clear message to contingent faculty about the importance and value they bring to the social work program (de Saxe Zerden et al., 2015; Strom-Gottfried & Dunlap, 2004).

Because of competing life demands, the expectation of part-time faculty to attend meetings, be present for conference calls, and even hold office hours for students may be difficult. The benefit of partnering with part-time faculty may be in their ability to engage in social work practice to help round out students' understanding of the *doing* of social work. A significant number of part-time faculty may be licensed, attend CEU events, and be up to date with current innovations in the field. The disadvantage is that these same responsibilities may interfere with their full assimilation into academic life.

Create opportunities for contingent faculty, especially adjuncts, to engage with social work programs in a way that values their contribution and strengthens the connection between them and the school. Opportunities such as attending discounted CEU programs or using feedback from community meetings in communication to the school's leadership team can help to minimize challenges a program director may encounter in trying to engage this group of faculty. A newsletter and soliciting volunteers for classroom speaking opportunities support the depth and breadth of the relationship and help to identify suitable candidates when openings for part-time faculty come up. As program director, the responsibility to engage may require creativity considering the aforementioned challenges with scheduling, time management, and managing multiple responsibilities.

> **PRACTICE TIP:** A well-planned and facilitated retreat could provide opportunities to enhance collegiality, strengthen teamwork, and develop stronger bonds between contingent faculty and program staff and administration (Cleary & Horsfall, 2015). Conduct outreach to bring faculty into the fold!

Anti-Racism, Diversity, Equity, and Inclusion (ADEI)

The year 2020 saw significant increase in activism, advocacy, and outreach to marginalized communities due to overpolicing, protests, riots, and the response of the Black Lives Matter movement. One of the many benefits of having adjunct faculty is that practicing social workers represent a wide diversity of ethnic and cultural perspectives and link academia to the community, increasing students' ability to practice as culturally responsive, human-rights-based, socially just practitioners (Fagan-Wilen et al., 2006). The attention given to diversity is important, as students may need, developmentally, to see representation in the faculty members in the same way they will be expected to practice across diverse populations.

Considering the contentious nature of political conversation, religious doctrine, and challenging students' understandings of marginalized and oppressed populations, uncomfortable conversations will arise (Strom-Gottfried & Dunlap, 2004). "Teaching students to be mindful of and sensitive to issues, from potential language barriers to recognizing various religious sects, plays a role in effective practice" (Hall & Lindsey, 2014, p. 1). Having a diverse faculty may be beneficial for framing some of these difficult dialogues, especially where race, privilege, and fragility are concerned.

In addition to racial and cultural diversity, program directors need to actively seek out and be inclusive of diversity in the broader sense when forming and cultivating full-time and adjunct faculty, including diverse areas of practice, years of practice, content expertise, and teaching strategies and activity. Given the importance of ADEI in the 2022 Educational Policy and Accreditation Standards (EPAS; CSWE, 2022), attention to this through the implicit curriculum is required.

As previously mentioned, creating a collegial and collaborative work environment enables contingent faculty to be included, feel valued, and form relationships with faculty, staff, and administrators with whom they may not otherwise come into contact (de Saxe Zerden et al., 2015). Such an environment, where contingent faculty are connected with healthy, diverse professional relationships, results in higher productivity and increased job satisfaction, and encourages program directors and contingent faculty to tap into the intrinsic motivators and rewards that call practitioners to accept and continue contingent appointments (Cleary & Horsfall, 2015; Flaherty, 2018).

Mentoring and Coaching Faculty From the Strengths Perspective

Social work embodies the principles of empowerment, as well as building trust, respect, and purposeful working relationships. Social work practitioners are taught to provide a safe environment and develop a relationship built on trust that encourages clients to open up and work with the practitioner. The same principles apply to program directors working with contingent faculty. As opposed to working with tenure-track/tenured faculty, the key concern for contingent faculty is a sense of security in the workplace. Although inherent in each semester appointment for adjuncts, for NTTE, this sense exists and heightens when their multiple-year contract may be coming to an end. At that point, the risk of nonrenewal is present, despite their efforts and achievements, particularly as budget exigencies are increasing at the institutional and governmental funding levels. To counter the insecurity of term contracts for both NTTE and adjunct faculty, it is imperative for the program director to develop a safe, trusting, professional relationship, rooted in the strengths perspective with each contingent faculty member. Some of the methods discussed in Chapter 13 for full-time faculty can be adapted here for contingent faculty.

This level of relationship building and mentorship can be accomplished by encouraging staff interaction between full-time faculty and adjuncts by facilitating working sessions to provide a professional link between the two groups. There are many innovative ways to accomplish this, including meeting around teaching methodologies, recent developments and rationales for curriculum development, creating contingent faculty committees, and inviting long-standing adjuncts to join standing academic ones (Fagan-Wilen et al., 2006).

Although establishing a mentoring program is highly effective to promote capacity building and inclusivity, mentoring alone should not be the entirety of contingent faculty support. Models exist that belay the traditional top-down management style to offer peer-support models, seen as more advantageous and beneficial to learning on a level playing field (de Saxe Zerden et al., 2015), as friendships formed outside of the formal faculty mechanism can solidify the working relationship (Seck et al., 2013).

Revisiting the earlier discussion about the lack of preparation for social work practitioners to teach, program directors should be prepared to provide a considerable amount of faculty development support. Conducting performance audits and class observations are helpful tools; however, they can also induce high levels of discomfort and anxiety. Program directors should conduct such observations as assessment tools with constructive feedback to improve course content delivery to match program goals, instead of evaluation measures focused on critiquing the individual faculty member's ability to teach.

Before the start of the course, during syllabus creation or review with the teaching faculty, ask how the faculty member plans to convey content that aligns with a program goal or with a specific CSWE competency. Program directors may provide suggestions for activities, particularly for first-time teachers, yet they need to remain open to learning new ways of thinking about connections between academic content and practice wisdom that contingent faculty can contribute.

Mark on your calendar the dates the faculty member expects to deliver connected lesson plans and be sure to have a follow-up conversation with them after that class session. During that follow-up, ask the faculty member how it went and whether they believe that the students were able to make the connection and integrate the learning and, upon reflection, if there are changes they would make for the next time they teach that lesson. Framing this type of a performance audit in the strengths and use of self in practice perspectives aligns with the social work practitioner aspect of the faculty member, thus providing another opportunity for both the program director–faculty relationship and the contingent faculty's confidence of teaching ability and value to the program to strengthen.

> **PRACTICE TIP:** Program directors may want to offer to co-teach a few lessons throughout the term, which will allow access into the classroom with a mutually prepared lesson. This should lower anxiety by having the program director co-teach alongside rather than solely observing from the back of the classroom.

Termination

One of the most difficult tasks of the program director's job is to manage a healthy termination process with a contingent faculty member. Hopefully, the program director has created a safe and inclusive environment with ongoing faculty development and support as suggested here. There are many reasons for a contingent faculty member's contractual appointment to end, from the member's personal reasons to the programmatic needs and decisions made by administration to budgetary issues of the institution. Regardless of whether the process is initiated by the administration or the faculty member, contract-ending processes should be carried out from the strengths perspective and in alignment with social work values and processes, as well as institutional policy.

Just as healthy termination occurs in social work practice with clients, so too should the contractual relationship end among the school, program director, and faculty member. In fact, just as the social worker begins termination in the planning and engagement phase of the helping relationship, so too would the program director do so during the recruitment and onboarding parts of the program director–faculty relationship development. For the ending of a faculty contract to be handled properly, discussions between the program director and faculty member should occur in advance and be addressed in a thoughtful and sensitive manner.

It is best that a contingent faculty member does not feel forsaken by the program director, program, or institution, and it is important to protect the reputation of both the social work program and the faculty member. Adherence to policy is essential. Reputation, an intangible entity based on behavior, others' perceptions of trustworthiness, and performance, along with reputation management are critical in higher education and in the social work profession (Tindall, 2016). In the social work profession, contingent faculty who end a teaching contract are likely still working in the field and have leverage and connections that influence future program success. Program directors able to navigate the ending of contracts in a healthy and positive manner will be able to maintain community-school-program relations and likely develop new ones.

Conclusion

Relationship building is a critical component of social work. This chapter underscores the importance of relationship-building skills for the program director to successfully work with contingent faculty, both NTTE and adjunct. Engaging with faculty from recruitment and continued cultivation of the relationship through the academic contract terms will assist the program director in developing a strong faculty base and reputable social work program. The contractual nature of contingent appointments in higher education proliferates a sense of insecurity in an ever-uncertain world. Practice tips are offered for program directors to promote the human rights of safety and security for contingent faculty under the purview of the directorship in efforts to increase job satisfaction and fulfillment of intrinsic motivators.

Suggested Readings

de Saxe Zerden, L., Ilinitch, T. L., Carlston, R., Knutson, D., Blesdoe, B. E., & Howard, M. O. (2015). Social work faculty development: An exploratory study of non-tenure-track women faculty. *Journal of Social Work Education, 51*(4), 738–753. https://doi.org /10.1080/10437797.2015.1076284

Gaye, L. (2018). Making visible our invisible faculty: Mentoring for contingent online faculty. *Journal of Higher Education Theory and Practice, 18*(2), 52–65. https://doi. org/10.33423/jhetp.v18i2.546

Hunnicutt, M. A. (2018). *Adjunct faculty satisfaction: Perceptions from the adjunct faculty and administrator perspectives at a large South Carolina technical college* (Publication Number 13425156) [Doctoral dissertation, Wingate University]. ProQuest Dissertations and Theses Global. Ann Arbor. http://gateway.proquest.com/openurl?url_ver=Z39 .88-2004&rft_val_fmt=info:ofi/fmt:kev:mtx:dissertation&res_dat=xri:pqm&rft_dat =xri:pqdiss:13425156

McNaughtan, J., García, H. A., & Nehls, K. (2017). Understanding the growth of contingent faculty. *New Directions for Institutional Research, 2017*(176), 9–26. https://doi.org/10.1002 /ir.20241

Nelson, G., Monson, M. J., & Adibifar, K. (2020). The gig economy comes to academia: Job satisfaction among adjunct faculty. *Cogent Education, 7*(1), 1–18. https://doi.org/10.1080 /2331186X.2020.1786338

Simmons, C. A., Weiss, E. L., & Schwartz, S. L. (2022). Job satisfaction indicators for tenure and non-tenure track social work faculty: Similar but not equal. *Social Work Education, 41*(2), 175–194.

References

American Association of University Professors (AAUP). (2014). *Contingent appointments and the academic profession*. https://www.aaup.org/report/contingent-appointments-and-academic-profession

American Association of University Professors (AAUP). (2018). *Data snapshot: Contingent faculty in US higher ed*. https://www.aaup.org/news/data-snapshot-contingent-faculty-us-higher-ed#.X_EdK9hKi72

Báez, J. C., Marquart, M., Chung, R. Y. E., Ryan, D., & Garay, K. (2019). Developing and supporting faculty training for online social work education: The Columbia University School of Social Work Online Pedagogy Institute. *Journal of Teaching in Social Work, 39*(4–5), 505–518. https://doi.org/10.1080/08841233.2019.1653419

Barbera, R., Ward, K., Mama, R., & Averbach, J. (2017). Improving teaching: Training program for social work adjuncts. *Journal of Baccalaureate Social Work, 22*(1), 17–30. https://doi.org/10.18084/1084-7219.22.1.17

Buquoi, B., McClure, C., Kotrlik, J. W., Machtmes, K., & Bunch, J. C. (2013). A national research survey of technology use in the BSW teaching and learning process. *Journal of Teaching in Social Work, 33*(4–5), 481–495. https://doi.org/10.1080/08841233.2013.833577

Carnegie Classification of Institutions of Higher Education. (n.d.). *About Carnegie classification*. http://carnegieclassifications.iu.edu/

Center for Community College Student Engagement. (2014). *Contingent commitments: Bringing part-time faculty into focus*. The University of Texas at Austin, Program in Higher Education Leadership. https://www.ccsse.org/docs/ptf_special_report.pdf

Chronicle Almanac 2020–21. (2020). Percentages of full-time faculty members who were non-tenure-track, by institutional classification, 2018–19. *The Chronicle of Higher Education*. https://www.chronicle.com/article/percentages-of-full-time-faculty-members-who-were-non-tenure-track-by-institutional-classification-2018-19

Clark, H. G., Moore, B. A., Johnston, L. B., & Openshaw, L. (2011). Using adjuncts in social work education: Challenges and rewards. *Social Work Education, 30*(8), 1012–1021. https://doi.org/10.1080/02615479.2010.534450

Cleary, M., & Horsfall, J. (2015). Teamwork and teambuilding: Considering retreats. *Issues in Mental Health Nursing, 36*(1), 78–80. https://doi.org/10.3109/01612840.2014.981432

Council on Social Work Education. (2020). *Information for deans and directors regarding regional accreditation standards for faculty qualifications*. https://www.cswe.org/Accreditation/RegionalAccreditors_GuidancetoPrograms-April-16-20.aspx

Council on Social Work Education. (2021). *2020 statistics on social work education in the United States*. https://www.cswe.org/getattachment/726b15ce-6e63-4dcd-abd1-35d2ea9d9d40/2020-Annual-Statistics-On-Social-Work-Education-in-the-United-States.pdf?lang=en-US

Council on Social Work Education. (2022). *2022 Educational policy and accreditation standards*. https://www.cswe.org/accreditation/standards/2022-epas/

de Saxe Zerden, L., Ilinitch, T. L., Carlston, R., Knutson, D., Blesdoe, B. E., & Howard, M. O. (2015). Social work faculty development: An exploratory study of non-tenure-track women faculty. *Journal of Social Work Education, 51*(4), 738–753. https://doi.org/10.1080/10437797.2015.1076284

Edwards, S. (2019, Fall). Supporting adjunct faculty. *The Department Chair*, 5–6. https://doi.org/10.1002/dch.30280

Fagan-Wilen, R., Springer, D. W., Ambrosino, B., & White, B. W. (2006). The support of adjunct faculty: An academic imperative. *Social Work Education, 25*(1), 39–51. https://doi.org/10.1080/02615470500477870

Flaherty, C. (2018). What motivates good teaching? *Inside Higher Ed.* https://www.insidehighered .com/news/2018/03/22/study-faculty-motivation-teaching-says-intrinsic-motivation-and -believing-teaching

Freire, P., & Moch, M. (Translator). (1990). A critical understanding of social work. *Journal of Progressive Human Services, 1*(1), 3–9. https://doi.org/10.1300/J059v01n01_02

Gappa, J. M. (2000). The new faculty majority: Somewhat satisfied but not eligible for tenure. *New Directions for Institutional Research, 2000*(105), 77–86. https://doi.org/10.1002 /ir.10507

Gappa, J. M., & Leslie, D. W. (1993). *The Invisible Faculty: Improving the Status of Part-Timers in Higher Education.* Jossey-Bass Inc.

Gaye, L. (2018). Making visible our invisible faculty: Mentoring for contingent online faculty. *Journal of Higher Education Theory and Practice, 18*(2), 52–65. https://doi.org/10.33423 /jhetp.v18i2.546

Hall, E., & Lindsey, S. (2014, Summer). Teaching cultural competence. *The New Social Worker,* 4–5. https://www.socialworker.com/feature-articles/ethics-articles/teaching-cultural -competence/

Hunnicutt, M. A. (2018). *Adjunct faculty satisfaction: Perceptions from the adjunct faculty and administrator perspectives at a large South Carolina technical college* (Publication Number 13425156) [Doctoral dissertation, Wingate University]. ProQuest Dissertations and Theses Global. Ann Arbor. http://gateway.proquest.com/openurl?url_ver=Z39.88-2004&rft _val_fmt=info:ofi/fmt:kev:mtx:dissertation&res_dat=xri:pqm&rft_dat=xri:pqdiss:13425156

Kumar, B., Swee, M. L., & Suneja, M. (2019). The ecology of program director leadership: Power relationships and characteristics of effective program directors. *BMC Medical Education, 19*(1), 436. https://doi.org/10.1186/s12909-019-1869-3

Leslie, D. W., & Gappa, J. M. (2002). Part-time faculty: Competent and committed. *New Directions for Community Colleges, 2002*(118), 59–68. https://doi.org/10.1002/cc.64

Maynard, B. R., Labuzienski, E. M., Lind, K. S., Berglund, A. H., & Albright, D. L. (2017). Social work doctoral education: Are doctoral students being prepared to teach? *Journal of Social Work, 17*(1), 91–114. https://doi.org/10.1177/1468017316637226

McMurtrie, B. (2020, November 5). The pandemic is dragging on. Professors are burning out. *The Chronicle of Higher Education.* https://www.chronicle.com/article/the-pandemic -is-dragging-on-professors-are-burning-out

McNaughtan, J., García, H. A., & Nehls, K. (2017). Understanding the growth of contingent faculty. *New Directions for Institutional Research, 2017*(176), 9–26. https://doi.org/10 .1002/ir.20241

Mehrotra, C. M., Townsend, A., & Berkman, B. (2013). Evaluation of a training program in aging research for social work faculty. *Educational Gerontology, 39*(11), 787–796.

Moor, K. S., Jensen-Hart, S., & Hooper, R. I. (2012). Small change, big difference: Heightening BSW faculty awareness to elicit more effective student writing. *Journal of Teaching in Social Work, 32*(1), 62–77.

National Association of Social Workers. (2021). *Code of ethics.* https://www .socialworkers.org/About/Ethics/Code-of-Ethics/Code-of-Ethics-English

Nelson, G., Monson, M. J., & Adibifar, K. (2020). The gig economy comes to academia: Job satisfaction among adjunct faculty. *Cogent Education, 7*(1), 1–18. https://doi.org/10.1080 /2331186X.2020.1786338

Page, K. (2018). Tell me what you want: Collective bargaining for adjunct faculty. *Journal of Collective Bargaining in the Academy, 0*(13), Article 42. https://thekeep.eiu.edu/cgi /viewcontent.cgi?article=1785&context=jcba

Peters, M. A., & Boylston, M. (2006). Mentoring adjunct faculty: Innovative solutions. *Nurse Educator, 31*(2), 61–64. https://doi.org/10.1097/00006223-200603000-00006

Pettit, E. (2020, October 26). Covid-19 cuts hit contingent faculty hard. As the pandemic drags on, some question their future. *The Chronicle of Higher Education.* https://www.chronicle.com/article/covid-19-cuts-hit-contingent-faculty-hard-as-it -drags-on-some-question-their-future

Pons Jr., P. E. (2015). *A preliminary study investigating motivational factors influencing part-time faculty to seek employment at community colleges* [Doctoral dissertation, Old Dominion University]. ODU Digital Commons. https://digitalcommons.odu.edu/cgi /viewcontent.cgi?article=1016&context=efl_etds

Pons, P. E., Burnett, D. D., Williams, M. R., & Paredes, T. M. (2017). Why do they do it? A case study of factors influencing part-time faculty to seek employment at a community college. *The Community College Enterprise, 23*(1), 43–59.

Reeder, H. (2020). Commitment among adjunct faculty. *Journal of Applied Research in Higher Education, 12*(5), 1209–1220. https://doi.org/10.1108/JARHE-04-2019-0079

Santisteban, L., & Egues, A. L. (2014). Cultivating adjunct faculty: Strategies beyond orientation. *Nursing Forum, 49*(3), 152–158.

Seck, M. M., McArdle, L., & Helton, L. R. (2013). Two faculty groups' process in delivering a joint MSW program: Evaluating the outcome. *Journal of Social Service Research, 40*(1), 29–38. https://doi.org/10.1080/01488376.2013.845125

Simmons, C. A., Weiss, E. L., & Schwartz, S. L. (2022). Job satisfaction indicators for tenure and non-tenure track social work faculty: Similar but not equal. *Social Work Education, 41*(2), 175–194.

Simmons, E. H. (2016, July 23). *What are the differences between teaching undergraduate and graduate students?* Quora. https://www.quora.com/What-are-the-differences-between -teaching-undergraduate-and-graduate-students-Does-the-preparation-differ-What -pedagogical-tools-and-materials-are-used-How-do-students-behave-and-interact -in-and-out-of-class/answer/Elizabeth-H-Simmons

Smith, M. (2019). Characterizing adjunct faculty members' call to teach in higher education. *Curriculum and Teaching Dialogue, 21*(1–2), 65–164.

Snook, A. G., Schram, A. B., Sveinsson, T., & Jones, B. D. (2019). Needs, motivations, and identification with teaching: A comparative study of temporary part-time and tenure-track health science faculty in Iceland. *BMC Medical Education, 19*(1), 349. https://doi.org/10.1186/s12909-019-1779-4

Strom-Gottfried, K., & Dunlap, K. M. (2004). Assimilating adjuncts: Strategies for orienting contract faculty. *Journal of Social Work Education, 40*(3), 445–452.

Suplee, P. D., & Gardner, M. (2009). Fostering a smooth transition to the faculty role. *The Journal of Continuing Education in Nursing, 40*(11), 514–520. https://doi.org/10.3928 /00220124-20091023-09

Teater, B., & Lopez-Humphreys, M. (2019). Is social work education a form of social work practice? *Journal of Social Work Education, 55*(3), 616–622. https://doi.org/10.1080 /10437797.2019.1567415

Tindall, N. (2016, July 25). How to resign. *The Chronicle of Higher Education.* https://community.chronicle.com/news/1473-how-to-resign

CHAPTER 15

The BSW Program Director's Role in Building an Effective Faculty Team

Jo Daugherty Bailey

The academe is a special place, an honored home to engaged inquiry in the pursuit of knowledge and truth. It is a complex organization, with its layers of bureaucracy, myriad of functions, and hierarchy of roles responding to external economic, market, and social pressures with governance by legislatures, accrediting bodies, and state and federal agencies. Institutions of higher learning are often criticized as inherently slow to make decisions and change. However, the many demands upon them, combined with a core commitment to shared governance, mean that actions must be sifted for known and unforeseen consequences and then thoughtfully deliberated among colleagues. This highly valued norm of active deliberation is perhaps one of the most unique features of the culture of higher education.

Nested within this larger organizational structure, baccalaureate social work programs must also comply with the rules of their accreditor—the Council on Social Work Education (CSWE) Board of Accreditation (the Accrediting Body)—as well as be responsive to the needs of their students, their communities, and the marketplace. These competing elements make the environment for decision making fraught with potential difficulty. Adding to this, professional ethics, program structures, policies, relationships, and personalities further inform and challenge the decision-making process.

Despite the potential challenges, BSW program directors who are committed to inclusive leadership can create, along with faculty, a healthy and productive work culture. Key elements of such a culture incorporate collaborative and solution-focused practices that engage faculty in efforts that facilitate the achievement of the program's mission. A collaborative culture also upholds the ideals of shared governance and the values of the social work profession. Standards of practice (National Association of Social Workers [NASW], 2021) include the notion that professional social workers have an ethical responsibility toward their colleagues. This responsibility includes treating colleagues with respect and working in a collaborative fashion.

The BSW program director who upholds and models the values of the profession is in an advantageous position to create and nurture a culture of respect, cooperation, and partnership that promotes and sustains the healthy functioning of the team and program. Developing such a culture begins with discussing, then developing consensus around group norms that, with periodic reminders of this agreement, will inform their work together. Such practices, through repetition and constancy, become normative, and therefore institutionalized, for the group.

Higher Education Context

Many of the challenges of the BSW program director's work are related to larger contextual issues in higher education. This context includes various market pressures, the regulatory environment, and the distinct values in the academe (see Figure 15.1). The uniqueness of colleges and universities lies in their "product," which, while not universally agreed upon, generally refers to providing the opportunity for the acquisition of knowledge and skills for employment, personal development, and civic participation. So, unlike corporate enterprises, which sell consumer products and services, colleges and universities are in the business of facilitating human growth and development.

FIGURE 15.1

Higher Education Context

Pressures	• Demand in services • Decreased funding • Increased competition
Oversight	• Federal & state • Regional accreditors • Professional accreditors
Values	• Shared governance • Academic freedom • Inquiry & debate

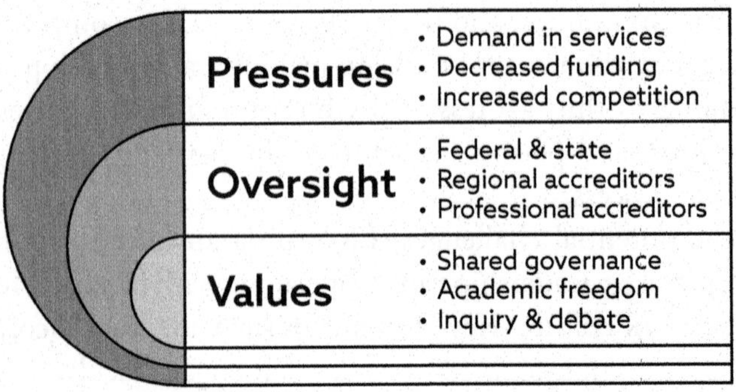

Despite their distinctive function of enhancing human potential, institutions of higher education must attend to operational elements common to other businesses (e.g., develop and enact marketing strategies, maintain statutory and regulatory compliance, etc.). Ongoing trends in higher education, such as the dramatic expansion of functions and services, increasing competition for students, and defunding by states, have presented significant challenges for administrative leadership (Kelchen et al., 2020). The specter of more than 700 college and university closures in the past two decades and impending decline in the population of high school graduates (Kelchen, 2020) exacerbate the pressures on current college and university leaders. Administration must steer the university to respond and adapt amid these dramatic challenges to higher education. Whether the adaptation undertaken is large and significant, like reorganization, or minor, like moving services to another unit, change can be disruptive and thus require a purposeful process (Hayes, 2014). To engage employees' sustained involvement in change efforts, leaders must demonstrate the need for change and then intentionally inspire, encourage, and reward continued efforts until the required change is solidified (Hayes, 2014; Kotter, 1996).

Faculty Role

Although university administrators have responsibilities similar to those of their counterparts in business (e.g., managing change efforts), their authority is circumscribed by the norm of shared governance in colleges and universities in the United States. While interpretation and implementation vary, shared governance typically means that university stakeholders, including administrators, staff, and faculty, actively collaborate and contribute to decision making. The conceptualization of shared governance recognizes that expertise and roles determine differing groups' capacities for decision making. Boards and presidents have the responsibility to ensure the financial viability of the institution (American Association of University Professors [AAUP], n.d.; Association of Governing Boards [AGB], 2017), and in order to do so, they have the power to make final decisions on the generation and allocation of funds. As scholastic ministers, faculty maintain a greater claim of authority over academic matters, such as "curriculum, subject matter and methods of instruction, research, faculty status, and those aspects of student life which relate to the educational process" (AAUP, n.d., The Academic Institution: The Faculty Section, para.1; Notes section, para. 4).

Within this culture of shared governance, the primary role of faculty—to advance truth and knowledge—gives rise to a peculiar orientation not seen in other professions. To advance truth, faculty must challenge the status quo and current understanding of their subjects (Buller, 2014). To effectively lead through many challenges, administrators (including BSW program directors) must understand and appreciate this culture of debate, knowledge seeking, academic freedom, and shared governance that is unique to higher education. A university leader who is culturally astute works well within these elements to advance institutional change. Faculty are likely to have a heightened sense of ownership of and commitment to their work that can lead to resistance to change, but which can also lead to active engagement in change activities when they see the need for change (Buller, 2014). Buller warned that the change process in a university is less a formulaic model than one of flexibility and discovery, guided by inquiry and investigation. To foster this process, leaders must help create a culture of innovation that is facile and characterized by a growth mindset oriented toward positivism and creativity (Buller, 2014).

Program Management and Team Leadership

In BSW social work programs, the program director is responsible for ensuring that the standards of social work education are delivered and met. In accordance with Educational Policy and Accreditation Standards (EPAS) 4.3.4(a), the program director *administers all program options* (CSWE, 2022, p. 30). Thus, the BSW program director has a number of critical responsibilities, including coordinating academic matters such as admissions, curriculum, and policy. Unfortunately, many BSW program directors receive little training or preparation for the position (Daley, 2008; Mapp & Boutté-Queen, 2021). It is therefore important for the new director to seek support and development opportunities, which could include mentorship by colleagues or training offered by their university (Daley, 2008; Mapp & Boutté-Queen, 2021). In fact, the support is so sparse that Daley (2008) advised BSW directors to "assume responsibility for their professional development in the position" (p. 395) and seek support from peer BSW directors in other programs. Regardless of the supports they seek, like any administrator, it is up to the BSW program director to commit to the ongoing development of their skills and knowledge in program management. While programs and program directors may differ in their approach to decision making about academic matters, I will discuss a team approach to most decisions, as it is most closely aligned with the ideals of shared governance.

Faculty are highly educated, informed, independent, and critical thinkers. To capture all they have to offer, to build a culture of innovation, and to channel the expertise and energy they bring, team decision making is optimal. The BSW program director must attend to the particulars of group building and functioning. Building and leading an effective team of faculty require a set of key skills, mostly related to planning, communication, and relationship building.

From a review of the literature, Holosko (2009) defined five core attributes for effective social work leaders (see Table 15.1). These attributes align with social work values and reflect the skills of effective management. By attending to these characteristics, program directors can direct the group's energies to achieving the program's mission while upholding the values of social work. The orientation and character of intentionality undergirds these skills. Intentionality implies a critical and methodical system of thoughtfulness. With intention, the director organizes and develops the road map for the group, creates clear and comprehensive strategies for information sharing and decision making, promotes social work values and ethics, and fosters relationships among and between group members. With intention, the BSW program director reflects on their own and the group's accomplishments and roadblocks.

TABLE 15.1

In Practice: Core Attributes

Attribute	Manifestation	Related Social Work Values
Vision	Defining goals and planning for achieving them	Competence, service
Influencing others to act	Promoting initiative	Social justice
Teamwork/ collaboration	Partnering to reach goals	Dignity and worth, importance of human relationships
Problem-solving capacity	Actively addressing problems	Competence, integrity
Creating positive change	Nurturing development and growth	Dignity and worth, importance of human relationships, integrity, social justice

Adapted from Holosko (2009).

Program Planning

For a program to function, it must have a mechanism to direct its activities. Decisions must be made about who is responsible for the work, what the group is doing, and when the work is to be done. Without a plan, the group does not have a course to set upon. Accordingly, it is definitive in the literature that planning is one of the core functions in an organization ("Management Functions," 2019). As the program's chief administrator, the BSW program director is responsible for program planning. To uphold the faculty's authority over academic matters, planning should be done in collaboration with the faculty. For example, the program's mission and goals must be determined by the team, as curriculum and admissions (i.e., those domains that fall within faculty responsibility) will be formed and guided by them. Sometimes, the planning will fall squarely upon the director. This may be most evident in operational planning including setting the agenda for the team's meetings (although team members may add to the agenda, the director must ensure inclusion of those issues necessary for the program's continued operation) or establishing deadlines to meet accreditation or regulatory review.

Planning has both operational and strategic facets, demanding a practical, instrumental focus along with the capability of forward thinking. It involves determining the group's short and long-term objectives (Dyer & Dyer, 2020), which will change over time as they are met and new ones need to be developed, and the means to achieve them ("Goals and Goal Setting," 2019). Many of the objectives, and therefore much of the team's work, are operational ("Goals and Goal Setting," 2019). They are focused upon achieving the mission and goals and delivering program elements as outlined in the self-study.

However, the overall functioning of the baccalaureate program is not static. The program will need to respond to changes in the university, evolving demands by regulatory and governing agencies, shifts in finances, new needs in the community, concerns expressed by students, and issues arising from program assessment and faculty's experiences. To effectively guide the team's work, the BSW program director must be monitoring and scanning for information, both internal and external to the program, to determine what may potentially affect the program's viability and relevance.

This fortune-telling may be one of the most difficult aspects of a BSW program director's job. The director must remain educated and attuned to cues to develop a programmatic response to the changing environment. For example, it seems fairly critical that program leaders understand demographic shifts, such as the now-declining traditional college-age cohort, as this will affect enrollments for the next decade and beyond (Western Interstate Commission for Higher Education, 2020). This trend is particularly problematic for those institutions that depend on state funding that is predicated on growth in enrollments, so programs must be ready to respond to these environmental changes. In sum, the BSW program director has to lead the development of the long-term strategic response of the program and has to monitor trends and events, help educate faculty about these trends, and then facilitate the team's planning and strategizing for them.

Team Rules and Decision Making

To begin the group's work, the BSW program director needs to help the group establish its rules for engagement. For conducting the meetings, some programs may follow Robert's Rules of Order (see Robert & Robert, 2011), and others may abandon all formality and structure. It is truly wise, given the timeliness of some of the decisions to be made, to establish some ground rules based on the ethics of respect and collaboration: rules pertaining to note taking, roll taking, turn taking, and decision making will help set the tone and structure of the group's activities and processes (Catalano, 2020; Dyer & Dyer, 2020; Franz, 2012; Pace, 2018; Schwarz, 2017; West, 2012).

The first two are rather straightforward, and the group may decide to rotate the responsibility or have a volunteer do these tasks. *Turn taking* refers to reminding the faculty to allow others their chance to speak, and the director can ensure that this happens by calling on a person who has indicated that they want to say something and by asking the group, from time to time, if anyone has anything to add to the discussion. The director must be continuously mindful of the impact of race, gender, ethnicity, class, and sexual identity upon faculty members' ability to speak and comfort level within the team setting. For those members who appear quiet, a private talk to find out what changes could be enacted to facilitate inclusion of their perspective could be helpful. Additionally, the director can periodically engage the team to review, assess, and revise their norms and practices to promote inclusivity.

The rules around decision making are undoubtedly vital. The parameters of the group's authority are typically addressed in the university and program governance documents and practices. Aside from any restrictions, faculty should have purview over academic matters, including curriculum and promotion and tenure guidelines. Promotion and tenure guidelines are incredibly important standards that serve as the tool for evaluation of all tenure-track and tenured faculty at some point in time. These guidelines include detailed and thorough explanation of the teaching requirements (e.g., number of courses, evaluation of teaching, etc.), research (e.g., number of publications, weight of various types of activities, etc.), and service (e.g., number of committee memberships, weighting of committee types and roles, etc.).

These discussions are more difficult because faculty members have a high personal stake (i.e., their future employment) in them. For decisions on academic matters, the faculty must have a mechanism for discussion and decision making (Pace, 2018; Schwarz, 2017). This is where Robert's Rules, or some version of them, may be helpful, especially for larger teams. Robert's Rules offer a clear guide for how a topic is introduced, how discussion and debate ensue and for how long, who gets to vote, and when and how votes are gathered. The clearer these rules are, the more productive team discussions will be (Franz, 2012). The BSW program director should seek to understand the team's preferred rules for decision making and ensure that the team has effectively established its norms. Once agreed upon (which could be clarified through a vote), the team becomes bound to the process and rules, and team members can be reminded of this occasionally as a way to maintain the group's integrity around decision making.

Additional rules that are highly advisable to determine relate to planning and agenda setting. Because the BSW program director has the responsibility for oversight of the program, they must provide direction for the work to be done. They ensure the work of curriculum management, policy development, and admissions is completed in accordance with university policies and schedules. They must be able, and encourage others, to identify issues that need to be worked on for program improvement and sustainability and bring these issues to the team for discussion. To the extent possible, that discussion will determine the team's plan for the work to be done. Relatedly, the BSW program director sets the agenda for meetings to ensure that discussion, decision making, and work distribution happen for issues that must be handled. Others should also be able to add to the agenda, bring matters up for discussion, and make suggestions for the structure of the work. An effective program director recognizes that they are primarily responsible for making sure that the planning and organizing of the work is done.

The catalyst for the decision-making process may be a result of known and planned needs for change or not. The decision-making process for both planned change (e.g., revising the curriculum in preparation of the next accreditation cycle) and unplanned change (e.g., responding to some newly gathered information about students' professional interests) is similar. The following outline for team decision making draws from the functional theory of group communication (see Gouran & Hirokawa, 1983), an inclusive, participatory model of group decision making, as it pertains to complex tasks.

To begin the process, the faculty must first have a sense of what the underlying problem or need is and what their goals are for the solution (Gouran, 2003; Hirokawa, 1990). It is easy to jump to solutions without fully exploring the goals and problems, but the BSW program director can help the group examine these thoroughly to check that any planned changes will address the actual issues and are in accordance with specific goals and objectives. Members must gather the necessary information regarding the problem (Gouran, 2003; Gouran & Hirokawa, 1983), which may mean collecting original data through interviews, surveys, or focus groups; conducting literature reviews; or contacting experts in the area.

Once a need or problem is investigated, the program director facilitates a conversation with the faculty to ensure that everyone has a keen understanding of the need. Then (or simultaneous to this) the group discusses their goals and objectives for the solution, creating the target that will help inform their final decision. Guided by problem identification and the goals, the group explores potential solutions. Again, members must gather sufficient information (Gouran, 2003) from the literature and maybe from other programs, institutions, and organizations to chart the realm of possibility. This collected information does not have to limit the group to certain outcomes but helps it to see how others have addressed the issues. The faculty share and discuss the information collected and discuss potential solutions and their potential consequences, both negative and positive (Hirokawa & Gouran, 1989). In search of innovation and to counter reductionistic thinking and groupthink, the BSW program director can introduce activities and exercises to expand creative problem-solving skills (Buller, 2014). With all of the information on the problem and a host of potential solutions, they then set upon negotiating the best solution (i.e., one that meets goals, considers costs, maximizes positive consequences, and minimizes negative consequences) for the program.

Communication

As effective planning guides the work to be done, the key tool for all of the program director's work involves communication skills and strategies. No matter how well planning is done, if we are poor communicators, the job is unlikely to be done right. To the extent that "communication is the process to create a shared understanding" (Barker, 2013, p. 12), program directors must attend to how information is shared and exchanged. At the most basic level, when sharing information, both written and oral, the program director's message should be inclusive (Jain, 2018), timely, clear, concise, and organized (Sullivan, 2016). Communicating in this fashion increases the likelihood that team members will understand the message. Good communication illustrates transparency and concern, which helps to build trust within the team.

When receiving information, BSW program directors should listen attentively and openly (Barker, 2013; Harrison & Mühlberg, 2014). They can demonstrate attentiveness and openness by not interrupting and by summarizing, without inserting judgment, what they think they hear. Other attributes of effective communication include assuming that others have something of value to contribute (Barker, 2013; Harrison & Mühlberg, 2014; Jain, 2018), attending to nonverbal behaviors to make sure they are consistent with intent (Jain, 2018; Lawton, 2006), and checking our understanding (and others' understanding) during the conversation (Barker, 2013; Jain, 2018; Sullivan, 2016).

The BSW program director's proficiency in communication and planning facilitates effective and productive team meetings. As stated previously, having the group establish meeting norms provides guidance for the members' behavior. The director provides the structure for the meeting by setting the schedule for the meeting and creating and following an agenda. The agenda should be manageable, and the time allowed should be long enough to get through the agenda while providing sufficient time needed for discussion. However, meetings that are too long can be counterproductive and should be avoided (Rogelberg, 2019).

There are important reasons for a BSW program director to help the team lay the groundwork for their rules and structure. First, the rules can help encourage participation and interaction in a productive way. When the conversation veers too far off-topic, the program director can easily redirect with a reminder of the meeting's purpose, if needed (and endeavor to include the new topic to be addressed in a future meeting). The rules also provide a set of expectations that help guide the group through contentious topics and discussions that could challenge them. Rules for participation also obligate the members to participate in a manner that promotes social work values pertaining to collegiality and respect. So, having the group establish these rules early on and occasionally reminding the group members of the rules can help them engage productively and avoid conflict.

Relationship Building

The BSW program director must also attend to building relationships between the team members and the director, and among the team members themselves. Healthy relationships with colleagues benefit the entire team, as they make for a better work environment, enhance productivity, increase effectiveness (Gilley et al., 2010; Gordon, 2018), and minimize potential conflict (Pruitt & Kim, 2004). Ideally, faculty will like and respect one another, but at the least, they must be collegial. In part, this can be facilitated by human resource training on the meaning of, and expectations for, collegiality in the institution. While civility is a necessary element for good working relationships, there is much more to a highly functioning team. The strongest, most effective teams are those in which members can rely on one another, have trust in one another, feel attached to one another, and feel committed to the team and the work (Dyer & Dyer, 2020; Franz, 2012; Gordon, 2018).

A director who follows the ethical, servant, transformational, or authentic leadership styles (Anderson & Sun, 2017; Northouse, 2019) exemplifies attributes that promote caring, positive relationships. BSW program directors can facilitate trust, commitment, and attachment by displaying transparency and authenticity (Gordon, 2018; Jiang & Men, 2017), acknowledging the value of members' input (Korsgaard et al., 1995; Jain, 2018), showing care and concern for members (Gordon, 2018; Jain, 2018), and behaving ethically (Treviño & Brown, 2014).

The director's consistent enactment of emotionally intelligent behavior, such as self-awareness, empathy, and social awareness, establishes norms for an emotionally intelligent team (Goleman et al., 2002). A director's authentic embrace, and thus actualization, of emotional intelligence requires intentional self-assessment and an ongoing commitment to their own growth and development. Active reflection and awareness can be conceptualized as a continuous process for improving one's actions, behaviors, and responses to a given situation (see Figure 15.2).

Continuous reflection is vital to a leader's growth and development and involves a number of elements: an *event*: an incident, interaction, or action that did not produce the desired response or outcome; *observation*: an examination of both the facts of the event and their own emotional response to the event, without judgment; *assessment*: an honest evaluation of the facts of the event and of their emotional response to that event; *learning*: sifting through the information from the observation and assessment in a way that leads to ideas for a difference in action and behavior; and *implementation*: carrying out a new response or new action that does not repeat those of the original event (Bozkuş & Göker, 2017).

FIGURE 15.2
Practice Tip: Self-Reflection and Self-Awareness

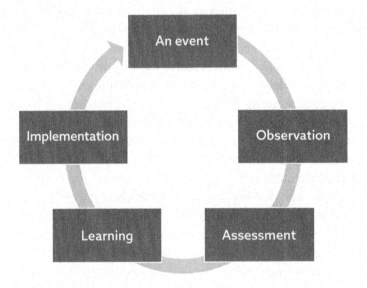

Adapted from Bozkuş & Göker (2017, pp. 27–45).

The BSW program director can also create opportunities for team members to develop and demonstrate emotionally intelligent behaviors. For example, the director can initiate team-building activities into faculty meetings. Such activities allow faculty to get to know one another, celebrate others' successes, and reaffirm their understanding and commitment to the program's mission. In individual meetings, the director can seek to understand a faculty member's concerns and talk more informally about family, hobbies, or interests (depending on the faculty member's comfort with sharing). It is also beneficial to discuss the faculty member's aspirations, help them to brainstorm ways that they would like to contribute to the team (e.g., lead activities, chair team meetings, etc.), and help them to locate professional development opportunities in ways that support the faculty's growth and ability to meet their goals.

These types of activities must be done authentically from a place of true interest and caring. Modeling and encouraging these behaviors help to create a positive culture that elevates people's commitment to the group, to the work, and to the organization (Gordon, 2018). Teams where cohesiveness and trust are high are able to engage in difficult conversations in a healthy manner (Franz, 2012; Gilley et al., 2010; Goleman, et al., 2002; Gordon, 2018; McCaffery, 2019; Simons & Peterson, 2000), so working on this early and often can help prevent destructive conflict in the group. Authentic and emotionally intelligent leadership increases the group's ability to engage in healthy debate and change (Alavi & Gill, 2017; Goleman et al., 2002) to both improve and maintain the program.

Conflict and Conflict Resolution

Despite earnest planning, clear and transparent communication, and consistent efforts at relationship building, conflict within a group is inevitable. In a group of faculty committed to their subject matter, diverse in backgrounds, experienced in teaching and the profession, and schooled in debate, there will be differences of opinion (Armstrong, 2012; Twale, 2018). As social work educators, we can appreciate the growth that can come from systems open to new and different ideas (Katz & Kahn, 1978). To do otherwise and manage autocratically, stifling conversation and debate, limits the potential of growth and creativity (McCaffery, 2019). Encouraging active participation on the part of faculty opens up the possibility not only for dynamic results but also for destructive conflict.

In the event that efforts to prevent destructive conflict do not work, strategies must be engaged to resolve differences in a way that maintains the integrity of the group and supports inclusivity. The earlier in the conflict this is done, the better, as conflicts left unattended are likely to grow wider and deeper and become seemingly intractable (Pruitt & Kim, 2004). Unresolved conflicts are also expensive, costing U.S. businesses approximately $359 million a year (CPP Inc., 2008). They negatively affect productivity, creativity, engagement, and team cohesiveness, and they increase stress, dissatisfaction, absenteeism, and turnover (Armstrong, 2012; CPP Inc., 2008; Liddle, 2017; Twale, 2018).

A significant factor in the persistence and escalation of conflict is the ineffectual management of disagreement. An avoidant leadership style is particularly problematic and likely to allow disagreements to spiral out of control (Twale, 2018). Avoidance is common; the hard truth is that most people are uncomfortable with conflict and do not handle issues directly, thereby contributing to the life of the conflict (CPP Inc., 2008; Patterson et al., 2012). As the person responsible for the team, the BSW program director must help the team navigate through disagreement and consistently and directly address conflict as it arises (Armstrong, 2012).

Thus, a BSW program director is best served by having a working model for conflict resolution. While any model will need to be adapted to properly suit the situation, having a model in mind can prepare the director to deal with conflict by providing an understanding of both the process for conflict resolution and the skills necessary to help move through conflict. The model in Table 15.2 was adapted from Moore (2014) and informed by Fisher and Ury (2011), and it can be applied to both intragroup and interpersonal conflicts.

TABLE 15.2
Model for Conflict Resolution

	Activity	Guiding Questions
Stage 1	Acknowledging the conflict	Is this happening?
Stage 2	Seeking understanding	What are the issues?
Stage 3	Deconstructing the concerns	Why is this important? What would this help accomplish?
Stage 4	Clarifying issues	What does all of this mean?
Stage 5	Negotiating solutions	What might fix the problem?
Stage 6	Reaffirming purpose	What are our goals?
Stage 7	Narrowing the options	What do we want?
Stage 8	Agreeing	Is this what we agreed on? How will this happen?
Stage 9	Feedback loop	Did we do it? Did it work?

The first stage of conflict resolution is recognizing and acknowledging that a conflict is occurring. The second stage is to seek understanding—that is, gather from the team members what they see as the issue(s). It helps to write these down in a way that all present at the meeting can see. It is the director's responsibility to ensure that every member who has a concern has an opportunity to talk without interruption from others. The director must keep the group from discussion at this point, because the objective is to gather information. After writing down the issues, the director will check to see if they have captured the concerns accurately and then revise as necessary.

In the third stage, the director must move the group to uncover the underlying interests. When people originally identify their concerns, oftentimes they present them as positions (e.g., "We should do this"). A key to resolution is to figure out what is driving the concern: What are the values, interests, needs, or desires that are shaping the stated positions? After delineating the underlying interests, the director moves to the fourth stage with the task of clarifying the issues and their interests, allowing for a question period to ensure that the team has a full accounting and understanding of the issues driving the conflict.

The fifth stage involves exploring potential solutions for all of the underlying problems. This is a brainstorming activity in which the entire team engages in identifying ways to resolve the identified problems. In the sixth stage, the program director steps back for a moment to remind the group of the program goals; this way, the team members can check potential solutions and their effects with the alignment of the goals. At this time, it is helpful for the director to remind everyone that the decision is a group one.

Then, the group members discuss the options; examine their consequences, outlining the various strengths and weaknesses of each; and remove any that the members easily agree are not tenable. Finally, the group can vote on the remaining options for resolution and determine how to execute what is agreed upon. This will involve deciding who is responsible for carrying out each of the action items needed to implement the solution. After implementation, the director will need to have some follow-up, checking on the status and effects of the change and reporting back to the group.

The BSW program director must make a number of decisions before engaging in the conflict resolution process. First and foremost, the program director needs to decide if the conflict should be addressed. Generally, a conflict needs to be addressed if it is affecting the team's functioning (McCaffery, 2019). The director also must decide if the conflict is best handled within a group process. Some conflicts, such as those that affect only a few of the faculty, particularly if they arise from personality or communication differences, may be better handled outside the group (Holmes & Marra, 2004). In such cases, as stated previously, the program director can employ the model for conflict resolution with only the faculty members involved in the dispute.

However, if the conflict is volatile, the program director may choose to meet with each faculty member separately, allowing the parties to vent a bit before bringing them together (Moore, 2014). When working on interpersonal conflicts among faculty, it can be helpful to bring relational elements into the conversation. That is, when inquiring about the nature of the conflict (Stage 2), the BSW program director can prompt the faculty members to see if they want to share how the conflict is affecting them personally. At times, disputes between and among faculty may be too unwieldy for the program director to address, in which case the director may consider other resources such as an ombudsperson or another trained specialist to facilitate the group conflict resolution process.

If the conflict involves the BSW program director, the director must decide on the proper course of action. Some conflicts can be addressed by meeting individually with the faculty members (Moore, 2014). In these cases, the program director should approach each faculty member with curiosity and authenticity and a commitment to the relationship. This means that the director must avoid defensiveness and instead attempt to understand the other person's perspective. To begin, they must engage in active listening. By first inviting the faculty member to share their concerns, the director can then openly reflect on what they think they heard and verify the accuracy of this reflection. After it is clear that they have a solid understanding of the faculty member's perspective, the program director then shares their understanding of the issues and problems. When doing so, the director must be careful to focus on specific actions and outcomes they have noticed, rather than characterizing any behavior.

The program director then shepherds the faculty member into dialogue to seek mutually acceptable and beneficial solutions, following the major elements of the conflict resolution process. Some situations may be too strained for the BSW program director to attempt to resolve alone. The director must acknowledge if they themselves cannot enter a conversation calmly and nondefensively. If the conflict seems unmanageable, the program director may bring in a trusted, neutral third party to facilitate the conversation.

Other issues, especially workplace civility issues, are best handled outside the group process. Because of their role in the program, a director may be the first person to know of allegations or concerns about faculty misconduct (e.g., harassment, bullying, or discrimination). Depending on the processes at the university, the director may be involved in initial conversations with the faculty members, but investigations and resolutions are likely to be managed by the administration. It is incumbent upon the director to refer the matter to the proper office and ensure that the person targeted has knowledge of and access to legal, health, and emotional supports. The subject of any such conversations would remain between the director and human resources or other designated university administrators. As protected by institutional, state, or federal regulations, investigations into faculty misconduct should remain confidential (Euben & Lee, 2006; Woska, 2013). Although there may not be legal requirements to do so, conversations with a faculty member regarding compliance with university policies and their job performance are best held in confidence.

Discussions of performance are grounded by the promotion and tenure guidelines developed by the team (as mentioned above). The BSW program director is aided in such conversations when the guidelines are thorough, comprehensive, and clear so that the comparison of standards to actual performance can be easily demonstrated. Concerns about a faculty member's performance (unless egregious) may lead to some form of improvement plan, offering mentorship, support, and clarity in order to help the faculty member achieve the team's expectations and standards for tenure and promotion. While discussions about the guidelines are held within the team, discussions about an individual faculty member's performance are private.

A BSW program director's indiscreet sharing of information about a faculty member can cause reputational harm to that person and will undermine the director's trustworthiness within the team (Kutsyuruba & Walker, 2015). Program directors can focus their efforts on preventive measures for employment-related concerns by arranging for ongoing team discussions on policies and procedures to ensure that faculty members are knowledgeable about university policies on misconduct as well as promotion and tenure guidelines.

The major goal in both conflict resolution and ongoing team decision-making efforts is to maintain a well-functioning faculty engaged in the process of program management. An engaged faculty use their authority to determine academic matters for the program. Voting procedures help to move the group forward on an issue when they are stuck. But after a vote, the "losing" members may hold grievances that later seep into future interactions. Once again, it is the BSW program director who must acknowledge the situation and speak directly with the faculty member(s) who appear discontented. For the whole group, the program director must encourage conversation about the agreed-upon goals and mission of the program, which should guide all their decisions. It may be that something has shifted within the program, and the team may need to revisit and revise the program's mission and goals. As the identified leader of the program, the director has the responsibility to ensure that the program is functioning to meet student needs, accreditation standards, and the university's requirements.

Social Work Values

Adhering to social work values (NASW, 2021) supports the successful fulfillment of the role and activities of the program director. First, the job of BSW program director is one of service: *service* to the program, university, and profession. In the proper conduct of the position, the program director places the needs and interests of the program before their own professional interests. The program director upholds *social justice* by promoting equitable practices in the program and enacting processes so that all faculty can fully participate in the decision-making process.

By treating members with respect, attending to relationships with and between faculty, and ensuring a collaborative working environment, the program director is honoring both the *dignity and worth of the person* and the *importance of human relationships*. In abiding by the faculty-determined norms and by being transparent and authentic in their actions, the director acts with *integrity*. The director demonstrates *competence* in organizing the work of the faculty to meet the program's requirements and seeking development opportunities as needed. Thus, the director's role encapsulates significant opportunities to employ the values of the profession.

Conclusion

The BSW program director's position is one of great rewards: It is energizing to work with smart and talented faculty who are committed to undergraduate students and to their craft. Harnessing faculty energy is both art and science and is exceedingly worthwhile for the program. The faculty members oversee and direct academic matters and can be solid supports for the program director to help meet the challenges of managing a baccalaureate program, which include navigating the shifting higher education landscape, sustaining enrollments in an increasingly competitive marketplace, monitoring the requirements of accreditors, assessing the needs of current and future students, evaluating the program's outcomes, and anticipating changes in the community and profession. To the extent that the program director, along with the faculty, is successful in nurturing a collaborative and innovative culture, the program, students, university, and profession benefit.

Management and Leadership: Internet Resources

Alliance for Nonprofit Management: https://allianceonline.org
American Public Human Services Association: www.aphsa.org
Association for Community Organization and Social Action: https://www.acosa.org
Association of Baccalaureate Social Work Program Directors: www.bpdonline.org
Association of Latina/Latino Social Work Educators (ALLSWE): https://www.allswe.com
Council on Social Work Education: https://www.cswe.org/
Latino Social Workers Organization: https://lswo.org
National Association of Asian American Professionals https://www.theatermu.org/news/naaap
National Association of Black Social Workers: https://www.nabsw.org
National Association of Puerto Rican Hispanic Social Workers: https://www.naprhsw.com/
National Association of Social Workers: https://www.socialworkers.org/
National Congress of American Indians: https://www.ncai.org/
The Network for Social Work Management: www.socialworkmanager.org

Suggested Readings

Brown, B. (2018). *Dare to lead: Brave work, tough conversations, whole hearts.* Random House.
Brown-Glaude, W. R. (2009). *Doing diversity in higher education: Faculty leaders share challenges and strategies.* Rutgers University Press.
Gunsalus, C. K. (2021). *The college administrator's survival guide.* Harvard University Press.
Hrabowski, F. A., Rous, P. J., & Henderson, P. H. (2019). *The empowered university: Shared leadership, culture change, and academic success.* Johns Hopkins University Press.
Johnson, S. K. (2020). *Inclusify: The power of uniqueness and belonging to build innovative teams.* Harper Business.
Patterson, K., Grenny, J., McMillan, R., & Switzler, A. (2012). *Crucial conversations: Tools for talking when stakes are high.* McGraw-Hill.
Sinek, S. (2014). *Leaders eat last: Why some teams pull together and others don't.* Portfolio/Penguin.

References

Alavi, S. B., & Gill, C. (2017). Leading change authentically: How authentic leaders influence follower responses to complex change. *Journal of Leadership & Organizational Studies, 24*(2), 157–171. https://doi.org/10.1177/1548051816664681
American Association of University Professors. (n.d.). *Statement on government of colleges and universities.* https://www.aaup.org/report/statement-government-colleges-and-universities#4
Anderson, M. H., & Sun, P. Y. T. (2017). Reviewing leadership styles: Overlaps and the need for a new "full-range" theory. *International Journal of Management Reviews, 19*(1), 76–96. https://doi.org/10.1111/ijmr.12082
Armstrong, J. (2012). Faculty animosity: A contextual view. *Journal of Thought, 47*(2), 85–103. https://doi.org/10.2307/jthought.47.2.85
Association of Governing Boards. (2017). *Shared governance: Changing with the times?* https://agb.org/sites/default/files/report_2017_shared_governance.pdf
Barker, A. (2013). *Improve your communication skills.* Kogan Page. https://www.koganpage.com/product/improve-your-communication-skills-9780749486273

Bozkuş, K., & Göker, S. (2017). Reflective leadership: Learning to manage and lead human organizations. In A. Alvinius (Ed.), *Contemporary leadership challenges* (pp. 27–45). InTechOpen. http://dx.doi.org/10.5772/64968

Buller, J. L. (2014). *Change leadership in higher education: A practical guide to academic transformation.* Wiley.

Catalano, E. M. (2020). Running effective meetings. In A. Viera & R. Kramer (Eds.), *Management and leadership skills for medical faculty and healthcare executives* (pp. 81–89). Springer International.

Council on Social Work Education. (2022). *Educational policy and accreditation standards.* https://www.cswe.org/accreditation/standards/2022-epas/

CPP Inc. (2008). *Global human capital report: Workplace conflict and how businesses can harness it to thrive.* http://img.en25.com/Web/CPP/Conflict_report.pdf

Daley, M. R. (2008). Managing baccalaureate social work education. In L. Ginsberg (Ed.), *Management and leadership in social work practice and education* (pp. 393–410). Council on Social Work Education.

Dyer, G., & Dyer, J. H. (2020). *Beyond team building: How to build high performing teams and the culture to support them.* Wiley.

Euben, D. R., & Lee, B. A. (2006). Faculty discipline: Legal and policy issues in dealing with faculty misconduct. *Journal of College and University Law, 32*(2), 241–308.

Fisher, R., & Ury, W. (2011). *Getting to yes: Negotiating agreement without giving in.* Penguin.

Franz, T. M. (2012). *Group dynamics and team interventions: Understanding and improving team performance.* Wiley.

Gilley, A., Gilley, J. W., McConnell, C. W., & Veliquette, A. (2010). The competencies used by effective managers to build teams: An empirical study. *Advances in Developing Human Resources, 12*(1), 29–45. https://doi.org/10.1177/1523422310365720

Goals and goal setting. (2019). In *Encyclopedia of management: Vol. I, A–K* (8th ed., pp. 487–492). Gale.

Goleman, D., Boyatzis, R., & McKee, A. (2002). The emotional reality of teams. *Journal of Organizational Excellence, 21*(2), 55–65. https://doi.org/10.1002/npr.10020

Gordon, J. (2018). *The power of a positive team: Proven principles and practices that make great teams great.* Wiley.

Gouran, D. S. (2003). Communication skills for group decision making. In J. O. Greene & B. R. Burleson (Eds.), *Handbook of communication and social interaction skills* (pp. 835–870). Lawrence Erlbaum.

Gouran, D. S., & Hirokawa, R. Y. (1983). The role of communication in decision-making groups: A functional perspective. In M. S. Mander (Ed.), *Communications in transition* (pp. 168–185). Praeger.

Harrison, E. B., & Mühlberg, J. (2014). *Leadership communication: How leaders communicate and how communicators lead in the today's global enterprise.* Business Expert Press.

Hayes, J. (2014). *The theory and practice of change management* (4th ed.). Palgrave.

Hirokawa, R. Y. (1990). The role of communication in group decision-making efficacy: A task-contingency perspective. *Small Group Research, 21*(2), 190–204. https://doi.org/10.1177/1046496490212003

Hirokawa, R. Y., & Gouran, D. S. (1989). Facilitation of group communication: A critique of prior research and an agenda for future research. *Management Communication Quarterly, 3*(1), 71–92. https://doi.org/10.1177/0893318989003001005

Holmes, J., & Marra, M. (2004). Leadership and managing conflict in meetings. *Pragmatics, 14*(4), 439–462. https://doi.org/10.1075/prag.14.4.02hol

Holosko, M. J. (2009). Social work leadership: Identifying core attributes. *Journal of Human Behavior in the Social Environment, 19*(4), 448–459. http://dx.doi.org/10.1080 /10911350902872395

Jain, N. (2018). Inclusive leadership and effective communication: An unbreakable bond. *Language in India, 18*(12), 207–215. http://www.languageinindia.com/dec2018 /neeluinclusiveleadershipeffectivecommunication1.pdf 3

Jiang, H., & Men, R. L. (2017). Creating an engaged workforce: The impact of authentic leadership, transparent organizational communication, and work-life enrichment. *Communication Research, 44*(2), 225–243. https://doi.org/10.1177/0093650215613137

Katz, D., & Kahn, R. L. (1978). *The social psychology of organizations.* Wiley.

Kelchen, R. (2020). *Examining the feasibility of empirically predicting college closures.* The Brookings Institution.

Kelchen, R. Ortagus, J., Baker, D., & Rosinger, K. (2020). *Trends in state funding for public higher education.* InformEd States. https://static1.squarespace.com/static /5d9f9fae6a122515ee074363/t/5f4d2ae0e8f13c2a2dabd9ea/1598892770478/IS_Brief _TrendsinStateFunding_Aug2020.pdf

Korsgaard, M. A., Schweiger, D. M., & Sapienza, H. J. (1995). Building commitment, attachment, and trust in strategic decision-making teams: The role of procedural justice. *The Academy of Management Journal, 38*(1), 60–84. https://doi.org/10.2307/256728

Kotter, J. P. (1996). *Leading change.* Harvard Business Review Press.

Kutsyuruba, B., & Walker, K. (2015). The lifecycle of trust in educational leadership: An ecological perspective. *International Journal of Leadership in Education, 18*(1), 106–121. https://doi.org/10.1080/13603124.2014.915061

Lawton, E. (2006). *Body language and the first line manager.* Chandos Publishing.

Liddle, D. (2017). *Managing conflict: A practical guide to resolution in the workplace.* Kogan Page.

Management functions. (2019). In *Encyclopedia of management: Vol. II, L–Z* (8th ed., pp. 677–682). Gale.

Mapp, S., & Boutté-Queen, N. (2021). The role of the US baccalaureate social work program director: A national survey. *Social Work Education, 40*(7), 843–860. https://doi.org/10.1080/02615479.2020.1729720

McCaffery, P. (2019). *The higher education manager's handbook: Effective leadership and management in universities and colleges.* Routledge.

Moore, C. W. (2014). *The mediation process: Practical strategies for resolving conflict.* Wiley.

National Association of Social Workers. (2021). *NASW code of ethics.* https://www.socialworkers.org/About/Ethics/Code-of-Ethics/Code-of-Ethics-English

Northouse, P. G. (2019). *Leadership: Theory and practice* (8th ed.). SAGE.

Pace, W. (2018). *Communication and work systems: Theory, processes, opportunities.* Cambridge Scholars.

Patterson, K., Grenny, J., McMillan, R., & Switzler, A. (2012). *Crucial conversations: Tools for talking when stakes are high.* McGraw-Hill.

Pruitt, D. G., & Kim, S. H. (2004). *Social conflict: Escalation, stalemate, and settlement.* McGraw-Hill.

Robert, H. M., & Robert, S. C. (2011). *Robert's rules of order newly revised* (11th ed). Da Capo Press.

Rogelberg, S. G. (2019). *The surprising science of meetings: How you can lead your team to peak performance.* Oxford University Press.

Schwarz, R. M. (2017). *The skilled facilitator: A comprehensive resource for consultants, facilitators, coaches, and trainers* (3rd ed.). Wiley.

Simons, T. L., & Peterson, R. S. (2000). Task conflict and relationship conflict in top management teams: The pivotal role of intragroup trust. *Journal of Applied Psychology*, *85*(1), 102–111. https://doi.org/10.1037/0021-9010.85.1.102

Sullivan, J. (2016). *Simply said: Communicating better at work and beyond*. Wiley.

Treviño, L. K., & Brown, M. E. (2014). Ethical leadership. In D. V. Day (Ed.), Oxford library of psychology. *The Oxford handbook of leadership and organizations* (pp. 524–538). Oxford University Press.

Twale, D. J. (2018). *Understanding and preventing faculty-on-faculty bullying: A psychosocial- organizational approach*. Routledge.

West, M. A. (2012). *Effective teamwork: Practical lessons from organizational research*. Wiley.

Western Interstate Commission for Higher Education (WICHE) (2020). *Knocking at the college door: Projections of high school graduates*. https://www.wiche.edu/wp-content/uploads/2020/12/Knocking-pdf-for-website.pdf

Woska, W. J. (2013). Legal issues for HR professionals: Workplace investigations. *Public Personnel Management*, *42*(1), 90–101. https://doi.org/10.1177/0091026013484568

Section Four

Student Issues

CHAPTER 16

Recruitment and Retention of Undergraduate Social Work Students

Kelly Ward

Melody Aye Loya

This chapter provides an overview of recruitment strategies aimed at a wide range of prospects, including high school students, community college transfers, and currently enrolled students. It discusses websites, social media, and program literature and giveaways. Retention is then discussed and insights shared regarding transfer students, off-campus instructional sites, financial and support needs, and pedagogical practices for a diverse student population. Drawing on the experiences of two former program directors/chairs, readers will gain ideas and strategies that are easily re-created within their programs' context.

The Council on Social Work Education (CSWE) (2021) reported that 19,474 undergraduate social work degrees were conferred during the academic year 2019–2020. This chapter may be especially apropos based on these numbers, given that the number of full-time students from undergraduate social work programs dropped from 2018–2019. Students may not declare social work as an incoming first-year student because they do not know about the major or may not be aware of the myriad of opportunities available in the profession. Misconceptions about social work abound, such as the stereotype of social workers as those people who take away other people's children, which make recruitment challenging.

Students rarely know the depth of opportunity that awaits them with an undergraduate degree in social work in hand. Oftentimes, students seem to find the major through word of mouth, through an advisor when they thought they wanted to be a nurse but struggled with chemistry courses, or after hearing about social work through targeted outreach. First, this chapter focuses on recruitment and offers concrete suggestions for recruiting students to the major. Second, the chapter explores retention challenges and offers potential solutions for retaining social work students. Much of the discussion is based on the two authors' personal experiences totaling more than 47 years in various social-work-program-related roles, including program director, field director, Title IV-E director, and department chair.

Recruitment

It is a rare social work faculty member who also has a marketing degree; however, undergraduate program directors must think about building and developing their program. Social work educators need to think about marketing tools and the students choosing to major in the discipline. Students can be viewed as customers or consumers in the marketing tradition. As stated earlier, recruiting students to the profession of social work can be challenging because of misconceptions and/or lack of knowledge about social work. In high school, many school districts offer electives in both sociology and psychology, which excites students about those degrees and career options. Rarely, if ever, is a social work survey course offered at the high school level. Thus, the discipline is at a disadvantage before students enter college.

It then becomes the social work program's responsibility to find ways to "advertise" the profession to the students and spark interest in the major. Also, some students have had negative interactions with child protective services in their personal life, leaving them with a limited and slanted view of the profession. Many students believe that the only career choice for a social worker is protective services. Having the opportunity to explore the wide array of career options can encourage students to reevaluate the major. Recruiting can take place in a wide array of formats, both on and off campus.

As social work educators, we also have to consider what and how we are marketing the major, and therefore the profession. Our marketing "tools" are faculty, course content, giveaways, written resources, social media, and our department and school web pages. However, our number one marketing tool consists of happy alumni who talk about their experience in the program and share their love of the profession. Our academic consumers are generally three different types: traditional, transfer, and posttraditional students who may be entering higher education for the first time or returning to finish what they started years ago.

> **PRACTICE TIP:** Have a presence on all the social media sites that your recruits may use. It may help to have a student cohost this site, recommending and posting relevant topics. At the time of this writing, TikTok and Instagram are popular, but this may change by the time of publication. Ask your students what social media they are using!

Marketing to each population is different, according to their age, their geographic location, and what they want from a degree. Traditional-age student-recruiting events need to connect with the student and the parent or caregiver attending the recruiting event with them. Current students who love the school and the major should be available to talk with prospective students, and relatable marketing materials should be given to them as well. Equally important is addressing concerns with parents and caregivers when they wonder about the quality of the program or if their student will graduate employment-ready, able to earn a living wage.

Transfer students are a mixed group of those in their early 20s to senior citizens returning to fulfill a life goal. As the cost of higher education continues to rise, many parents and financially savvy students realize that attending the local community college saves a significant amount of money. Many students, especially in states that offer free community college to students with a high grade point average (GPA), are opting to complete their general education credits at the local community college and then transfer to a 4-year institution. One such program is the NJ Stars (2021) program. Free community college has become part of the political landscape in recent years; thus, programs across the United States may be facing a decline in first-year enrollment.

Traditional-aged students may find themselves in courses with a diverse group of students who are returning to school after a leave of absence to build careers and raise families. Many community colleges offer programs to encourage their return, such as the Displaced Homemakers Program (Brookdale Community College, 2021). These programs prepare students to enter the workforce or attend community college classes. Having a strong relationship with the local community colleges in your area, especially those with human services and psychology programs, will provide opportunities for you to talk with their students about social work and consider attending your university. The 20-something student may be flexible in their plans after attending community college, but many posttraditional students are less likely to be geographically mobile. Students may rely heavily on their advisors' and teachers' comments about your program to decide about the viability of the degree at your college or university.

> **PRACTICE TIP:** Develop strong relationships with community colleges. Participate in transfer days; invite their advisors, professors, and students to your campus; and offer to be a guest speaker.

The final group of prospective students are those adults who have chosen the major to start a second career. Many have been successful in their first career and are looking for a second career that sings to their soul or helps their communities. These changes may have occurred after major current national or international events like 9/11, the Great Recession of 2008–10, or the start of COVID-19. Sometimes change is triggered by a significant life event such as a divorce or sending their last child to college. These students are generally not geographically mobile, and they will look for a program with a good reputation and may even review the credentials of your faculty.

Marketing Tools

When marketing anything, having a specific plan and a targeted audience is essential. Sometimes an all-out marketing campaign ensues; for instance, everyone has experienced being bombarded with advertisements for a new TV show or a new item at the grocery store. Consider the commercials on Super Bowl Sunday, which may be big launches for a new product: A 30-second commercial in 2021 cost $5.5 million (Heyen, 2021). As social work educators, we need to recruit using targeted marketing but without the Super Bowl ad budget! Program directors have several marketing tools at their disposal, but may not think of these items as marketing tools. These tools consist of a survey course (usually Introduction to Social Work), printed materials, electronic tools including the program or department web page, social media sites, giveaways, the faculty (especially those who love the profession), and the secret weapon: the students and alumni! It is important to think about why these tools are relevant and how they can be used to recruit.

Survey Courses

Introduction to Social Work, which may be called by various names, is the undergraduate students' foray into the major. Trying to cover all of the content on social problems and the history of the profession, which are frequently found in introductory textbooks, usually requires a very fast pace. One approach may be to structure the course as a true survey course and not worry so much about getting through all of the content. It is more important to communicate about social work's core values, types of issues in which social workers intervene, and why the professor is passionate about the profession. Providing a strong foundation of what a social worker does on a day-to-day basis, the variety of populations served, and the enormous choice of settings where social workers work can help students decide if social work is for them. This class is where you want your strongest, most passionate faculty (full- or part-time), who understand the importance of securing new majors and minors, and even helping to recruit future MSW students. This class aims to engage the students in conversations about social work values and career opportunities. Having a faculty with strong teaching skills, varied experience, and lots of stories based on real practice enhances the course content and may intrigue students, leading them to want to learn more.

> **PRACTICE TIP:** Assign your strongest faculty (adjunct or full-time) to teach your Introduction to Social Work course. Consider adopting Grobman (2019) for your survey course on social work to give students a broad view of what it is like to be a social worker.

Social Work Program Website

Every university has a website, but faculty may be unaware that the primary purpose of a website is to recruit students, not solely as a resource for current students or faculty. Too often, social work educators write their department web page without recruitment in mind; faculty do not usually write their biographical profiles linked from the website with the intent of attracting BSW students. Graduate students may choose a school based on the faculty's research, but undergraduates look for information on the program (e.g., what classes do I have to take?) and for ways to connect with faculty who are aligned with their interests. Students choosing your university may also be looking at the campus environment and gauging the potential for engagement during their college years. Once prospective students find your web page and ask questions or reach out to a faculty member, connect with them as soon as possible. If you are perceived as unresponsive, the student may quickly move on to another school or a related major.

> **PRACTICE TIP:** When building a website for your department or program, consider an FAQs (frequently asked questions) page, pictures of recent events with students and faculty (keep these up to date), news of recent and upcoming events, and easy connections to the field and program directors. Review and edit your web page, course catalog, and student handbook at least annually.

Consider the information that would be important to potential majors and their parents looking at your website. For instance, highlighting career opportunities, perhaps through the sharing of alumni stories, can help dispel the myths discussed earlier and give students a better understanding of the breadth of our profession. In addition, content should include links to sites that explore career choices, such as the Help Starts Here site, offered by the National Association of Social Workers (NASW, 2021), or the information found on the Social Work Guide website (Social Work Guide, 2020).

Additionally, consider including information such as curriculum and sequence charts to guide students who may be navigating college for the first time; students should be able to get an idea of the required classes and the order in which to take those classes. Obviously, students will meet with an advisor to review these items, but they should be informed ahead of time about requirements and so forth so they can prepare for that meeting. Finally, many students and their parents will want to know about the hands-on experience that students garner not only in many of their classes but also through the field practicum experience. Highlighting social work's signature pedagogy—field practicum—is what sets it apart from the other helping professions at the undergraduate level. Connecting students to information about field internship opportunities can be important in the recruiting process.

> **PRACTICE TIP:** Ask yourself the following questions regarding your program's main web page. Is the information easy to find? How engaging is the website? Is the webmaster familiar enough with the profession to portray it accurately? Are pictures current? Does the site have any broken links? Are tabs correctly labeled?

Your program website may also include student involvement activities like student organizations (social work club and honor society), accreditation status, and, of course, links to the current assessment data. Pictures with people wearing current fashions (and, ideally, actual social work majors) show potential students that you keep your site current. Students being able to relate to the pictures can help in their decision process. Prospective students need to be able to see themselves doing what your current students are doing. We hope to encourage excitement about the opportunities and focus on what makes our program different from others they may be considering. For example, highlighting recent study abroad programs may encourage a student to look further into your program. Showcasing volunteer activities and internships, and highlighting alumni success stories may be vital to converting those browsing potential students into actual enrolled students.

Use of Social Media

It may be difficult to keep track of which social media apps are the new "in" thing. However, using apps to highlight incoming students, recent graduates, department activities, and accomplishments can work to your advantage. Facebook, Instagram, Snapchat, TikTok, and Twitter provide platforms to engage with prospective students and parents. Know what social media tools are connecting with which customer groups. Today, Facebook may no longer be a college student tool, but it might connect with older students, parents, and/or alumni. Currently, TikTok is the platform of choice for younger people, but by the time you are reading this chapter, that trend may be over. Ask your current students or admissions office what social media they are using, and be sure you keep a current presence there.

Prospective Student or Transfer Days

As mentioned earlier, social work educators recruit multiple types of students: traditional-age, posttraditional students, and transfer students. Within those groups, there is even more diversity, such as the changing-the-major student, the athlete, the midlife change-of-career person, persons of color, international students, different-ability students, and students from LGBTQ+ communities. With that much diversity, one cookie-cutter marketing plan will not work. This chapter cannot cover specialized approaches for all groups (and with a quickly moving target, the information may have changed by the time of publication).

We also have not mentioned the dreaded word *COVID*. COVID-19 has thrown educators many curveballs and has made the words *unprecedented* and *pivot* ever present in our daily vocabulary. No one has the answer on how to best recruit during a pandemic, and hopefully by the next recruiting event at your school, this will not even be a consideration. However, the tools that educators acquired during the pandemic include recruiting with virtual open houses, Zoom interviews with prospective students, and campus events using streaming services for those interested in the program. Recruiting students remains important to the program's life, the university, and the profession, so it must be successful however it is done.

> **PRACTICE TIP:** Track responses to your events and/or methods, be nimble enough to change course, and always ask for feedback from participants. Consider using a QR code for virtual sign-in!

Recruiting on campus looks a little different everywhere. Some pull out all the stops, including the marching band, balloons, and big welcomes by the university or college president. Others have award-winning marketing materials, tons of food and beverages, and lots of university or college swag. Be sure you know what the administration is planning and always present a complementary message. Open houses and other recruiting events are the perfect time to wear university and/or department clothing and name tags—and bring plenty of business cards, swag, and especially high energy! Program representatives at your marketing events should be your most upbeat, pro-social-work, pro-university students, staff, and faculty.

Always follow up with attendees. Having names, email addresses, and phone numbers to follow up allows you to send additional information and arrange for a phone call from a current student to answer a potential student's questions, both of which help to develop relationships and connections to the program. You can also invite prospective students to sit in on a class, either virtually or in person. It is always a good idea to send a follow-up email a week or two after the event to see if the students have additional questions and call them to see if they have made their decision after being accepted. Also, check with your centralized admissions staff on their recommendations for the next steps.

Establish open communication with recruiters and meet with admissions staff on a regular basis to make sure they have the most up-to-date information about the program. Share your preferred talking points, which might include highlighting new faculty, successful accreditation, or a new curriculum that you would like them to mention when talking to prospects. Ensure that new admissions staff know what social work is and how to talk about it with the student who states that they want to "help people" or "make the world better." The most obvious recruiting events are open houses (face-to-face or virtual) and tours targeting high school students, community college or other transfer students, and post-traditional students. Each participant has their own particular interests and needs and will want to hear about what pertains to them specifically. Some universities invite admitted students to spend the day or even stay overnight at the university. During any of these events, be sure that current social work students are available to talk to the prospective students about why they like the school or program and why they chose social work. Most students will appreciate those conversations; having diverse representation among your students who are present can be helpful, too.

> **PRACTICE TIP:** Find or create opportunities for smaller groups of students to talk informally about a social work career—for example, a "Chat and Chew" event. If there are no formal opportunities to recruit, consider creating your own event, such as a "Get the Scoop on Social Work" ice cream social or "Waffle Wednesday" for students waffling on their major! Students can be invited to have a waffle breakfast with the social work faculty and current students.

High School Students

Events attracting high school students are often large, and someone should be there who can answer questions not only from prospective students but also, and perhaps more important and more common, from their parents or caregivers. Parents, especially those of younger students who are the first to go to college (the oldest or a first-generation student), have many questions and need to have a good idea to whom they are entrusting their child. Developing a short presentation about why social work is a diverse and exciting profession with growing job prospects can help students define and/or redefine their career aspirations. The staff or faculty person should be energetic, enthusiastic, and knowledgeable, and that person should be your best program and university cheerleader. They should also be well versed in the program and the university in general. Even if students do not choose your program, they may leave with a broader idea of what social workers do, thus contributing to knowledge about our profession. Handouts can refer students to other resources about social work and describe quick facts about your program in an aesthetically yet engaging way by using infographics, pictures, and/or brightly colored paper.

PRACTICE TIP: Don't feel the need to rotate among all your faculty to "even out" the burden of these events. Align service with people's skill sets. You want your best representatives attending these events!

Recruitment to a specific degree or program is different from general recruitment to the university. More specifically, targeted recruitment of students should focus on the benefits of the degree, including employability, graduate school options, and the wide range of career paths within the profession. As discussed previously, one way to recruit outside the college setting is by offering an Introduction to Social Work course at local high schools. Many high schools offer Introduction to Sociology, Introduction to Psychology, and general education through dual credit agreements, designed for students to earn college credit while completing high school requirements. Students may be introduced to information about working with or understanding people in these classes, but Introduction to Social Work is strangely absent. This could potentially be offered as a dual-credit course located at the university where the students earn elective credits in high school and college credits as well. Another option is to offer the course for college credit but located at the high school for ease of access to students. Both ways can be successful.

There are several questions to consider when selecting a high school partner or partners. For instance, is there a school with which you have a healthy relationship because the social worker has supervised interns? Which high school has sent you the most social work majors in the last 5 years? Which high schools have a schedule conducive to a college course that meets once or twice a week? What high school has the best demographic that you want to recruit? Where can you go to recruit as diverse a group as possible of incoming students? Is there a vocational high school offering a career-oriented curriculum that mirrors social work? Maine Career and Technical Education (2021) has a social services program for high school students; if there are similar vocational schools in your area, they may be your best partners in the area. Could an alternative high school in your area find students who want to help children who need the help they received?

Once you have identified a high school, the work begins with both your university and the high school administration. Details like tuition, who pays for the textbooks, and who teaches the course need to be discussed. It may be useful for community relations if the course is offered for free; recruiting just one student per year will more than pay for a faculty member's cost to be present in the school and teach the course. Finally, parents may have questions about the tuition and the course's transferability if their child does not want to choose a social work major or attend your college or university. Be candid, letting them know that there is no guarantee that another college will accept the credits. However, convey that the course can help the student learn how to pace themselves and work at a college level. Other ways to partner with high schools include presenting at career days, being a guest lecturer in a class, or setting up a table at the high school to answer specific questions about the major and career options with the social work undergraduate degree.

Community College Students

Community college students pursued their education by a different route for various reasons. These may include but are certainly not limited to finances, academic eligibility, flexibility needed in scheduling, and/or uncertainty in their degree path. Their choice of major frequently happens before they enter the university, having taken introductory courses at community colleges. When they are admitted to a university, they may have completed most of their general education requirements, so they might be ready to jump right into major classes. Recruiting community college students can occur through guest lectures at community colleges, individual conversations discussing internship opportunities, and transferring as many of their community college credits as possible. For example, majors at community colleges may go by a different name (e.g., human services or social services). Transfer students will appreciate connecting with program faculty about required coursework, admissions requirements, and career options. Making information available about the profession, as discussed previously, may also help recruit transfer students.

For community college students, articulation agreements are helpful. These agreements show students the pathway to the social work major, transferring as many credits as possible. Articulation agreements (also called 2+2 or transfer agreements) with community colleges may focus on specific social-work-related programs such as human services, psychology, pre-social-work, or similar majors. A 2+2 agreement outlines the student's first 2 years at a community college and final 2 years at the university level. A specific agreement regarding transferability allows for a clear and easy transfer of credits. Working with program leaders, faculty, and advisors at the community college on a course-by-course comparison can offer the most transfer credits possible while maintaining the integrity of the undergraduate curriculum. Examples of this course-by-course comparison include human development as equivalent to human behavior in a social environment (HBSE) and Introduction to Human Services as equivalent to Introduction to Social Work.

One issue with community college transfer students may be the credentialing of instructors; transferring courses to a university may require that instructors meet the same requirements as the university's regional accrediting body regarding the instructors' degrees earned and years of experience. For example, some community colleges may offer workforce or technical courses with bachelor's prepared instructors, but those courses may not transfer to the 4-year college because of the university's credentialing requirements as outlined by their regional accreditor. Credits may transfer as a block into an associate of applied science (AAS) or an associate of applied arts (AAA), but those credits will not generally lead to an accredited degree in social work. Transfer students may not understand the ins and outs of credentialing, academic versus workforce credit, and why some courses will or will not transfer. Outlining the guidelines through articulation agreements can save students (and program faculty) frustration over the long term.

> **PRACTICE TIP:** Clear guidelines, transparency about transfer credits, and a good relationship with the community college will help ease the path for your transfer students.

Posttraditional Students

Universities have identified and named adult students "nontraditional students" determined by their age, typically 25 and older. Updated terminology may more accurately reflect the current profile of students: "posttraditional" may be preferred. According to the American Council on Education (ACE) (2021), 60% of enrolled undergraduates balance life, work, and education. A majority of university students are now older than 25 and may be caring for dependents, may be working fulltime, and/or may be veterans. These students are driven by a goal or a dream that they finally have time to realize. Some of them have been full-time caregivers; they may be change-of-career adults who have opted to leave their first profession and start a social work career, or those who have slowly but surely taken one course every semester for the last umpteen years. Sometimes a change of career is initiated by a major event like 9/11, Hurricane Sandy, COVID-19, or another disaster.

The authors have had students who were parents who have volunteered for years, and we have also had marketing executives, TV broadcasting managers, and dentists in our classes. Veterans may be interested in a career path that includes military or health care social work.

Sometimes personal events lead adults to change occupations midcareer; they may have been exposed to social workers through their own life circumstances or may be pursuing their dream career. Their needs are different, their direction is frequently already established, and they may only want information about course sequencing and networking opportunities. As with community college students, sharing information about the profession, such as the NASW's Help Starts Here website (discussed earlier), will help students make an informed decision. These students may be very goal-directed and may have already explored options within the profession. In these cases, you will serve as a broker of information rather than a marketer.

Program Literature and Giveaways

All of the meetings and opportunities to meet potential students that have been discussed may be more successful with swag or handouts. Respectfully, if you are reading this chapter, you are probably too old to select the swag items for traditional-age students! That should be left to your current social work majors, as they will be more likely to know what is popular and likely to lure prospects to your table. Laptop stickers or cell phone wallets might be great this year but could look old and tired next year. However, tying swag to the profession might increase the life of the product. A little creative marketing can get a prospect to your table even if your swag is the least expensive you could find.

> **PRACTICE TIP:** Don't put dates on your swag or you could find that you have "old" stuff in storage that you can't give away. When possible, spend money on giveaways, especially for on-campus recruiting events. Be creative! For example, sunglasses can represent how social workers see things through a different lens; a fan may represent fanning the flames of advocacy, and a stress ball shaped like the Earth can be tied to our desire to improve global functioning for all. Also, never recruit without candy!

Display colorful infographics that highlight different career opportunities or statistics about the major. Various websites, such as the Social Work Guide, provide helpful resources. Presenting information from the

U.S. Bureau of Labor Statistics (2021) can reassure parents or students that a social work degree is marketable and that you can live well on the salary (poor wages being one of those myths that need shattering!). Additionally, literature should reinforce the possibility of advanced standing in an MSW program after earning a BSW. Achieving an MSW in a year or less may be very appealing. Finally, all marketing materials and literature should help students know where to find you on campus when they have questions or are ready to change their major.

Recruiting Currently Enrolled Students

Once on campus, each of the groups discussed here, including incoming high school students, community college students, and posttraditional students, may opt to change their major after they find out about social work. However, actively recruiting students already on campus is a very different process, with many more items to consider before moving forward with a plan of action. First, there may be other program leaders worried that you are trying to "steal" their majors. The larger your program gets, the smaller their numbers become, moving valuable resources such as faculty posts and adjunct funds from them to you. If you are in a multidisciplinary department or college, caution is advised to protect your relationships with colleagues. You also have to be sure that recruiting events focus on all students, not just one group or major.

Exploring neutral campus events like a "Choose a Major Day," a career fair, or an opportunity to talk with undeclared majors individually or collectively can be a great way to reach a broader audience. For instance, if faculty advise first-year students, placing a faculty member in the advising center can provide access and the opportunity to suggest the major to an uncertain student. Your school may also have professional advisors; meeting with advisors regularly to update them about program changes can help build relationships. Different advising models abound, but knowing the specific model for your campus can help you build the appropriate bridges with professional advisors.

You also cannot underestimate your Introduction to Social Work course as one of your strongest marketing tools. Selecting the instructor, involving committed social work students, and creating interactive content in your survey class are of utmost importance; the combination of the three has a synergistic effect. The class needs to be engaging and upbeat, and provide a solid and accurate view of the major. Hosting guest speakers, having virtual events, bringing agency personnel into the classroom, and establishing mentoring partnerships with your junior, senior, or MSW students (if you have an MSW program) can serve to recruit students to your major and help them understand what social workers can accomplish.

Another option is having Introduction to Social Work considered a social or behavioral science course in your university's general education requirements, and thus being able to offer it to a broader range of students. Be forewarned, however, that you may be asked by college and university administrators to have more sections than you are prepared to staff. Be sure you are prepared to offer as many Introduction to Social Work sections as there are Introduction to Psychology or Introduction to Sociology courses because you may need to help the university fulfill the general education seats and mission. For one of the authors, this would be a difference of offering two sections of Introduction to Social Work at 25 students a class to 30 sections of Introduction to Social Work with 50 students each. The work to scale to this level of activity may or not pay off at your university.

Off-Campus Learning Sites

With state funding of public universities declining, many universities have expanded to multiple campuses (also called branches, off-campus learning sites, or satellites), thus increasing recruitment and retention challenges. Although this model is not new, more universities seem to be moving toward offering courses and/or degrees at multiple locations. Groenwald (2018) outlined challenges with these multicampus universities and distinguished between a "system," where multiple campuses in the same system each have a large degree of autonomy, and multiple sites covered by one accreditation and centralized governance. Off-campus learning sites away from a main or flagship campus often recruit transfer students, who are coming into the program with their general education courses largely completed. Recruitment in these settings may have to focus on the community colleges in the program's area that offer lower-level (first-year and sophomore) courses using the tips described earlier. Some of these courses may include gateway courses such as Introduction to Social Work and Social Welfare; thus, it is essential for the program, department, and university to collaborate and establish trust with community college partners.

Campuses are likely to be geographically separated, thus increasing the challenge of providing consistency across the curriculum. Recruiting can be difficult, with faculty spread thin, and one size will probably not fit all. Each campus may have its own personality, and the demographic profiles

of students may vary widely. Transferability of courses can be a significant recruitment challenge; each community college may teach gateway
courses (such as Introduction to Social Work) differently. Students may
be taking courses to satisfy the requirements for a certificate or an associate
degree, but those classes may not be required or may lack transferability to
a 4-year social work undergraduate degree. Students who lose large blocks
of credit may be less likely to choose social work because there are usually
many credits to acquire, considering the range of HBSE, policy, research,
practice, and field courses needed to graduate.

Once again, partnerships with the transferring college are important, and
the development of 2+2 plans can ease the transfer process. As previously
discussed, developing relationships with your university's admissions office,
recruiters, and advisors is essential. Know the pathway that students must take
to reach your program and then eliminate barriers. Expeditious application
processes, a review of the transferability of courses, and establishing relationships early on, whether with professional advisors or with faculty, are essential.

Diversity and Inclusion

A chapter on recruitment is not complete without talking about a few
other considerations. First, what is your university, college, and/or program's commitment to diversity? If you desire more diversity in your
student population, whether that be race, sexual orientation, religion,
ableness, or any other form of diversity, have you brainstormed where to
find those students you hope to recruit? Could a high school social work
class be offered for free in the high schools with the most diversity to
introduce those students to the profession? Are there targeted scholarships?
Are there clubs or organizations on campus that attract and support the
diversity you are looking for in your majors? For instance, you might try
to present to an organization for young people aging out of foster care or
involve other organizations in community-service-based events.

There also seems to be an increase in students with different learning
abilities and/or mental health issues. Does your university have enough
staff in these areas to help all students be successful? If support programs
are not adequate, should the program encourage the university to increase
the availability of services? Do we have an ethical responsibility as a social
worker to advocate on behalf of the students with mental health and learning disability issues? Where does the program stand on accepting and
working with students who find their way to the major because of their
personal mental health challenges or disabilities, or a personal background

that may present barriers (i.e., a criminal history)? Is the program willing to support students who need extra support in these areas? All of these questions should be explored by program faculty, establishing short- and long-term goals for the recruitment of a diverse student population.

Retention

Once you have invested the time and energy in recruiting majors, the focus shifts to retaining those students. The retention of students is as important as recruitment; it also requires an investment of time, money, and energy. Unfortunately, there is no one-size-fits-all or magic bullet to retaining students. Moriarty et al. (2009) addressed barriers to retention, including transitioning into a university setting, lack of academic support for at-risk students, and demographic factors (such as being a first-generation student). Students who are working and/or juggling family responsibilities may not have the time to form and develop supportive relationships. Students at some stages of their academic career may need additional support, such as while they are in their internships. Moriarty et al. (2009) pointed out that retention should be a focus of the institution; addressing systemic and institutional challenges is key. Retention does not happen in isolation; social work programs can lead the way but should be advancing the cause of retention while supplementing what is happening at an institutional level. Programs need to seek out reliable data about who is leaving without graduating or why they are leaving the major.

> **PRACTICE TIP:** Make friends with your office of retention or your institutional research office on campus and ask for help diving deep into the data, especially if you are in a larger program. Often, reports are available by major and demographic breakdowns if you know where to look and how to access them.

Ongoing Support

The profile of college students is changing; students with more diverse backgrounds are seeking higher education. Getting students in the door is only the first step. Providing ongoing support and helping them balance work, family, and finances is part of today's reality. Be sure to have a clear pathway to matriculation, including earlier and accurate advising. For some students, nonacademic factors (finances, work, and family) may play a much larger role in leaving the program than academic factors (Priode et al., 2020). Specifically, Priode et al. cited developing a circle of support (friends, both in their classes and outside the university; family; and faculty) and adequate living and transportation resources as ways to retain these students.

Moriarty et al. (2009) discussed the need for mentors from varied backgrounds; faculty and mentors should represent diverse backgrounds. Programs should seek to hire diverse faculty to represent the students whom they are trying to recruit and recognize the additional barriers these students face, including being underprepared and underresourced (Ghose et al., 2018). Students may need academic, financial, and social support to successfully complete their social work education (Weng & Gray, 2017). Simple encouragement from faculty, peer mentors, and tutors can help develop relationships and help students feel connected. One critical area of support that may be needed within social work programs is when students enter their practicum; placing at least two students per agency may offer the students a built-in peer-support group.

> **PRACTICE TIP:** When students enter their practicum, they may be placed alone in an agency, without their natural support group. Robust seminars can help engage students, and ongoing communication from a faculty or a seminar leader is important. One possibility, if you have an MSW program, is to assign an MSW student to provide a support group for undergraduate interns. This works well if an MSW student is assigned to your undergraduate field office for their practicum.

Off-Campus Learning Sites

As discussed previously, the growth of outreach or satellite campuses adds additional layers to the issue of retention. Students may feel that they do not have parity in support services at multiple sites. Consistency and rigor may be an issue, and a lack of contact with faculty from different sites may affect retention. Groenwald (2018) discussed similar issues relating to the challenges of leadership in multicampus systems; when leadership is challenged, the overall climate of the campus may affect student retention. With the growth of online interactions, whether through web-based video platforms or online courses, students talk and compare, and they may become dissatisfied if they feel there are discrepancies or inequities.

Outreach campuses may be more likely to suffer from low enrollment (Groenwald, 2018), thus putting these students at risk of canceled classes or engaging in alternative instruction methods. Students on outreach campuses may feel disadvantaged and may not have access to the same level of services as flagship campus students. For example, counseling services may be available only through telehealth (which may also be influenced by where the student lives, depending on state laws), a comprehensive health clinic may not be available, or a food pantry may not be as well stocked. Students attending classes widely separated by distance may not feel connected to their peers on other campuses. Additionally, the pandemic forced classes online; thus, students may lack a feeling of connection to their peers in general. For information relating to support of students in online programs, please see Chapter 7.

It's Not Just the First Year That Matters

Many universities provide first-year experience programs focusing on retaining students from their first year to their sophomore year. These programs generally focus on college success, making connections, and easing the transition from high school to college. Fewer schools have focused on sophomore or second-year experience programs. A quick Google search using the phrase "first-year experience" yielded more than 7 billion results. When searching using the phrase "second-year experience," results fell to less than half: 3.2 billion hits. "Sophomore experience" results fell to just over 48.5 million hits.

Moriarty et al. (2009), in a qualitative study of British social work students, suggested that students could benefit from ongoing programs focusing on support during subsequent years of college. This becomes even more important if a program recruits transfer students; they may have had their first-year experience at their community college, and they may not feel connected to the university if there are no formal programs welcoming them. University-wide transfer student orientations can be one way to bring those students into their new university family, or, perhaps even better, a programwide orientation at a critical point in their quest for a degree in social work, such as entry to their junior year or to field placement. For example, hosting an orientation that brings students together from all locations can increase the students' feelings of connectedness. Programs can offer information on sequencing, internships, and study abroad, and may even include breakout sessions for professionalism, how to approach faculty, and the importance of good study habits.

Eliminating Silos

Groenwald's (2018) suggestions for leadership, which are relevant here, include breaking down silos, establishing good communication, providing equal access to support systems, and communicating a shared vision.

Once again, if silos exist, communication among faculty and leadership is inconsistent or poor, and if there is no shared vision, then it is reasonable to assume that the campus climate and student outcomes may also be affected. The program director's presence on a regular basis, whether physically or virtually, can provide reassurance to outreach-based students that they are receiving the same amount of attention and are just as important as the main campus students. Students on outreach campuses may be housed on a community college campus or in an office building, both of which may lack the feeling of being at a university. Engaging in communication that actually connects with students (through social media, messages in the course platform, or video messages posted in a class shell) helps to break down silos and establishes open communication.

Having all faculty meet students can be helpful. One of the authors teaches in a program offered on three campuses; all faculty travel to each campus on a given night once per semester and engage with those students. They may have had the students in an online class, but meeting with each campus cohort of students over pizza has helped break down barriers and has enhanced communication. Campus involvement may be a factor in retaining students, but that can be complicated when multiple off-campus learning sites are part of the program's makeup or the program has a large number of posttraditional students. Creating similar experiences and shared traditions may be an essential part of retaining outreach students.

Barriers

Economic barriers and a lack of funds for food, transportation, or daily living may factor into a student's inability to matriculate and persist. Campuses with a higher percentage of underserved, first-generation, or posttraditional students may be more at risk for lower retention rates. Pressure from families who may not see the value in higher education creates stress for students who wish to continue. Social work may be viewed as an underpaid career where someone cannot make a decent living, thus reducing familial support for students who choose social work as a path. Students who have children or become pregnant may have challenges in juggling multiple responsibilities.

Hybrid, Online, and Creativity in Instruction

One helpful approach to working with today's students is developing hybrid, online, or more flexible approaches to instruction. The COVID-19 pandemic has, perhaps, reshaped how we view the delivery of coursework.

Faculty had to quickly pivot and strategize in creating effective online classes or present classes via online platforms such as Zoom. Although it remains to be seen what the lasting effects will be on approaches to teaching post-COVID, some faculty may have figured out that online is not horrible and that providing students with flexible ways to access content can actually benefit working or parenting students. College professors have been forced to review hegemonic approaches to education as face-to-face, in a specified time slot two days per week, with the instructor at the center of the learning. Using asynchronous approaches for at least some classes or within parts of classes offers ultimate flexibility and encourages students to take control of their own learning.

However, faculty need to be cognizant of pedagogical challenges and need to engage in best practices. Universities offer varied opportunities for learning how to teach online; at times, faculty need to advocate for or search out additional resources to help them create engaging content (see Chapter 7). According to Davis et al. (2019), effective online faculty are able to shift from being the "keeper of all knowledge … to [being] facilitator[s] of learning" (p. 37). Some faculty (primarily those who have not taught online) may see online teaching as easier—it is not. Creating opportunities for collaboration and interaction, establishing clear guidelines for participation, and providing prompt and specific feedback are ingredients for success (Davis et al., 2019). Faculty must work hard to create content that includes cognitive, social, and teaching presence. Integrating social media, incorporating support services, developing relationships, and using various communication techniques are essential to online teaching. Again, please refer to Chapter 7 for further content related to online programs.

PRACTICE TIP: Teaching pedagogy in the classroom needs to go far beyond simply using canned resources from the publisher of the text. One free tool to explore when teaching online is Perusall (https://perusall.com).

Building Relationships and Encouraging Involvement

Students' needs regarding persistence may vary, and different programs will attract different types of students. However, in general, students need to feel supported personally and academically. Having relationships with faculty or an advisor where they feel comfortable sharing the barriers that impede their ability to successfully complete school may increase retention. If they can feel comfortable sharing about their difficulties in access to technology, food and housing insecurity, employment, and medical issues that prevent their full attention to school, faculty may be able to refer them to campus resources for assistance, such as reserving computer time at the library or a food pantry.

Students also need opportunities to get involved in campus activities, and financial barriers may affect retention. Students may need to work more hours than is ideal. As the cost of a 4-year degree skyrockets, students are adversely affected by rising tuition and housing costs. According to Mitchell et al. (2016), costs are rising as many states cut support to public higher education following the last recession. The Institute of Education Sciences (IES, 2019b), which compiles statistics through the U.S. Department of Education, estimates that the cost of a 4-year degree rose by 31% at public institutions in the 10 years from 2007–2008 to 2017–2018. At private institutions, the cost rose by 23%. Both of these figures have been adjusted for inflation.

Finances

Students may be burdened with student loans; they may have not considered the financial ramifications of accepting all financial aid, including unsubsidized loans, every semester. The number of students receiving aid has steadily risen, correlating with the rise in the cost of a 4-year degree across public and private nonprofit institutions. In 2000–2001, 75% of total students received federal aid, and in 2017–2018, 86% received federal aid (IES, 2019a). The cost of a college education has grown appreciably faster than the median income (Mitchell et al., 2016).

PRACTICE TIP: Know what the process is for searching for and obtaining on-campus employment. Most universities have an office that works with students who need on-campus jobs; some jobs may be tied to financial need, so understanding the where and how for student employment could help you point students toward a campus job that could make a difference in their ability to remain in school. Added bonuses are the connections they make around campus as well as the opportunity to build professional skills.

Although the latest CSWE (2021) report shows that the percentage of students incurring loan debt has decreased from 81.3% in 2015 to 70.7%

in 2020, the average loan debt for BSW graduates is 10% higher than it was 10 years ago. Students graduating in 2020 with their BSW had an average loan debt of $27,264. Increasing loan debt is also present among students earning an MSW degree; 73.1% of MSW students graduate with an average debt of $47,965 (CSWE, 2021). Looking at data on MSW graduates, debt load is substantially higher for those from racially minoritized groups, especially those who are Black (Fitzhugh Mullan Institute for Health Workforce Equity, 2020). While this chapter focuses primarily on undergraduate recruitment and retention, helping students in BSW programs matriculate with less debt should correlate with lower debt at the MSW level. When looking nationwide at overall undergraduate graduation rates, compared with their White counterparts (67.2%), only 45.9% of Black students and 55% of Latinx students completed their studies, which has important implications for debt (Banks & Dohy, 2019).

Open Educational Resources

With the development of open educational resources (OERs), the cost of course materials to students can be decreased or eliminated altogether. Books are one of the largest expenses for students, and most of us have heard students complain that the professor did not use the book or lament that they could not afford to purchase the book. Focusing on finding reasonably priced books, or using open-access articles, readings, websites, and so forth, is a social justice issue. If we are, indeed, serving a more diverse student population (including first-generation and/or students coming from backgrounds of poverty), then making education affordable should be our focus.

PRACTICE TIP: Examples of OERs include an entry-level research text titled *Scientific Inquiry in Social Work* (DeCarlo, 2018), which is 100% free, downloadable, and customizable. DeCarlo has also created a website, https://opensocialwork.org/textbooks/, that lists many social work OERs. Also, explore *Human Behavior and the Social Environment*, by Tyler (2020). Many universities have thier own websites to search for OERs created there as well.

McCarty et al. (2021) discussed how their university "identified 'lack of money' as the variable most predictive of 'dropping out'" (p. 37). As stated previously, the cost of education continues to rise, thus putting an increasing financial burden on students who may be relying on student loans. OERs can help to level the playing field as all students will have access to course materials.

PRACTICE TIP: Your university's librarians may be a valuable resource when deciding to transition to OERs. Linking these resources through your learning management system and using an open-access site such as Perusall can decrease costs for students while also increasing student communication and collaboration.

Diversity

Diversity is a strength of the social work classroom; however, it may also be a barrier to retaining students from traditionally oppressed or marginalized backgrounds who may not feel that their voices matter and may not feel represented. According to the most recent data from the U.S. Census Bureau (2021), 59.3% of the population is White non-Hispanic, 18.9% Latinx, 13.6% Black, and 6.1% Asian. However, demographics are shifting in the United States. Schaeffer (2019) stated that the populations of color have an average age younger than non-Hispanic Whites. Thus, it makes sense that social work students are more diverse than the population as a whole. According to CSWE (2021), fewer than half of BSW graduates are White. Although 49.2% of graduates are White (non-Hispanic), 20% are Black, and 16.3% are Latinx. Asian students are underrepresented at only 2.7% of undergraduate social work graduates. According to Banks and Dohy (2019), students of color have lower graduation rates, with Black students being the least likely to matriculate into a major whether they entered a university as first-year students or transferred from a community college.

Latinx students may benefit from mentorship but may also need enhanced institutional support. As more institutions strive to become Hispanic Serving Institutions, it is incumbent upon them to provide a culturally sensitive learning environment and explore and integrate various types of cultural capital (Olcoń et al., 2018). They focused on six types of cultural capital and outlined specific strategies that BSW programs can use; pedagogical techniques may influence retention of all students. One example of leveraging social capital is encouraging bilingual students to frame their linguistic abilities from a strengths-based perspective.

In a study specific to social work students (both undergraduate and graduate), Deepak et al. (2016) found that engaged learning and building social capital helped to retain students. Engaged learning involves evidence of questioning, application of knowledge beyond the classroom, and essentially encouraging students to take responsibility for their own learning. Schreiner and Louis identified engaged learning as "meaningful processing, focused attention, and active participation" (as cited in Deepak et al., 2016, p. 311). Students who think about their learning beyond the classroom are more likely to continue their quest for a degree (Deepak et al., 2016).

> **PRACTICE TIP:** Bilingual materials should be offered (as appropriate to your context) during college orientation workshops, family weekends, or other events. Interaction with families from bilingual staff and faculty should be encouraged.

Posttraditional Students

As discussed in the "Recruitment" section of this chapter, posttraditional students may face additional pressure from family or work responsibilities. In many social work programs, the typical social work student is older and is more likely to have familial responsibilities. CSWE (2021) reported that at least a third of BSW students fell into the 25 and older age range, with an additional 11.2% reported as "unknown." Although 85.3% of all BSW students were enrolled as full-time students, posttraditional students were disproportionately represented in the number of part-time students, with only 28.7% being full-time students (CSWE, 2020).

Attending a university part-time may increase the overall cost of attendance because of tuition and fee structures. Some universities offer lower tuition for enrolling in more classes; thus, the per-credit cost of 18 credit hours may be lower than the per-credit cost for 6 credit hours. Program faculty should discuss with students what they can realistically handle in terms of course load and finances. Many struggling students who are juggling multiple responsibilities would be better served by taking fewer hours, but this can be challenging in programs requiring a strict sequence of courses. Program leaders may need to review strict sequencing and determine alternative pathways.

> **PRACTICE TIP:** Whenever possible, gather data from students leaving your program, whether they are leaving the university or are changing majors. Automating withdrawals to an online process, for example, may give universities solid data as to why students choose to leave. These data may help programs better serve their students.

Practical Tips for Retaining Students

Often, one of the first questions students ask when considering a degree path is, "When can I graduate?" Having a formal matriculation plan developed with input from the student that considers their unique needs is an essential first step in retention. Although some universities may push students to enroll fulltime, some students may benefit from a part-time plan. State funding for public universities may be tied to graduation rates, which incentivizes timely graduation. Some universities offer progressively lower per-class tuition when registering above a certain level. When considering the number of hours students should take, multiple factors need to be considered by advisors and students. Whether course advising is done by professional advisors or social work faculty, students need to understand prerequisites, sequencing, and schedule rotations. For example, some classes may be offered only one time per year; thus, knowing when those courses are offered is vital to planning ahead. Accurate advising is essential, and developing well-articulated transfer agreements (2+2 plans) may also help with retention.

Early Intervention and Support

Having a system in place to raise an early alert about students who appear to be struggling, are not engaged in the classroom (if they come at all), or may have professional behaviors to address (like boundaries and inappropriate language or dress) can help with retention. Programs may recruit students who have lived through hard times; students may be drawn to the profession because they have been in a difficult life situation. Consistent communication among faculty is important. If a student is struggling in one class, they may be struggling in multiple classes. Early intervention, whether through an informal meeting with a caring faculty member or in a more formal program or university system, may help a student salvage their semester. It may take only one conversation to help a student express their concerns or needs and navigate their choices. More schools are offering support programs to meet tangible needs such as access to food pantries, day care support, or transportation difficulties. Providing resources such as counseling (often already included in students' fees) may help students deal with life issues and stressors. Being proactive with students may help them maintain their enrollment and not end up with a semester of failing grades.

As previously mentioned, having support services available for students and ensuring that students know about those services is essential to retaining students. Rates of anxiety and depression continue to climb, and the pandemic has only exacerbated these statistics (McAlpine, 2021). Additional factors increasing these mental health issues, according to McAlpine (2021), include "political unrest, and systemic racism and inequality" (para. 1). Students need clear and consistent communication from faculty and advisors about counseling services; social work programs should be at the forefront of promoting mental health services and reducing the stigma associated with seeking help. At times, our students believe that the helper should not need help. It is up to us to emphasize that seeking counseling does not mean someone cannot be an effective helper. In fact, those who are willing to seek help may be much better prepared in the long run to work with clients.

Additionally, a food pantry that is not well advertised will not help food-insecure students. Making sure that support services meet the specific needs of each student, no matter which site they are attending, is essential. All sites may not need a food pantry, but all sites need something. Each off-campus learning site may have a different demographic and thus have different needs. Therefore, each site does not have to have the same resources, but the university should provide the resources needed to encourage and assist students in timely matriculation. Social work programs should lead the charge when advocating for students to have the support they need. For example, it is unethical to encourage students to take out student loans but not help those students to graduate in a timely manner.

Developing Clear Pathways

Universities are developing clear pathways for all students, whether the first time in college or posttraditional or veterans. With the tightening of financial aid regulations and legislative input in many public university systems, faculty and program administrators are essential elements in assisting with clear pathways. When a student declares a social work major, they should meet with an advisor, whether a faculty member or a professional advisor, to learn about opportunities for involvement, prerequisites, or sequencing challenges. Even if professional advisors are used, students should always be connected to faculty within the program. Although academic advising in some universities may occur outside of the department or program, the CSWE 2022 Educational Policy and Accreditation Standards (EPAS) stipulate that programs have a plan for both academic and professional advising. This should be more than a "tick the box" meeting with someone just to get clearance to register for courses. Some universities may offer an orientation at a certain point in a student's degree plan, triggered by a specific course, and others may use student groups to connect.

As stated previously, diversity is a strength of social work programs in general. However, the graduation rate gap needs to be addressed, considering the demographic characteristics of baccalaureate social work graduates. According to Banks and Dohy (2019), students need to feel a sense of belonging, and the curriculum, especially considering the divisiveness present in today's society, must be culturally appropriate and culturally responsive. Some ideas presented by Banks and Dohy in their review of the literature included establishing peer groups, making sure that students have high-quality mentoring from a faculty member of color, and approaching diversity from a strengths-based perspective. Creating safe spaces for students of color is paramount, along with an honest examination of institutional and program barriers for these students. The 2022 EPAS focuses on the integration of anti-racism, diversity, equity, and inclusion (ADEI) approaches across the curriculum. These foci need to be present in all recruitment activities, addressing the needs of a broad population of students.

At the end of the day, retention happens through active involvement in the matriculation plans of students. Retention can be increased by helping students with professional development, encouraging them to become involved in campus and/or social work program activities, and creating an inclusive environment that validates diverse students' lived experiences. Students should have access to a diverse faculty, but diversity should be represented in many ways. Programs may need to focus on supporting students who work by offering a clearly articulated part-time matriculation plan, developing paid internships, or establishing endowed scholarships. Program faculty should form relationships with the financial aid and scholarship office, as those entities can sometimes "find" money if a faculty member intervenes when a student is struggling financially. On-campus work-study programs can be beneficial in alleviating financial stress, and often the jobs go to students who qualify for financial aid, perhaps reducing the burden of student loans.

Working Students

Working students may benefit from a blend of online or asynchronous and face-to-face classes, even in a primarily face-to-face program. Connections made with faculty can give students the tools they need to be successful and help them plan for the professional world or graduate school. These connections should be available to students regardless of program options (off-campus learning sites or online programs). Social work is a profession that requires hands-on learning and the ability to form relationships as a foundation for training; this, of course, reflects our profession's core value of the importance of human relationships. This happens first within the program as faculty help students set goals and focus on their future. For many students, finding ways to help students persist in their education changes the trajectory of their lives and the generations to follow.

Conclusion

As this chapter is being written, we are still experiencing a worldwide pandemic. Thus, recruitment and retention efforts may continue to shift and change rapidly because of its continuing effects. The challenge for faculty and administrators to retain students is huge; technology issues, mental health impacts, financial challenges, and the possibility of illness will probably change our conversations for the foreseeable future. For successful recruitment, creativity in marketing and putting your best foot forward will require your university's and program's concentrated and coordinated efforts. Hosting smaller preview days for prospective students or adding virtual open houses may help the school recruit from a broader geographic range. Addressing barriers on a systematic basis and paying attention to psychosocial issues are what social workers do best. Using our social work knowledge and skills in academia to address recruitment and retention challenges will help put the profession in good hands for the future.

Suggested Readings and Resources

Articles

Bowie, S. (2018). An assessment of social work education efforts to recruit and retain MSW students of color. *Journal of Social Work Education, 54*(2), 270–286. https://doi.org /10.1080/10437797.2017.1404531

Britt, S. L., Ammerman, D. A., Barrett, S. F., & Jones, S. (2017). Student loans, financial stress, and college student retention. *Journal of Student Financial Aid, 47*(1), Article 3. https://ir.library.louisville.edu/jsfa/vol47/iss1/3

Hemy, M., Boddy, J., Chee, P., & Sauvage, D. (2016). Social work students "juggling" field placement. *Social Work Education, 35*(2), 215–228. https://doi.org/10.1080/02615479 .2015.1125878

Nsonwu, M., Welch-Brewer, C., Folarin, O. M., Jernigan, Q., Durham, L., Marshall, A., & Bailey, G. (2019). Unity is our strength: Perspectives on recruitment and retention of African American male social work students. *Urban Social Work, 3*(S1). https://doi.org /10.1891/2474-8684.3.S1.S129

Olcoń, K., Pantell, M., & Sund, A. C. (2018). Recruitment and retention of Latinos in social work education: Building on students' community cultural wealth. *Journal of Social Work Education, 54*(2), 349–363. https://doi.org/10.1080/10437797.2017.1404530

Silver Wolf (Adelv unegv Waya), D. A. P., Perkins, J., Butler-Barnes, S. T., & Walker, T. A., Jr. (2017). Social belonging and college retention: Results from a quasi-experimental pilot study. *Journal of College Student Development 58*(5), 777–782. https://doi.org/10.1353/csd.2017.0060

Websites

4 Imprint: https://www.4imprint.com/
AudioGo for HigherEd: https://www.audiogo.com
Penji.co: https://penji.co/marketing-strategies-for-universities/
Print Tech: https://www.printtechofwpa.com/top-10-tips-for-promoting-your-university/

References

American Council on Education. (2021). *Post-traditional learners.* https://www.acene.edu/Research-Insights/Pages/Student-Support/Post-Traditional-Learners.aspx

Banks, T., & Dohy, J. (2019). Mitigating barriers to persistence: A review of efforts to improve retention and graduation rates for students of color in higher education. *Higher Education Studies, 9*(1), 118–131. https://doi.org/10.5539/hes.v9n1p118

Brookdale Community College. (2021). *Displaced homemakers program.* https://www.brookdalecc.edu/continuinged/displaced-homemakers

Council on Social Work Education. (2021). *2020 statistics on social work education in the United States.* https://www.cswe.org/getattachment/726b15ce-6e63-4dcd-abd1-35d2ea9d9d40/2020-Annual-Statistics-On-Social-Work-Education-in-the-United-States.pdf?lang=en-US

Council on Social Work Education. (2022). *Educational policy and accreditation standards.* https://www.cswe.org/accreditation/standards/2022-epas/

Davis, C., Greenaway, R., Moore, M., & Cooper, L. (2019). Online teaching in social work education: Understanding the challenges. *Australian Journal of Social Work, 72*(1), 34–46. https://doi.org/10.1080/0312407X.2018.1524918

DeCarlo, M. (2018). *Scientific inquiry in social work.* Open Textbook Library. https://open.umn.edu/opentextbooks/textbooks/591

Deepak, A. C., Wisner, B. L., & Benton, A. D. (2016). Intersections between technology, engaged learning, and social capital in social work education. *Social Work Education, 35*(3), 310–322. http://doi.org/10.1080/02615479.2016.1154661

Fitzhugh Mullan Institute for Health Workforce Equity. (2020). *The social work profession: Findings from three years of surveys of new social workers.* https://www.cswe.org/getattachment/a75b244d-5831-4d51-b59c-1e51de32b93e/SW-Workforce-Book-2020.pdf?lang=en-US

Ghose, T., Ali, S., & Keo-Meier, B. (2018). Diversity in social work doctoral programs: Mapping the road ahead. *Research on Social Work Practice, 28*(3),265–271. https://doi.org/10.1177/1049731517710725

Grobman, L. (2019). *Days in the lives of social workers* (5th ed.). The New Social Worker Press.

Groenwald, S. L. (2018). The challenges and opportunities in leading a multi-campus university. *Journal of Professional Nursing, 34,* 134–141. https://www.semanticscholar.org/paper/The-challenges-and-opportunities-in-leading-a-Groenwald/d4a948bff3ec360e1fec7ff86cd6db71fcaec5e2

Heyen, B. (2021). Super Bowl commercials 2021: How much does an ad cost for Super Bowl 55? *Sporting News.* https://www.sportingnews.com/ca/nfl/news/super-bowl-commercials-cost -2021/1bdelznuzr47c1jiimnz1l8j4z

Institute of Education Sciences. (2019a). *Financial aid: Fast facts.* https://nces.ed.gov/ fastfacts/display.asp?id=31

Institute of Education Sciences. (2019b). *Tuition costs of colleges and universities: Fast facts.* https://nces.ed.gov/fastfacts/display.asp?id=76

Maine Career and Technical Education. (2021). *Westbrook regional vocational center.* http://westbrook.mainecte.org/

McAlpine, K. J. (2021). Depression, anxiety, loneliness are peaking in college students. *The Brink.* Boston University. https://www.bu.edu/articles/2021/depression -anxiety-loneliness-are-peaking-in-college-students/

McCarty, D., Smith, D. S., & Goltz, H. H. (2021). Practicing what we teach: Open access in the classroom. *Journal of Baccalaureate Social Work, 26*(1), 35–44. https://doi.org /10.18084/1084-7219.26.1.35

Mitchell, M., Leachman, M., & Masterson, K. (2016). Funding down, tuition up: State cuts to higher education threaten quality and affordability at public colleges. *Center on Budget and Policy Priorities.* https://www.cbpp.org/research/state-budget-and-tax/funding -down-tuition-up

Moriarty, J., Manthorpe, J., Chauhan, B., Jones, G., Wenman, H., & Hussein, S. (2009). Hanging on a little thin line: Barriers to progression and retention in social work education. *Social Work Education, 28*(4), 363–379. https://doi.org/10.1080/02615470802109890

National Association of Social Workers. (2021). *Help starts here.* http://www .helpstartshere.org/

NJ Stars. (2021). State of New Jersey Higher Education Student Assistance Authority. *New Jersey Student Assistance Rewards Program.* https://www.hesaa.org/Documents /NJSTARS_program.pdf

Olcoń, K., Pantell, M., & Sund, A. D. (2018). Recruitment and retention of Latinos in social work education: Building on students' community cultural wealth. *Journal of Social Work Education, 54*(2), 349–363. https://doi.org/10.1080/10437797.2017.1404530

Priode, K. S., Dail, R. B., & Swanson, M. (2020). Non-academic factors that influence non-traditional nursing student retention. *Nursing Education Perspectives, 41*(4), 246–248. https://doi.org/10.1097/01.NEP.0000000000000577

Schaeffer, K. (2019). The most common age among Whites in US is 58—more than double that of racial and ethnic minorities. *Pew Research Center.* https://www.pewresearch.org /fact-tank/2019/07/30/most-common-age-among-us-racial-ethnic-groups/

Social Work Guide. (2020, September 11). *Careers in social work.* https://www.socialworkguide .org/careers/

Tyler, S. (2020). *Human behavior and the social environment I.* University of Arkansas Pressbooks. https://open.umn.edu/opentextbooks/textbooks/880

U.S. Bureau of Labor Statistics. (2021). *Occupational outlook handbook.* https://www.bls.gov /ooh/community-and-social-service/social-workers.htm

U.S. Census. (2021). *Quick facts: Population estimates.* https://www.census.gov/quickfacts /fact/table/US/PST045221

Weng, S. S., & Gray, L. A. (2017). Advancement in social work education: Fostering a supportive environment for students of non-dominant racial and ethnic backgrounds. *Social Work Education, 36*(6), 662–677. https://doi.org/10.1080/02615479.2017.1335700

CHAPTER 17

Don't Pass the Buck
Gatekeeping's Role in Social Work

Leah Lazzaro
Kelly Ward

Gatekeeping is a process that takes place from the time a person decides to be a social work major until the day that social worker retires from practice. Along this continuum are multiple natural stopping points for the social work student to reflect and assess whether this is the right career choice, and faculty aid in that process. Gatekeeping has been defined as a continuous process in which educators assess students' appropriateness for the social work profession (Lafrance et al., 2004). Opportunities for such assessment include application processes for accepting students into a social work major, social work practice and field courses, and the field practicum itself. Field education is considered the signature pedagogy of social work education and offers multiple opportunities for assessing a student's suitability for professional practice (Martin & Ciarfella, 2015; Miller & Koerin, 2001; Sowbel, 2012).

This chapter illuminates the need for continued research about gatekeeping practices in social work education and the student development process required in the 2022 Educational Policy and Accreditation Standards (EPAS) of the Council on Social Work Education (CSWE, 2022). Standards 4.1.6–4.1.7 specify that a program needs to have policies around advisement, retention, and termination, creating a mandate to develop a process the program can follow if and when it becomes necessary to terminate a student. The EPAS section on termination aligns with the Code of Ethics of the National Association of Social Workers (NASW, 2021), which discusses the need to be fit for duty in Section 2,

Social Workers' Ethical Responsibilities to Colleagues. Because the field internship is where students are in contact with vulnerable populations, a discussion regarding the importance of field supervisor training and rapport is included.

Typically, before many of us social workers and our colleagues were in leadership roles in college and universities, we were social work faculty. Before many colleagues were faculty, they were social workers, and before they were social workers, they were social work students. In each of these roles, we were likely engaged with people of whom we thought to ourselves, "Why are they in this profession?" And we worried to ourselves, "Should that person even enter or work in the field?" We all can share stories about those social workers about whom we wondered in the past. As social work leaders, we have an ethical duty to gatekeep for the profession. This chapter's goal is to lay out this duty to gatekeep to protect clients and the steps needed to make sure there is a road map on how to legally and ethically take on the gatekeeping role ascribed to social work educators and leaders.

By the end of this chapter, you will be able to:

- Connect the NASW Code of Ethics and CSWE competencies to inform gatekeeping practices.

- Enhance your program's faculty and field supervisors' ability to assess students' competence.

- Create a gatekeeping process for your department or make improvements to an existing policy.

Literature Review

Much of the literature on gatekeeping in social work education focuses on the administrative approaches and admissions process. Yet, developing policies is not the primary concern; it is more about developing a culture around excellence in social work practice that puts the client in the forefront while students' needs are also considered. BSW program directors can learn from the students' and other stakeholders' perspectives to build an inclusive environment where student well-being is key, along with keeping clients safe (Street, 2018). Striking a balance between the approaches of "screening in"—using a strengths-based approach to allow adult learners the ability to grow—and "screening out" students who have problems abiding by the Code of Ethics is a challenge.

Tam and Coleman (2011) emphasized the strengths perspective, which takes the view that students have the potential for positive change, thus making it particularly challenging to screen students out of social work. To overcome this, some empirical studies suggest that using multiple stakeholders to inform the policies of the program will promote representation and model professional values (Cervero & Wilson, 1994; Street et al., 2019). Field supervisors, employers, and adjunct faculty members are typically not involved in the admissions process of students, but they would like their needs considered, including professional suitability, indicators of educational quality, and progress of students' professional socialization as social workers (Street et al., 2019). This can be particularly important when considering the needs of adult students, such as taking into consideration social context, power relationships, and a commitment to include those who will be part of the program (Cervero & Wilson, 1994).

When students enter social work, they are doing more than simply declaring a major. They are entering a profession that has a set of core values that dictate how to approach their work. This new identity can become more deeply realized as students complete field internships in agencies that identify them as "social work interns." Social work faculty and field supervisors need to use their relational and professional skills to aid in this transformational process from "student" to emerging "social worker." This role can sometime blur the professional boundaries between educator and practitioner as faculty and field supervisors work with students to connect theory to practice and also provide supportive supervision regarding professional use of self and emotional maturity (Street, 2018).

Students sometime share with faculty and field supervisors personal issues that stand in the way of their progress in the classroom and in the field. It is easy to slip back into the role of social worker and lose sight of the role of an educator or supervisor, especially in the first few years of being in a new role. Faculty and supervisors need to remember that the students still need to be accountable to complete the work to the best of their ability and follow through on their commitments in the classroom and in the social work agency in order to fulfill the first principle of the Code of Ethics: Commitment to Clients (NASW, 2021). When extenuating circumstances happen, creating a plan that helps the student complete the work or take time off to address this issue would be useful. While the instructor and the supervisor can assist the student and express empathy, their first and foremost responsibility is to ensure the safety and care of the clients (Molina et al., 2018).

Faculty educate students about the NASW Code of Ethics in coursework and are expected to model those values in action (Reamer, 2012).

The Code is based on six standards that address ethical responsibilities (1) to clients, (2) to colleagues, (3) to the practice setting, (4) as professionals, (5) to the profession, and (6) to the broader society (NASW, 2021). As students are completing fieldwork, it is essential that they understand the Code of Ethics and what they need to abide by in their professional relationships with agencies and their clients. This includes, but is not limited to, boundary violations, self-disclosure, and confidentiality. Though it is hoped that any student concerns are identified and addressed early in the coursework, field education is a likely place for students to have difficulties in these areas if they are unable to carry out their duties (Sowbel, 2011).

By promoting the professional use of self throughout supervision, field supervisors can build a relationship to learn about students' emotional and mental health, as well as personal life stressors—including marital or relationship problems, financial problems, substance abuse, personal illness, death of a loved one, or legal problems. Awareness of personal life stressors can help the student and field supervisor be on alert for and respond to potential impairment, minimizing threats to violation of ethical standards (Reamer, 2012). Considering that tragic life events or changes in relationships, mental health, and physical well-being change over time, professors and field supervisors must continually and consistently emphasize the nature of competent and ethical practice. The challenge for social work education is to develop a policy that values the student's unique experience and strengths yet articulates a process to intervene and provide accommodations and respectful gatekeeping practices if necessary (Todd et al., 2019).

Suitability and Competence

According to Educational Policy 4.1.1, programs must identify inclusive admissions policies and processes to admit students to the social work major (CSWE, 2022). Admission policies need to define the criteria for "suitability" and "competence." It is important to create standards that are clearly communicated to students, field supervisors, and full- and part-time faculty members. Though these terms are similar in meaning, the literature describes suitability as "fit or appropriate for the purpose or task" (Oxford University Press, 2020, para. 1). The focus is on the qualities of the individual. When considering suitability, educators are required to make an ethical judgment about someone's professional fit. Madden (2000) defined an unsuitable student as "one who exhibits emotional or mental instability that poses a risk of harm to the student or to potential clients or whose values are in clear and direct conflict with those of the social work profession" (p. 141).

The call for ethical judgment of another's suitability requires self-awareness, honesty, and accountability to the profession's Code of Ethics. There may be conflict between one's subjective experiences and the professional value system that requires a gatekeeper to make complex decisions about the qualities that make a student unsuitable for professional practice. For example, personality traits such as agreeableness and conscientiousness affect performance in field (Sowbel & Miller, 2015).

Competence focuses on performance or capabilities. It is a behavioral approach that shifts the emphasis away from personal qualities and toward more objective behaviors. According to the EPAS (CSWE, 2022), "Social work competence is the ability to integrate and apply social work knowledge, values, skills, and cognitive and affective processes to practice situations in a culturally responsive, purposeful, intentional, and professional manner to promote human and community well-being" (p. 7). The move to competency-based practice behaviors in the 2008 EPAS informed gatekeeping policies that explicitly state that students are to be competent or "able to be successful" first and foremost in professional and ethical behavior. Assessing students using a competency-based approach to view growth can minimize bias (Steinke & Fitch, 2017). Using the CSWE competencies as a guide in the application process, classroom assignments, and field practice expectations ensures clarity and consistency in the gatekeeping process and focuses on the student's performance rather than the student's personal qualities.

A student may be an excellent candidate based on academic performance and competency admissions requirements, but face life changes or a decline midway through a program that negatively affects their field or classroom abilities and needs to be addressed. The literature on gatekeeping consistently describes the NASW Code of Ethics as the central benchmark for assessing suitability and competence (Elpers & FitzGerald, 2013; Reamer, 2012; Urwin et al., 2006). Because social work practice is complex, and education is a place to promote growth and transformation, it can be challenging to determine when it is necessary to intervene. The areas of "gross" misconduct where a student's behavior is dangerous or damaging to themselves, their classmates, or their clients, or where there are serious ethical violations—though disheartening—may be the easier situations to end in a termination of program or counsel out of the social work major (Currer & Atherton, 2008). More commonly, educators deal with problems that are less explicit and may challenge their roles of "supportive educator" and "gatekeeper of profession."

In addition, there may be pressure from college administration on student enrollment and retention that is in direct conflict with gatekeeping policies. It may take time and multiple university partners to explain the responsibility that professional faculty (e.g., social work, psychological counseling, nursing, and education) have with students working with clients in the field. Helping university administrators understand the ethical and legal responsibilities of the program and the program faculty is an essential training that needs repeating as many times as necessary for them to understand the responsibility to clients.

PRACTICE TIPS:
- Engage with university general counsel when writing gatekeeping policies.
- Meet with colleagues or departments that have strong gatekeeping practices and review their policies.
- Review gatekeeping polices periodically to ensure that they align with legal requirements.

According to EPAS, programs must create "initiatives designed to further student professional identity and comportment as well as student preparation for professional practice" (CSWE, 2022, p. 24). Have protocols in place to continually assess student competence through a student-centered approach that supports students' well-being even when that means terminating a student earlier in their education rather than continuing to enroll them if it is unlikely the student will succeed. This decision cannot and should not be made by one person. Having a committee of people who implement the gatekeeping policy can provide a less biased and more fact-based approach to reviewing a student's performance and determining, together, a fair outcome that protects clients and the social work profession and that supports the student's well-being—even if that means determining that social work is not the right fit for the student. Making this decision earlier in a student's educational career can save the student from incurring education debt when they may be unlikely to be successful in a social work career. To do this in an effective and consistent manner, good policy is required.

Ensuring an Effective Gatekeeping Policy

To hold students to ethical standards, programs must have policies and processes grounded in the EPAS and NASW Code of Ethics. Just as the

EPAS provides standards for admissions (B4.1.2), explicit curriculum (3.0), and advisement (4.1.6), it also requires policies on termination and due process (4.1.7). Previously, EPAS required "policies and procedures," but the necessity of specific due process policies "for reasons of academic performance, professional performance, and termination from the program" is a new CSWE requirement in the 2022 EPAS (CSWE, 2022, p. 26) (see Chapter 18 for more detail on due process, student rights, and legal protections).

Urwin et al. (2006) provided guidelines for effective gatekeeping approaches that emerged from court cases. Their findings suggest that program directors need to provide written criteria for students to meet academic and behavioral standards, a process for reviewing and evaluating student performance, an opportunity for students to express grievances, and a due process that sets criteria for clear decisions made in good faith. The gatekeeping policy should be applicable at all points of a student's educational career.

If a program does not have a committee of people to review and make decisions regarding ethical violations, then one should be formed (Royse, 2000). The gatekeeping policy and practices should be written and practiced using a strengths-based approach and integrate anti-oppressive practices in the organization. The people within the organization create the culture through their policies and practices (Pender Green et al., 2016). The culture frames how the policy is viewed. Sound gatekeeping policy is meant to guide students to reflect on the profession and their fit into the profession. It should not be viewed as punishment but rather clear and firm guidance. A gatekeeping policy must be thoroughly developed with, and vetted through, the faculty, who must understand it and use it. If they do not believe in the policy or understand its process, they will not use it. The policy also must be enforceable above the department, so the dean of your college, administration, and the university lawyer need to agree with and approve of the policy. College administrators may not be familiar with the need of the profession to protect clients, follow the Code of Ethics, and assess students' academic and professional performance even if they are not yet working in the field.

PRACTICE TIP: To achieve a well-rounded and culturally diverse Gatekeeping Committee, consider adding adjuncts, advisory council members, and other members of the campus community. This is known as intentional inclusivity.

Social work educators need to be able to assess students for competence in ethical behavior without fear they will be accused of discrimination (Lafrance et al., 2004). Policies such as those developed in response to the Americans With Disabilities Act (ADA) can be used as a supportive guide for writing a gatekeeping policy. For instance, the ADA provides protections for "a person who has a physical or mental impairment that substantially limits one or more major life activities, a person who has a history or record of such an impairment, or a person who is perceived by others as having such an impairment" (ADA, 1990, p. 1). Receiving input from the university disabilities services office and general counsel can provide resources for your team as you develop your policy and integrate supportive services for students with disabilities.

Now is a time to remember what was mentioned at the beginning of the chapter, that the faculty members using the gatekeeping policies are still social work educated professionals, whose primary responsibility is to clients, which is clear in the NASW Code of Ethics. When we faculty members review students who are applying to be social work majors, and then monitor their progress as they continue through the program, we have to keep clients in mind. Social work students are a very close secondary concern, but we (faculty and students) must ensure that they are healthy and fit for duty. It does not matter if a student is in recovery from addiction (drugs or alcohol), has a learning disability, or has been diagnosed or treated for any other mental or behavioral issue. If they are to earn a social work degree and practice in the field, those issues need to be addressed and should never negatively affect the care of clients.

The policy must meet the needs of all stakeholders: the students, the program, faculty, field directors, and field supervisors. It needs to have depth and clarity so that it will handle simple to serious issues when they arise, and it needs to have reasonable consequences that are enforceable if they are recommended. An example of a gatekeeping policy is that shared by Monmouth University School of Social Work (2021). Developed by the BSW director and the field director more than a decade ago, it has been revised and vetted through university counsel. We offer it here as a starting point for those who do not have a policy. We welcome you to use it, providing proper credit is given to Monmouth University in your version of the policy.

A gatekeeping model should include a communicated plan of action based on a student-centered team approach. There are several things to consider when developing a gatekeeping policy, and it is best to seek support from the university from the very beginning. Other departments, including student affairs, may have strong models that you can adapt to suit your department's needs.

Here is an outline of sections to include in a gatekeeping policy:

1. Rationale: Define what gatekeeping is and the reasons it is critical for social work education. Refer to the Code of Ethics and the EPAS expectations for ethical, competent practice, and university code of conduct.

2. Committee Composition: Name committee members who will review concerns and act as appropriate.

3. Mission and Goals of the Committee: Provide a clear mission and related goals of the committee. This will give students, parents, field supervisors, and others an understanding of what the committee does.

4. ADA Statement: Include a statement regarding the Americans With Disabilities Act and the university office that helps to implement student accommodations. This statement provides information about the ADA and the steps students need to take to access accommodations.

5. Referral Process: Provide a transparent process and a form for faculty, field supervisors, or students to complete to refer another student to this committee.

6. Review Hearing: Share a step-by-step process about the timeline of events and what will happen during the student hearing meeting. Identify who will be present so all parties know what to expect. At this point in the process, legal counsel is not needed for either side. The hearing is intended to prevent the need for legal counsel.

7. Potential Outcomes: Give clear guidance about what happens after the hearing is over. Provide the student with a written plan about the next steps. The policy includes a list of potential outcomes from "no action" to "dismissed from program." This section offers information on additional support from specific faculty or an advisor, probation and suspension options, and recommending but not requiring counseling.

BSW program directors can use a team approach to develop and implement a gatekeeping policy that communicates clear expectations for ethical, competent practice, as well as to provide a student-centered review process that respects and upholds students' rights simultaneously. Figure 17.1 shows an example of a flowchart of a referral made to the gatekeeping committee. Remember that you are not alone. Seek support in creating or updating the gatekeeping policy for your school, so that you will be able to provide support to all the stakeholders who are important in the education process. Gatekeeping at the beginning of the continuum is a way of practicing our social work values by protecting clients and our profession.

FIGURE 17.1

Flowchart of Referral Process

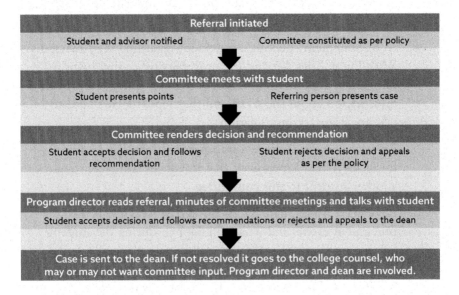

The Gatekeeping Continuum

It is hard to know the best time to begin gatekeeping or when it should occur, as programs have standards (CSWE, 2022) for admissions, advising, evaluation, and termination. The NASW Code of Ethics speaks to this responsibility in the professional standards, ranked in order of importance: We have responsibilities (1) to clients, (2) to colleagues, (3) to the practice setting, (4) as professionals, (5) to the profession, and (6) to the broader society (NASW, 2021). Inherent in those standards is accountability to what seems to be the entire world, but first and most important to our clients. Thus, when we, as social work educators, send a student to an internship, graduate a student, or write a reference letter for a student, we have an ethical imperative to be sure that we can do that easily and without much hesitation because we know the student will adhere to the Code of Ethics. If we keep gatekeeping in the forefront of our minds in each of the touchpoints laid out in the continuum, we can welcome new members of the profession proudly and with certainty that we have done our jobs well.

Although not every program or student will fit the continuum in Box 17.1, this information suggests that assessing for competency is an ongoing process and student advising throughout the program is important. For instance, not all colleges or schools have an MSW program, and some do not let students take any social work classes prior to admission. Likewise, there are several spots along the continuum where students can be reflective and opt out of the major. Each of these points must be clearly communicated and documented for the benefit of both the students and the program.

BOX 17.1

Gatekeeping Continuum

The gatekeeping continuum addresses issues of performance no matter what the cause or when the issues occur. The NASW (2021) Code of Ethics Standard 4.05 addresses the issue of personal impairments and sets the expectation that such impairments must be addressed when they interfere with professional performance. According to NASW (2021), "Impairments include personal problems, psychosocial distress, legal problems, substance abuse, or mental health difficulties that interfere with professional judgment and performance that jeopardize the best interests of the people for whom a social worker has a professional responsibility" (p. 44). The issue of impairment applies equally in social work education, given that the graduates will be future practitioners (Cole & Lewis, 1993). Consider the following case example, which several programs around the country must have faced in one form or another.

CASE EXAMPLE

A student named Jennifer has straight A's, attends every class, and does quite well with the structure and routine of the semester. She is drawn to talk to faculty and shows up for office hours frequently. In those office hours, she shared her mental health history and medication regiment. The university ADA officer strongly supports Jennifer and says she cannot be stopped from being a major because of her self-disclosure of mental health issues. Over summer break, after having gone off her medication, she ends up in the hospital for suicide ideation.

(continued)

The student selects an internship in mental health. Midsemester, you find out that her supervisor is her former social worker, who reports that she is doing well in the internship. What can be done? What is your thought of the dual role that the internship supervisor accepted? Can you trust the supervisor's report of the student's favorable internship performance? Is the supervisor acting as a social worker or an intern supervisor? Do you trust the student not to go off her medication, as you know she has done that during every break in the semester? What do you do about the repeated hospitalizations and the student's stability while in internship? How do the EPAS and the NASW Code of Ethics frame this case?

BSW directors and faculty need to grapple with these scenarios, and there are no right answers, making gatekeeping particularly intricate when using the same policy.

Entry-level courses provide an opportunity for reflection and introspection for students and faculty members because of the ongoing interaction. Whether this is a first-year seminar course or an introductory course on social work, faculty have a chance to get to know the students better. They see written work, interaction with other students, and how the student presents in class. Over the semester, whether in an on-campus, hybrid, or online course, there are opportunities to assess and reflect on each student and help the students self-reflect on the work and values described in the classes and imagine themselves working in settings with the populations as they are covered in the course material.

During this time, some students will self-select out, and others may be sitting on the fence and just need encouragement to think more deliberately about the profession. Faculty can encourage or discourage students in the first-year seminar or introductory course to think about a particular major, keeping in mind that many traditional-aged first-year students come to the university with their family's values and are still developing their social and cognitive skills. Both will change rapidly as they are exposed to different cultures, different values, and independent thinking during their college years. These early touchpoints are useful for recruiting but not necessarily the most essential points in gatekeeping. However, the opportunity does exist to pose the question, "Does this student have the potential to be a good social worker?"

PRACTICE TIPS:
- Discuss gatekeeping regularly in faculty meetings as part of academic advising.
- Provide space for faculty to discuss approaches to student advising in order to create a culture of support when challenges arise.

An important touchpoint is when the student officially applies to the major. Each program has a different process and a different timeline for the official application to meet Educational Policy B4.1.2. Sometimes there is an application, while others interview or ask for letters of reference from other faculty or supervisors. Other programs have a faculty meeting to discuss the applicants. Some programs may utilize all these components for the application to the major.

Yet, regardless of the process, as social work educators, we all want to know the same information. We look for the ability to do the work including, but not limited to, writing for documentation; critically analyzing information; and the ability to engage, assess, intervene, and evaluate at all levels of practice. How will this student work with clients? Is the student capable of handling the rigor of the work, as a student and as a social worker? Will they uphold the values of the profession? These concerns include not only the knowledge, the skills, and the values of the profession, but also the stress and volume of work that we know comes with the profession. In addition, the application to the major is an excellent time to discuss and assess how the student's personal values align with social work values and ethics.

Faculty's last official gatekeeping opportunity is during the all-important senior year internship experience. Some programs have other field experiences in earlier courses, so a field supervisor may have already provided some feedback from observing the student's practice and their capabilities before the student has been officially accepted into the program. However, for many programs, the first feedback from the field is during senior year. Many students are strong in the classroom, but their strength may not be reflected in reports from observation in the field. Vice versa, some students perform marginally in the classroom but are naturals in the field and thrive as practitioners. All of the data we collect about the student from the classroom or the field should be considered academic and professional performance. Some programs try to separate the actions shown in the field as personal, emotional, or behavioral, and they can be labeled as such, but they are still academic. They are part of the curriculum and should be defined as such in student and field handbooks. Think about this case example.

CASE EXAMPLE

During the last week of November, you, the BSW program director, received a frantic email from your student Alex, who is in their senior year of the BSW program. Alex alerted you that they were told by their field placement supervisor that they cannot return to the field site next spring. Upon discussing the

(continued)

situation over the phone, you come to understand that Alex had a rocky start to the semester. Here is what you know from Alex.

They started their field placement late—3 weeks into the semester—and knew they needed to make up time. But because of a packed class schedule and a part-time job during evenings and weekends, Alex continued to be behind during hours. To make matters worse, Alex had to "call out" three times because of car trouble or "personal situations" at home that they did not feel comfortable talking about with their supervisor. They insist that they communicated their schedule changes as soon as they knew—but that it was within 10–15 minutes of the usual start time of their field placement.

They said they got the impression that the supervisor did not like them and that she was not supportive of them because of their nonbinary gender identity. During their first day at the agency, Alex told their supervisor that their preferred pronouns are "they, them." Alex said that their supervisor hesitated in responding, and she said that she was okay with this but not sure how other staff and clients at the agency would receive the information.

Their supervisor told Alex that she was concerned about Alex's commitment to their clients and the agency. They were not as reliable at taking on independent work as the other students who started on time. Alex was shadowing the social worker and given menial projects that did not align with the learning agreement. You hear from the supervisor that she was going to provide Alex with one more chance, but if they missed another day of field, they would be terminated.

Your field director approaches you because Alex's supervisor called to say she can't complete the field evaluation because Alex has not had enough exposure to the work for her to rate their competence. She said Alex will get caught up on hours over winter break, but she also suggests that Alex find a placement that might be a "better fit" for them next semester. The field director suggests this is a "soft termination" and wants to know how to handle it. Does Alex get penalized, fail field, and repeat the course?

As the BSW program director, you realize that Alex has spent most of the semester at an agency that was not providing opportunities for skill development, partly because Alex was unreliable. Is this a student performance problem or an agency problem? Is the student capable of doing the work, or is the supervisor withholding higher-level work to protect the clients? Is Alex facing discrimination, and do they need extra support with transportation or other needs, so they can eliminate barriers to getting field work done? Should they "pass" field seminar for the fall semester?

These are the questions you have, and you cannot answer these questions on your own. You suggest to the field seminar teacher that she submit a referral to a committee of the department that reviews student performance. This group of faculty can collaborate to learn about Alex and their experiences to make a determination about their ability to pass the field seminar and move forward in a new field placement. Conversations should be about the student's capability and the agency's lack of early action and should examine whether there is proof of discrimination based upon the student's gender orientation. How do the Code of Ethics and the EPAS come into support for the student in this situation?

As social work educators, once we have graduated students, we have officially recognized them as qualified entry-level social work professionals. Further gatekeeping opportunities are not the purview of BSW faculty. These graduates will be in MSW programs, employment, and/or the social work licensing process. At this point, we must rely on our peers in MSW programs, employers, and clinical supervisors to do their parts in the process and point out, try to correct, and assign appropriate evaluative criteria for the student or employee for whom they are responsible. Gatekeeping appropriately at the beginning of the continuum can prevent potential problematic behavior or unethical practices to continue or worsen as social work students gain more independence in practice beyond their BSW education.

Roles in the Gatekeeping Continuum

Much of the focus of gatekeeping lands squarely on the program director (Barlow & Coleman, 2003; Currer & Atherton, 2008; Street, 2018). Framing the process along the continuum from a strengths-based approach, where the student's learning and development are prioritized in the educational environment (whether in field placement or classroom), is central to the role of gatekeeping (Street, 2018). However, it is important to use an inclusive model that involves anyone engaged with the student, including other students, if they have witnessed something of concern and inform program faculty of it.

Each BSW program director can develop a diverse and inclusive team based on the program's size and context. Even small programs with just two faculty members can seek support from each other, adjunct faculty, or professional advisors. When considering the response process, this can also include a support person of their choosing for the student of concern to help organize and compose their explanation. The roles of the student, program director, faculty members, field director, and field supervisor are further explained next.

Students

The student's performance is at the center of the process, and the emphasis is on viewing the student as a learner. The student may be at the very beginning of their social work education or may be in their last semester of the program. Regardless, even if the student is screened out of the social work program, they can learn about themselves through the approaches implemented in the gatekeeping process that are congruent with social work values (Street, 2018). From the student's point of view, each opportunity to reflect helps them examine their goodness of fit for the profession they desire. Examples of situations that may need to be addressed through the gatekeeping process include a demonstrated lack of fit with social work's stated values; ethical violations including academic dishonesty, poor communication skills, and active behavioral health issues including substance abuse; and any illegal activity that would preclude the student's ability to meet licensing requirements in their state or be hired in the field.

BSW Program Director

The BSW program director provides students and faculty with guidance and oversight at every point along the continuum from admission to BSW graduation. Depending on the program's size, the BSW director may or may not know the student well and may or may not have had the student in class. Regardless, the program director has the responsibility of knowing what issues arise for the students. Some program directors deal with this by talking about students of concern in regular meetings or by receiving documentation that is generated after negative behavior exhibited by the student.

An example of a supportive review policy can be reviewed in Monmouth's *School of Social Work Handbook* (Monmouth University School of Social Work, 2021). The policy is contained in the student handbook and is carried out by the Student Review Committee. The written policy is given to the students with a referral, which provides transparency and support all the way through the process, from referral to disposition and any corrective action. Students can bring in witnesses to substantiate their versions, and students can submit documentation of the same. Creating an environment where the program director and the faculty can communicate about students of concern (and their witness or other material) in a confidential, respectful way will ensure that students have support and are meeting the expectations for the major.

CASE EXAMPLE

You have an adult student, Samantha, who performs well in class, straight A's. She has exhibited good performance in her internship, and the people at this internship are even talking about hiring her when she completes it. However, a faculty member teaching senior seminar believes that her final work for the class was plagiarized. A quick search reveals that the faculty member is accurate. However, Samantha states that she did not plagiarize and cannot be failed for that because she purchased the paper from another student. She begs not to be terminated from the program as she bought the piece because her husband had COVID, her son needed her support with homeschooling, and she was working more hours at her full-time job. The faculty in the program have mixed emotions; the vote is evenly split, and it is the BSW director's decision on what to do. What are the solutions you can think of, and how do the Code of Ethics and EPAS help here?

Faculty Members

Full- and part-time faculty members who know the students' academic work, classroom behavior, and interpersonal skills play an important role in gatekeeping. The professors know the students best, know the program's criteria for meeting the competencies, and promote ethical standards. Grading students' academic work using rubrics and set criteria can minimize grade inflation or bias (Miller, 2014). Besides grading students accurately and fairly, faculty members—as school stewards—can support or halt a student's progress. Faculty members who teach the Integrative Seminar course or are field liaisons function as connections between the field supervisor and the school and thus can share field supervisor concerns about students' field performance.

CASE EXAMPLE

Stacey is a senior social work major placed in a nursing home. Her field supervisor indicated that Stacey struggled with fulfilling anything but the most basic tasks, such as asking patients if they had signed their bill of rights. The supervisor did not want to hurt the student's feelings and thus had not dealt with this issue. Dr. Jackson was the field liaison who taught the Integrative Seminar. From Stacey's class discussion, Dr. Jackson recognized the concern and spoke to the field supervisor. The three of them were then able to craft a corrective plan to get Stacey on track to fulfill the competencies by graduation.

Field Director

The field director provides orientation, support, and training to field supervisors and field Integrative Seminar professors or faculty field liaisons (if applicable). Depending on the size of the program, the field director may know the students well and may teach the Integrative Seminar classes. The key to this role is that the field director is responsible for supporting all of the stakeholders in field education. They recruit and orient field supervisors, oversee placing students, provide administrative support for field evaluations, and so forth. Though many ethical and professional practice breaches may happen in the field placement, a few of the reasons evaluating field performance is so challenging stem from inconsistency in expectations and understanding of student roles, along with a desire by the field supervisor to have a positive relationship with the program (Bogo et al., 2014; Reamer, 2012). This can lead to uncertainty and conflict about determining when a student's behavior or lack of competency is concerning enough to bring to a review committee. When the program director has good rapport and open communication with field supervisors or liaisons about students of concern, then the field supervisors or liaisons can feel free to share vital details about students' progress without fear of harming their relationship with the university.

Field Supervisor

Social work education places a significant emphasis on students' training through agency-based field experiences. The field supervisor is likely external to the university structure and one of the greatest assets to field education. They provide the student with supervision on behalf of the agency, and they provide educational experiences on behalf of the university. Field supervisors are integral as gatekeepers, as they are directly observing and assessing the student's performance (Molina et al., 2018). Field supervisors must have support and reassurance from the university so that they are able to voice ethical and professional performance concerns without fear of tarnishing the relationship between the field agency site and the university.

Field supervisors are the foremost observers of students in the practice setting as the students engage with clients. The gatekeeping burden falls primarily on them to communicate feedback to the student, the field liaison, and possibly others at the school—especially when problems arise (Ketner et al., 2017). However, field supervisors do not always want the gatekeeper role and can be uncomfortable with feedback and the formal evaluation process. This is a challenge when there are indicators that the student is having difficulty mastering the expected skills or is not displaying appropriate alignments with values and ethics. Rather than respond to what they view as inappropriate behavior, they may suggest that students find a new internship that will be a "better fit." Field directors must orient supervisors from the beginning about their role as gatekeepers and the need for regular, consistent, and honest feedback to the students and involving the field liaison at an early stage with concerns and in written evaluations.

Program faculty and staff need to work together to ensure that agency partners understand the school's expectations. Competency-based education provides standards for practice skills. Learners in the field are required to be competent in what Bogo et al. (2014) described as *complex practice behaviors*, which include the integration of skills; self-regulation of emotions, reflections, and self-awareness; knowledge about the theory that is both generic and specific; and judgment in making sound decisions and using critical thinking skills. Social work students receive a great deal of their education about how to think and behave as social workers through the field education experience with supervision and feedback from their field supervisors. Integrating these deep, transformative learning experiences requires self-reflection (Molina et al., 2018). Student behaviors can be identified in the classroom; however, Gibbs (1994) stated that

> support from field supervisors was the factor most likely to make termination for non-academic reasons possible. This suggests that when a student "slips through the gates" of the academic program, program faculty can count on field supervisors to address issues of un-suitability as demonstrated by the student during hands-on experience in the field. (p. 15)

A reflective field internship experience teaches students how to think like social workers. The field supervisor needs to make explicit for themselves what their personal and professional values are. Then they need to teach the ability to differentiate professional and personal values to the students, so that in the end, the student is making ethically informed decisions. The challenge with this is that the field supervisor shares their implicit beliefs based on their social identities, social work practice experience, and life experiences. Modeling cultural humility and critical self-reflection is key to addressing bias (Charles et al., 2017). Allowing students to reflect in supervision and through process recordings, journaling, or reflective discussions can aid the field supervisor in assessing the student's ability to separate personal and professional values, as well as their thought process and ability to exemplify social work values in action.

To work toward mastery, students need to be able to practice a skill, have the tools to reflect on it, and receive peer or supervisor feedback about the observed practice. Providing feedback about actual observed practice and thus ensuring appropriate gatekeeping can be challenging in an environment where agencies rely on "task" supervisors (who may or may not be social workers) to provide a portion of the hands-on observation and student support. Having an engaged field supervisor to provide meaningful feedback is vital, especially for a student who is struggling with integrating complex practice behaviors. Students learn when they receive immediate, evaluative feedback related to their social work skills and then incorporate that into their progress toward their overall goals and performance. Overall, it is best to give feedback in a collaborative discussion about what to do better and how to think differently about a situation.

Conclusion

Upholding the gatekeeping responsibility of the profession is hard work. As social work educators, we want to support and help students. Yet when students are not meeting the academic and performance standards or ethical principles, the best way to help them is to hold them accountable for their actions, create a behavioral contract, hold up their progress in the program, or dismiss them entirely. Through the use of a strong and clearly written policy and ongoing communication throughout the program with students, faculty, field directors, supervisors, and the university administration, gatekeeping becomes a supportive and protective process for all involved.

Suggested Readings

Holley, L. C., Charles, J. L. K., Kondrat, D. C., & Walter-McCabe, H. Q. (2022). Supports and gatekeeping experiences of schools of social work with students with mental health conditions. *Journal of Social Work Education, 58*(1), 76–95. https://doi.org/10.1080/10437797.2020.1798312

Hylton, M. E., & Messick, S. G. (2017). Gatekeeping and competency-based education: Developing behaviorally specific remediation policies. *Journal of Teaching in Social Work, 37*(3), 249–259. https://doi.org/10.1080/08841233.2017.1313359

Monmouth University School of Social Work. (2021). *School of social work handbook.* https://www.monmouth.edu/school-of-social-work/student-resources/student-handbooks/

Sussman, T., Sacha, B., Richardson, K. B., & Granner, F. (2014). How field instructors judge BSW student readiness for entry-level practice. *Journal of Social Work Education, 50*(1), 84–100. https://doi.org/10.1080/10437797.2014.856233

Tam, D. M. Y., Kwok, S. M., Brown, A., Paz, E., & Birnbaum, R. (2018). Challenges faced by Canadian social work field instructors in baccalaureate field supervision. *Journal of Teaching in Social Work, 38*(4), 398–416. https://doi.org/10.1080/08841233.2018.1502228

References

Americans With Disabilities Act of 1990, 42 U.S.C. § 12101 *et seq.* (1990). https://ada.gov

Barlow, C., & Coleman, H. (2003). Suitability for practice guidelines for students: A survey of Canadian social work programs. *Social Work Education, 22*, 151–164. https://doi.org/10.1080/0261547022000058206

Bogo, M., Rawlings, M., Katz, E., & Logie, C. (2014). *Using simulation in assessment and teaching: OSCE adapted for social work (objective structured clinical examination).* Council on Social Work Education.

Cervero, R. M., & Wilson, A. L. (1994). *Planning responsibly for adult education: A guide to negotiating power and interests.* Jossey-Bass.

Charles, J. L. K., Holley, L. C., & Kondrat, D. C. (2017). Addressing our own biases: Social work educators' experiences with students with mental illnesses. *Social Work Education, 36*(4), 414–429.

Cole, B. S., & Lewis, R. G. (1993). Gatekeeping through termination of unsuitable social work students: Legal issues and guidelines. *Journal of Social Work Education, 29*, 150–160.

Council on Social Work Education. (2022). *Educational policy and accreditation standards for baccalaureate and master's social work programs.* https://www.cswe.org/accreditation/standards/2022-epas/

Currer, C., & Atherton, K. (2008). Suitable to remain a student social worker? Decision making in relation to termination of training. *Social Work Education, 27*(3), 279–292.

Elpers, K., & FitzGerald, E. A. (2013). Issues and challenges in gatekeeping: A framework for implementation. *Social Work Education, 32*(3), 286–300. https://doi.org/10.1080/02615479.2012.665867

Gibbs, P. (1994). Screening mechanisms in BSW programs. *Journal of Social Work Education, 30*(1), 63–74.

Ketner, M., VanCleave, D., & Cooper-Bolinskey, D. (2017). The meaning and value of supervision in social work field education. *Field Educator, 7*(2), https://fieldeducator.simmons.edu/article/the-meaning-and-value-of-supervision-in-social-work-field-education/

Lafrance, J., Gray, E., & Herbert, M. (2004). Gatekeeping for professional social work practice. *Social Work Education, 23*, 325–340.

Madden, R. G. (2000). Creating a bridging environment: The screening-in process in BSW programs. In P. Gibbs & E. H. Blakely (Eds.), *Gatekeeping in BSW programs* (pp. 135–148). Columbia University Press.

Martin, E. M., & Ciarfella, T. M. (2015). The devil is in the details: A content analysis of field manuals. *Field Educator, 5*(2). https://fieldeducator.simmons.edu/article-tags/cswe-epas/

Miller, G. (2014). Grade inflation, gatekeeping, and social work education: Ethics and perils. *Journal of Social Work Values and Ethics, 11*(1), 12–22.

Miller, J., & Koerin, B. (2001). Gatekeeping in the practicum: What field instructors need to know. *The Clinical Supervisor, 20*(2), 1–18.

Molina, V., Molina-Moore, T., Smith, M. G., & Pratt, F. E. (2018). Building education and practice with a competency-based learning contract. *Journal of Teaching in Social Work, 38*(1), 18–27.

Monmouth University School of Social Work. (2021). *School of social work handbook.* https://www.monmouth.edu/school-of-social-work/student-resources/student-handbooks/

National Association of Social Workers. (2021). *Code of ethics of the National Association of Social Workers.* https://www.socialworkers.org/About/Ethics/Code-of-Ethics/Code-of-Ethics-English

Oxford University Press. (2020). Suitability. In *Oxford learner's dictionaries.* https://www.oxfordlearnersdictionaries.com/us/definition/english/suitability

Pender Green, M., Bernabei, S., & Blitz, L. (2016, Summer). Achieving racial equity through social work: Gatekeeping and manifestations of racism. *The New Social Worker.* https://www.socialworker.com/feature-articles/practice/gatekeeping-and-manifestations-of-racism/

Reamer, F. G. (2012). Essential ethics education in social work field instruction: A blueprint for field educators. *Field Educator, 2*(2), 1–15.

Royse, D. (2000). The ethics of gatekeeping. In P. Gibbs & Blakely E. (Eds.), *Gatekeeping in BSW programs* (pp. 22–44). Columbia University Press. https://doi.org/10.7312/gibb11050

Sowbel, L. R. (2011). Field note: Gatekeeping in field performance: Is grade inflation a given? *Journal of Social Work Education, 47*(2), 367–377.

Sowbel, L. R. (2012). Gatekeeping: Why shouldn't we be ambivalent? *Journal of Social Work Education, 48*(1), 27–44. https://doi.org/10.5175/JSWE.2012.201000027

Sowbel, L. R., & Miller, S. E. (2015). Gatekeeping in graduate social work education: Should personality traits be considered? *Social Work Education, 34*(1), 110–124. https://doi.org/10.1080/02615479.2014.953046

Steinke, P., & Fitch, P. (2017). Minimizing bias when assessing student work. *Research and Practice in Assessment, 12*(2), 87–95.

Street, L. A. (2018). Selective BSW admission: Experiences and expectations of students and alumni. *Journal of Baccalaureate Social Work, 23*(1), 123–143. https://doi.org/10.18084/1084-7219.23.1.123

Street, L. A., MacGregor, C. J., & Cornelius-White, J. H. (2019). A stakeholder analysis of admission in a baccalaureate social work program. *Journal of Social Work Education, 55*(1), 34–49. https://doi.org/10.1080/10437797.2018.1513877

Tam, D. M., & Coleman, H. (2011). Validation study of a gatekeeping attitude index for social work education. *Journal of Teaching in Social Work, 31*, 505–522. https://doi.org/10.1080/08841233.2011.615259

Todd, S., Asakura, K., Morris, B., Eagle, B., & Park, G. (2019). Responding to student mental health concerns in social work education: Reflection questions for social work educators. *Social Work Education, 38*(6), 779–796. https://doi.org/10.1080/02615479.2018.1556591

Urwin, C. A., Van Soest, D., & Kretzschmar, J. A. (2006). Key principles for developing gatekeeping standards for working with students with problems. *Journal of Teaching in Social Work, 26*(1/2), 163–180. https://doi.org/10.1300/J067v26n01_10

CHAPTER 18

Student Rights and Legal Protections

Kathryn S. Krase

Any discussion of the rights and protections afforded to students in the United States should flow from this important quote from the U.S. Supreme Court decision in the case of *Tinker v. Des Moines Independent Community School District* (1969): "It can hardly be argued that either students or teachers shed their constitutional rights to freedom of speech or expression at the schoolhouse gate."

In *Tinker,* a junior high school student in Iowa in 1965, Mary Beth Tinker, sought to enforce her First Amendment right to protest U.S. involvement in the Vietnam War while in school, by wearing a black armband. In the *Tinker* decision, a seven-justice majority of the U.S. Supreme Court concluded that students, even minors, have fundamental rights, including First Amendment rights, that cannot be infringed upon by their schools. The *Tinker* case is the first in a series of Court decisions related to the rights of students. Additional laws, most often in the form of major federal legislation and executive orders, have provided the framework that ultimately guarantees students of all ages equal protection and rights to due process.

The Basics: Constitutional Rights to Due Process and Equal Protection

Due Process

You have likely heard the term *due process* before, probably in a courtroom and/or police-related drama you can stream on a subscription service or watch late at night on cable. However, you might not have considered *due process* as a term directly relevant to your role as a social work program administrator. This term is *very* relevant to much of what you do as a program administrator, so you need to understand it.

Due process is found twice in the U.S. Constitution (1789). Both the Fifth and Fourteenth Amendments of the Constitution make clear that the government cannot deprive anyone of "life, liberty or property without providing due process of law." In the context of government responsibility, the Constitution guarantees that the government cannot charge someone a fee or restrict their rights (e.g., incarcerate them, limit their movement) without providing a process through which the person can challenge the government's action. For instance, the government can issue me a parking ticket and demand that I pay money for my infraction, but it must also provide me the opportunity to challenge the ticket as unfair or unjust. This challenge must be overseen by a neutral arbiter (e.g., a hearing officer), who is tasked with determining the outcome of the challenge.

Public colleges and universities are considered government actors. Thus, if you are the administrator of an undergraduate social work program at a public college or university, you need to ensure that your program does not deprive a student of any benefit they receive as part of the program without providing due process. This means that if you are removing a student from a field placement against their wishes, you need to provide due process for them to challenge the decision. If you are terminating a student from the program, you must provide due process to challenge the decision, consistent with Accreditation Standard 4.1.7 of the Educational Policy and Accreditation Standards (EPAS) (Council on Social Work Education [CSWE], 2022). If you are giving a student a grade they do not think they deserve, you must provide due process for them to challenge the decision.

Due process in these contexts should generally require a written declaration by the student of their challenge to the program's decision and a clearly outlined procedure through which the challenge will be considered, by whom the challenge will be considered, and the timeline through which a decision will be provided. All of these procedures should be clearly outlined in any student handbook and/or field education manual. These policies should ideally be approved by upper administration and/or university counsel or lawyers before being distributed to students.

What if you teach at a private college or university? Does that mean that you do not have to consider, or provide, due process? Not so fast!

The relationship between a student and a private college or university is, generally, governed by contract law. The contract between a student and the school includes all written policies and procedures provided, or made available, to students, including student handbooks and field manuals. CSWE (2022) requires accredited programs to include various policies in their student handbooks and field manuals, and to include such manuals in their initial accreditation and reaffirmation of accreditation self-study process. If a student were to sue a social work program for failing to provide them due process, they would need to show that the school did not follow its own procedures. So, make sure you get your student handbooks and field manuals approved by upper administration and/or university counsel or lawyers, *and* make sure you follow those procedures carefully and apply the procedures equally to all students.

CASE EXAMPLE

An undergraduate social work student contacts you, as program director, by email days after the spring semester ends. They are very upset about the grade they received in their Social Work Research class: a B–. The student is sure that this grade will make them unable to earn admission, with advanced standing, to the master's in social work program that they have their heart set on attending. They are begging you to talk to their faculty member and have their grade adjusted to at least a B. They are even willing to do extra credit to get their grade up, but their faculty member has not responded to their email correspondence in the past 24 hours requesting the same. What should you do to ensure due process?

ANSWER

Check your university and program policies related to challenging a course grade. Such a policy would likely require the student to outline their case to adjust their course grade in writing to their course instructor. (Please note that the requirement for correspondence "in writing" is generally considered to be met through email. However, program administration, in particular, should make a regular practice of sending correspondence of import, like denials of appeals, by both email and the U.S. Postal Service). If the student does not receive the answer they were hoping for from the faculty member, in writing, the policy should outline to whom they could appeal that determination.

Program administrators should make clear that they cannot replace, or overturn, the grading decision of a faculty member. Due process guarantees that students are given the opportunity to challenge inaccurate grading or inappropriate application of a grading policy. However, an appeals process cannot substitute academic judgment afforded to individual faculty when they are assigned their courses. Program administrators should pay special attention to avoid any situation where they might later be accused of differential treatment.

PRACTICE TIP: If an administrator gives a benefit to one student that is not provided for in written policy, they are opening up the door to later claims for the same treatment by future students. Remind students about the admissions requirements of various programs for advanced standing and that final grades are determined through student achievement according to the policies of the course syllabus.

Equal Protection

The Equal Protection Clause of the Fourteenth Amendment of the Constitution prohibits the government from denying to individuals "equal protection of the laws." Generally speaking, the Equal Protection Clause has been interpreted to mean that the government, including institutions of public education (including public colleges and universities), cannot treat members of different racial or ethnic backgrounds and other protected classes differently unless the discriminatory action is necessary to achieve what is called "a compelling government purpose," as in the case of affirmative action.

The Civil Rights Act (1964) was used to extend this prohibition to private colleges and universities. Title VI of the Civil Rights Act prohibits discrimination on the basis of race in public accommodations, federally funded programs, and employment. The "federally funded programs" clause makes the law applicable to almost all colleges and universities, because most receive some sort of federal funding in the form of grants. A decision by the Supreme Court (*Grove City College v. Bell*, 1984) clarified this connection further by finding that even institutions receiving no direct federal aid may be subject to the clause, if they have a significant proportion of students who receive federal financial aid, including subsidized loans. Because of the increasing dependence of students on these loans, it would be hard to find an institution of higher education that does not have a significant proportion of their students who receive federal financial aid or participate in the subsidized federal loan programs. Protection from discrimination in employment decisions on the basis of race, color, religion, sex, and national origin is provided in Title XII of the Civil Rights Act.

CASE EXAMPLE

As the new program director for an undergraduate social work program, you start reviewing the past few years of admissions practices. You realize that a higher proportion of applicants of color (specifically Black and Hispanic/Latinx students) have not been accepted, as compared with White students. You are concerned that your program's admissions policies might not have been applied equally across groups. What should you do?

ANSWER

First, you should review the policies and procedures that have been outlined in the student handbook and other materials shared with applicants and students. Note any requirements that might be differentially experienced by students of color as compared with White students. As social work program administrators, it is imperative for us to consider the true role as gatekeepers to our profession and question if our practices have been intentionally, or unintentionally, keeping certain students from accessing our field. This is not just a legal imperative as per law but also a professional ethical imperative.

PRACTICE TIP: Perhaps, upon examination, you find that the writing samples provided by White students are perceived, on average, as higher quality than those of students of color. If so, you should revisit how these appraisals were determined. Make sure there is a uniform set of criteria used to evaluate writing samples. Consider what considerations are made, such as what is deemed important. Consider how grades are, in general, considered in your application process. Perhaps you could provide students an opportunity to explain their grades. For instance, what if a student explains that they are putting themselves through school while working full-time and supporting their family?

Sex/Gender Discrimination and Rights of Transgender and Nonbinary Students

Student protections from gender discrimination largely come from a different area of federal law: Title IX of the Education Amendments Act (1972) specifically protects students against sex discrimination, sexual assault, and sexual violence. Section 1681(a) of Title IX states:

> No person in the United States shall, on the basis of sex, be excluded from participation in, be denied the benefits of, or be subjected to discrimination under any education program or activity receiving federal financial assistance.

Those familiar with Title IX know the provision in relation to providing women with equal opportunity to sports in college. But the provision was originally enacted to ensure that women would receive equal treatment in regard to many education-related activities by prohibiting discrimination based on sex by educational institutions or programs receiving federal funding. Title IX applies to all schools receiving federal funds, whether public or private. Title IX has been interpreted through Court decisions and guidance from policies set forth by the U.S. Department of Education to include a wide range of issues such as sexual harassment; sex-related violence; sexual preference discrimination; transgender discrimination; discrimination due to pregnancy, parenting, or marital status; and more. Title IX protections have been found to apply across the scope of higher education decisions, include recruitment, admissions, housing, field of study (e.g., the STEM fields: science, technology, engineering, and mathematics), and many others.

All students should be safe from harassment and violence. However, students who identify as female and/or LGBTQ+ are more likely to be victimized, especially in educational settings (Kann et al., 2018). Sexual harassment is generally defined as "unwelcome conduct of a sexual nature" (Equal Employment Opportunity Commission [EEOC], n.d.). The term *sexual harassment* includes not only all forms of sexual assault and violence but also aggressive acts through written statements, verbal acts, cyberbullying, unwanted advances, sexual touching, spreading sexual rumors, stalking, voyeurism, exhibitionism, and physical threats (EEOC, n.d.). The perpetrator could include school officials, faculty and program staff, clients and staff at field placement, as well as fellow students and peers. Courts have confirmed an obligation of institutions of higher education to protect students from sexual harassment regardless of who is the perpetrator (U.S. Department of Education, 1997).

The administration under President Donald Trump intended to roll back a number of protections afforded to transgender students through executive actions. In response, the Supreme Court confirmed some employment rights for transgender people through a 2020 Court case, *Bostock v. Clayton County* (2020). This decision signaled that similar rights should be similarly protected in other aspects of law, including education. President Joe Biden used his authority under executive order, in the early days of his term in 2021, to ensure that the rights of LGBTQ+ students are protected under federal law.

While federal law applies most broadly across all states, it is also generally most conservative about protecting the rights of historically oppressed groups. Social work program administrators should become familiar with state and local statutes, such as antibullying and antidiscrimination laws that may apply. For instance, a growing number of states and the District of Columbia have laws in place prohibiting discrimination based on sexual orientation or gender identity (Warbelow et al., 2020).

As a general rule, your program should take extra care to avoid differential treatment of students on the basis of race, color, religion, sex, ability, and national origin, or even the appearance of differential treatment, unless there is a compelling interest that would justify the difference. In Standard 3.0 of the 2015 edition of EPAS (CSWE, 2015), programs were held responsible for ensuring that diversity of student identity is valued and respected. CSWE's 2022 EPAS expanded this responsibility, requiring attention to anti-racism, equity, and inclusion, as well as diversity. Social work programs must work diligently to ensure that equal protection rights of students are enforced in the classroom and in the field.

CASE EXAMPLE

A faculty member reports to you that they recently reached out to a student who missed a number of classes, including a graded assignment. The student reported to the faculty member that they were pregnant and experiencing severe morning sickness. The faculty member is seeking guidance on whether the student's absences and missing assignment should be excused. You later realize that the student is likely to deliver during the subsequent semester, when they are in field placement. How can you support this student?

There was a time when female college students were expected, if not required, to postpone their studies if they became pregnant. Thankfully, this is no longer the standard. However, there remain logistical and legal implications of the rights of pregnant students that need to be understood by program directors.

Students are protected against pregnancy-related discrimination by federal law, including Title IX and the Pregnancy Discrimination Act. In order for students to be protected by these laws, the pregnancy must be reported to the college or university. In the case described previously, the student's absences due to morning sickness, or other pregnancy-related conditions, could be excused, and they could receive the opportunity to replace the missed assignment without penalty. Although the professor and/or program could require the student to submit documentation from a medical professional that confirms pregnancy-related conditions resulted in the missed classes and assignment, such communication does not need to be required by the faculty or program to provide the accommodation to the student.

Many universities have a Title IX office responsible for coordinating communications of this nature. However, if not, the program director should communicate directly with the student to ensure that the student is aware of their rights and work with the student to make a plan that supports student success and accommodates the realities that pregnancy and parenting may require.

> **PRACTICE TIP:** Student manuals, handbooks, and syllabi should highlight the rights of students, including freedom from discrimination and harassment. These program policies should also provide guidance on the procedures necessary for students to bring concerns about discrimination and harassment to the appropriate authorities.

Contract Law in Social Work Education

There are not many law students who report admiration for their required first-year contract law course, but law school graduates often acknowledge that this course made them acutely aware of how contracts, explicit and implicit, surround them in their everyday lives. As social workers, we learn about contracts, too. We learn about contracting with clients in our practice classes. Through the contracting phase with clients, we, as social workers, work to clarify the issues our clients want to address, set goals for treatment or services, and make plans to achieve those goals (Nelken, 1987). Through our social work practice, sometimes we write these goals and plans down on paper; sometimes we just discuss them verbally. It is the same with legal contracts; some are written, and others are discussed, but not written; and others are implied (Nelken, 1987).

In social work programs, as social work educators, we often work with contracts without even realizing that is what we are doing. A contract does not have to be signed by two parties to be a contract. Anytime we write down our program policies and procedures, such as in a handbook or manual, and even through our course syllabi, we are essentially authoring a contract. We are telling students: If you choose our program or take this course, these are the policies and procedures to which you are agreeing.

When students implicitly agree to be subject to this contract of policy and procedures, we are now bound to follow those policies and procedures. When we do not follow the policies and procedures we have outlined through our handbooks, manuals, syllabi, and websites, we can be held accountable for breaching the contractual terms.

For instance, when we outline admissions procedures on our websites and in our student handbooks, we need to follow them. When we outline in our field manuals the processes for removing a student from field placement because of concerns regarding quality of work, professionalism, and the like, we need to follow them. When we provide in the syllabus a breakdown of what percentage of a student's final course grade comes from the grade of each individual assignment, we need to use that formula to calculate the final course grade. If we do not, we open up the program and the college or university to legal liability.

CASE EXAMPLE

Continuing from the due process case example, the same student contacts you about their interest in appealing their grade in their Research Course. This time, the student clearly follows the process outlined in the student handbook, outlining in writing (via email) to the faculty member that they believe the faculty member incorrectly calculated their grade for the course. The faculty member responds to the student, denying the request for a change in their grade because the student performed poorly on a series of pop quizzes. In the student's written appeal to you, as appropriate to the process outlined in your program's student manual, they explain that the pop quizzes were not included in the syllabus provided to students at the beginning of the semester. The student provides a copy of the syllabus that confirms that the pop quizzes were not included on the original breakdown of assignments that make up the final grade for the course. What do you do?

ANSWER

The student's analysis of the syllabus as a contract is correct. The pop quizzes were not outlined in the syllabus and thus can be considered ungraded assignments, at best. The faculty member should recalculate the grade based on the original syllabus and correct the student's final grade, accordingly.

Rights of Students With Disabilities in Higher Education

The Code of Ethics of the National Association of Social Workers (NASW, 2017) outlines the core values of social workers, including "dignity and worth of the person." There are various sections of the Code that refer to special responsibilities of social workers to ensure the rights of people with disabilities. People with disabilities have the right to access an education at all levels. The term *disabilities* includes physical disabilities (e.g., visual impairments, hearing impairments, orthopedic impairments or limitations of physical condition), as well as specific and nonspecific learning disabilities, autism spectrum disorders, speech and language impairments, and emotional disturbance, among other categories. There are various federal laws that apply to the rights of students with disabilities, which are outlined in the following sections.

IDEA

The Individuals With Disabilities Education Act (IDEA) is a federal law, originally passed in 1975 as the Education for All Handicapped Children Act. IDEA established the right of children with disabilities to a free and appropriate public education (FAPE). IDEA provided the regulations and related funding for states to develop programs in public schools to meet the educationally related needs of children from ages 3 to 21 (Congressional Research Service, 2019).

Families of children with disabilities in preschool, elementary, and secondary schools are likely quite familiar with the concept of FAPE and the benefits and services afforded them through IDEA. However, IDEA does not apply to the rights of students with disabilities in higher education. Federal law provides protections that are similar, but not identical, to IDEA for students with disabilities in higher education through Title II of the Americans With Disabilities Act (ADA, 1990) and Section 504 of the Rehabilitation Act of 1973.

ADA, Title II

Title II of the Americans With Disabilities Act (ADA, 1990) prohibits state and local government entities, including public institutions of higher education, from discriminating against "qualified individuals with disabilities" in the programs, services, and activities provided by those entities. Title II of the ADA does not apply to private colleges and universities. The ADA, in general, is widely known for requirements to provide physical access to spaces for people with disabilities, like requiring ramp access. However, in the context of educational entities covered by the ADA, the law requires equality of "access" beyond the physical. For instance, students with visual or hearing impairments would need to be provided accommodation necessary to access readings or lecture content, respectively.

Rehabilitation Act of 1973, Section 504

Section 504 of the Rehabilitation Act of 1973 is a civil rights law that prohibits discrimination in the participation in programs and activities of students with a physical or mental disability by educational institutions receiving federal funding or other federal assistance. Section 504 requires most private and all public colleges and universities to make the "appropriate academic adjustments" or accommodations necessary to ensure the equal opportunity of students with disabilities to participate in a school's programs. Some private colleges and universities are exempt from this act because they do not accept federal funding or other federal assistance.

Possible accommodations that should be provided to students with disabilities include textbooks with large format text or braille; note-taking services; computer-aided instruction; schedule accommodation; substitution of nonessential courses to complete degree requirements; audio/video recording of classes; extra time to complete tests or assignments; and physical modifications of classrooms, campus housing, and other campus facilities to accommodate physical and mental health disabilities. In some cases, an institution can challenge an accommodation based on the "undue financial burden" that would be caused by such accommodation (Section 504, Nondiscrimination on the Basis of Handicap, 45 C.F.R. §§ 84.31-39, 41-47, 1998).

Accessing Rights to Accommodation for Students With Disabilities

Although federal law protects the rights of students with disabilities through antidiscrimination protections and accommodation requirements, students with disabilities must identify as such to receive these protections. As a result, each institution of higher education should have an office and an officer or administrator responsible for helping students with disabilities register their disabilities and determine appropriate accommodations.

Social work programs should work diligently to ensure that the rights of students with disabilities are protected in the classroom and in the field. Student manuals, handbooks, and syllabi should highlight the rights of students with disabilities, including freedom from discrimination and the right to accommodations. These program policies should also provide guidance on the procedures necessary for students to access educational accommodations through campus services.

CASE EXAMPLE

As you are reviewing applications for your undergraduate social work program, you find an applicant whose personal statement describes the challenges in their life experiences as a deaf person who uses American Sign Language (ASL). While you are impressed by the student's academic achievement and commitment to the values of the social work profession, you are unclear about whether your program will be able to meet the needs of this student in the classroom and concerned you will not be able to find a field placement for the student. What should you do?

ANSWER

Assuming that your institution is covered by Section 504, you cannot discriminate against the student on the basis of their hearing impairment. If they meet the admissions requirements that are applied to all other applicants, then you must admit them to the program. The responsibility to provide classroom accommodations is on the program and the institution at large. You should communicate with the appropriate officer or administrator at your institution who handles educational accommodations. They will likely be able to coordinate for ASL interpreters to be at classroom sessions. They will also be able to help you brainstorm field placement opportunities for the student that either have existing accommodations to meet the needs of the student or would be able to provide new accommodations without undue financial burden.

If your institution of higher education is not covered by the requirements of Section 504, the values and ethics of the social work profession would implore you to work with your institution anyway to provide the accommodations necessary to support the matriculation and successful program completion of this student in your program.

Student Privacy in Higher Education

In the days of social media and oversharing, it might seem like everyone has lost their right to privacy, but that is simply not true. Students, in particular, have rights to privacy embedded in federal law. Social work program administrators must understand the laws, namely, the Health Insurance Portability and Accountability Act (HIPAA, 1996) and Family Educational Rights and Privacy Act (FERPA, 1974), and the regulations pertinent to your role as program director and educator.

HIPAA

Everyone who has ever gone to a doctor's appointment in the United States in the past 30 years has heard about HIPAA (1996), but many people do not really know when HIPAA applies. HIPAA covers the confidentiality and protection of patient medical records. HIPAA gives patients the right to exert a level of control over when and how their health information is shared and for what purposes.

As social workers, we are acutely aware of HIPAA, largely because many of us work for entities that are explicitly covered by the law (e.g., hospitals and mental health clinics). Therefore, when we consider concerns related to confidentiality, we often might consider HIPAA first, but does HIPAA apply to our work in institutions of higher education? The general answer is no, but sometimes maybe.

Generally, HIPAA does not apply to institutions of higher education because they are not included in the list of HIPAA-covered entities. However, there are some situations where an institution of higher education can be a covered entity. When an institution of higher education provides physical, sexual, or mental health care services to students, then HIPAA applies to the students' medical records. Such medical records should be kept separate from students' educational records. HIPAA protections do not apply to situations related to student educational records. The protections of student educational records are covered by FERPA.

The right to privacy per HIPAA likely does not apply to students in a social work program in classroom or field education, because HIPAA relates to medical records. However, the HIPAA privacy rights of the clients of social work faculty and social work student interns are covered by HIPAA, both in the classroom and through student field education. Students and faculty who hold confidential client/patient information through their service (paid or volunteer) to a HIPAA-covered entity should ensure that they keep that information confidential. HIPAA, however, does not necessarily stop a student or faculty member from sharing their client experiences for educational purposes.

Confidentiality means that information about clients cannot be shared in an identifiable way. Real client names should never be used in the classroom, course materials, or student assignments. Although it may be legal to share identifiable information with client permission secured, that is not advisable.

Confidentiality allows the sharing of client information (e.g., some case facts, presenting problems) as long as the information does not allow for identification of the client in any way. For instance, to help maintain confidentiality, clients should be given pseudonyms when information about client experiences is shared for educational purposes. However, faculty and students should still limit the amount of information about the client, so that the client cannot be identified by their unique characteristics or presenting problems.

FERPA

FERPA (1974) is a federal law enacted to protect the privacy of students' educational records. The law applies to all schools, from preschool through graduate and professional programs, that receive funds under an applicable program of the U.S. Department of Education. As discussed in the "Equal Protection" section earlier, this means that all institutions of higher education, public and private, should be considered to fall under the requirements of FERPA.

FERPA focuses on the rights of parents to have access to their minor children's educational records. These rights transfer from the parents to the student when the student reaches the age of 18 or graduates from high school. When a student turns 18, their parents *no longer* have a right to access the student's educational records. Parents can access their adult child's educational records only if the adult child provides a release to the educational institution for that purpose, or if the parent assumes decision-making rights over the adult child through guardianship proceedings. The second scenario usually occurs when the child has a cognitive or psychological condition that impairs their ability to make sound decisions for themselves, either permanently or temporarily.

FERPA provides that students of an institution of higher education have the right to inspect and review their educational records maintained by the school. Materials included in the concept of educational records include grades, disciplinary records, class schedules, transcripts, and contact information. Schools are not required to provide copies of records unless, for reasons such as great distance, it is impossible for the student (or parents, when they have appropriate permission) to review the records. Whenever a school is providing actual copies, they may charge a reasonable fee for the service. Therefore, schools are allowed to charge a fee to process transcript requests, even when done electronically, for the purposes of graduate school admissions processes.

FERPA gives students of an institution of higher education the right to request that the school correct records that they believe to be inaccurate or misleading. If the school decides not to amend the record, the student then has the due process right to a formal hearing. After the hearing, if the school still decides not to amend the record, the student has the right to place a statement within the educational record with their own view about the contested information.

Generally, institutions of higher education must have written permission from the student to release any information from the student's educational record. However, FERPA allows schools to disclose certain records, without consent, in certain situations. Most of the situations involve reporting to internal and external educational authorities, including financial aid agencies and accrediting bodies. Faculty and staff of the same social work program can share protected student information among themselves to meet the needs of the program. For instance, during a meeting of program faculty and staff, someone can raise concerns about a particular student with other members of the faculty and staff to seek guidance or to determine if similar concerns are arising in other situations.

Social work program directors should also know that they can release student educational records without permission to comply with an order issued by a judge or a lawfully issued subpoena. Social work programs can also disclose student educational records in defense of themselves during a legal proceeding brought about by the student. If a program is seeking to determine if a field placement can accommodate a student with a particular disability, it is advisable to talk to the agency about accommodations without providing identifiable student information or to ask permission from the student to disclose their disability information to the extent necessary to ensure a placement that can accommodate their needs.

Student Privacy in the 21st Century

HIPAA and FERPA are the major federal laws that relate to student privacy, but they were both designed to meet the needs of late-20th-century health care and educational systems. Privacy issues are more complex than they were in the past, even just 5–10 years ago. FERPA became law when information transfers mainly happened in person or by mail. When HIPAA was passed, the major electronic means of sharing patient information was the fax machine. Fast-forward 25 years, and information travels via email, text/SMS (short message service), and other forms of electronic file sharing through apps (applications) and websites. Undergraduate social work program directors need to consider the privacy consequences of the use of the latest forms of technology to share student information.

Email is a regular business function for all members of our college and university communities. We use email to communicate between individuals and among groups about things we used to use the telephone for, as well as many in-person negotiations. We schedule meetings, share documents, make plans, and talk about our professional lives, all over email. The important questions are: When is sharing over email inappropriate? Unethical? Illegal?

FERPA-protected information, especially grades, grade point averages, social security numbers, and/or transcripts should *never* be sent by email without student permission. Email, unless sent through encrypted services, is not considered a secure method of communication. If a student asks for their transcript information or other FERPA information to be sent to them over email, you should confirm with them that they are giving you permission to release their information to them through this means.

Email can be used to communicate with students about their general status in a program. You can feel comfortable, generally, recognizing exemplary student achievement through email communication, both individually to the student, and/or including other members of the school community on the message. When communicating with students about concerning behavior or failure to meet program standards, an initial email is appropriate, but full discussion of a concern should be done by phone, by videoconference, or in person when possible.

In cases where a student's concerning behavior or academic challenges become the subject of disciplinary proceedings, the findings of such a process can be sent by email but should also be sent by regular USPS mail. While email can provide a digital record of sending and receipt, the legal standard for communication has long been the use of USPS because of its legal protections against tampering. If a student has a school address versus a home address, the sender should make sure to send the mail to the appropriate address based on the timing of the communication. In cases where the sender is unsure where the student is residing, sending the correspondence to both addresses would be appropriate.

Communicating with colleagues about student conduct can be done through email initially, but telephone communication or an in-person meeting is preferred. Email communication can be effectively used to summarize phone conversations for the purpose of creating a record, but make sure to not share FERPA-protected student information in email communications with colleagues.

Texting is a newer technology used for communication between individuals and groups. It involves sending information over cellular phone signals. This technology does not provide secure connection between two parties. For instance, the content of your texts is technically being shared with your service provider. So, you are not really communicating directly and privately with the person you are messaging. A safer method for communicating through text messages is to use a service that encrypts your messages, such as WhatsApp. However, even when using more secure methods of texting, FERPA-protected student information should never be shared.

Social media is a more complicated form of communication, bringing a special set of concerns related to privacy and confidentiality. Social media includes current applications such as Facebook, Twitter, Instagram, SnapChat, and TikTok, and new services are created every year. Social media is successful as a form of sharing information, though the veracity of the information is not always guaranteed. Although there are some forms of control over who gets to access the information you share on some forms of social media, FERPA-protected student information should never be shared through social media.

Many people use social media to express their feelings about events in their life: They share great news through social media, and they also complain through social media. What should be shared about work or school over social media? A good general rule would be to share nothing! However, some sharing is not necessarily problematic. General praise for situations, or even for nonspecific students, is generally acceptable over social media and does not present a conflict with FERPA. General complaints about one's work or annoying situations in employment that do not involve the sharing of identifiable information might not be counter to FERPA, but should be avoided whenever possible.

CASE EXAMPLE

You are an undergraduate social work program director; one of your students emails you to express concern about what another student in the program is sharing over social media. The student reports that the other student has been complaining about one of your faculty members, saying that the faculty member isn't fair in their grading and that their lectures are boring. The student also reports that the other student has been making fun of one of their clients from the fieldwork placement. How should you respond?

ANSWER

Call the student who emailed you on the telephone, and schedule a time for a videoconference or to meet in person as soon as possible. Avoid communicating with this student about another student over email. That would be a direct FERPA violation on your part. The student sharing information with you is *not* violating FERPA by communicating with you over email. The student does not have an obligation to the other student covered by FERPA. The student in question's troubling behavior of sharing disparaging information about program

(continued)

faculty does not violate FERPA or HIPAA, but it *does* violate professional norms and ethical standards. The student-in-question's troubling behavior of making fun of their client on social media might also implicate HIPAA, if they included any potentially identifiable information about their client in their posts.

Ideally, your program's student manual includes a policy that outlines the obligation of all students to maintain professional norms and ethical standards, as provided in the NASW Code of Ethics. This student manual should also provide guidance on the appropriate use of social media and other forms of communication. Clearly, what is reported, if true, would be a violation of such norms. The student's behavior should be reviewed by a committee brought together for the purpose of determining how to respond to the situation.

Possible repercussions for this behavior include (1) issuing a letter of reprimand outlining what the student did wrong and clarifying expectations for future behavior, (2) placing the student on a probationary status that requires subsequent reviews of their professional behavior at a higher level of inspection than provided to other students, and (3) terminating the student from the program. The final option of termination from the program should only be considered as a last resort, reserved for cases in which a student does not accept responsibility for their behavior and seems incapable of changing their behavior. Regardless of which of the outcomes is chosen by the committee, it is essential that the process arrives at a decision that is transparent, provides the student with the ability to respond to the accusations against them, and allows for an appeal to an additional decision maker of a higher authority, whose role is to ensure that appropriate due process was provided and not to reevaluate the information already considered by the committee.

Conclusion

This chapter outlines students' rights and the responsibilities of institutions of higher education to protect those rights. This information was presented in such a way that would be most helpful to undergraduate social work program directors, but the legal doctrines and relevant federal law do not apply equally to all programs in institutions of higher education. Social work program directors, however, have a special obligation to support social and racial justice. Please keep these ethical values in mind when applying your authority in your role as social work program director.

Program directors need to keep abreast of emerging trends in federal policy and related technology. As social work educators, pay attention to updates in the CSWE EPAS and the NASW Code of Ethics to stay informed and responsive.

Suggested Readings

Attal, L. (2018). *Student data privacy: Building a school compliance program.* Rowman & Littlefield.

U.S. Department of Education. (2022). *Family Educational Rights and Privacy Act (FERPA).* https://www2.ed.gov/policy/gen/guid/fpco/ferpa/index.html

References

Americans With Disabilities Act of 1990, 42 U.S.C. § 12101 *et seq.* (1990). https://ada.gov

Bostock v. Clayton County, 590 U.S. ___ (2020).

Civil Rights Act of 1964, Pub. L. No. 88-352, 78 Stat. 241 (1964).

Congressional Research Service. (2019). *The Individuals With Disabilities Education Act (IDEA) funding: A primer.* https://fas.org/sgp/crs/misc/R44624.pdf

Council on Social Work Education. (2015). *2015 Educational policy and accreditation standards (EPAS) for baccalaureate and master's social work programs.* https://www.cswe .org/accreditation/standards/2015-epas/

Council on Social Work Education. (2022). *2022 Educational policy and accreditation standards (EPAS) for baccalaureate and master's social work programs.* https://www.cswe .org/accreditation/standards/2022-epas/

Education Amendments Act of 1972, 20 U.S.C. ch. 38 § 1681 *et seq.* (1972).

Equal Employment Opportunity Commission. (n.d.). *Sexual harassment.* https://www.eeoc .gov/sexual-harassment

Family Educational Rights and Privacy Act (FERPA), 20 U.S.C. § 1232g; 34 CFR Part 99 (1974).

Grove City College v. Bell, 465 U.S. 555, 104 S. Ct. 1211, 79 L. Ed. 2d 516 (1984).

Health Insurance Portability and Accountability Act of 1996, Pub. L. No. 104–191 (1996).

Individuals with Disabilities Education Act (IDEA), 20 U.S.C. 1400, *et seq.*

Kann, L., McManus, T., Harris, W. A., Shanklin, S. L., Flint, K. H., Queen, B., Lowry, R., Chyen, D., Whittle, L., Thornton, J., Lim, C., Bradford, D., Yamakawa, Y., Leon, M., Brener, N., & Ethier, K. A. (2018). Youth risk behavior surveillance—United States, 2017. *Morbidity and Mortality Weekly Report. Surveillance Summaries, 67*(8), 1–114. https://doi.org/10.15585/mmwr.ss6708a1

National Association of Social Workers. (2017). *Code of ethics of the National Association of Social Workers.* https://www.socialworkers.org/About/Ethics/Code-of-Ethics /Code-of-Ethics-English

Nelken, D. (1987). The use of "contracts" as a social work technique. *Current Legal Problems, 40*(1), 207–223. https://doi.org/10.1093/clp/40.1.207

Section 504 of the Rehabilitation Act of 1973, Pub. L. No. 93-112, 87 Stat. 394 (1973).

Tinker v. Des Moines Independent Community School District, 393 U.S. 503 (1969).

U.S. Constitution. (1789). https://constitutioncenter.org/interactive-constitution/full-text

U.S. Department of Education. (1997). *Sexual harassment guidance: Harassment of students by school employees, other students, or third parties.* https://www2.ed.gov/about/offices/list /ocr/docs/sexhar01.html

Warbelow, S., Avant, C., & Kutney, C. (2020). 2020 state equality index. *Human Rights Campaign Foundation.* https://hrc-prod-requests.s3-us-west-2.amazonaws.com/resources /HRC-SEI2020.pdf?mtime=20210124164058&focal=none

Sample Job Description

▶ SOCIAL WORK BSW PROGRAM DIRECTOR

The social work program director is the chief administrator of the social work program and provides leadership in ensuring a quality social work education is provided to the program's students. The director is expected to initiate and sustain action toward achieving program goals and objectives and to stimulate initiative in that regard on the part of faculty and students; foster a professional and inclusive working atmosphere; and welcome and encourage diversity in faculty and student composition. The director is expected to actively consult faculty and students and involve them in participatory decision making, to be open to fair criticism, and to maintain professional objectivity. The director is expected to exercise professional leadership within the program, within the social work profession, and within the field of social work education. The director is expected to demonstrate a commitment to achieving excellence in teaching and research through continuing activity as a teacher and as a scholar. In performing the duties of the position, it is assumed that the social work program director will exercise considerable discretion while complying with college policies and procedures and operating within the limitations imposed by the availability of resources. Among the expectations of the social work program director is that they will adhere to established timelines and deadlines in performing their duties. The social work program director is expected to periodically recommend updates to this statement of duties, following consultation with the social work faculty and the administration.

ADMINISTRATIVE FUNCTIONS

Curriculum

1. Promote instructional quality.
2. Maintain oversight of courses offered within the program to ensure alignment with social work accreditation standards.

3. Ensure that all syllabi meet standards for both the institution and accreditation.

4. Facilitate curriculum change to reflect evolving academic and professional standards of practice. Lead the social work program faculty in all discussions and deliberations related to curriculum design and implementation of the social work program.

5. Facilitate program effectiveness through compliance with accreditation standards, positive student outcomes, and adequate resources for instruction.

6. Coordinate with the field director to support program field education.

7. Submit catalog information to the registrar upon approval of the social work faculty.

8. Submit materials for new and changed courses and program materials to Academic Council. Coordinate with Academic Council as needed until approval is achieved.

9. Develop the schedule of class offerings, in coordination with the social work faculty, in accordance with deadlines.

10. Monitor retention performance and enrollment trends in courses and programs in order to address performance issues. Recommend and act on necessary changes to improve total enrollment and retention metrics.

11. Understand and monitor the impact of industry standards and accreditation needs on course and program design, development, assessment, and revision. Provide evidence as required for new and ongoing accreditation efforts.

12. Recommend, in collaboration with social work faculty members, library resources for purchase.

13. Evaluate courses for transfer credit.

Supervisory

1. Supervise the program's administrative assistant. Perform a yearly evaluation.

2. Supervise the program's student assistant.

3. Ensure the maintenance of effective and confidential program administrative records, including a system of student files and a student information database, records of fieldwork placements and fieldwork instructor information, records of student fieldwork placement evaluations, records of fieldwork agency visits, etc. Ensure that all such records are maintained in the program offices and are available for review.

4. Provide oversight to and remain apprised of the development of the field education program, including the status of the development of field placements; the recruitment, orientation, and training of field instructors; the outcome of field agency visits; the outcome of the assignment of students to placements; and the outcome of semester evaluations of students.

5. Meet as needed with the director of field education in order to remain so apprised as well as to be available to assist in the resolution of any problems that arise within the field education program concerning agencies, field instructors, or students.

6. Facilitate faculty discussions aimed at achieving program goals and objectives and at the regular review of the program's mission, goals, and objectives.

7. Facilitate faculty discussion aimed at achieving the effective and equitable distribution of program responsibilities among program faculty and staff.

8. Facilitate faculty discussion aimed at ensuring that the program is actively striving toward achieving accessibility, diversity, equity, and inclusion in the explicit and implicit curricula and creating an atmosphere of collegiality and professionalism among program faculty and students of diverse backgrounds, consistent with college and CSWE policies and procedures.

9. Convene regular program meetings, including planning schedules, setting agendas, and developing minutes.

10. Maintain the program's membership in the Phi Alpha Honor Society. Ensure that student notification and induction into the honor society are coordinated by the Phi Alpha advisor.

Fiscal

1. Oversee the program budget, recordkeeping, and the requisition of supplies, equipment, materials, and other instructional needs.

2. Consult with social work faculty about major budget priorities and major expenditures.

3. Develop the program's annual budget.

4. Approve purchases and expenses.

5. Allocate and manage assets assigned to the program.

Accreditation and Assessment

The program director is responsible for taking the lead on accreditation. They will ensure that the program is meeting standards as set by CSWE and is adjusting requirements as necessary to maintain accreditation.

1. Maintain the accreditation schedule.

2. Oversee the accreditation timeline and process.

3. Write self-study for accreditation, delegating sections as needed.

4. Ensure that appropriate data collection occurs each semester/year as appropriate.

5. Ensure that the program is implementing new accreditation standards.

6. Coordinate and supervise program compliance with CSWE accreditation policies and procedures.

7. Ensure yearly assessment of social work competencies.

8. Ensure assessment of the implicit curriculum.

9. Oversee development of interventions to address anywhere the program is not meeting goals.

10. Maintain training on CSWE competencies as they evolve.

11. Participate in CSWE feedback sessions on draft standards, as appropriate.

12. Communicate with the CSWE accreditation specialist as needed.

13. Have assessment results placed on the program's website each year.

14. Coordinate and supervise program participation in the college's program review procedures.

15. Foster the development of short- and long-term program goals and monitor their achievement.

FACULTY-RELATED FUNCTIONS

Assessment

1. Oversee regular review of the program's standard performance expectations (SPEs) for faculty.

2. Develop and oversee the peer review plan each year within the program.

3. Coordinate the recommendation of the social work full-time faculty regarding hiring, reappointment, tenure, promotion, and leaves of absence, and the hiring and reappointment of full-time and part-time temporary faculty.

4. Evaluate pretenure faculty each semester and all faculty each year.

5. Conduct pretenure reviews.

6. Serve as review chair for promotion and tenure reviews.

7. Handle cases of faculty misconduct/nonadherence to SPEs.

8. Recruit and assess part-time faculty.

9. Write requests for emeritus status.

Professional Development

1. Encourage improvement of faculty performance by fostering good teaching, stimulating research, and encouraging faculty research, scholarly writing, and other forms of professional and creative activity, as well as by promoting faculty professional development.

2. Conduct regular observation of faculty.

3. Encourage faculty service to the program and the college, as well as to the social work profession and to the field of social work education.

4. Assist faculty with identification of performance goals.

5. Mentor faculty, as needed, in any areas where they are experiencing difficulty/ need further development.

6. Review and approve professional development plans.

7. Review and approve professional development expense requests.

8. Review and approve IRB applications.

9. Write sabbatical recommendations.

Recruitment

1. Write position requests for new faculty hires.

2. Coordinate searches for full-time faculty, including placing advertisements, responding to inquiries, screening interviews, coordinating on-campus interviews, and making recommendations for hire.

3. Exercise leadership in recruiting and retaining capable social work regular and temporary faculty.

4. Make a recommendation to the social work regular faculty regarding the hiring and reappointment of part-time temporary faculty.

5. Provide program orientation, training, and supervision of new faculty. Mentor new faculty and assist in their acclimation to the program and the college.

LIAISON FUNCTIONS

The social work program director has primary responsibility for representing the program to the program, the college, the profession, and the community at large, as well as for encouraging the participation of other faculty and staff in such representation as appropriate. The specific duties for which the social work program director is responsible and accountable include:

1. Serve as the program's primary spokesperson and represent the program to the program, college, and community.

2. Maintain collegiality, keeping open lines of communication and resolving conflict among social work faculty and between social work faculty and other program faculty.

3. Attend program chair meetings.

4. Cooperate with programs, schools, and other units in accomplishing program goals and objectives.

5. Coordinate the development of a committed social work advisory board, consisting of faculty (full- and part-time), current students and alumni, and field supervisors. Facilitate regular meetings of both the full board and the student advisory board, including planning the meeting, developing the agenda, and taking minutes.

6. Prepare the program's annual report at the conclusion of each academic year.

7. Fulfill public relations responsibilities and enhance the program's image and reputation on and off campus.

8. Facilitate the maintenance of effective and ongoing relationships with other programs offering majors and minors in social work relevant subjects.

9. Participate in the annual meeting of CSWE and/or BPD nationally, as resources permit.

10. Encourage the participation of faculty and students in the NASW state chapter.

11. Develop and maintain relationships with the college library in order to maximize faculty and staff access to and utilization of books, journals,

and other information resources, as well as to maximize the development and utilization of library science skills as part of the skill and knowledge development of social work students.

12. Maintain office hours such that the social work program director is available several days of the week.

13. Ensure that the student handbook and fieldwork manual are kept up to date and available to all stakeholders.

14. Oversee the program's social media accounts.

STUDENT-RELATED FUNCTIONS

Current Students

1. Assign advisees to faculty, ensuring a good distribution.

2. Coordinate regular assessment of advising.

3. Ensure effective administration of the required student community-based learning experience, including development and maintenance of a list of preapproved placements.

4. Ensure that students have access to up-to-date information about the program curriculum, program policies and procedures, program-sponsored events, and other important extracurricular events.

5. Encourage student clubs and organizations that foster achievement and professional development.

6. Encourage student participation in professional association conferences and other professional activities.

7. Implement compliance with procedures for resolving student complaints about faculty, courses, and/or programs, consistent with college policies, program bylaws, and social work program policies and procedures.

8. Inform students of special program course registration procedures, enrollment criteria, etc., and administer those procedures as appropriate.

9. Ensure that students pursuing programs in the program have available to them appropriate courses to allow satisfactory progress toward their degrees.

10. Encourage appropriate student participation in program governance.

11. Oversee admission to the major. Ensure that all students are sent a letter informing them of the outcome of their application.

12. Serve as a resource for students with concerns about faculty, in or out of the program, and serve as a resource for problem solving.

13. Meet with students who have violated the program's social work student handbook or who are demonstrating one of the behaviors of concern listed therein to discuss the issue and consequences.

14. Dismiss students from the program who have demonstrated an inability to follow the professional standards set forth in the program's social work student handbook.

15. Facilitate activities to ensure students' overall academic performance, personal growth, and professional development.

16. Plan a welcome session for incoming intended majors in August.

17. Plan a session for intended majors in October.

18. Plan a yearly social work banquet to celebrate graduating seniors, induct Phi Alpha members, and celebrate the close of the academic year.

19. Handle exceptions pertaining to program academic policies and standards, as well as meet with students regarding appeals/grievances occurring within the program.

20. Write letters of recommendation for graduate schools, as many schools require a letter from the program director.

21. Respond to parent concerns.

22. Oversee the program's mentor program.

Prospective Students

1. Assist in recruiting prospective students, including conducting in-person meetings during tours. Facilitate the contact of all prospective students to inform them about the program.

2. Develop a schedule for staffing open house events, including admitted student days.

3. Ensure that social work program marketing materials are up to date and stocked for distribution.

4. Be the contact person for questions for new or transferring students. Assist in the development of their schedule as needed.

Alumni

1. Oversee maintenance of the alumni database.

2. Coordinate the annual reunion at homecoming.

3. Ensure the annual alumni survey is conducted and the results are shared with the program.

Author Profiles

Co-editors

Needha Boutté-Queen, PhD, is a Professor of Social Work at Texas Southern University, where she serves as the Dean of the College of Liberal Arts and Behavioral Sciences. She was Chair of the Social Work Department and BSW Program Director for more than a decade and has also served as a Field Director and Field Liaison in the University of Houston system. She has more than 20 years of assessment, quality enhancement, and assurance experience. Dr. Boutté-Queen served as a site visitor and Commissioner for the Council on Social Work Education Commission on Accreditation and is currently her institution's Liaison for the Southern Association of Colleges and Schools Commission on Colleges Associate Accreditation. She has participated in the writing of self-studies that led to successful initial accreditation and reaffirmation decisions, at both the programmatic and institutional levels.

Susan Mapp, PhD, MSSW, is a Professor of Social Work and the Associate Provost for Institutional Effectiveness and Innovation at Elizabethtown College. She served as the Social Work Department Chair and BSW Program Director for more than a decade and also has served as a Field Director and Field Liaison. On the national level, she served two terms on the CSWE Board of Directors and one term on the Association of Baccalaureate Social Work Program Directors (BPD) Board of Directors. She is the author of numerous articles and books, primarily on human rights and global social work, and she has presented her research at national and international conferences. Her work has been recognized through institutional and national awards.

Chapter Authors

Kathleen Arban, LCSW, is a Clinical Associate Professor at Salisbury University. She has been in practice for more than 25 years in a variety of settings, including child welfare, community-based practice, and child maltreatment prevention. She joined the School of Social Work in 2013 as Site Coordinator for social work programs at the Southern Maryland satellite location.

Jo Daugherty Bailey, PhD, MSW, is the Associate Dean of the College of Health and Human Sciences, a Professor of Social Work, and the former MSW Program Director at Metropolitan State University of Denver. She was the founding BSW Program Director at the University of Houston–Downtown, which began her teaching and research interest in leadership. She is committed to supporting effective and inclusive teams, policies, and systems in all of her roles.

DuWayne Battle, PhD, MSW, is a Teaching Professor, the Director of the Baccalaureate Social Work (BASW) Program, and the Campus Coordinator of the Baccalaureate Child Welfare Education Program (BCWEP) on the Rutgers Camden and New Brunswick campuses. Dr. Battle's areas of practice include all aspects of student advising and engagement; program administration, management, and development; curricula development; leadership development; cultural humility and anti-racism, diversity, equity, and inclusion (ADEI) training; fundraising; and teaching and research in the areas of diversity, racial and social justice, spirituality and social work, and child welfare. He has worked collaboratively to create and develop courses to be delivered both in person and online.

Candyce Berger, PhD, MSW, is an Emeritus Professor of Social Work at University of Texas at El Paso. Dr. Berger held positions as the Associate Dean in the College of Health Sciences, Chair of the Department of Social Work, and Coordinator of the MSW Program at the University of Texas at El Paso. Her areas of expertise include organizational behavior, administration and leadership, and health care. She brings more than 40 years of social work experience as a practitioner, hospital social work director, hospital administrator, and social work faculty member.

Stacey Borasky, EdD, has more than 25 years of experience in social work education in various roles, including the Director of Accreditation for the Council on Social Work Education and Department Chair for Sociology, Social Work, and Criminology at St. Edward's University. Dr.

Borasky is the co-author of two textbooks: *Caught in the Storm, Navigating Policy and Practice in the Welfare Reform Era* (2010) and *Navigating Policy and Practice in the Great Recession* (2018). Dr. Borasky has practice expertise in child welfare and community organizing.

Lori Darnel, JD, MSW, is an Assistant Professor in the Department of Social Work at Metropolitan State University (MSU) of Denver teaching in the Macro Content Area. Before she began teaching at MSU in 2013, Ms. Darnel was an adjunct at the University of Denver Graduate School of Social Work starting in 1999. Combining a theoretical knowledge with practical experience, Ms. Darnel focuses on teaching advocacy skills and interdisciplinary education with an emphasis on legal issues and policy. Ms. Darnel is a Qualified Administrator for the Intercultural Development Inventory and has supported professionals as they develop their cross-cultural competence.

Heather Diehl, MSW, is a Clinical Assistant Professor of Social Work and the former MSW Program Director at Salisbury University, where she provided academic oversight to five hybrid campuses, the MSW Online program option, and the University of Maryland Global Campus (UMGC) partnership program in Europe. She has a long record of being a strong advocate for nontraditional and military-connected students to reach their academic goals at satellite and in distance education programs.

James Drisko, PhD, LICSW, is a Professor Emeritus at Smith College School for Social Work. He has written on competencies and their assessment and on holistic competencies. He has chaired or served on five Smith program reviews and served 6 years on the CSWE Commission on Accreditation, which reviews program self-studies. Drisko has also written on curriculum issues, qualitative research methods, and evidence-based practice.

Stephen "Arch" Erich, PhD, is a Professor Emeritus with the University of Houston–Clear Lake (UHCL). He served as the Program Director of the UHCL BSW Program for more than 18 years and played a pivotal role in the formation, development, and growth of the program.

Warren K. Graham, LCSW, ACSW, CASAC, is the Associate Dean for Field Education and a Clinical Assistant Professor at the Stony Brook University School of Social Welfare. In this role, he supports a number of contingent and adjunct faculty. In addition, he is a forensic social worker in private practice conducting court-ordered evaluations and is active in NASW.

Tanya Greathouse, PhD, LCSW, is an Associate Professor, the MSW Program Director, and the Co-coordinator of diversity, equity, and inclusion (DEI) programming at Metropolitan State University (MSU) of Denver's Social Work Department. She teaches at both MSU Denver and Smith College School for Social Work. Her research interests include developing culturally responsive integrative health interprofessionals, promoting multicultural awareness in supervisory relationships, assessing and supporting multicultural organizational development, and developing anti-oppressive curriculum. She is a Qualified Administrator for the Intercultural Development Inventory and has served as Steering Committee Leader responsible for coordinating content on engaging diversity and difference in practice for two CSWE curriculum guides (Substance Use and Health).

Laurel Iverson Hitchcock, PhD, LICSW, is the BSSW Program Director and Associate Professor of Social Work at the University of Alabama at Birmingham. One of her research interests includes the role of technology in social work education and practice. She blogs about her work at Teaching & Learning in Social Work at www.laureliversonhitchcock.org. In 2012, Dr. Hitchcock received the SAGE/CSWE Award for Innovative Teaching for her work incorporating social media into social work pedagogy.

Jennifer R. Jewell, PhD, LCSW, serves as the Dean of the School of Humanities, Arts, and Social Sciences at Columbia College in Missouri. Formerly, she served as a Professor and the Director of the School of Social Work at Salisbury University. Both schools have a strong commitment to delivering high-quality education in distance education formats. In her leadership roles, Dr. Jewell has developed and launched distance education program options at both the bachelor's and master's levels and spearheaded the creation of comprehensive mentoring programming for faculty and students.

Heather Kanenberg, PhD, LMSW, is an Associate Professor of Social Work at the University of Houston–Clear Lake (UHCL). She has worked for more than 17 years in higher education and social work, and 15 of those years were in a small BSW program of only two faculty. She has served as Director of Field Education and Program Director while also teaching across the curriculum.

Kathryn Krase, PhD, JD, MSW, is a lawyer, a social worker, and an educator. Currently principal at Krase Consulting, in Brooklyn, NY, Dr. Krase previously served as the undergraduate Program Director, MSW Program Director, and Department Chairperson, as well as the Associate Dean of the School of Health Professions at Long Island University Brooklyn. Dr. Krase is also a longtime member of the SWEAP (Social Work Education Assessment Project) Team.

Leah K. Lazzaro, DSW, LSW, is the Assistant Dean in the School of Social Work at Monmouth University. With 16 years of social work education administration experience and a strong focus on field education, Dr. Lazzaro has collaborated closely with faculty colleagues to create policies, programs, and models that support student success.

Melody Loya, PhD, LMSW-IPR, is currently serving as the Associate Dean of University College and is a Professor of Social Work at Tarleton State University. She earned her BSW, MSSW, and PhD in Social Work & Community Services. She has more than 20 years of experience in social work education, including having served as the Department Chair for the BSW and MSW program.

Consuelo Elizabeth Mendez-Shannon, PhD, MSW, is a national consultant in diversity, inclusion, and equity initiatives. Her work has included the Diversity and Inclusion Community Engagement Lead for the American Rescue Plan Act (2021) and Disaster Recovery Divisions for Boulder County leading strategic planning in community engagement involving regional partnerships, collaborations with other community organizations, and integration of programs across multiple departments in the county. Her areas of specialization include community development; programmatic leadership including start-up development; clinical practice development; and cross-cultural organizing such as with local police, nonprofit organizations, and universities, all while integrating efforts toward creating a welcoming workplace.

Judith Kay Nelson, PhD, MSW, is Dean Emerita of The Sanville Institute for Clinical Social Work, where she was also on the core faculty and served as Accreditation Liaison Officer to Western Association of Schools and Colleges (WASC). She has taught and presented throughout the United States and Europe on topics related to attachment and grief and is the author of numerous books and articles on those topics, including "Loss and Grief in an Age of Global Trauma." She was adjunct faculty at Smith College School for Social Work, where she currently co-teaches a professional education seminar for doctoral students focused on applying an anti-oppressive and intersectional lens to clinical theory and practice.

Cathryn C. Potter, PhD, MSW, is the Dean and Distinguished Professor at the Rutgers School of Social Work. Dr. Potter previously served as Associate Provost for Research at the University of Denver, overseeing research policy and strategic planning for research. A proven leader in social work education and research, Dr. Potter also served as executive director of the Butler Institute at the University of Denver. As an administrator, Dr. Potter is guided by her recent scholarly work on organizational culture and climate. Other areas of research focus on children and families at risk, especially those served in the child welfare, children's mental health, and juvenile justice systems. She also has a particular interest in minority overrepresentation and service disparity in child and family serving systems.

Carolyn J. Tice, DSW, ACSW, is a Professor Emeritus at the School of Social Work, University of Maryland, where she served as the Associate Dean of the BSW program. She previously served as the Chair of the Department of Social Work at Ohio University. She earned a BSW from West Virginia University, an MSW from Temple University, and a DSW at the University of Pennsylvania, along with a Certificate in Administration from the Wharton School. The co-author of numerous books and peer-reviewed articles, Dr. Tice focuses primarily on the development of critical thinking skills and social policy. As a Fulbright Specialist, she traveled to Mongolia to assist in the development of social work programs.

Suzanne Velázquez, PhD, LCSW, is the BSW Program Director and a Clinical Associate Professor at the Stony Brook University School of Social Welfare. In her role, she works with a number of contingent and adjunct faculty. She serves on the CSWE Committee for Human Rights and is a strong advocate for integrating a rights-based approach into social work education.

Kelly Ward, PhD, LCSW, LCADC, earned her social work degrees from Eastern Michigan University, Rutgers University, and Fordham University. She has a license to practice clinically in social work and addictions. She has been teaching for more than 25 years and during that time has held multiple positions in several different schools and is presently at Saint Mary's University of Minnesota.

Index

Boxes, figures, and tables are indicated by *b*, *f*, and *t* following the page numbers.

student retention, 15, 419–431
  advisement and, 182
  barriers for students and, 422
  diversity and, 420, 426–427
  early intervention and, 428–429
  financial issues and, 424–425
  first-year programs, going beyond, 421
  gatekeeping in conflict with, 440
  hybrid, online, and creative instruction, 422–423
  inclusive culture and, 131
  off-campus learning sites and, 420–421
  ongoing support and, 419–420
  open educational resources and, 425–426
  overview, 419
  pathway development and, 429–430
  posttraditional students and, 427
  practical tips for, 428
  relationship building and, 423–424
  silos, elimination of, 421–422
  student-centered approach and, 204
  technology for, 267
  working students and, 430–431
student rights and legal protections, 16, 457–475
  case examples, 459b, 461b, 463b, 465b, 468b, 473–474b
  contract law, 464–465
  due process, 457–460
  equal protection, 460–461
  First Amendment, 457
  gender discrimination, 461–464
  privacy and confidentiality, 468–474
  students with disabilities, 465–468
students. See also academic advisement; grades
  academic integrity and, 270
  assessment of learning, 83–87, 89–91, 220
  awards and recognition for, 186
  cost of college and, 47–48, 205, 424–425
  course evaluations of, 211
  curriculum revisions and development, 211
  digital divide and, 142
  with disabilities. See people with disabilities
  diversity and demographics, 139–140, 233
  employment of, 414, 424
  faculty evaluations, 334
  faculty-to-student ratios, 120
  field education for. See field education
  gatekeeping and, 435–458. See also gatekeeping
  institutional supports for, 131–132, 155–156, 418–419
  large BSW programs and, 204–211
  market considerations for new BSW programs and, 118–119
  mental health issues and. See mental health issues
  mentoring of, 420, 426
  portfolios of, 85, 89, 185–186, 266–267
  reaffirmation process participation and, 180
  recruitment of, 404–419. See also student recruitment
  retention of, 419–431. See also student retention
  rights and legal protections for, 457–475. See also student rights and legal protections
  self-assessments of, 69, 91
  small BSW programs and, 181–184
  termination of, 9–10, 435–436, 439–441
Style, E., 227, 237, 239, 241
Sullivan, W. P., 22–23
summative assessments, 83–85
supervision of faculty, 330–337
  classroom observation, 334–337
  effective evaluation, 333–334
  models for, 331–333
Supreme Court, U.S.
  on employment discrimination, 230, 462
  on equal protection, 460
  on First Amendment rights of students, 457
Survey Monkey, 266
Suto, I., 89–90
swag and handouts, 415–416
Swaine, R., 8
SWEAP (Social Work Education Assessment Project), 178, 274
Sykes, S., 207

T

Tam, D. M., 436–437
teaching
  classroom observation, 334–337
  contingent and adjunct faculty experience, 360–362
  co-teaching, 374
  philosophy of, 326, 330
  portfolios of, 334–335
  training in methods for, 326–327, 365
team-building activities, 390–391
technology, 14–15, 249–279. See also online education
  accreditation and reaffirmation, 70
  applicant tracking system for prospective faculty, 304
  assessment and ongoing feedback, 274–275
  case examples, 264b, 269b
  communication with diverse student body and, 208–209
  digital portfolio software, 85, 266–267
  disruptions to, 252, 263
  for explicit curriculum, 257–258, 259–260t, 262b, 264b
  for implicit curriculum, 265–274, 268b
  innovation adoption curve, 256–257, 257f